ABOLITION, THE UNION, AND THE CIVIL WAR

by
Clement Laird Vallandigham

THE CONFEDERATE
REPRINT COMPANY
✩ ✩ ✩ ✩
WWW.CONFEDERATEREPRINT.COM

Abolition, the Union, and the Civil War
by Clement Laird Vallandigham

Originally Published in 1863
by J. Walter and Company
Cincinnati, Ohio

Reprint Edition © 2015
The Confederate Reprint Company
Post Office Box 2027
Toccoa, Georgia 30577
www.confederatereprint.com

Cover and Interior Design by
Magnolia Graphic Design
www.magnoliagraphicdesign.com

ISBN-13: 978-0692350638
ISBN-10: 0692350632

"Do right; and trust to God, and truth, and the people. Perish office, perish honors, perish life itself, but do the thing that is right, and do it like a man.... I appealed to Time, and right nobly hath the Avenger answered me."

– C. L. Vallandigham
Speech of January 14, 1863

CONTENTS

☆ ☆ ☆ ☆

Preface 7

Chapter One 9
History of the Abolition Movement

Chapter Two 47
There is a West: For the Union Forever; Outside of the Union, For Herself

Chapter Three 69
How Shall the Union Be Preserved?

Chapter Four 107
Executive Usurpation

Chapter Five 127
Charges of Disloyalty Triumphantly Repelled

Chapter Six 139
Columbus Democratic Convention

Chapter Seven 153
State of the Country

Chapter Eight 173
Political Campaign of 1862

Chapter Nine 181
Democratic Jubilees

Chapter Ten 191
The Great Civil War in America

Chapter Eleven 231
The Conscription Bill

Supplement 257

PREFACE

This work offers, in a convenient form, the principal speeches of Hon. C.L. Vallandigham, on the Constitution, the Union, and the Civil War. Extracts from other speeches are added; also, a variety of facts and incidents. The object is to furnish the means of forming a correct judgment in relation to a man who, through the malignant assaults of his enemies, and the esteem of his friends, has become one of the most generally talked-of men of these times.

This Record shows why Mr. Vallandigham has so many enemies, and all of one class — why negrophilistic fanaticism includes, as one of its essential qualities, an intense hatred of Vallandigham. This fact is explained by showing that, not only his six years in Congress, but his whole public life, has been a clear, uniform, and unequivocal expression of a deep and true love of his country, the Union, and that he has ever been among the foremost to stand by and defend its institutions and laws.

In the darkest and most trying hours of the great national conflict, still pending, Mr. Vallandigham has never deviated a moment from the old and true principles of Democracy, whereby the Union was formed and preserved, and by which alone it can be saved from destruction, restored, and perpetuated. If his words and acts have been treason, then was the Government itself, through the whole period of its history, down to the inauguration of Mr. Lincoln, one continued act of treason. In common with all democratic and conservative statesmen, he had, before the commencement of the war, and formerly, maintained that the principles around which the Abolition party was organized, were hostile to the Union, and would endanger its peace and perpetuity, if permitted to get control. Those warnings were not heeded, and the fatal mistake was committed of placing in power men whose cherished principles were enemies of the Union. A deadly national conflict ensued; and then Mr. Vallandigham did differ from many in whom the people had reposed full faith and confidence. He stood by his principles, held his position unmoved, while the strong current of a raving fanaticism, that swept by and around him, bore off many of his old companions, knocked from their feet.

Of the war, its causes and attending circumstances, many have said more than Mr. Vallandigham; but few, if any, have said so much that comes square up to the record of events, as history unfolds them. The doctrines announced by him, and the few who have stood with him, are rapidly forming themselves into the public sentiment of the country. The conviction that those men have been right thus far, gives value to their opinions in relation to the probable course of coming events.

Those who have been accustomed to denounce Mr. Vallandigham as a traitor and disunionist, will not take a favorable interest in this Record, for they will find their slanderous accusations nailed to the wall, and hung up to the gaze of the public. This work will, however, be gladly welcomed by a large number of honest men, who have hitherto been deceived by false reports, continuously and persistently circulated. They will discover a pure, able, consistent patriot, a devoted friend and defender of the Union, in one, whom, through slander and misrepresentation, they had been led to regard as a traitor, to whom permission to live was an extra and unmerited allowance. To that immense circle of friends who, with inflexible firmness, have adhered to Mr. Vallandigham, amidst all the malignant and deadly assaults of his enemies, this Record will be a sure testimony that their confidence has not been misplaced. And they will here be furnished with the means, not only to correct the misjudgments of those who have been honestly deceived, but to silence the slanders of those who delight in falsehood and injustice.

The above remarks tell why this Record has been prepared, and is now offered to the public.

J.W. & Co.
Cincinnati, April 13, 1863.

CHAPTER ONE
History of the Abolition Movement
Speech Delivered at a Democratic Meeting
Held in Dayton, Ohio, October 29, 1855

We open this Record with a copy of the speech delivered by Mr. Vallandigham, at a Democratic meeting held in Dayton, on the evening of the 29th of October, 1855, a few days after the election which resulted in the choice of Salmon P. Chase as Governor of Ohio. Three hundred and one thousand votes had been east at that election, of which Mr. Chase, the "Free Soil" candidate, received one hundred and forty-six thousand, being less than half, but enough to elect him. The Democratic candidate received one hundred and thirty-one thousand, and the remaining twenty thousand were given to Mr. Trimble, whom the old-line Whigs supported. The Democratic party being thus temporarily defeated, and thrown out of power, an excellent opportunity was offered for giving the history of the causes which led to the defeat, and for indicating, also, the means which would *"restore it to sound doctrine and discipline, and, therefore, to power and usefulness."* This task was performed by Mr. Vallandigham, on the occasion referred to, in a speech characterized by extraordinary logical accuracy and clearness of statement, as well as extensive and thorough historical research. The general purpose for which the meeting had convened was to consider "The Present State of the Democratic Party in Ohio, and Its Duty."

After some preliminary remarks, explanatory of the object of the meeting. and the reasons why it was proper and expedient thus early to discuss before the people the great question which must make up the chief issue in the campaign of 1856, and to organize preparatory thereto, Mr. Vallandigham said that he proposed as the text or "rubric" of what he had to say tonight, the following inquiries:

> Why has the Democratic Party suffered defeat in Ohio?
> Why is it so greatly disorganized? What will restore it to sound doctrine and discipline, and, therefore, to power and usefulness?

These, Mr. President, are grave questions. I propose to answer them plainly – boldly – not as a partisan, but as a patriot; and for the opinions which I shall this night avow, I alone am responsible. I speak not to please, but to instruct, to warn, to arouse, and, if it be not presumption, to save, while to be saved is yet possible. The time for plain Anglo-Saxon out-speaking is come. Let us hear no more the lullaby of peace, when there is no peace; but rather the sharp clang of the trumpet stirring to battle; at least, the alarm bell in the night, when the house is on fire over our heads. Or, better still, give us warning while the incendiary is yet stealing, "with whispering and most guilty diligence," and flaming torch, toward our dwelling, that we may be ready and armed against his approach.

First, then: The Democratic party of Ohio suffered defeat because it became disorganized; and it was disorganized because it held not, in all things, to sound doctrine, vigorous discipline, and to true and good men. It began to tamper with heresy and with unsound men – to look after *policy,* falsely so called, and forget sometimes the *true* and *honest;* not mindful, with Jackson, that the right is always expedient – at least, that the wrong never is; and that an invigorating defeat is ever better than a triumph which leaves the victor weaker than the conquered. This is a law of nature, gentlemen, and we may claim no immunity from punishment for its infraction. I speak of the Democratic party of Ohio, because we are our own masters, and have a work of our own to perform. But the evil, in part, lies outside the State. It infects the whole party of the Union, as such. It ascends into high places, and sits down hard by the throne. But I affect the wise caution of Sallust, remembering that *concerning Carthage it is better to be silent, than speak too little*. Yet we, as members, must partake of the weakness and enervation of other parts of the system; and atrophy is quite as fatal, though it may not be so speedy, as corruption and gangrene.

The inquiries, gentlemen, which I have proposed, assume the truth of the facts which they imply. Are they not true? That we have been defeated, is now become history. But defeat did not disorganize us. Had not discipline first been lost, we could not have been overpowered. I know, indeed, that some have affirmed that we, too, are an effete party, ready to be dissolved and pass away. It is not so. Dissolution and disorganization are wholly different things. The Democratic party is not a thing of shreds and patches, organized for a transient purpose, and thrown hap-hazard together, in undistinguishable mass, without form, consistency, or proportion, by some sudden and temporary pressure, and passing away with the occasion which gave it being; or catching, for a renewed, but yet more ephemeral existence, at each flitting exigency, as it arises in the State; molding itself to the form of every popular humor, and seeking to fill its sails with every new wind of doctrine, as it passes, either in zephyr or tempest, over the waves of public caprice – born and dying with the breath which made it. No, sir. The Democratic party is founded upon principles which never die: hence it is itself immortal. It may alter its forms; it must change its measures – for, as in principle it is essentially *conservative,* so in policy it is the party of *true progress* – its individual members and its leading spirits, its representative men, cannot remain the same. But wherever there is a people wholly or partially free, there will be a Democratic party more or less developed and organized. But no party, gentlemen, is at all times equally pure and true to principle and its mission. And whenever the Democratic party forgets these, it loses its cementing and power-bestowing element; it waxes weak, is disorganized, is defeated – till, purging itself of its impurities, and falling back and rallying within its impregnable entrenchments of original and eternal principles, it returns, like "eagle lately bathed," with irresistible might and majesty, to the conflict, full of hope, and confident in victory. Sir, it is this recuperative power – this *vis medicatrix* – which distinguishes the Democratic party from every other; and it owes this wholly to its *conservative element, fixed political principles.* I say *political* principles – principles dealing peculiarly with government – because it is a *political* party, and must be judged according to its nature and constitution. Recognizing, in their fullest extent, the imperative obligations of personal religion and morality upon its members, and also that, in its aggregate being, it dare not violate the principles of either, it is yet neither a Church nor a lyceum. It is no part of its mission to set itself up as an expounder of ethical or divine truth. Still less is it a mere philanthropic or eleemosynary institution. All these are great and noble, each within its peculiar province, but they form no part of the immediate business and end of the Democratic party. And it is because that party sometimes will forget that it is the first and highest duty of its mission to be the depositary of immutable political principles, and steps aside after the dreams and visions of a false and fanatical progress – sometimes political, commonly philanthropic or moral – that it ceases to be powerful and victorious; for God has ordained that truth shall ever, in the end, be vindicated, and error chastised.

    Forgetting the true province of a political party, the Democracy of France and Germany has always failed, and ever must fail. It aims at too much. It invokes government to regenerate man, and set him free from the taint and the evils of sin and suffering; it seeks to control the domestic, social, individual, moral, and spiritual relations of man; it ignores or usurps the place of the fireside, the Church, and the lyceum: and, emulating the folly of Icarus, and spreading its wings for too lofty a flight into upper air, it has melted like wax before the sun. *Indirectly,* indeed, government will always, sir, affect more or less all these relations for good or evil. But departing from its appointed orbit, confusion, not less surely or disastrously, must follow, than from a like departure by the heavenly bodies from their fixed laws of motion. And, indeed, the greater, and by far the gravest part of the errors of Democracy everywhere, are to be traced directly to neglect or infraction of the fundamental principle of its constitution – that man is to be considered and dealt with by government strictly in reference to his relations as *a political being*.

These reflections, Mr. President, naturally lead me to the first inquiry.

Personal dissension: a turning aside after mere temporary and miscalled expediency; a faith in and following after weak, or uncertain, or selfish, or heretical men; neglect of party tone and discipline as essential to the *morale,* and hence the success of a party, as of an army, and just as legitimate; these, and the like minor causes of disorganization and defeat, I pass over. They are incident to all parties, and although never to be too lightly estimated, yet rarely occasion lasting or very serious detriment. Commonly, indeed, sir, they are but the *diagnostic,* or visible development of an evil which lies deeper – just as boils and blotches upon the surface of the body show that the system is tainted and distempered within. Neither do I pause, gentlemen, to consider how far the final inauguration of the grand scheme of domestic policy, which the Democratic party so many years struggled for, and the consequent prostration and dissolution of the Whig party, have contributed to the loss of vigilance and discipline; since an organization healthy in all other things must soon recover its wonted tone and soundness. Sir, the Democratic party has principle to fall back upon; and it has, too, a trust to execute not less sacred, and almost as difficult, as its first work. It is its business to preserve and keep pure and incorrupt that which it has established. And this, along with the new political questions which, in the world's progress, from day to day spring up, will give us labor enough, and sweat enough, without a wild foray into the province of the benevolent association, the lyceum, or the Church; to return thence laden, not with the precious things, the incense, and the vessels of silver and gold from off the altar, but the rubbish and the offal – the bigotries, the intolerance, the hypocrisies, the persecuting spirit, and whatever else of unmixed evil has crept, through corruption, into the outer or the inner courts of the sanctuary.

I know, indeed, gentlemen, that every political party is more or less directly affected, as by a sort of magnetism, by all great public movements upon any subject; and it is one of the peculiar evils of a democracy, that every question of absorbing, though never so transient interest – moral, social, religious, scientific, no matter what – assumes, sooner or later, a political shape and hue, and enters into the election contests and legislation of the country. For many years, nevertheless, sir, questions not strictly political exerted but small influence upon parties in the United States. The memorable controversies which preceded the American Revolution, and which developed and disciplined the great abilities of the giants of those days – founded, indeed, as all must be, upon abstract principles drawn from the nature of man considered in his relation to government – were yet strictly legal and political. The men of that day were not cold metaphysicians, nor wicked or mischievous enthusiasts – else we had been subjects of Great Britain to this day. Practical men, they dealt with the subject as a practical question; and deducing the right of *revolution,* the right to institute, alter, or abolish *government,* from the "inalienable rights of man," the American Congress summed up a long catalogue of injuries and usurpations wholly *political,* as impelling to the separation, and struck out of the original draught of the Declaration of Independence the eloquent, but then mistimed, declamation of Jefferson against the African slave-trade. Sir, it did not occur to even the Hancocks and the Adamses of the New England of that day, that the national *sins and immoralities* of Great Britain could form the appropriate theme of a great state paper, and supply to a legislative assembly the most potent arguments wherewith to justify and defend before the world a momentous political revolution. Discoveries such as these are, belong to the patriots and wise men – the Sewards, the Sumners, the Hales, and the Chases – of a later and more enlightened age.

Our ancestors went to war, indeed, about a preamble and a principle: but these were political – the right of the British Parliament to tax America. And they did not stop to inquire whether war was humane and consistent with man's notion of the Gospel of Peace. Their political rights were invaded, and they took up arms to repel the aggression. Nor did they, sir, in the temper and spirit of the pharisaic rabbins and sophisters of '55, ask of each other whether, morally or piously, the citizens of the several Colonies were worthy of fellowship. They were resolved to form a *political Union,* so as to establish justice and to secure domestic tranquility, the common defense, the general welfare, and the blessings of liberty to themselves and posterity. And the Catholic of Maryland and Huguenot of Carolina, the Puritan Roundhead of New England and the Cavalier of Virginia – the slavery-hating, though sometimes slave-trading, saint of Boston and the slave-holding sinner of Savannah – Washington and Adams, Rutledge and Sherman, Madison and Franklin, Pinckney and Ellsworth, all joined hands in holy brotherhood to ordain a Constitution which, silent about *temperance,* forbade *religious tests and establishments, and provided for the extradition of fugitive slaves.*[1]

The questions which engaged the great minds of Washington and the men who composed his cabinets were, also, purely political. *"Whiskey,"* indeed, sir, played once an important part in the drama, threatening even civil war; but it was as the creature of the tax-gatherer, not the theme of the philanthropist or the ecclesiastic. Even the *Alien and Sedition Laws* of the succeeding administration – renascent now by a sort of Pythagorean *metempsychosis,* in the form of a secret, oath-bound conspiracy – were defended then solely on political grounds. "The principles of '98," which, at that time, convulsed the country in the struggle for their predominance, were, indeed, *abstractions,* though of infinite *practical* value – but they were constitutional and political abstractions. Equally is it true that all the capital measures, in every administration, from '98 to 1828 were of a kindred character, except only the *Missouri Question,* that "fire-bell in the night" which filled Jefferson with alarm and despair. But this was transient in itself; though it left its slumbering and treacherous ashes to kindle a flame, not many years later, which threatens to consume this Union with fire unquenchable.

But within no period of our history, gentlemen, were so many and such grave political questions the subject of vehement, and sometimes exasperated, discussion, as during the administrations of Jackson and his successor, continuing down, many of them, to 1847. Among these I name Internal Improvements, the Protective System, the Public Lands, Nullification, the Removal of the Indians, the United States Bank, the Removal of the Deposits, Removals from Office, the French Indemnity, the Expunging Resolutions, the Specie Circular, Executive Patronage, the Independent Treasury, Distribution, the Veto Power, and their cognate subjects. Never were greater questions presented. Never was greater intellect or more abundant learning and ingenuity brought into the discussion of any subjects. And never, be it remembered, was the Democratic party so powerful. It was the power and majesty of principle and truth, working out their development through machinery obedient to its constitution and nature. True, Andrew Jackson was then at the head of the party, and his name and his will, moving all things with a nod, were a tower of strength. But an hundred Jacksons could not have upheld a party one day which had been false to its mission.

Within this period, indeed, Anti-masonry rose, flourished, and died; the first, in the United States, of a long line of *third* parties – the *tertium quid* of poli-

---

1. Both of these provisions were carried unanimously, without debate and without vote. – 3 *Mad. Pap.*, 1366, 1447, 1456, 1468.

tical sophisters – based upon but one tenet, and devoted to a single purpose. But even in this, the professed principle was solely political.

Following the great questions of the Jackson era, came the Annexation of Texas, the Oregon question, and the Mexican War; during, or succeeding which, that pestilent and execrable sectional controversy, *Respublicæ portentum ac pœne funus,* was developed and nurtured to its present perilous magnitude.

Here, gentlemen, a new epoch begins in our political history. A new order of issues, and new party mechanism are introduced. At this point, therefore, let us turn back and trace briefly the origin and history of those grievous departures from the ancient landmarks, which, filling the whole country with confusion and perplexity, have impaired, more or less seriously, the strength and discipline of the Democratic party.

In the State of Massachusetts – not barren of inventions – in the year 1811, at a meeting of an ecclesiastical council, a committee was appointed, whereof a reverend doctor, of *Salem,* was chairman, to draught a constitution for the first "Temperance Society" in the United States. The committee reported in 1813, and the society was established. It languished till 1826; and, "languishing did live." Nathan Dane was among its first presidents. In that year of grace, sir, at *Boston,* died this association, and from its ashes sprang the "American Society for the Promotion of Temperance" – the parent of a numerous offspring. This association was, in its turn, supplanted by the Washingtonian Societies of 1841, and they, again, by the Sons of Temperance. The eldest of these organizations taught only *temperance* in the use of ardent spirits; their successors forbade, wholly, all spirituous, but allowed vinous and fermented liquors. The Washingtonians enjoined *total abstinence* from every beverage which, by possibility, might intoxicate, and so, also, did the Sons of Temperance. But all these organizations, gentlemen – in the outset, at least – professed reliance solely upon "moral suasion," and denied all political purpose or design in their action. They were voluntary associations, formed to *persuade* men to be temperate. This was right; was reasonable; was great, and noble; and immense results for good rewarded their labors. The public was interested, everywhere. The cause became popular – became powerful. Designing men, not honest, were not slow to discover that it might be turned into a potent political engine for the advancement of personal or party interests. Weak men, very honest, were dazzled and deluded by the bright dream of intemperance expelled, and man restored to his original purity, by the power of human legislation. And lo, in 1855, in this, the freest country upon the globe, fourteen States, by statute – bristling all over with fines, the jail, and the penitentiary – have prescribed that neither strong drink nor the fruit of the vine shall be the subject of contract, traffic, or use within their limits. Temperance, which Paul preached, and the Bible teaches as a religious duty, and leaves to the Church, or the voluntary association, is now become a controlling element at the polls and in legislation. Political parties are perverted into great temperance societies; and the fitness of the citizen for office gauged now by his capacity to remain dry. His palm may itch; his whole head may be weak, and his whole heart corrupt; but if his tongue be but parched, he is competent.

And now, sir, along with good, came evil; and when the good turned to evil, the plague abounded exceedingly. I pass by that numerous host of lesser *isms* of the day, full – all of them – of folly, or fanaticism, and fit only to "uproar the universal peace, confound all unity on earth," which, nevertheless, have excited much public interest, numbered many followers, and, flowing speedily into the stream of party politics, aided largely to pollute its already turbid and frothy waters. I come to that most recent fungus development of those departures from original and wholesome political principle, *Know-Nothingism* – as barbarous in name, as, in my judgment, it is dangerous in essence.

The extraordinary success, gentlemen, which had attended political temperance and abolition, revealed a mine of wealth, richer than California *placer,* to the office-hunting demagogue. Ordinary political topics were become stale – certainly unprofitable. But he, it now appeared, who could call in the aid of moral or religious truths, touched an answering chord in the heart of this very pious and upright people – a people so keenly sensitive, too, each one, to the moral or religious *status* of his neighbor.

Not ignorant, sir, of the corroding bitterness of religious strife, and mindful of the desolating persecutions, for conscience' sake, of which governments, in times past, had been the willing instruments, the founders of our Federal Constitution forbade, in clear and positive language, all religious tests and establishments: and every State, in terms more or less emphatic, has ordained a similar prohibition. The Constitution of Ohio, declaring that all men have a *natural and indefeasible right* to worship Almighty God according to the dictates of their own conscience, provides that "no preference shall be given, by law, to any religious society, nor shall *any interference* with the rights of conscience be permitted; and no *religious test* shall be required as *a qualification for office."*

By prohibitions, positive and stringent as these are, gentlemen, our fathers, in their weakness, thought to stay the flood of religious intolerance. Vain hope! The high road to honor and emolument lay through the "higher law" reforms of the day. Moral and religious issues alone were found available. The roll of the "drum ecclesiastic" could stir a fever in the public blood, when the thunders of the rostrum fell dull and droning upon the ears of the people. It needed but small sagacity, therefore, to foresee that the *prejudices* of race and sect must prove a still more powerful and wieldy engine. The Pope of *Pilgrim's Progress* grinned still at the mouth of the cave full of dead men's bones; and Foxe's *Book of Martyrs* lay shuddering yet, with its hideous engravings, under every Protestant roof. How easy, then, to revive, or, rather, to fan into a flame, this secret but worse than goblin dread of Papacy and the Inquisition. Add to this, that a majority of Catholics are foreigners – obnoxious, therefore, to the bigotry of race and birth also; add, further, that silence, secrecy, and circumspection are weapons potent in any hands: add, still, that to be over-curious is a controlling element in the American character. Compound, now, all these with a travesty upon the signs, grips, and machinery of already existing organizations, and you have the elements and mechanism of a great and powerful, but assuredly not enduring party.

In the month of January, 1854, the telegraph, on lightning wing, speeds through its magic meshes the astounding intelligence that, at the municipal election of the town of Salem (not unknown in history), in the Commonwealth of Massachusetts, men not known to be candidates were, by an invisible and unknown agency, said to be a secret, oath-bound society, without even so much as a name, elected by heavy majorities over candidates openly proclaimed. In March, and in April, similar announcements appear from other quarters. The mystery is perplexing – the country is on fire – and lo, in October, nine months after this Salem epiphany, from Maine to California, the mythic "Sam" has established his secret conclaves in every city, village, county, and State in the Union.

And here, again, sir, the Protestant clergy, forgetting, many of them, their divine warrant and holy mission – I speak it with profoundest sorrow and humiliation – have run headlong into this dangerous and demoralizing organization. They have even sought, in many places, to control it, and through it, the political affairs of the country: and, sad spectacle! are found but too often foremost and loudest and most clamorous among political brawlers and hunters of place. I rejoice, sir, that there are many noble and holy exceptions – ministers mindful of their true province, and preaching only the pure precepts and doctrines of that Sacred Volume, without which there is no religion, and no stability or virtue worth the name, in either Church or State. Nevertheless, covertly or openly, the Protestant clergy and Church have but too much lent countenance and encouragement to the order. And the truth must and shall be spoken both of Church and of Party.

In seizing upon the Temperance and other moral and religious movements, party invaded the territory of the Church. The Church has now avenged the aggression, and gone into party – not with the might and majesty of holiness – not to purify and elevate – but with distorted feature, breath polluted, and wing dripping and droiling in mire and stench and rottenness, to destroy and pollute, in the foul embrace, whatever of purity remained yet to either Church or the hustings. The Church has disorganized and perverted party; and, in its turn, party has become to the Church as "dead flies in the ointment of the apothecary." Church and State, each abandoning its peculiar province, and meeting upon the common ground of fanaticism and proscription, have joined hands in polluting and incestuous wedlock. The Constitution remains, indeed, unchanged in letter; but this unholy union has rendered nugatory one among its wisest and most salutary enactments.

But, gentlemen, all these are, in their nature and from circumstances, essentially ephemeral. No powerful and controlling interests exist to cement and harden them into strength and durability. They are among the epidemic diseases which for a season infect every body politic – leaving it, if sound in constitution and not distempered otherwise, purified and strengthened. In all these, too, the Democracy, as a party, has stood firm and uncontaminate; although, indeed, individual members have, in every State and county, been beguiled and led astray, and thereby the aggregate power and influence of the party greatly impaired.

Especially, sir, is the present order of "Know-Nothings" evanescent. Even now it totters to the earth. In the beginning, indeed, it was, perhaps, the purpose of its founders to hold it aloof from the great sectional controversy between the North and the South, and to mold it into a permanent national party. But circumstances are stronger than men – and already throughout the North it has become thoroughly abolitionized. Hence, it must speedily dissolve and pass away, or remain but a yet more hateful adjunct of that one stronger and more durable organization, in which every element of opposition to the Democratic party must, sooner or later, inevitably terminate – *the Abolition horde of the North;* for, however tortuous may be its channel, or remote its fountain, into this turbid and devouring flood will every brook and rivulet find its way at last.

The consideration of this great question, Mr. President, I have naturally and appropriately reserved to the last. It is the gravest and most momentous, full of embarrassment and of danger to the country; and, in cowering before, or tampering with it, the Democratic party of Ohio has given itself a disabling, though I trust not yet mortal, wound.

I propose, then, sir, to trace fully the origin, development, and progress of this movement, and to explore, and lay open at length, its relations, present and prospective, to the Democratic party and to the Union.

Slavery, gentlemen – older in other countries also than the records of human society – existed in America at the date of its discovery. The first slaves of the European were natives of the soil; and a Puritan governor of Massachusetts – founder of the family of Winthrop – bequeathed his soul to God, and his Indian slaves to the lawful heirs of his body. Negro slavery was introduced into Hispaniola in 1501, more than a century before the colonization of America by the English. Massachusetts, by express enactment, in 1641, punishing "man-stealing" with death – and it is so punished to this day under the laws of the United States – legalized yet the enslaving of captives taken in war, and of such "strangers," *foreigners,* as should be acquired by purchase; while confederate New England, two years later, providing for the equitable division of lands, goods, and *"persons,"* as equally a part of the "spoils" of war, enacted also the first fugitive slave law in America.[2] White slaves – convicts and paupers some of them; others, at a later day, prisoners taken at the battles of Dunbar, and Worcester, and of Sedgemoor – were, at the first, employed in Virginia and the British West Indies. Bought in England by English dealers, among whom was the queen of James II, with many of his nobles and courtiers – some of them, perhaps, of the house of Sutherland – they were imported and sold at auction to the highest bidder. In 1620, a Dutch man-of-war first landed a cargo of slaves upon the banks of James river. But the earliest slave-ship belonging to the English colonists was fitted out, in 1645, by a member of the Puritan Church, of Boston. Fostered still by English princes and nobles, confirmed and cherished by British legislation and judicial decisions, even against the wishes, and in spite of the remonstrances, of the Colonies, the traffic increased; slaves multiplied, and, on the Fourth of July, 1776, every Colony was now become a slave State; and the sun went down that day upon four hundred and fifty thousand of those who, in the cant of eighty years later, are styled "human chattels," but who were not, by the act of that day, emancipated.

Eleven years afterward, delegates, assembling at Philadelphia, from every State except Rhode Island, ignoring the question of the sinfulness and immorality of slavery as a subject with which they, as the representatives of separate and independent States, had no concern, founded a Union and framed

---

2. Slavery in Massachusetts. – "There shall never be any bond slavery, villeinage, or captivity among us, unless it be lawful captives taken in just wars, and such strangers as willingly sell themselves, or are sold to us." – *Massachusetts Body of Liberties,* 1641: § 91.

"It is, also, by these confederates agreed, that, etc and that according to the different charge of each jurisdiction and plantation, the whole advantage of the war, (if it please God so to bless their endeavors,) whether it be in lands, goods, or *persons,* shall be proportionably divided among said confederates." – *Articles of Confederation, etc.,* May 19, 1643; § 4; and *Bancroft's United States,* vol. 1, p. 168.

The New England Fugitive Slave Law. – "It is also agreed that if *any servant run away from his master* into any of these confederate jurisdictions, that, in such case, *upon certificate* of one magistrate in the jurisdiction out of which the said servant fled, or upon due proof, the said servant *shall be delivered up* either to his master or *any other that pursues* and brings such certificate or proof." – *Ibid,* § 8.

a Constitution, which, leaving with each State the exclusive control and regulation of its own domestic institutions, and providing for the taxation and representation of slaves, gave no right to Congress to debate or to legislate concerning slavery in the States or Territories, except for the interdiction of the slave-trade and the extradition of fugitive slaves. The Plan of Union proposed by Franklin, in 1754, had contained no allusion, even, to slavery; and the Articles of Confederation of 1778, but a simple recognition of its existence – so wholly was it regarded then a domestic and local concern. In 1787, every State, except, perhaps, Massachusetts, tolerated slavery either absolutely or conditionally. But the number of slaves north of Maryland, never great, was even yet comparatively small – not exceeding forty thousand in a total slave population of six hundred thousand. In the North, chief carrier of slaves to others, even as late as 1807, slavery never took firm root.[3] Nature warred against it in that latitude; otherwise every State in the Union would have been a slaveholding State to this day. It was not profitable there, and it died out – lingering, indeed, in New York, till July, 1827. It died out; but not so much by the manumission of slaves as by their transportation and sale in the South. And thus New England, sir, turned an honest penny with her left hand, and with her right modestly wrote herself down in history as both generous and just.

    In the South, gentlemen, all this was precisely reversed. The earliest and most resolute enemies to slavery were Southern men. But climate had fastened the institution upon them; and they found no way to strike it down. From the beginning, indeed, the Southern colonies especially had resisted the introduction of African slaves; and, at the very outset of the revolution, Virginia and North Carolina interdicted the slave-trade. The Continental Congress soon after, on the 6th of April, 1776, three months earlier than the Declaration of Independence, resolved that no more slaves ought to be imported into the Thirteen Colonies. Jefferson, in his draught of the Declaration, had denounced the king of England alike for encouraging the slave-trade, and for fomenting servile insurrection in the provinces. Ten years later, he boldly attacked slavery, in his *Notes on Virginia*; and in the Congress of the Confederation, *prior to the adoption of the Constitution, with its solemn compacts and compromises upon the subject of slavery*, proposed to exclude it from the territory north-west of the river Ohio. Col. Mason, of Virginia, vehemently condemned it, in the Convention of 1787. Nev-

---

3. The North and the Slave Trade. – The number of African slaves imported into the port of Charleston, S. C, alone, in the years 1804, 1805, 1806, and 1807– the last year of the slave-trade – was 39,075. These were consigned to *ninety-one* British subjects, *eighty-eight* citizens of New England, *ten* French subjects, and only *thirteen* citizens of Charleston. – *Compend. of U. S. Census,* p. 83.

ertheless, it had already become manifest that slavery must soon die away in the North, but in the South continue and harden into, perhaps, a permanent, uneradicable system. Hostile interests and jealousies sprang up, therefore, in bitterness, even in the Convention. But the blood of the patriot brothers of Carolina and Massachusetts smoked yet upon the battle-fields of the Revolution. The recollection of their kindred language and common dangers and sufferings, burned still fresh in their hearts. Patriotism proved more powerful than jealousy, and good sense stronger than fanaticism. There were no Sewards, no Hales, no Sumners, no Greeleys, no Parkers, no Chases, in that Convention. There was a Wilson, but he rejoiced not in the name of Henry; and he was a Scotchman. There was a clergyman – no, not in the Convention of '87, but in the Congress of '76; but it was the devout, the learned, the pious, the patriotic Witherspoon; of foreign birth, also – a native of Scotland, too. The men of that day and generation, sir, were content to leave the question of slavery just where it belonged. It did not occur to them, that each one among them was accountable for "the sin of slaveholding" in his fellow; and that to ease his tender conscience of the burden, all the fruits of revolutionary privation, and blood, and treasure – all the recollections of the past, all the hopes of the future – nay, the Union, and with it, domestic tranquillity and national independence – ought to be offered up as a sacrifice. They were content to deal with political questions, and to leave cases of conscience to the Church and the schools, or to the individual man. And, accordingly, to this Union and Constitution, based upon these compromises – execrated now as "covenants with death and leagues with hell" – every State acceded; and upon these foundations, thus broad and deep and stable, a political superstructure has, as if by magic, arisen, which, in symmetry and proportion, and, if we would but be true to our trust, in strength and durability, finds no parallel in the world's history.

Patriotic sentiments, sir, such as marked the era of '89, continued to guide the statesmen and people of the country, for more than thirty years, full of prosperity; till, in a dead political calm, consequent upon temporary extinguishment of the ancient party lines and issues, the Missouri Question, resounding through the land with the hollow moan of the earthquake, shook the pillars of the Republic even to their deep foundations.

Within these thirty years, gentlemen, slavery, as a system, had been abolished by law or disuse, quietly and without agitation, in every State north of Mason and Dixon's line – in many of them lingering, indeed, in individual cases, so late as the census of 1840. But, except in half a score of instances, the question had not been obtruded upon Congress. The Fugitive Slave Act of 1793 had been passed without opposition, and without a division, in the Senate; and by a vote of forty-eight to seven in the House. The slave-trade had been declared piracy, punishable with death. Respectful petitions from the Quakers of Pennsylvania, and others, upon the slavery question, were referred to a committee, and a report made thereon, which laid the matter at rest. Other petitions, afterward, were quietly rejected, and, in one instance, returned to the petitioner. Louisiana and Florida, both slaveholding countries, had, without agitation, been added to our territory. Kentucky, Tennessee, Louisiana, Mississippi, and Alabama, slave States each one of them, had been admitted into the Union, without a murmur. No Missouri Restriction, no Wilmot Proviso, had as yet reared its discordant front to terrify and confound. *Non-intervention* was then both the practice and the doctrine of the statesmen and people of that period; though, as yet, no hollow platform enunciated it as an article of faith, from which, nevertheless, obedience might be withheld, and the platform "spit upon," provided the tender conscience of the recusant did not forbid him to support the candidate, and help to secure the "spoils."

Once only, sir, was there a deliberate purpose shown, by a formal assault upon the compromises of the Constitution, to array the prejudices of geographical sections upon the question of slavery. But, originating within the secret counsels of the Hartford Convention, it partook of the odium which touched every thing connected with that treasonable assembly,[4] till, set on fire by a live coal from the altar of jealousy and fanaticism, it burst into a conflagration, six years later. And now, sir, for the first time in our history under the Constitution, a strenuous and most embittered struggle ensued, on the part of the North – the Federalists of the North – to prevent the admission of a State into the Union; really, because the North – the Federalists of the North – strove for the mastery, and to secure the balance of power in her own hands; but ostensibly because slaveholding, which the Missouri Constitution sanctioned, was affirmed to be immoral and irreligious. In this first fearful strife, this earliest departure from the Constitution and the ancient sound policy of the country, *the North* – for the truth of history shall be vindicated – the North was the aggressor; and that, too, without the slightest provocation. Vermont, in New England, Ohio, Indiana, and Illinois, out of

---

4. The Hartford Convention. – "*Resolved,* That it is expedient to recommend to the several State legislatures certain amendments to the Constitution, viz.:

"That the power to declare or make war, by the Congress of the United States, be restricted. That it is expedient to attempt to make provision for restraining Congress in the exercise of an unlimited power *to make new States, and admit them into the Union. That an amendment be proposed respecting slave representation and slave taxation.*" – The third resolution of the Hartford Convention, reported Dec. 24, 1814, and subsequently adopted.

It was also resolved "that the *capacity of naturalized citizens to hold offices* of trust, honor, or profit, ought to be restricted."

territory once the property of slaveholding Virginia, had been admitted into theUnion; and Michigan organized into a territorial government, without one hostile vote from the South given upon the ground that slavery was interdicted within their limits. Even Maine had been permitted, by vote of Congress, to slough off from Massachusetts, and become a separate State. But now Missouri knocked for admission, with a constitution not introducing, but continuing slavery, which had existed in her midst from the beginning; and four several times, at the first, she was rejected by the North. The South resisted, and the storm raged. Jefferson, professing to hate slavery, but living and dying himself a slaveholder, or, in the delicate slang of to-day, a "slave-breeder," loving yet his country with all the fervid patriotism of his early manhood five and forty years before, heard in it "the knell of the Union," and mourned that he must "die now in the belief that the useless sacrifice of themselves by the generation of 1776, to acquire self-government and happiness to their country, was to be thrown away by the unwise and unworthy passions of their sons;" consoling himself – the only solace of the patriot of fourscore years – that he should not live to weep over the blessings thrown thus recklessly away for "an abstract principle;" and the folly and madness of this "act of suicide and of treason against the hopes of the world."[5]

---

5. The Missouri Question a Federal Movement – the North the Aggressor. – "The slavery agitation took its rise during this time (1819-'20), in the form of attempted restriction on the State of Missouri – a prohibition to hold slaves to be placed upon her as a condition of her admission into the Union, and to be binding upon her afterward. *This agitation came from the North, and under a Federal lead,* and soon swept both parties into its vortex.... The real struggle was political, and for the balance of power, as frankly declared by Mr. Rufus King, who disdained dissimulation. The resistance made to the admission of the State, on account of the clause in relation to free people of color, was only a mask to the real cause of opposition.... *For a while this formidable Missouri question threatened the total overthrow of all political parties upon principle, and the substitution of geographical parties, distinguished by the slave line,* and, of course, destroying the just and proper action of the Federal Government, *and leading* eventually *to a separation of the States.* It was a *Federal movement,* accruing to the benefit of that party, and, at first, was overwhelming, sweeping all the Northern Democracy into its current, and giving the supremacy to their adversaries. When this effect was perceived, the Northern Democracy became alarmed, and *only wanted a turn or abatement in popular feeling at home, to take the first opportunity to get rid of the question, by admitting the State, and re-establishing party lines upon the basis of political principles....* It was a political movement for the balance of power, balked by the Northern Democracy, who saw their own overthrow, and the eventual separation of the States, in the establishment of geographical parties divided by a slavery and anti-slavery line.... In the Missouri controversy, the North was the undisputed aggressor." – Benton's *Thirty Years,* pp. 5, 10, and 136, of Volume First.

But the incantations of hate and fanaticism had evoked the hideous specter, and it ought to have been quelled, never to re-appear. The appalling question was now stirred; and it should have been met and re-settled forever, by the men of that day, on the original basis of the Constitution – not left, as a legacy of discord, a Pandora's box full of all evil, of mischief and pestilence, to the next generation. They were not true to themselves; they were not true to us. They cowered before the goblin, and laid before it peace-offerings and a wave-offering, and sent us, their children, to pass through the fire in the valley of Hinnom. Setting aside the compromises of the Constitution, and usurping power not granted to Congress, they undertook to compromise about that which had already been definitely and permanently settled by that instrument. This was the beginning, sir, of that line of paltry and halting compromises; of fat-brained, mole-eyed, unmanlike expedients, which put the evil day off only to return laden with aggravated mischief. They hushed the terrible question for a moment; and the election machinery moved on, and the spoils of the Presidency were divided as before. But it was "a *reprieve only, not a final sentence.*" The "geographical line" thus once conceived for the first time, and held up to the angry passions of men, was, as Jefferson had foretold, never obliterated, but rather, by every irritation, marked deeper and deeper. And, after fifteen years' truce, it re-appeared in a new and far more dangerous form; and, enduring already for more than half the average life-time of man, has attained a position and magnitude which neither demands nor will hearken to any further compromise. Nevertheless, sir, but for the insolent intermeddling of the British government and British emissaries – continued to this day, with the superaddition now of Napoleon the Third – it might have slumbered for many years longer.

In England, gentlemen, the form of personal bondage disappeared even to its last traces from her own soil, about the beginning of the seventeenth century; its legal existence continued till 1661; its worst realities remain to this day; for although, in that very humane and most enlightened Island, there be no involuntary, servitude except as a punishment for crime, yet in England, poverty is a crime, punishable with the worst form of slavery, or by starvation and death. Three hundred years ago, she began to traffic in negro slaves. Queen Elizabeth was a sharer in its gains. A hundred and fifty years later, at the peace of Utrecht, England undertook, by compact with Spain, to import into the West Indies, within the space of thirty years, one hundred and forty-four thousand negroes, demanding, and with exactest care securing, a monopoly of the traffic. Queen Anne reserved one-quarter of the stock of the slave-trading company to herself, and one half to her subjects; to the king of Spain, the other quarter being conceded. Even so late as 1750, Parliament busied itself in devising plans to make the slave-trade still more effectual, while in 1775, the very year of the Revolution, a noble earl wrote to a colonial agent these memorable words: "We can not allow the Colonies to check or discourage, in any degree, a traffic so beneficial to the nation." Between that date, and the period of first importation, England had stolen from the coast of Africa, and imported into the new world, or buried in the sea on the passage thither, not less than three and a quarter millions of negroes – more, by half a million, than the entire population of the Colonies. In April, 1776, the American Congress resolved against the importation of any more slaves. But England continued the traffic, with all its accumulated horrors, till 1808; for so deeply had it struck its roots into the commercial interests of that country, that not all the efforts of an organized and powerful society, not the influence of her ministers, not the eloquence of all her most renowned orators, availed to strike it down for more than forty years after this, its earliest interdiction in any country, by a rebel congress. Nevertheless, sir, slavery in the English West Indies continued twenty-seven years longer. But the loss of her American Colonies, and the prohibition of the slave-trade, had left small interest to Great Britain in negro slavery. Her philanthropy found room now to develop and expand in all its wonderful proportions. And accordingly, in 1834, England – England, drunk with the blood of the martyrs, stoning the prophets, and rejecting the apostles of political liberty, in her own midst – robbed, by act of Parliament, one hundred millions of dollars from the wronged and beggared peasantry of Ireland, from the enslaved and oppressed millions of India, from the starving, overwrought, mendicant carcasses of the white slaves of her own soil, to pay to her impoverished colonists, plundered without voice and without vote in her legislature, the stipulated price of human rights; and with these, the wages of iniquity, in the outraged name of God and humanity, mocked the handful of her black bondsmen in the West Indies with the false and deluding shadows of liberty. Exeter Hall re sounded with acclamation; bonfires and illuminations proclaimed the exultant joy of an aristocracy fat with the pride and lust of domination. But in that self-same hour – in that self-same hour, from the furnaces of Sheffield and the manufactories of Birmingham; from the wretched hovels of Ireland, full of famishing and pestilence; from ten thousand work-houses crowded with leprous and perishing paupers, the abodes of abominable cruelties, which not even the pen of a Dickens has availed to portray in the full measure of their enormity, and from the mouths of a thousand pits and mines, deep under earth, horrid in darkness, and reeking with noisome vapor, the stupendous charnel-houses of the living dead men of England, there went up, and ascends yet up to heaven, the piercing wail of desolation and despair.

But England became now the great apostle of African liberty. Ignoring, sir, or putting under, at the point of the bayonet, the political rights of millions of her own white subjects, she yet prepared to convict the world of the sinfulness of negro slavery. Exeter Hall sent out its emissaries, full of zeal, and greedy for martyrdom. The British government took up the crusade – not from motives of religion or philanthropy. Let no man be deceived. No, sir. Since the days of Peter the Hermit and Richard the Lion-hearted, England, forgetting the Holy Sepulcher, had learned many lessons: and none know better now their true province and mission, than English statesmen. But the American experiment of free government had not failed. America had grown great – had grown populous and powerful. Her proud example, towering up every day higher, and illuminating every land, was penetrating the hearts of the people, and threatening to shake the thrones of every monarchy in Europe. Force against such a nation would be the wildest of follies. But to be odious is to be weak, and internal dissension had wasted Greece, and opened even Thermopylæ to the Barbarian of Macedon. The Missouri Question had revealed the weak point of the American Confederacy. Achilles was found vulnerable in the heel. *In spem ventum erat, intestina discordia dissolvi rem Romanam posse.*

The machinery which had effected emancipation in the British West India Islands, of use no longer in England, was transferred to America. Aided by British gold, encouraged by British sympathy, the agitation began here, in 1835; and so complete was it in all its appointments, so thorough the organization and discipline, so perfect the electric current, that, within six months, the whole Union was convulsed. Affiliated societies were established in every Northern State, and in almost every county; lecturers were paid, and sent forth into every city and village; a powerful and well supported press, fed from the treasuries, and working up the cast-off rags of the British societies, poured forth a multitude of incendiary prints and publications, which were distributed by mail throughout the Union, but chiefly in the Southern States, and among the slaves. Fierce excitement in the South followed. And so great became the public feeling and interest, that President Jackson, so early as the annual message of 1835, pressed earnestly upon Congress the duty of prohibiting the use of the mail for transmitting incendiary publications to the South. But, prior to the sitting of Congress, the Abolition societies, treading again in the footsteps of the emancipationists in England, had prepared, and now poured in a flood of petitions, praying Congress to take action upon the subject of slavery. The purpose was to obtain a foothold, a fulcrum, in the Capital; for without this, the South could not be effectually embroiled, and little could be accomplished, even in the North. But no appliances were left untried. Agitators, their breath was agitation; quiescence would have been a sentence of obscurity and dissolution. And accordingly, in May, 1835, the American Anti-Slavery Society was established in New York, its object being the immediate and unconditional abolition of negro slavery in the United States. It was a permanent organization, to be dissolved only upon the consummation of its purpose. The object of attack was the South, the seat of war the North. Public sentiment was to be stirred up here against slavery, because it was a moral evil, and a sin in the sight of the Most High, for the continuance of which, one day, the men of the North were accountable before heaven. Slaveholders were to be made odious in the eyes of Northern men and foreign nations, as cruel tyrants and task-masters, as kidnappers, murderers, and pirates, whose existence was a reproach to the North, and whom it were just to hunt down and exterminate, as so many beasts of prey, to whom even the laws of the chase extended no indulgence. To hold fellowship and union with slaveholders, was to partake of all their sins and enormities; it was to be "in league with death, and covenant with hell." The Constitution and Union were themselves sinful, and, as such, they ought forthwith to be abrogated and dissolved. And thus, sir, the earlier Abolitionists, who were zealots, began just where their successors of to-day, who are traitors, have ended.

A separate political organization was not, at the first, proposed, and each man was left to his ancient party allegiance. The revolution was to be a moral and religious revolution, and its principles, propagated by petitions, lectures, societies, and the press, in the North, were, through these instrumentalities, to penetrate Congress and the legislatures of the South, and if not hearkened to there, then to effect a dismemberment of the Union by secession of the North, or secession forced upon the South.

Slavery, gentlemen, had, before this, been the subject of earnest and sometimes angry controversy in Congress, and elsewhere. But a powerful and permanent organization, founded for such a purpose, and working by such appliances, had never yet existed. Coming thus in such a questionable shape, even the North started back aghast, as at "a goblin damned;" and it was denounced as treason and madness from the first. Its presses were destroyed, its assemblies broken up, its publications burned, and its lecturers mobbed everywhere, and more than one among them murdered in the midst of popular tumult and indignation. The churches, the school-houses, the court-houses, and the public halls were alike closed against them. Misguided men, fanatics, emissaries of England, traitors – these were among the mildest of epithets which, in every place, and almost from every tongue, saluted their ears. The very name of "Abolitionist" became a by-word and a hissing. Not an advocate, and scarce even an apologist, for the men, or their course, was found in either hall of Congress. Members presented their petitions with great reluctance; and, as late as the twenty-eighth of December, 1837, Mr. Calhoun rejoiced that "every senator, without exception," had confessed himself opposed to the agitation. A bill to punish, by severe penalties, any post-master who should knowingly put into the mail any incendiary publication directed to the South, had, by the casting vote of Vice-President Van

Buren, been ordered to a third reading. The Senate declined to refer, or in any way act upon, the numerous petitions presented, while the House, refusing to read, print, or refer, laid them forthwith upon the table. In January, 1838, the Senate, by a majority of four to one, adopted a series of resolutions denouncing the Abolition movement "on whatever ground or pretext urged forward, political, moral, or religious," as insulting to the South, and dangerous to her domestic peace and tranquillity; and further, condemning all efforts toward the abolition of slavery in the District of Columbia and the Territories as a breach of good faith, a just cause of serious alarm to the States in which slavery exists, and of most mischievous tendency. At the following session, the House of Representatives, by a majority of more than one hundred and fifty, passed resolutions, stronger, if possible, than these, and, some time later, censured, and almost expelled, John Quincy Adams, for presenting an abolition petition looking to a dissolution of the Union.

Outside of Congress, also, sir, Abolition received, up to this period, just as little countenance or support. By both of the great political parties it was utterly and indignantly repudiated; while from none of the political, and scarce any of even the religious journals and periodicals of the day, did it find either aid or comfort. Especially, sir, was the Democratic party then sound on this question. General Jackson had already denounced, in strong language, officially, the "wicked and unconstitutional attempts of the misguided men, and especially the emissaries from foreign parts," who had originated the Abolition movement. President Van Buren, in his inaugural address, had volunteered a pledge to veto any bill looking to the abolition of slavery in the District of Columbia. Benton, Buchanan, Wright, Allen, all concurred; and voted, also, for the resolutions which passed the Senate. In Ohio, the Democratic State Convention of January 8, 1840, planted itself firmly upon the rock of the Constitution, and taking high and patriotic ground, condemned the efforts then being made for the abolition of slavery in the District of Columbia, "by organizing societies in the free States, as *hostile to the spirit of the Constitution, and destructive to the harmony of the Union*": and resolving that, "We, as citizens of a free State, had no right to interfere" with slavery *elsewhere,* denounced the Abolition movement and Abolition societies, declaring, that while they "ought to be discountenanced by every lover of peace and concord, *no sound Democrat* would have any part or lot with them." It was, also, further resolved, as if in the very spirit of prophecy, that "political Abolitionism was but *ancient Federalism,* under a new guise, and only a new device for the overthrow of Democracy."

These resolutions, sir, were adopted with but three dissenting voices, in a more numerous assemblage of delegates than had ever before met in the State.

George W. Ells, Esq., one of the old Liberty (Abolition) Guard, hero interrupting, said, that historical statements ought to be correct; that he had been a member, from Licking county, of the convention referred to, and that he knew that the resolutions quoted had never passed, but were smuggled into the proceedings, in order to be circulated through the South, to aid Mr. Van Buren.

Mr. Vallandigham. Sir, I have before me the official record of the proceedings of that convention, signed by the late lamented Thomas L. Hamer, president of the convention, a man too candid, too brave, and too true to lend himself to so base and detestable a fraud for any such purpose. You libel the gallant dead; and it is quite too late in the day, after the lapse of *fifteen years,* for you, sir, by your own parol testimony, to seek to impeach the absolute verity of the record. And I repeat now again, and desire you to hear and understand it, that these resolutions *did* pass that convention, and pass, too, with but three dissenting voices, in that, the largest State convention ever before assembled in Ohio. And if you, sir, happened to be one of the *three* who voted against these resolutions, I can only say that you had the misfortune to find yourself in a very small and most inglorious minority. I assert further, that three weeks after that convention, Benjamin Tappan, then a senator in Congress from Ohio, quoting these same resolutions, and affirming the statement which I have just made, concluded a speech of remarkable precision and clearness, by declining even to present a petition from citizens of the State, praying for the abolition of slavery in the District of Columbia.

A few months later – mark you, Mr. President, Ohio then took the lead in denouncing the treason and fanaticisms of Abolition – the Democracy of the Union, assembled in general convention at Baltimore, passed, without a dissenting vote, that memorable resolution, penned by that pure and incorruptible patriot, Silas Wright; and which penetrated then the heart also, and not the ear only, of every Democrat, to the full and utmost significancy of every word and letter, repudiating "incipient steps," even by Congress, in relation to "questions of slavery," of every sort, as calculated to lead to the most alarming and dangerous consequences, and such as ought not to be countenanced by any friend of our political institutions.

Such, Mr. President, was Abolition in the North, fifteen years ago – *such it is not now*. To the philosophic historian, who, in a future age, shall sit amid the ruins of my country, to write her decline and fall, I leave the sad but instructive office of tracing its progress, and exploring the causes, which, step by step, have lead to its present portentous development. I propose but a brief and hasty summary.

Slowly emerging from obscurity and odium, Abolition began to fix attention, not as hitherto, by its sound and fury, but, losing none of these, rather now by its increasing numbers and influences. Designing men soon foresaw that, of all the movements of the day, none promised so abundant and perhaps durable a harvest to him who should organize and discipline its wild crusading forces into a regular political party. Fanaticism, and a false, religious zeal, conjoined with that pestilent, but ever-potent, spirit, which is so sorely offended at the mote that is in our brother's eye, and which makes each man jealous over his neighbor's conscience, could easily be arrayed under the banner of sectional hate and bigotry, and thus a distinct political faction be compounded out of these elements. Such a party, sir, united by these, the strongest, though not most durable ties, was soon shuffled together, and not long after, supplanted the system of affiliated societies. It formed separate tickets, and, in 1844, supported a candidate for the Presidency. But, prior to 1848, it attained, as a party, comparatively small weight in elections. The vehement contests and grave political questions which convulsed the two great parties of the country, overshadowed all interest in the feeble, but still earnest and active Abolition band; but that band, meantime, was steadily increasing, by accessions, now and then from the Democrats, but chiefly from the Whigs; some honest men, and the discontented and rejected spirits of each, naturally dropping off, and falling into its ranks. Abolitionists, many of them styling themselves, at this period in their history, the "Liberty Party," gained now, in some counties, the balance of power; and hence became there an object of courtship to the other parties; in New England yet earlier, but all over the North, in 1844, the Whig party began to trim and falter upon the question. The defeat of Clay, and the annexation of Texas, gave a new impetus to Abolition, and many more, upon these pretexts, fell into its ranks. Meantime, the steady, persistent, never-wearying labors of its orators and press, full of grossly false and exaggerated portraitures of slavery, and libels upon Southern society, working by day and by night, in the Church, the schools, and the lecture-room, at the public meeting, the fireside, and the sick bed, fomenting thus hate and jealousy of the South everywhere, and that, too, for the most part, without counteracting influence from any quarter, had poured the leprous distillment deep into every vein and artery of the Northern body politic.

Just at this point, sir, in the history of the Abolition movement, came the Oregon controversy, and after that the Mexican war, embroiled by the now terrible question of the acquisition of a very large tract of Mexican territory. Pride or vanity, wounded by the settlement of the Oregon boundary at forty-nine, ambition, disappointed of office, the nomination of Generals Cass and Taylor in 1848, and the manifestly approaching dissolution of the Whig party, all contributed to throw a large portion of that party in the

North, and not a few from the Democratic host, into the ranks of the Abolitionists; who, swelled now by such great accessions, threw off wholly the odious name of Abolition, and, organizing into one body, under a new title, at Buffalo, announced Martin Van Buren as their candidate for the Presidency. In the midst of all this chaos in the political elements, arose that pernicious bubble, the "Wilmot Proviso," which, convulsing the country for more than four years, in its various forms, had well nigh precipitated us headlong into the bottomless gulf of disunion.

    Assuming now the specious name of "Free Soil," and disguising its odious principles and its true purposes, under the false pretense of No Extension of Slavery, the Abolition party addressed itself to minds full now of hate toward the South and her institutions, and ready alike to forget the true mission of a political party, and the limitations of the Constitution. But the united patriotism, talent, and worth of the North and South rallied to the rescue of this the last grand experiment of free government, from the thick darkness of failure and of ruin by the parricidal hands of its own children. The Compromise of 1850 followed: intended and believed to be a final adjustment of this appalling controversy. It was designed to be a covenant of peace forever – sealed and attested by the self-sacrifice of Webster, Clay, and Calhoun, the most illustrious triumvirate of great men and patriots, in any age or any country. But to no purpose: the yawning gulf did not close over them. The origin of the evil lay deeper, and it was not reached. No great question of a like nature and magnitude was ever adjusted by a legislative compromise, in a popular government. The evil lay in that great and most pernicious error which pervaded and penetrated so large a portion of the Northern mind, that the men of the North, if not under the Constitution, yet, by some "higher law" of conscience, had a right, and, as they would escape that fire which is not quenched, were bound to intermeddle, and, in some way, to legislate for the abolition of the "accursed system." No act of Congress, no number of acts, could heal a malady like this, rooted in presumptuous self-righteousness, and aggravated by the corroding poison of sectional jealousy and hate. For such, sir, there is no sweet oblivious antidote in legislation. Set on fire by these passions, applied now to that case which, coming nighest home, appealed most plausibly and most strongly to their impulses and their prejudices, a large part of the North resolved to render nugatory the chief slavery compromise of the Constitution, by trampling under foot and resisting or obstructing the execution of the Fugitive Slave Act of 1850. And three years later, re-enforced now by many recruits from the Democratic ranks, and by almost the entire Whig force of the North, disbanded finally by the overthrow of 1852, but re-organized in part under the banner of Know-Nothingism; the Abolition handful of 1835, swelled now to a mighty host, rallied in defense of the Missouri Restriction, and shook the whole land with a rocking tempest of popular commotion, more dangerous than even the storm of 1850.

Here, then, gentlemen, let me pause to survey the true nature and full extent of the perils which thus encompass us, and to inquire: What remains to be done, that they may be averted?

In January, 1838, Mr. Calhoun spoke, with alarm – then derided as visionary – of the danger which, to him, seemed already as certain as it would be disastrous, from the continued, persevering, uncounteracted efforts of the Abolitionists, imbuing the rising generation at the North with the belief that the institutions of the South were sinful and immoral, and that it would be doing God service to abolish them, even should it involve the destruction of half her inhabitants, as murderers and pirates at best. Sir, what was then prophecy, is now history. More than half the present generation in the North have ceased to look upon Southern men as brethren. Taught to hate, first, the institutions of the South, they have, very many of them, by easy gradations, transferred that hatred to her citizens. Learning to abhor what they are told is murder, they have found no principle either in nature or in morals, which impels them to love the murderer with fraternal affection. Organized bands exist in every Northern State, with branches in Canada, which make slave-stealing a business and a boast: and that outrage which, if any foreign state, or any State of this Union even, in anything else, were to encourage or permit in any of her citizens, would, by the whole country, with one voice, be regarded as a just cause of instant war or reprisals, is every day consummated without rebuke, or by connivance, or the direct sanction of many of the members of this Confederacy; by school-books, and in school-houses; in the academies, colleges, and universities; in the schools of divinity, medicine, and law – these same sad lessons of hate and jealousy are every day inculcated. Even the name and the fame of a slaveholding Washington have ceased to cause a throb in many a Northern heart. The entire press of the North, in journals, newspapers, periodicals, prints, and books, with not many manly and patriotic exceptions, has either been silent or lent countenance and support, knowingly or carelessly, to the systematic and treasonable efforts of those who are resolved to pull down the fabric of this Union. Literature and the arts are put under conscription, for the same wicked purpose. Not a Northern poet, from Longfellow and Bryant, down to Lowell, but has sought inspiration from the black Helicon of Abolition: and the poison from a hundred thousand copies of false and canting libels, in the form of works of fiction, is licked up from every hearthstone, while the *Tribune* of Greeley – one among ten thousand "sold to do evil," at once the tool and the compeer of Seward in his traitorous purpose to make himself a name in history – the antithesis of Washington – by the subversion of this Republic – gathering up, with persevering and most devilish diligence, every murder, every crime, every outrage, every act of cruelty, rapine, or lust, upon white or upon black, real or forged, throughout the South, sends it forth winged with venom and malice, as a faithful witness of the true and general state of Southern society, and the legitimate fruit of slaveholding. In the public lecture, and anniversary address; at the concert hall, and upon the boards of the theater; nay, even at the festivals of our ancient charitable orders, this same dark spirit of mischief is ever present, dropping pestilence from his wings. Even history is corrupted, and figures marshaled into a huge lie, to compass the same treacherous end.

Here, again, too, the clergy, and the Church, gentlemen, mindful less than ever of their true province and vocation, have, one by one, joined in the crusade, till nineteen-twentieths of Northern pulpits resound every Sabbath, in sermon or prayer, with imprecation upon slaveholders. Already has disunion and consequent strife ensued in all the chief religious sects, three only excepted. Outside of these – and sometimes within them, too – the religion of the Bible is but too often superseded by the gospel of Abolition, and the way of salvation taught to lie through sympathy with that distant portion of the African race which is held in bondage south of Mason's and Dixon's line. Thus the spirit of persecution is superadded to the jealousies of sectional position, and the furnace of hate heated seven times hotter than is wont.

They who would not turn a deaf ear to the express requirements of the Constitution, are beguiled and drawn astray by the hollow pretense of Opposition to the Extension of Slavery – a pretense alike false and unmanly, and opposed to the spirit of the Constitutional compact, and the principle which forbids to intermeddle with slavery in the States.

Others, sir, who may care nothing for the sinfulness or immorality of slaveholding, are wrought to jealousy by the false and impudent outcry against the "aggressions of the slave-power," "the grasping spirit of the South," "Southern bluster and bravado;" and many an arrant coward hires himself to be written down a hero, for his wondrous courage in lending the eye a terrible aspect on his own hustings, at the mention of a "fire-eater" from the Carolinas, or repelling, indignantly, six weeks after the offense, on the floor of Congress, the insolence of some "slave-dealing" member from Virginia, who is, perhaps, at the moment, a hundred miles from the capitol. Thus the claim of the South to participation in the common territory purchased by the common blood and treasure of the Union – nay, even her demand that the solemn compact of the Constitution be fulfilled and her fugitives restored to her – are denounced alike as arrogant "slave-driving" assaults and aggressions upon the rights of the North.

Others, again, are persuaded that the South is weak, is unwilling, and dare not resist – is afraid of insurrection, and dependent for safety and bread and existence upon the proverbial fertility and magnanimity of New England. As if no Henry, no Lee, no Jefferson, no Pinckney, no Sumpter, no Hayne, no Laurens, no Carroll, no George Washington had ever lived – as if the spirit of Marion's men lingered not yet upon the banks of Santee, and the fierce courage of the Butler who rode pale and corpse-like from the bed of death, to lead the Palmetto regiment to battle at Cherubusco, foremost in the ranks and "nearest the flashing of the guns," was already become extinct.

The political parties, also, at the North, gentlemen, have faltered, and some of them fallen, before Abolition. The Whig party, bargaining with, courting, and seeking to absorb it into its own ranks, has, itself, at last, been swallowed up and lost. Political Temperance and Know-Nothingism are rapidly drifting into the same vortex. The spirit of Anti-Masonry transmigrated, some years ago, into the opaque body of Abolitionism. Fourierism, Anti-Rentism, the party devoted to Women's Rights, and all the other isms of the day, born of the same generating principle, are already fully assimilated to their common parent: for all these isms, sir, like the nerves of sense, run in pairs. Even the Democratic party, never losing its identity, never ceasing to be national, and even now the sole hope of the country, if it will but return to its ancient mission and discipline – the only organized body round which all true conservatives and friends of the Constitution and Union may rally – has, nevertheless, in whole or in part, at some period or another, in every State, cowered before or tampered with this dark specter.

Just such, too, as public feeling in the North is, so is its legislation. Vermont has passed a law repealing, in effect, within her limits, the Fugitive Slave Act of 1850, and abrogating so much of the Constitution as requires the rendition of fugitives from service. Connecticut, enacting a similar statute, has gone a step farther, and outraged every dictate of justice, in the effort to make it effectual. Massachusetts, the "model Commonwealth" of the times, improving yet upon the work of her sister States, provides, also, that whatsoever member of her bar shall dare appear in behalf of the claimant of a fugitive slave, shall ignominiously be stricken from her court rolls, and forbidden to practice within her limits. Legislation of a kindred character exists, sir, in other States also; and New England will, doubtless, yet find humble imitators even in the West. Already, indeed, the Supreme Court of Wisconsin has deliberately released from her penitentiary, upon *habeas corpus,* a prisoner convicted, on indictment before a United States court, of resisting the laws and officers of the United States in a slave case. Judges, elsewhere, have held that no citizen of the United States living South may dare set his foot, with a slave, upon the north-west shore of the Ohio, at low-water mark even, without by that act, though but for a moment, and from necessity, working instant emancipation of the slave. Not many months ago, a mingled mob of negroes, white and black, at Salem, in Ohio, entered a railroad train, and by violence tore from the family of a slaveholder, passing through the State from necessity, and at forty miles an hour, the nurse of his infant child. A Massachusetts legislature has demanded of her Executive the removal of an able, meritorious, and upright judge, for the conscientious discharge, within her limits, of the duties of an office which he held under authority of the United States; and a Massachusetts ecclesiastical conclave, three hundred in number, rose as one man on the announcement of the outrage, and shouted till the house rang again with their plaudits. And a Massachusetts university rejected, also, the same judge, for the same cause, when proposed for a professorship in the institution.

This, sir, within little more than two years from the death of her noblest son – whose whole life, and whose dying labors were exhausted in defending the Union and holding the Commonwealth of his adoption up to the full measure of her Revolutionary patriotism and greatness – has the star of Massachusetts been seen to fall from heaven and begin to plunge into the utter blackness of disunion. In vain now, sir, from the grave of the Statesman of Marshfield there comes up the warning cry, "Let her shrink back; let her hold others back, if she can; at any rate, let her keep herself back from this gulf, full at once of fire and blackness – full, as far as human foresight can scan, or human imagination fathom, of the fire and the blood of civil war, and of the thick darkness of general political disgrace, ignominy, and ruin." No; she is fallen. Sumner has supplanted Winthrop; and a Wilson crawled up into the seat which Webster once adorned.

And add, now, to all this, gentlemen, that, already, that portentous and most perilous evil, against which the Father of his Country so solemnly and earnestly warned his countrymen, a party bounded by geographical lines – a Northern party, standing upon a Northern platform, doing battle for Northern issues, and relying solely for success upon appeals to Northern prejudices and Northern jealousies, is now, for the first time in our history, fully organized and consolidated in our midst. Add farther, that, to the Thirty-Fourth Congress, fourteen Senators and a majority of Representatives have been chosen who, in name or in fact, are Abolitionists; Ohio contributing to this dark host her entire delegation in House and Senate, one only excepted; and thus, for the first time, also, since the organization of our Government, has the House of Representatives been converted into a vast Abolition conventicle, full of men picked out for their hatred of the South, and who cannot be true to the Constitution and the Union without treachery to the expectations and the purposes of those who elected them. And then reflect yet further, that this vast and terrible magazine of explosive elements is gathered together just upon the eve of a Presidential election, with all its multiplied and convulsing interests; and that soon Kansas will knock for admission into the Union, thus surely precipitating the crisis; and who, tell me, I pray you, may foresee what shall be the history of this Republic at the end of two years from to-day?

All this, gentlemen, the spirit of Abolition has accomplished in twenty years of continued and exhausting labors of every sort. But, in all that time, not one convert has it made in the South; not one slave emancipated, except by larceny and in fraud of the solemn compacts of the Constitution. Meantime, public opinion has wholly, radically changed in the South. The South has ceased to denounce, ceased to condemn slavery – ceased even to palliate – and begun now, almost as one man, to defend it as a great moral, social, and political blessing. The bitter and proscriptive warfare of twenty years has brought forth its natural and legitimate fruit in the South. Exasperation, hate, and revenge are every day ripening into fullest maturity and strength; and, throughout her entire extent, she awaits now but the action of the North to unite in solemn league and covenant to resist aggression even unto blood.

But the South, sir, has forborne a little. I say, she has forborne a little. She has not yet associated and formed political parties to put down Masonry and Odd Fellowship in the free States and in the Territories, upon the pretext that these institutions are sinful and immoral. She has not yet organized societies, and fostered and protected them by her legislation, to steal that which our law recognizes as property, and refused restitution on the pretext that by the "higher law" of conscience, no right of property exists in the thing stolen. Neither, sir, has any Southern State, no, not even "fire-eating" South Carolina, sought as yet to compensate herself for the fugitives which we have abducted, by enacting laws to encourage the slave-trade, by punishing with fine and imprisonment in her penitentiary for years any one of her citizens who should aid in enforcing the laws of the United States against the traffic, striking from her court rolls any attorney within her limits, who should appear in behalf of the prosecution, and excluding all who hold the office of United States Commissioner or Judge, from any office or appointment under her authority. How long before all this shall have been done, is known to Him only whose omniscient eye penetrates and illumines the clouds and thick darkness of the future.

Thus, then, Mr. President, by little and little at first, but now, as with a flood, fraternal affection is wasted away; hate and jealousy and discord, nourished and educated into maturest developments; and, one by one, the real and strong cords which bind us together as a confederacy snapped asunder, or stretched to their utmost tension. It needs no spirit of prophecy, not even a human sagacity above the ordinary level, to foretell just how long the habits, forms, and paper parchments of a union can last when its life-giving principle and nourishing and sustaining virtue are wasted and gone.

Sir, he is yet but in the swaddling bands of infancy, who does not already see that there is wanting but some strong convulsion, or even but some sudden jar in the system, to hurl us headlong down into the abyss of disunion.

I know, gentlemen, that to many all this is as "a twice-told tale, vexing the dull ear of a drowsy man." They hearkened not to the voice of Webster, Clay and Calhoun, while yet among the living; neither would' they believe, though these three men rose from the dead. Being dead, they yet speak. The dead of all ages speak. All history lifts up its warning voice. Livy and Tacitus are full of saddest and most instructive teachings. But let us not deceive ourselves. It is not in their pages that we are to read the lessons of that danger which threatens us with destruction. There has been to us no slow and gradual progression of five hundred years to the full growth and stature of a great nation; neither is it in reserve for us to pass through the mellowing and softening gradations of luxury, vice, corruption, and enervation for five hundred years more, to our final fall as an empire. No. The history of Greece is the true study for the American statesman. There he will find the chiefest lessons of political wisdom, adapted to our peculiar exigencies. He will learn there how internal dissension and discord may prostrate a state in the full vigor of its manhood; and, indeed, that it is only in the manhood of a confederacy that there is strength enough, and energy enough, in the members, to rend each other in pieces, and that in the decadence of a state, in decay and atony, it is a Cæsar within, or a Macedonian phalanx, or Roman legions from without, which overwhelm the state. In Thucydides, he may learn how a thirty years' civil war exhausted Greece, and prepared her first for the haughty domination of the conquering member of the confederacy; and finally, for that yoke of foreign despots which galls and burns into her neck to this day.

Let us improve these lessons. It is not yet too late to be saved. The current may still be turned back, and the Union restored to its former sound and healthy condition, though many a gaping scar shall attest the wounds she has received from the hands of her own children.

What then remains to be done? – I answer this momentous question, Mr. President, by declaring first, what will not heal the sick man of America.

First, then, closing our eyes and our ears to the truth, and laughing all danger to scorn, will not do it. The scoffs and derision of the diluvian world did not stay the fountains of the great deep, nor seal up the windows of heaven.

Professions and resolutions of love for the Union and Constitution, whether hypocritical or sincere, will not do it, while, at the same moment, we strike the blow which destroys both. Nor will legislative compromises and finalities, nor yet national conventions and presidential elections. None of these.

Least of all, sir, will platforms, of themselves, avail anything. Time was when they had a meaning, and when the partisan who repudiated or doubted even an abstract principle, was stricken down by a surer and heavier blow of popular wrath than he who "bolted" a nomination. But that day is past. The best of platforms is now too often but a spider's snare; the weak and unsuspecting house-fly is caught and devoured, the stout, blue-bottle, carrion insect breaks through its meshes. A sound system of faith is, indeed, still proclaimed, but mental reservation is now tolerated. The thirty-nine Articles are subscribed, but a wide margin and much space between the lines allowed for liberal interpretation. Obedience is no longer expected or required to the platform, if the professor will but support the candidate. And thus, sir, the aged worshiper who lingers yet around the altar, and the simple-minded convert of yesterday, whose burning faith receives the creed as an enunciation of eternal principles, the sacred canon of political scripture, are alike amazed to learn from the organ of the ecumenical council, interpreting by authority, that it is only the gospel according to Judas, whereby a general amnesty is proclaimed to all rebels and deserters; – a cumbrous but convenient piece of machinery, whereby apostates may be restored, if not to favor, at least to position and office in the party. Witness the bold and impudent fraud of the platform promulgated by the Grand Council of Know-Nothings at Philadelphia, which yet a subordinate State Council of the same Order, assembled at Cleveland, and bound by the most stringent oaths to obedience, had assumed, in advance, to repudiate. And need I but allude to that State Democratic Convention of Ohio, which, resolving to adhere to and support the Baltimore platform, rugged all over as it is, with denunciations of all and every attempt, of whatsoever shape, or color, or pretense, in Congress or out of it, to keep up the slavery agitation, did yet, with amiable and most refreshing consistency, resolve that the Democracy of Ohio would use all power, under the Constitution, "to prevent the increase, to mitigate, and *finally to eradicate* – tear up by the roots – the evil of slavery."

Either away then with platforms, at least, as a sanative process, and until a sounder public virtue be restored, or require a strict and ready and honest obedience to the principles which they proclaim.

What then remains to be done? – I answer, first, that whatever it may be, it is to be done by and through the *Democratic party,* and the national Whigs and others who may act with it in this crisis; for "when bad men combine, good men must associate." There is no hope, none, in any other organization. To that party, therefore, and through it, to all true patriots and conservatives, I address myself, and answer further: We must return to the principles, follow the practice, imitate the good faith and fraternal affection, and restore the distinctions with which our ancestors set out at the commencement of this government. We must learn a wise and wholesome conservatism; learn that all progress is not reform, and that the wildest and most pernicious and most dangerous of all follies is to attempt to square our political institutions and our legislation by mere abstract, theoretical, and mathematically exact, but impracticable truths. We must remember, also, our true mission as a political party, and retrace our steps from outside the territories of the lyceum and the Church, and drive back the clergy and the Church to their own domain. We must build up again the partitions which separate sacred things from profane, and begin once more to *"Render unto Cæsar the things that are Cæsar's, and unto God the things that are God's."* We must set out again to pronounce upon political questions, without essaying to try them by the touchstone of our own peculiar notions of moral or divine truth, and thus relegate temperance to the voluntary association, religion to the Church, and slavery to the judgment and conscience of those in whose midst it exists, or is sought to be established, casting aside that false and dangerous and most presumptuous self-delusion, that we are to give account, each one as citizens, for the sins or immoralities of our fellow-men. Slavery, indeed, sir, where it exists, or to the people among whom it is proposed to introduce it, may be, and it is to them, a political subject in part. To us of the North, it is and can be none other than an ethical or religious question. For, disguise and falsify it as you will; marshal and array your figures and your facts to lie never so grossly, it is the sinfulness and immorality of slaveholding as viewed by the Northern mind, and this alone, which has stirred the people of the North to such a height of folly and madness. And yet, if immoral, it concerns only the people of the States and Territories where it exists; if sinful, they only are the offenders, and even if a political evil, it is they alone who feel the curse. It is, therefore, and can be of no possible concern to us, except, indeed, upon the principle of that self-sufficient, self-righteous and most pernicious egoism which it is time now to purge out of the system.

But a high and imperative constitutional obligation, also, Mr. President, devolves here upon the Democratic party.

The accidents and the necessities of its settlement determined the political character of this continent, and divided it into separate colonies, as perfectly independent, one of the other, as any foreign states. A common subjection to the crown of Great Britain gave the first notion of a common Federal Government; and the aggressions of that crown, and of Parliament, compelling civil war, forced our fathers into a union and articles of confederation. The Constitution of '89 extended the powers and the efficiency, but did not alter the nature of the General Government. That instrument, sir, was framed by delegates appointed not by the old Congress, but by the States, as sovereign and independent communities. State conventions ratified it; and it was binding only as between those States which acceded to it. They consented to yield up to a common government, certain delegated powers, for the good of the whole; reserving all others, each to itself. We are a confederacy, sir, of sovereign, distinct, independent States; in all things not brought into the common fund of power, just as thoroughly foreign to each other (except only in a common language and fraternal affection), and as subject to the obligations and comities of the law of nations, as France and England. With the domestic police and institutions of Kentucky, or any other State, the people of Ohio have no more right to intermeddle, than with the laws or form of government in Russia. Slavery in the South is to them as polygamy in the Turkish Empire; and for the political evils, or the sinfulness and immorality of the one, they are in no wise more responsible than for the other. Or – to select the same subject-matter – they have no more right to interfere with, nor are they in any degree more accountable for, the continuance of slavery in Virginia, than for its existence in Persia. Neither, sir, have the people of the Northern States any greater right, under the Constitution, to deny admission into the Union to a State, because its laws sanction involuntary servitude, or to prescribe that slavery shall not be tolerated in a territory, than to abolish it in a State already in the Union. The converse of this proposition is sheer, rank, unmixed, unanointed *Federalism* – just the Federalism of Alexander Hamilton, who, in the convention of '87, would have made the States wholly subordinate to the General Government – mere adjuncts – "corporations for local purposes." The reasons, sir, are obvious, and they are conclusive. It is a fundamental principle of the Democratic theory, and of our institutions, that to the people of each particular State, county, township, city, and village, shall be committed, as far as possible, the exclusive regulation of their more immediate and local affairs. In other words, that power, whenever it is practicable, shall be diffused to the utmost, and never centralized beyond urgent necessity. Again, the only limitation prescribed in the Constitution, for the fitness of a State for fellowship with us, is that such State shall establish a "republican" or representative form of government. Now, it is too late to allege, at this day, and quite too absurd, that the existence of the domestic institution of slavery in a State makes its form of government anti-republican, and, therefore, unconstitutional. Such an argument is not worth a serious refutation. Again: The Territories are the common property of the States in their Federal capacity, purchased by the common blood and treasure of all, and as much the property of South Carolina as of Massachusetts. They are tenants in common of this property; and for one State to demand the exclusion of another from participation in their use in common, in every respect, is arrogant and unfounded assumption of superiority; and fifty-fold more offensive, when the pharisaic pretense is set up that they are more holy than that other State, whose inhabitants are sinners before God exceedingly, and who would pollute the territory, by the introduction of their wickedness upon its soil; assuming thus to be keeper of the conscience and custodian of the morals of the people of the territory, putting on the robes, and ascending into the judgment-seat of the Almighty. Sir, if the inhabitants of Cape Cod are not satisfied with the coparcenary, let them seek, by partition, to hold in severalty; and, obtaining thus the very small and almost infinitesimal portion which is their share, exert over it such acts of ownership as to them may seem meet; but not attempt insolently to take possession and control of the whole.

Manifestly, then, sir, the agitation of the slavery question finds no warrant or countenance, but direct and emphatic condemnation, in the Constitution. That part of the instrument which apportions the representation and taxation of slaves, for the most part executes itself, and admits only of direct attack by amendment or nullification. The clause which empowers Congress to prohibit the slave-trade, has long since been quietly carried into effect; and the South has never sought to disturb it. The sole remaining instance in which Congress may legislate in reference to slavery, is for the extradition of fugitives. From its very nature, sir, this presents a capital point for assault by Abolitionists. Long before the act of 1850, they had, by State legislation, or public odium, rendered nugatory the act of 1793, and were laboring for its direct repeal by Congress. They openly repudiated that part of the Constitution upon which it was founded; and, as early as 1843, a general convention of Abolitionists, assembled at Buffalo, and composed of the ablest and most distinguished members of the party, resolved that whenever called upon to swear to support the Constitution, they would, by mental reservation, regard that clause in it as utterly null and void, and forming no part of the instrument.[6] Nevertheless, sir, in the adjustment of 1850, provision was made to enforce this solemn compact. And hence, the popular tumults, the mobs, the forcible rescues, and the nullifying acts of the New England States, and other parts of the North, which yet find countenance and applause even from a thousand presses and tens of thousands of citizens, upon the pretext that the rendition of fugitives is distasteful and revolting to the

---

6. The Buffalo Resolution, 1843, *offered by a committee of which Salmon P. Chase, of Ohio, was a member.* – "*Resolved,* That we hereby give it to be distinctly understood, by this nation and the world, that, as *Abolitionists,* considering that the strength of our cause lies in its righteousness, and our hopes for it in our conformity to the laws of God, and our support for the rights of man, we owe to the sovereign Ruler of the Universe, as a proof of our allegiance to him, in all our civil relations and offices, whether as friends, citizens, or as public functionaries, sworn to support the Constitution of the United States, to regard and treat the third clause of that instrument, whenever applied in the case of a fugitive slave, *as utterly null and void,* and, consequently, as forming no part of the Constitution of the United States, *whenever we are called upon as sworn to support it.*"

North. Yes, Abolitionist, it is the Constitution which you attack, not the act of 1850. It is the extradition of "panting fugitives," under any circumstances, or by virtue of any law, at which you rebel. Be manly, then, and outspoken, and honest. Act the part of cowards and slave-stealers no longer. Assail the Constitution itself, and do it openly – it is the Constitution which demands the restoration – and cover not up your assaults any longer, under the false and beggarly pretense that it is the act of Congress which you condemn and abhor.

I know, sir, that it is easy, very easy, to denounce all this as a defense of slavery itself. Be it so; be it so. But I have not discussed the institution in any respect – moral, religious, or political. Hear me; I express no opinion in regard to it; and, as a citizen of the North, I have ever refused, and will steadily refuse, to discuss the system in any of these particulars. It is precisely this continued and persistent discussion and denunciation in the North, which has brought upon us this present most perilous crisis; since to teach men to hate, is to prepare them to destroy, at every hazard, the object of their hatred. Sir, I am resolved only to look upon slavery outside of Ohio, just as the founders of the Constitution and Union regarded it. It is no concern of mine – none, none – nor of yours, Abolitionist. Neither of us will attain heaven by denunciations of slavery; nor shall we, I trow, be cast into hell for the sin of others who may hold slaves. I have not so learned the moral government of the universe; nor do I presumptuously and impiously aspire to the attributes of Godhead, and seek to bear upon my poor body the iniquities of the world.

I know well, indeed, Mr. President, that in the evil day which has befallen us, all this, and he who utters it, shall be denounced as "pro-slavery;" and already, from ribald throats, there comes up the slavering, driveling, idiot epithet of "doughface." Again; be it so. These, Abolitionist, are your only weapons of warfare; and I hurl them back defiantly into your teeth. I speak thus boldly, because I speak in and to and for the North. It is time that the truth should be known and heard, in this the age of trimming and subterfuge. I speak this day, not as a Northern man, nor a Southern man; but, God be thanked, still as a United States man, with United States principles; and though the worst happen which can happen – though all be lost, if that shall be our fate, and I walk through the valley of the shadow of political death, I will live by them, and die by them. If to love my country; to cherish the Union; to revere the Constitution; if to abhor the madness and hate the treason which would lift up a sacrilegious hand against either; if to read that in the past, to behold it in the present, to foresee it in the future of this land, which is of more value to us and the world for ages to come, than all the multiplied millions who have inhabited Africa from the creation to this day – if this it is to be pro-slavery, then, in every nerve, fiber, vein, bone, tendon, joint, and ligament, from the top-most hair of the head to the last extremity of the foot, I am all over and altogether a *pro-slavery man*.

To that part now, Mr. President, of the Germans who have been betrayed upon this question, I address a word of caution. Little more than a year ago, availing themselves of the Nebraska question as the pretext, mischievous and designing demagogues, just at the moment they prepared to deny you the full enjoyment of your own political rights here in Ohio, persuaded some of you to trail in the dust at the heels of the Abolition rout. They told you, and you believed it, some of you, that, failing to establish civil liberty against the crowned oppressors of your fatherland, and seeking for it as exiles in America, you had the right, nevertheless, to intermeddle with personal liberty among the inhabitants of other States and Territories, to form political associations exclusively German, to adopt platforms of your own as such, to instruct us in the science of government, the nature of free institutions, and the value of freedom, to require of us to give away our public lands to all alike, naturalized or alien, white or *black,* to denounce the people of the South, because of the "curse of slavery," to repeal the Fugitive Slave Law, to abolish slaveholding *throughout the States, in conformity with,* as you alleged, and perhaps by virtue of power *derived from,* the Declaration of Independence, and finally to propose to convert your good old German May festival into an Abolition mass meeting, in our very midst. These things, they persuaded some of you to believe and to do. But at this very moment, and by the self-same demagogues, was the knife put to your own throats, and you were quietly guillotined, and your heads thrust into the basket, upon just the principles they had persuaded you that you had the right to intermeddle with the domestic, moral, and religious concerns of other States and Territories. Opening now your eyes to the fraud thus practiced upon you, learning the true character of the men who beguiled you, and remembering that the first State which breasted and turned back the torrent which was sweeping you, and your hopes, and your rights before it, was the *slaveholding* State of Virginia, through the Democratic party of Virginia, followed up by every Southern State, Kentucky alone excepted, retrace your steps now into the ranks of that party, stand fast to your true interests and true position, concern yourselves no longer with the business of others, but quietly enjoy, and calmly defend, your own rights, remembering always those who have ever sustained you in whatsoever truth and liberty and justice demand for you.

Addressing myself now, finally, Mr. President, to the Democratic party of Ohio, I say: You are a political party; hence, all your principles must as well take shape and color, as reflect them, from the fundamental institutions of the country; and those principles which belong to Democracy, universal and theoretical, are to be modified and adjudged by the Constitution. It has always been your boast, that you are peculiarly the party of the Constitution and of that Union which results from, and exists only, by the Constitution. And just in proportion as you value these, will you mold and modify your doctrine, and your practice, to sustain and preserve them in every essential element. Sure I am, at least, that you will not, for the sake of an abstract principle, purely, or mainly moral, or religious, and to us not political, and urged now in the very spirit of treason and madness, and far removed from every personal concern of yours, sacrifice or even imperil these priceless legacies of a generation at least as good and as wise as we. Trust not to past success. Times have changed. For four years you filched inglorious triumphs by fomenting dissensions among your enemies, and by exhausting all the little arts of partisan diplomacy, to keep the Whig and Abolition parties asunder. You wasted your time striving to pluck out of the crucible of politics the fluxes which they threw in, seeking thus vainly to prevent or impede a fusion which was inevitable, and which, when it came, overwhelmed you as with a flood of lava, in disastrous, if not ignominious defeat. Was this conduct befitting a great and enduring party – conduct worthy the prestige of your name? Learn wisdom from Virginia, your mother State; she is ever invincible, because she is always candid and manly and true to principle. Look no longer now to availability; above all, be not deceived by the false and senseless outcry against that most just, most Constitutional, and most necessary measure – the *Kansas-Nebraska Act*. The true and only question now before you is: Whether you will have a Union, with all its numberless blessings in the past, present, and future, or disunion and civil war, with all the multiplied crimes, miseries, and atrocities which human imagination never conceived, and human pen never can portray?

    I speak it boldly – I avow it publicly – it is time to speak thus, for political cowardice is the bane of this, as of all other republics. To be true to your great mission, and to succeed in it, you must take open, manly, one-sided ground upon the Abolition question. In no other way can you now conquer. Let us have, then, no hollow compromise, no idle and mistimed homilies upon the sin and evil of slavery in a crisis like this, no double-tongued, Janus-faced, delphic responses at your State conventions. No; fling your banner to the breeze, and boldly meet the issue. "Patriotism above mock philanthropy; the Constitution before any miscalled higher law of morals or religion; and the Union of more value than many negroes."

    If thus, sir, we are true to the country, true to the Union and the Constitution, true to our principles, true to our cause and to the grand mission which lies before us, we shall turn back yet the fiery torrent which is bearing us headlong down to the abyss of disunion and infamy, deeper than plummet ever sounded; but if in this, the day of our trial, we are found false to all these, false to our ancestors, false to ourselves, false to those who shall come after us, traitors to our country and to the hopes of free government throughout the globe, Bancroft will yet write the last sad chapter in the history of the American Republic.

CHAPTER TWO
There is a West: For the Union Forever; Outside of the Union, For Herself
Speech Delivered in the House of Representatives, December 15, 1859

More than four years had intervened between the delivery of the preceding speech and the one that here follows. Meantime the evil agencies, there so clearly depicted, and against which those earnest warnings were given, had been steadily maturing their work of mischief. Like some vile insects, which consume and destroy the foundations of houses, working silently and unseen, and permitting the occupants to receive the first intimations of danger when they feel their dwellings crumbling and falling around them, so were those industrious fanatics consuming and destroying the foundations of the Union.

The John Brown raid into Virginia gave the first public and distinct intimation of the coming trouble. Moved by the same spirit, and aiming at the same end as that whole great army of fanatics to which he belonged, only having less than an average share of prudence and sagacity, he broke from the ranks, and rushed forward in advance of the lines. It has been said that "coming events cast their shadows before," and it might have been added, that those coming events sometimes send forward miniature representations, from which may be seen, by substituting great things for small, what will be the character of those events when they come.

To all who hated that dear old Union which God gave to our fathers, John Brown's raid was a signal for rejoicing, while it sent a thrill of horror to the heart of every true patriot. The whole country was startled, and, for a brief period, deeply aroused. Men took sides, and showed, by their words and deeds, either that they were leagued in sympathy with those who had resolved on the destruction of the Union, or else that the Union was held in the firm grasp of their strongest and deepest affections.

Among those who took a prominent place in this latter class was Mr. Vallandigham, of Ohio. On many occasions he had predicted the very dangers whose first loud note of alarm was now sounding. Especially had he predicted and portrayed those dangers in that speech on the 29th of October, 1855. He had described the character and form of the coming trouble, as if seen with the keen eye of prophecy. And now, as the danger draws nearer, we find him still at his post. Congress had assembled at its first meeting after that notable and ominous event; a Speaker was to be elected, and the question was, should he be one who had lent the sanction and influence of his name to principles involved and illustrated in the late raid of John Brown.

It was under these circumstances – the general question before the House being the election of a Speaker – that Mr. Vallandigham obtained the floor, but yielded it for the purpose of a ballot. No choice having been made, he resumed the floor, but proposed again to yield for another ballot. Objection being made, he proceeded to address the House, as follows:

> Mr. Clerk: Desiring to speak at some length, and with some regard to method, upon the more important subjects which have been introduced into this debate, I cannot consent to yield the floor except upon a point of order, or for a strictly personal explanation. I claim no right myself to interrupt others for the purpose of interrogatory or catechising, and in return acknowledge no right in them to subject me to cross-examination as a witness upon this floor. I trust, along with other reforms, to see the ancient decorum and propriety of legitimate debate restored within these walls. In nothing, therefore, which I propose to say, do I mean to offend, by personal reflection upon any member of this House.
>
> And now, in the first place, Mr. Clerk, allow me to say that I do not regret this discussion. I lament, indeed, that it has not, at all times, been conducted in a better temper. Had it been possible to avoid it altogether, certainly it would have been preferable that it had never been commenced; but no one familiar with the temper of the whole country, reflected back in the Representatives of the country, and concentrated here into one intense focus, could have expected a week to pass after organization without an explosion more formidable, perhaps, and in a more questionable shape. This, in my judgment, is a better time and mode in which to meet it than any other. But, gentlemen of the House of Representatives, let us conduct it at all times with the temper and courtesy which become a legislative assembly. And yet the admonition is almost needless here. Although within these walls are as-

sembled the two hundred and forty-two Representatives and Delegates from the thirty-eight States and Territories of the Union, bringing with them every variety of personal and sectional temper and peculiarity; assembled, too, in the midst of a popular feeling more pervading and more deeply stirred up than at any former period, in one-half at least of these States, and upon the eve of startling, and, it may be, disastrous events, yet without organization, without rules, without a Speaker to command, or a Sergeant-at-Arms to execute – without gavel or mace – the instinct of self-government peculiar to the Anglo-Saxon race, and the habit of self-command and of obedience to but the shadow even of law and authority, have, for now these ten days past, secured us not only from collision and violence, but, for the most part, from breach even of the strictest decorum observed by our predecessors in this Hall at any period of our history. How sublime the spectacle! how grand this illustration of the spirit of free government! There is but one other country upon the globe where a similar spectacle could be exhibited.

I do not, then, regret this debate; it is fit and proper in itself; it is strictly parliamentary. You have a right by English precedent; you have a right by American precedent; by the usages of this House, to discuss the qualifications of your candidates for Speaker. If any member of this House has indorsed and recommended a book full of sentiments insurrectionary and hostile to the domestic peace and tranquillity of this country – a book intended or tending to stir up discord or strife between the different sections of this Union, or servile or other insurrection in any one or more States of this Union – and refuses still to disavow sympathy with the sentiments and purposes of such book, he is not fit to be Speaker or member of this House. Whether any one who has recommended such a book for wholesale circulation, not knowing, or caring to inquire into its character and contents – who has indorsed insurrection and violence in blank, and given a cordial letter of credit to whatsoever the Abolition authors of the "Helper book" might choose to say and to circulate throughout the South – is competent for Speaker, or fit to be trusted in the Speakership, this House must determine; and the country, gentlemen, must sit in judgment upon the decision.

But, Mr. Clerk, this whole subject and controversy has assumed a character and magnitude which impel me to break the silence which I thus fur have observed. Sentiments have been avowed and statements made upon this floor which demand notice and reply.

At this point Mr. Vallandigham gave way to a motion to adjourn, which was negatived. He then said that he should decline to pursue any farther that night the line of remark which he had proposed to himself; and, the House having again refused to adjourn, he proceeded to read and refer to matters which, forming no part of what he designed to say in the first place, are omitted here. (See *Congressional Globe*, page 150.) The House, after several other motions, having finally adjourned, the next morning he resumed as follows:

>Though a young man still, I have seen some legislative service. One of the earliest lessons which I taught myself as a legislator, and which I have sought to exemplify in every department of life, was so to be a politician as not to forget that I was a gentleman. There is a member of this House, now present, with whom, some years ago, I served in the legislature of my State, and to him I might with perfect confidence appeal to verify the assertion that no man ever was more exact in the observance of every rule of courtesy and decorum, not only in debate, but in private intercourse with his fellows. I might appeal, also, to the members here present of the last Congress, and to every member of this House of Representatives, and demand of them whether I have offended in anything, in public or private, in word or by deed.
>
>Now Mr. Clerk, that courtesy which I thus readily extend to others I am resolved to exact for myself, at all times and at every hazard. I had a right, yesterday, especially after yielding for a ballot, at a time when the Republican party with confidence anticipated the election of their candidate for Speaker, to expect the usual courtesy, scarce ever refused, of an adjournment. If any gentleman, this morning, after a night's calm reflection, sees, in anything that I have ever said or done, here or elsewhere, any justification for the extraordinary yet very discreditable scenes of yesterday, enacted by grown-up men and Representatives, I do not envy him the mental or moral obliquity of his vision.
>
>Mr. Clerk, I heard it said, many years ago, and my reading and observations of the proceedings of this House and of the Senate have taught me the truth of the declaration, that there was a marked difference between the deportment of the anti-slavery men in Congress toward slaveholders and their own Democratic colleagues from the free States. Sir, I want no better evidence of that fact than the occurrences of yesterday.
>
>I said then, that if any member of this House had indorsed a book full of sentiments which were insurrectionary and hostile to the domestic peace and tranquillity of this country – a book intended or tending to incite servile insurrection in one or more of the States of this Union – and refused still, either by himself or through another, to disavow all sympathy with such sentiments, he was not fit to be Speaker or member of this House. That judgment I, this morning, deliberately reaffirm in all its length and breadth and significance. The other day the gentleman from Virginia (Mr. Millson), a slaveholder, distinctly declared upon this floor, with all the emphasis he could command, that any one who would incite a servile insurrection, or knowingly distribute books or papers with that design, was not only not fit

to be Speaker, but not fit to live. There was then upon that side of this Chamber no sign, not even a whisper, of indignation or resentment. No, gentlemen, you sat in your seats, under that just but scathing denunciation, as mute as fishes and as gentle as lambs. Even your candidate for Speaker started to his feet, and, with manifest trepidation, disavowed every purpose and sentiment of the kind. Now, gentlemen of the Republican party, once for all and most respectfully, not in the language of menace, but as sober truth, receive this message from me, greeting: I am your peer; I represent a constituency as brave, as intelligent, as noble, and as free as the best among you upon this floor – and in their name and in my own name, I tell you that just whatsoever rights, privileges, courtesies, liberties, or anything else, you – whether from apprehension of personal danger or from any other cause – you, brave men at home vaunting arrantly there your rebukes here of Southern insolence and bravado – you, who return to your constituents at the end of every session bearing with you the scalps of half a score of fire-eaters from Alabama, Mississippi, or the Carolinas – you are accustomed to extend to slaveholders and Southern men upon this floor, I, as your peer, demand and will have at your hands. If you think otherwise, you have much yet to learn of the character of the man with whom you have to deal. I am as good a Western fire-eater as the hottest salamander in this House. (Laughter and applause.)

I have been served with a notice this morning that the Republican party here do not intend to listen to any further discussion. Very respectfully, I care not whether they listen or not. Let me tell them that the country holds its breath in suspense at the lightest word uttered in this Hall. The people of the United States are listening, at this moment, to catch every syllable which falls from the lips of the humblest member here.

I propose, now, sir. to address myself to those subjects only which I designed, from the beginning, to discuss.

I have said, and repeat, that the sentiments which have been avowed and the statements made upon this floor, demanding notice and reply, impel me to break the silence which I have thus far observed. The North and the South stand here arrayed against each other. Upon the one side, I behold numerical power; upon the other, the violent, even fierce, spirit of resistance. Disunion has been threatened. Sir, in all this controversy, *so far as it is sectional,* I occupy the position of *armed neutrality*. I am not a Northern man. I have little sympathy with the North, no very good feeling for, and am bound to her by no tie whatsoever, other than what once were and ought always to be among the strongest of all ties – a common language and common country. Least of all, am I that most unseemly and abject of all political spectacles – "a Northern man with Southern principles;" but, God be thanked, still a United States man with United States principles. When I emigrate to the South, take up my abode there, identify myself with her interests, holding slaves or holding none; then, and not till then, will I have a right, and will it be my duty, and no doubt my pleasure, to maintain and support Southern principles and Southern institutions. Then, sir, I am not a Southern man, either – although, in this unholy and most unconstitutional crusade against the South, in the midst of the invasion, arson, insurrection, and murder, to which she has been subject, and with which she is still threatened – with the torch of the incendiary and the dagger of the assassin suspended over her – my most cordial sympathies are wholly with her.

Mr. Clerk, I have heard a good deal said, here and elsewhere, about "Southern rights." Sir, I have no respect – none – none – for Southern rights merely because they are Southern rights. They are yours, gentlemen – not mine. Maintain them here, within the Union, firmly, fearlessly, boldly, quietly – do it like men. Defend them here and everywhere, and with all the means in your power, as I know you will and as I know you can. Yorktown and New Orleans – the end of the Revolution and the end of the War of 1812 – are both yours, and there is no power on earth that can subdue or conquer you.

But, while I have no respect for Southern rights simply because they are Southern rights, I have a very tender and most profound and penetrating regard for my own obligations. Your rights impose upon me corresponding obligations, which shall be fulfilled in their spirit and to the very letter – three-fifths rule, fugitive slave law, equal rights in the Territories, and whatsoever else the Constitution gives you. (Applause.) Our fathers made that compact, and I will yield a cordial, ready, and not grudging, obedience to every part of it.

I have heard it sometimes said – it was said here two years ago, not on this floor, certainly, but elsewhere – that there is no man from the free States, North or West, who is "true to the South." Well, gentlemen, that depends upon what you mean by being true to the South, If you mean that we, the Representatives of the free States of this Union, North and West, shall sit here within this Chamber, uttering Southern sentiments, consulting Southern interests, sustaining Southern institutions, and giving Southern votes, reckless of our own identity and our own self-respect, then I never was, am not now, and never will, while the Representative of a free State, be "true to the South;" and I thank God for it. If that be what is meant by "rottenness," in the other end of the capitol, commend me to rottenness all the days of my life.

But if you mean – and I know that a large majority of you do mean – true to the Constitution, without which there cannot be, and ought not to be, any Union – true to our own obligations – ready and sedulous to fulfill every article of the compact which our fathers made, to the extremest inch of possibility, and yielding, gracefully and willingly, as in the earlier and better days of the Republic, everything which comity and good fellowship, not only as between foreign States, but among brethren, demands at our hands, then, I tell you, and I tell the gentleman from Tennessee (Mr. Nelson), that the great mass of the Democratic party in the free States, and especially in the West, and thousands and tens of thousands of others, not members of that party, are now, and, I trust, ever will be, true to the South.

Allow me to illustrate my proposition. There are in this Hall, as elsewhere, three classes of men. The Republican or anti-slavery man – and you, gentlemen, have, or have had, not a few of that number in the South – asks, whenever a measure is proposed here, Will it tend to injure and hem in the institution of slavery, or rather will it weaken or offend the South, because it is the South? and he subordinates every other consideration to the great object of suppressing slavery, and of warring on the South. Upon the other hand, the merely Southern man, and especially the Southern extremist, asks, How will this measure advance the interests of slavery, or, rather, how will it aggrandize the South as South? and his vote is determined or insensibly influenced by this consideration. There is yet another, a third class, who ask none of these questions, and are moved by none of these considerations; political Gallios, perhaps, the gentlemen from Ohio (Mr. Corwin) would call them, who care for none of these things. To that class, Mr. Clerk, I am glad to belong. Outside of my own State, and of her constitution, I am neither pro-slavery nor anti-slavery; but maintain, as was said upon a memorable occasion, "a serene indifference" on this subject between these two sections. And here I stand upon the ancient, safe, constitutional, peaceable ground of our fathers. For many years after the foundation of this Republic was laid by wiser and better men – pardon me, gentlemen – than I see around me, no man ever thought of testing any measure here by its effects upon the institution of slavery. Never till the fell "Missouri question" reared its horrid front, begotten in New England, and brought forth in New York, was slavery made the subject of partisan and sectional controversy within this capitol. And we had peace in the land in those days, and patriotism and humanity and religion and benevolence; faith and good works. We neither had, nor demanded then, an anti-slavery Constitution, an anti-slavery Bible, nor an anti-slavery God; but the Constitution of the land, the Bible of our fathers, and that great and tremendous Being, who, from eternity, has ruled in the armies of heaven, and among the children of men.

Then, sir, I am not a Northern man, nor yet a Southern man; but I am a *Western man,* by birth, in habit, by education; and although still a United States man with United States principles, yet within, and subordinate to the Constitution, am wholly devoted to Western interests. Sir, this is no new enunciation of mine here. I proclaimed it upon this floor one year ago, and now congratulate myself and the West in having found so able and eloquent a coadjutor in the person of the distinguished gentleman from the seventh district of Ohio (Mr. Corwin). Sir, I am of and from the West; the great Valley of the Mississippi; of the free States of that valley, seated in queenly majesty at the head of the basin of that mighty river; yet one in interest, and one by the bonds of nature, stronger than hooks of steel, with every other State in that valley, full as it is, of population and riches, and exultant now in the hour of her approaching dominion. Seat yourself, denizen of the sterile and narrow, but beautiful hills and valleys of New England, and you, too, of the great cities of the North, whose geography and travel are circumscribed by the limits of a street railroad; seat yourselves upon the summit of the Alleghanies, and behold spread out before you a country stretching from the Alleghany to the Rocky Mountains – from the Gulf of Mexico to the Canada frontier – with limitless plains, boundless forests, fifteen States, a hundred rivers, ten thousand cities, towns, and villages, and twelve millions of people. Such a vision no man ever saw; no, not even Adam, when, in the newness and grandeur of God-made manhood, he stood upon the topmost hill of Paradise, and looked down upon a whole hemisphere of the yet unpeopled world. That, sir, is my country; if I may speak it without profanity, God's own country; yet, in this war of sections, I am of the free States of that valley.

Mr. Clerk, when I came to this city, two years ago, I brought with me an intense nationality; but I had been here only a little while till I learned that a man without a section to cling to, was reckoned but as a mere cipher in the account; and from that hour, subordinate always to the Constitution, I became and am a *Western sectionalist,* and so shall continue to the day of my death. I, too, propose, with the Leather Stocking of the "Prairie," to fight fire with fire. I learned here, Mr. Clerk, that while there was a North and a South, there was no West. I found her individuality sunk in the North. I saw that you of New York and New England entertained a profound respect for the citizen of South Carolina or Georgia, slaveholder though he might be, because he was east of the Alleghanies; and that you of Georgia and South Carolina reciprocated the good opinion, Abolition aside, because the New Yorker and the Yankee lived very near to the rising of the sun; while the Western man was held to be a sort of outside barbarian, very useful to count in a trial of numerical strength, but of no value for any other purpose. We of the great valley of the Mississippi are perpetually ignored. Sir, if all this were done of studied purpose, it would at least be tolerable; but not so; there is no design in it. It is a cool, silent, persistent, unobtrusive, but most offensive disparagement. Gentlemen, you do not know us. It is but a few months ago that a great paper in the city of New York spoke of Judge Douglas as attempting – and it was in the very capital of the State – "to impose his absurd theories upon the honest foresters of Ohio." And about the same time another great paper in the North referred to Governor Chase as a public man of merely "provincial reputation."

Let not the gentleman from the Mansfield district (Mr. Sherman) flatter himself that he is to be an exception. No, sir; he sees the parting rays of the setting sun too late in the day. A distinguished predecessor of his attained once the same point of greatness, but only to be let down gently in favor of Cape Cod. Do not deceive yourself. You were only put forward to be killed off; you were merely detailed as a forlorn hope, to be shot down in front of that Malakoff which you never will capture. Oh no! though two thousand miles east of the Rocky Mountains, you are quite too far West. Your distinguished colleague from the seventh district (Mr. Corwin) is gazing now wistfully through a spy-glass in the direction whither your eyes are turned; but he, alas, any more than you, will never wake up from that delicious reverie in which he now sits buried, to realize that –

> 'Tis distance lends enchantment to the views,
> And robes the Speaker's tribune in its radiant hue.

We did, indeed, gentlemen, once elect a Western President; but him you killed in a month – and a South-western President, too, and he survived you but fifteen months.

But, gentlemen of the West, the day-spring of our deliverance begins to dawn. Let us rejoice. The long period of our minority is about to terminate. Within the Union, after the next census, we of the Mississippi Valley will hold in our own hands the political power and the destinies of this country, and we will administer them for the benefit of the whole country. The day of our political independence is right now, while I speak. If you of the North and South-east will conspire, as for the last seventy years, to control the power and patronage of this Government for your own benefit, we of the Mississippi Valley will combine to rescue them from your hands. If you of the whole North will continue your sectional warfare upon the whole South, know ye that we of the North-west hold the political balance of power between you, and that we will use it to crush out and annihilate forever the fanaticism and treason which are threatening now to overspread the whole North, and very speedily to destroy this Republic. We will be ignored no longer. And here let me warn the Republican representatives from the West, that they have loaned themselves too long already to this proud and domineering North. You permit yourselves to be identified with the North, and to make common cause with her against slavery. *Cui bono?* Not yours; ah, no! You help to win the fight; you make good soldiers – excellent food for powder – but your Northern officers and Northern masters will divide the spoils. When William H. Seward threatens the South with the power and domination of the North, he means you; but when he would distribute office and patronage, he will know no West. Some of you dream that your Governor Chase will be the candidate of the Republican party for the next Presidency. Miserable infatuation! Cease, then, I beseech you, this unmanly vassalage to the North. If you will not hearken to the voice of patriotism, listen, at least, to the demands of independence and self-respect. If you will be sectionalists, lay aside this pestilent fanaticism on the subject of slavery, which you borrow servilely from the clergy, lecturers, and other demagogues of the North, and which they use for the purpose of their own aggrandizement – lay it aside, and be Western sectionalists. Talk not to me about humanity and benevolence. I have as profound and delicate an appreciation of them as you can have, but I will not be insulted with the miserable pretense. Are there no objects of charity in your own midst – no poor, no sick, no lame, no halt, no blind, no widows and orphans – to whose necessities you may administer, and thus find vent for that abounding river of humanity which wells up and flows out from the fountain of your hearts? Pardon me, but I despise and contemn your vassalage to the North as much as you can contemn and despise any man's servility to the South.

And now, one word to the gentleman from Pennsylvania (Mr. Hickman), who took refuge, the other day, in the "engine-room" of the left side of this Chamber, whence, through new and rudely-constructed port-holes, to send his missiles whistling into the camp which he so lately deserted. I admire his discretion – the better part of valor. Sir, he spoke about precipitating eighteen millions of people upon eight millions. Whence does he propose to get his eighteen millions? Did he mean to include us of the North-west? Does he imagine that we are militiamen to be drafted, or conscripts to be enrolled, and march forth at the sound of his drum, or to the notes of his bugle? I tell him that, if he means to raise the black standard of internecine war upon the South, he must find his recruits nearer home.

> Mr. Florence (in his seat). He will not find them there. (Applause in the galleries.)

Mr. Vallandigham. I rejoice to hear it. But I tell the gentleman further, that, if the Territories of this Union are to become the subject of controversy after dissolution, we of the Mississippi Valley propose to keep them ourselves, and then to make fair and honest partition with each other.

I approach now, Mr. Clerk, a painful and most difficult subject – *periculosæ plenum opus aleæ*. A word which, for very many years after the organization of this Government, no man ever dared to breathe within this capitol, has now become as familiar as the most ordinary words of salutation. Not a day nor an hour passes, but the hoarse croaking of this raven is heard, piercing the fearful hollow of our ears with moaning and dirge-like wail, the "never more" of the Union of these States. Sir, in this war of sections, standing here between the living and the dead, we, the Democratic representatives of the West, and I, as one of that number, have a duty to perform, which, in all humbleness, but in all faithfulness, shall be fulfilled. But too many of you of the North are striving with might and main to force the South out of this Union; and too many of you of the South are most anxious to be forced out. Do not deny it, either of you. I know it. Sir, if any member should rise here and tell me that there are no disunionists in the South, could I believe it? And when the gentleman from New York (Mr. Clark), or any one else, would persuade the South that there are no Abolitionists, or disunionists, in the North or the West, he only insults the intelligence of the men upon whom he would impose. Sir, if any colleague of mine, or any other gentleman from the free States, upon this floor, will so far forget the solemn responsibilities of his office, in the midst of the great and most alarming dangers wherewith we are at this moment encompassed, and unintentionally, of course, misrepresent the true state of public sentiment and public action in the North and the northern portions of the West, I, at least, will not consent to be a party to the deception. I tell gentlemen of the South that the doctrines of Hale, Banks, Seward, Giddings, Chase, Lincoln, and, above all, of the New York *Tribune*, are the doctrines of a large majority of the people of the North, and of a powerful and, for all efficient purposes of political action, a controlling minority, just now, in the West. One column of editorial in the recognized organs of the Republican party of Ohio, circulating every day among the masses of the people, penetrating into the homes and hearts of every family, acting and reacted upon by the public opinion which they help to create, and by which the public men of this country are set up, or pulled down, at the ballot-box, is better evidence of the true Republican sentiment of Ohio than a thousand speeches from the distinguished member for the seventh District of that State (Mr. Corwin). Sir, I listened the other day, as I always listen, with very great pleasure, to the genial and gushing eloquence from the lips of that gentleman, touched, as they are, as with a live coal from the altar of oratory. In the sentiments which he uttered here, there is much, very much, which meets my hearty concurrence; but I regret that truth and candor compel me to say that he does not represent the opinions and sentiments of the party to which he belongs. He claims, indeed, the leadership of that party. Pardon me – he is not only not a leader, but not even a respectful follower of the Republican party in that State. (Applause in the galleries.) Kentuckian as he is by birth, nobleman by nature – patriot as he is, and Whig as he! once was, I know that he never will consent to "guard the baggage" of that vandal host. Yet am I sorry to say that, to him, more than to any other man in the State, the Republican party to-day are indebted for their political supremacy in Ohio. He it was, who, without power in his own party, yet controlled, at the late election, the fifty thousand conservative voters of that State who are not of the Democratic party, and misled them into the support of an organization and of principles with which he has no real sympathy at all. He went into the Republican party to control it for good – but he was only as a straw before the whirlwind. He finds now a barren scepter in his grip; and let me, with great respect, remind him that it is not conservative speeches which are needed here to save us, but conservative votes at home. Certainly, the vast majority of the people of Ohio, of all parties, are at heart opposed to insurrection and disunion; but I tell the gentleman that, if he would conquer Abolition and sectionalism, he must fight them at the ballot-box.

Mr. Clerk, I do not propose to follow the gentleman into a discussion of the local politics of Ohio. I resolved, a good many years ago, to make no speech within a legislative assembly fit only to be spoken upon the "stump;" and to that resolution I propose steadily to adhere. But, inasmuch as the mere partisan politics of my State have already been drawn into debate here, a passing remark may not be inappropriate from me as a Representative, in part, from that State – though, in truth, I can add little to what has been fitly, strongly, eloquently spoken by the gentleman from the twelfth District (Mr. Cox).

Something has been said – more, I understand, is to follow – in regard to the soundness of the Democratic party in Ohio, and in other States of the Union. Sir, I will spare gentlemen all trouble upon that point. The Democratic party in Ohio, some years ago, was not sound, as men count soundness now. You need not go back to the records, and reproduce them here. Open confession is good for the soul, and I make it. I speak the more freely, because I think – and there are hostile witnesses here present to attest it – that my own record, from the very beginning of this whole controversy concerning slavery as a political question, is as unimpeachable as the record of any man in the North or the West, and, I may add, the South, too; for let me admonish gentlemen from that section that many of the people of the free States were for a good while misled by the precepts, if not the practice, of some of the earlier, and the later fathers, too, of the Southern political church. A little charity, I pray you, upon this subject. The Democratic party of Ohio, very much after the fashion described by the gentleman from the seventh district (Mr. Corwin), adopted, in 1848, a certain resolution, in which they denounced slavery in the abstract, and, with valorous earnestness, declared that the *people* of Ohio would use all power clearly given in the constitutional compact to "eradicate," tear up slavery by the roots; *but* – there is much virtue in "but," as well as "if" – they further resolved, with refreshing consistency, protesting the highest regard for the Union, the Constitution, and the rights of all the States, that the *Democracy* of Ohio were of opinion that no power was conferred by the constitutional compact to institute any process of eradication at all. Sir, I am not here to commend the superior honesty of such a platform. The gentleman (Mr. Corwin), who is well posted and of mature years, has explained luminously how these things are done, even in Republican conventions; but I will not disingenuously pretend – of course, I have no allusion to my colleague – that these resolutions did not at that time express the sentiments of the Democracy of my State. I think that, so far as they were supposed to be anti-slavery in their character, they did express both the opinions and the feelings of a very large majority of the people of the State. Sir, I was a member of that convention, and of the committee on resolutions, and voted many times in committee, during a protracted session of two days, against any and every expression of opinion upon the question of slavery in any form. Like my colleague, I was overpowered; like him, I endeavored to make the best of it, seeking consolation in the second and sound part of the resolution, and whiling away my idle hours in the delicate task of reconciling the two branches with each other. My success in this somewhat difficult work was just about equal to the success of the gentleman (Mr. Corwin) who undertook a similar contract here, the other day. But, Mr. Clerk, at every subsequent convention I exerted myself to the utmost to procure a recission of these resolutions; and, finally, in January, 1856, they were rescinded, and a sound platform adopted in their stead. From that hour the Democratic party has steadily gained strength. I pass by the election of Mr. Chase to the Senate, in 1848, the refusal by a State Convention to indorse the Baltimore platform, in 1853, and other unsound things, in faith or in practice, whereof the Democracy of my State were guilty in times past. "Let the dead past bury its dead." *Ernst ist das Leben.* Our business is to grapple manfully with the living realities of the present moment. Sir, in my judgment, the wisest man that ever lived was the author of the statute of limitations; all things adjust themselves equitably in periods of just about six years. Politicians, indeed, in later times, require, and, perhaps, are entitled to a shorter limitation. No man's record ought to be revived or called in question after the lapse of six months.

Allusion has been made to the present state of parties and of public sentiment in the North and West. Sir, I do not propose to speak at any length upon this subject. The events are recent, and no public man anywhere can have failed to observe them. It is folly to deny that, all through the North, and in many portions of the West, distinct and very earnest sympathy has been exhibited for John Brown in his recent insurrectionary and murderous invasion of Virginia; and that, too, not by the vulgar and low, but by men very high in political, social, and religious positions. Funeral processions, halls draped in mourning, tolling of bells, sermons, eulogies, orations, public meetings, adjournment of courts of justice, attempted adjournment of Senates and Houses of Representatives, and all the other usual insignia of public sorrrow, bestowed only hitherto upon the great and the good, the patriots, the heroes, and martyrs of the world – all these tributes, and more, have been paid to the memory of a murderer and felon. Even in my own native State, and in a part of my own district, I lament to say that these sad evidences of a corrupted public sentiment have been exhibited. In Cleveland, fertile in revolutionary conventions, in Akron, in Cincinnati, and elsewhere, in public assemblages, and by other means equally public and significant, the sympathy of thousands has been expressed. Sir, it is vain to attempt to conceal what all this means. There is a public sentiment behind it all, or it never would be tolerated. Thirty years ago, John Brown, hung like a felon, would have been buried like a dog.

Allusion has been made also to the Union meetings held, or to be held, in the great cities of the North. Sir, I would not abate one jot or tittle from the true value, least of all, from the patriotism of these assemblages. When public meetings run along with public sentiment, they are powerful to mold and to give it efficiency; but when they do not beat responsive to the popular heart, they are of no value. No one single page of election returns is worth more, as an index of real public sentiment, than all the Union resolves which shall be passed between this and the 4th of March, 1861. Let no man be deceived. If the distinguished gentleman from Tennessee (Mr. Nelson) be sincere – and I know that he is – in believing that the great mass of the people of the free States are opposed to the agitation of the slavery question in any form, and are ready to strike hands with any party which will put it down forever; if he really thinks that but a very small part of the people of the North sympathize with John Brown, or yield assent – a cordial and working assent – to the doctrines of William H. Seward, the "irrepressible conflict" included, full as it is of insurrection, treason, and murder; if he believes that, without the strong arm of the Federal Government, powerfully and in good faith stretched forth, fugitive slaves could be recaptured in one half the free States of this Union, under any law of Congress, I can only say, that he has the mild virtue of an honest heart – most marvelous credulity. Sir, I entertain for that gentleman the very highest respect, but he must allow me to say that, aside from that portion of his remarks the other day, which breathed so much of earnest, sincere, and eloquent eulogy upon the Union – one such speech, blinding the eyes of the people of the free States to the real public sentiment at the South, does more thus to keep alive the flames of civil discord between the South and the North and West, than a hundred speeches, vehement and impassioned though they may be, of the gentleman from South Carolina (Mr. Keitt). Sir, when a member of this House, of fine personal appearance, of sonorous voice, of classic education, and approved rhetorical excellence, tells us, with a magnificence of rhythm which regurgitates through these aisles, peals along these galleries, pierces the ceiling, and loses itself amid the columns and scaffolding of the unfinished dome of the capitol, that he will shatter this Republic "from turret to foundation stone," we are apt to understand that he is executing a grand rhetorical fugue, and that he is not half so much in earnest as he would have us imagine. But when a gentleman, mature in years, with a cold logic, a calm demeanor, but a sincere heart and earnest purpose, tells us, in the midst of invasion and murder – the legitimate and inevitable fruit of the "irrepressible conflict," which has been proclaimed against his own section – that he is not alarmed, and believes that no mischief is intended, we only understand that he invites aggression.

Sir, I am this moment reminded, by the appearance of the gentleman before me (Mr. Briggs), that I need no better illustration of the melancholy change in public sentiment, at the North, within the past few years. Here he sits, upon the only national side of this chamber, sole exemplar of the "lost politics" of the Whig party, faithful among the faithless, only he sole representative of the flag of our country, solitary and alone, *E Pluribus Unum*. (Laughter.) Sir, does not all this mean something?

But I will pursue this subject no further. I find no pleasure in it. I have said, and I think the dullest among us cannot fail to discern it now, that there is danger, great and most imminent danger, of a speedy disruption of the Union of these States. Too many of you of the South desire it, and but too many of you of the North are either striving for, or reckless whether it comes or not.

Sir, I will not consent that an honest and conscientious opposition to slavery forms any part of the motives of the leaders of the Republican party. In the earlier stages of the Abolition agitation, it may have been otherwise, but not so now. This whole controversy has now become but one of mere sectionalism – a war for political domination, in which slavery performs but the part of the letter x in an algebraic equation, and is used now, in the political algebra of the day, only to work out the problem of disunion. It was admitted, in 1820, in the beginning, by Rufus King, who hurled the first thunderbolt in the Missouri controversy, to be but a question of sectional power and control. To-day it exists, and is fostered and maintained, because the North has, or believes that she has, the power and numbers and strength and wealth, and every other element which constitutes a State, superior to you of the South. Power has always been arrogant, domineering, wrathful, inexorable, fierce, denying that constitutions and laws were made for it. Power now, and here, is just what power has been everywhere, and in every age. But, gentleman of the North, you who ignorantly or wittingly are hurrying this Republic to its destruction, you who tell the South to go out of the Union if she dare, and you will bring her back by force, or leave her to languish and to perish under your overshadowing greatness, did it never occur to you that when this most momentous but most disastrous of all the events which history shall ever to the end of time record, shall have been brought about, the West, the great West, which you now coolly reckon yours as a province, yours as a fief of your vast empire, may choose, of her own sovereign good will and pleasure, in the exercise of a popular sovereignty, which will demand, and will have non-intervention, to set up for herself? Did you never dream of a Western Confederacy? Did that horrid phantom never flit across you in visions of the night, when deep sleep falls upon men? Sir, we have fed you, we have clothed you, we have paid tribute to, and enriched you, for now these sixty years; we it is who have built up your marts of commerce; we it is who have caused your manufacturing establishments to flourish. Who made Boston? What built up New York, till now, like Tyre of old, she sits queen of the seas, and her merchant-princes and traffickers are among the honorable of the earth? *The cotton of the South, and the produce of the West.* Maintain this Union, and you will have them still. Dissolve this Union, if you dare; send California and Oregon to the Pacific, compel the South into a Southern confederacy, force us of the West into a Western confederacy, and then tell me what position would you assume among the powers of the earth? Where then would be your pride and arrogance, your trade and business, your commerce and your dominion? Look at the map spread out before you. Behold yourselves, as Mr. Webster said of Austria, "a mere patch upon the earth's surface." And, gentlemen of New England, let me ask you, What if New Jersey, Pennsylvania, and New York should refuse to go with you? They may refuse. You are a peculiar people. (Laughter.) I cannot say God's peculiar people; for you have dethroned Jehovah, and set up a new and anti-slavery god of your own; and before one year, you will inaugurate the statue of John Brown in the place where the bronzed image of Webster now stands. (Applause and hisses.) But, suppose these three States refuse your fellowship. Then would be fulfilled the prophecy, uttered many years ago, of the re-annexation of New England to the British crown.

    I know well, Mr. Clerk, that within the Union, we of the West are now, and so far as business and trade are concerned, must ever remain, tributaries to the North. You have made us so by that magnificent net-work of railroads which stretches now from the Atlantic to and beyond the Mississippi. But be not deceived. That "vast inland sea" is *mare nostrum* – it is our Atlantic ocean. Once cut off from the powerful and controlling ties of a united Government, aliens and foreigners to each other, with police and espionage and armed force at every depot upon the frontiers, nature, stronger than man, would reassume her rights and her supremacy. You made the railroad and the telegraph, but God Almighty made the Mississippi and her hundred tributaries.

    Is it not, I appeal to you, better then for you of the North, better for you of the South, better for us of the West, better for all of us, that this Union shall endure forever? Sir, I am for the Union as it is, and the Constitution as it is. I am against disunion now, and forever; against disunion, whether for its own sake or for the sake of anything else, equal, independent, constitutional liberty alone excepted. Do you ask me when the hour for disunion will come? I tell you never, never, while it is possible to avert it; never, while we can have, within the Union, the just constitutional rights which the Union was first made to secure; never certainly, till the hour shall come wherein to vindicate the glorious right of revolution. I speak not of the abstract right of secession. Do you ask me when that hour will come? I cannot tell you. Of that every State and every people must judge for themselves, before God and the great tribunal of history. Our fathers, in their day and generation, judged of it for themselves in our great Revolution. There, gentlemen, is one precedent, at least, hallowed by success, and canonized in the world's history. American citizens dare not call it in question. I commend it to you. Study it; ponder over it; profit by it. I know, indeed, that it has been sometimes said that our fathers went to war about a preamble, and fought seven long years to vindicate a principle. But, gentlemen, I am not sure that there is not, in all this, somewhat of the flourish of rhetoric and the flash of history; a little of the "glittering generalities" of the Declaration of Independence. I fear it may not be safe for you to follow that precedent too closely.

Do you ask me whether the election of an anti-slavery, sectional, Republican president, upon a sectional platform, pledged to administer the Government for sectional purposes, would, *per se,* be a justifiable cause of disunion? I cannot tell you. But I do tell you, as a Western man, and I tell the gentleman from Tennessee (Mr. Nelson), that, when you of the South shall have attained the numerical power and strength in this Union, and shall then organize a Southern party, on a Southern basis, and, under the forms of the Constitution, shall elect a Southern President, for the purpose of controlling all the vast power and patronage and influence of the Government, by action or non-action, for the advancement of Southern interest, and above all, for the purpose of extending slavery into States now free, with the design of making them all slave States, I will meet you as the Irish patriot would have met the invaders of Ireland – with the sword in one hand, and a torch in the other; dispute every inch of ground, burn every blade of grass, till the last intrenchment of independence shall be my grave. (Applause.) I will not wait for any overt act. What! Do I not know that fire will burn, that frost will congeal, that steel and poison will do their work of destruction to the human system, that I shall await the slow process of experiment to ascertain their natural and inevitable effects? Never – never! *Experimentum in corpore vili.*

These, Mr. Clerk, are no new doctrines in the country whence I come. Stronger sentiments, if possible, were uttered here upon this floor, ten years ago, by a distinguished predecessor of mine, the Hon. Robert C. Schenck, of Dayton, my fellow-citizen still, and the familiar friend of the eloquent gentleman before me (Mr. Corwin), an old-line Whig now, with a slight, very slight varnish of Republicanism.

Allow me, sir, to read what he said in a similar, though not so alarming, crisis in public affairs, on the 27th of December, 1849:

> If we of the Northern States –

We had no West then, sir; her existence and geography have been ascertained, and settled since –

> If we of the Northern States would not vote for a Southern man, merely because he is a Southern man, and men of the South will not vote for a Northern man, merely because he is a Northern man; and if that principle is to be carried out from here into all our national politics and elections, what must be the result? Disunion. *That itself is disunion.* You may disguise and cover up as you please, but that it will be. It may, perhaps, be regarded as but the first step in disunion; but its consequence follows as inevitable as fate. One section – the North or the South – must always have the majority. Disfranchise all upon the other side, and the Union could not hold together a day; *it ought not to hold together upon such conditions a day.* On this floor we now have from the free States one hundred and forty Representatives, and ninety from the slave States. Suppose the relative numbers were reversed; would we submit to be denied all participation in privileges here? *Not for an hour.* And should we ask for such submission from others? *Never!* the Whig party say – never. The true people of the North say – never.

That, sir, was good Whig doctrine ten years ago. It was good American doctrine in 1856; and I aver here, upon my responsibility as a Representative, that it is good sound Democratic doctrine everywhere, and all the time.

Then, sir, I am against disunion. I find no more pleasure in a Southern disunionist than in a Northern or Western disunionist. Do not tell me that you of the South have an apology in the event and developments of the last few months. I know you have. War – irrepressible war – has been proclaimed against your institution of slavery; it has been carried into your own States; arson and murder have been committed upon your own soil; peaceful citizens have been ruthlessly shot down at the threshold of their own doors. You avenged the wrong; you executed the murderer and the felon; but he has risen from the dead a hero and a martyr; and now the apostles of this new Messiah of Abolition, with scrip and purse, armed with the sword, insolent from augmenting numbers, apostles rather of Mahomet, disciples of Peter the Hermit, are but gathering strength, and awaiting the hour for a new invasion.

Certainly – certainly, in all this you have ample justification for whatsoever of excitement and alarm and indignation pervade now the whole South, from Mason and Dixon's line down to the Gulf of Mexico. But will you secede now? Will you break up the union of these States? Will you bring down for ever, in one promiscuous ruin, the columns and pillars of this magnificent temple of liberty, which our fathers reared at so great cost of blood and of treasure? Wait a little! Wait a little! Let us try again the peaceful, the ordinary, the constitutional means for the redress of grievances. Let us resort once more to the ballot-box. Let us try once again *that weapon, surer set, and better than the bayonet.*

      Mr. Clerk, I am not, perhaps, so hopeful of the final result as some other men; but I was taught in my boyhood that noblest of all Roman maxims – never to despair of the Republic. I was taught, too, by pious lips, a yet higher and holier doctrine still – a firm belief in a superintending Providence, which governs in the affairs of men. I do believe that God, in his infinite goodness, has foreordained for this land a higher, mightier, nobler destiny than for any other country since the world began; *Time's noblest empire is the last*. From the Arctic ocean to the Isthmus of Darien; from the Atlantic to the Alleghanies; stretching far and wide over the vast basin of the Mississippi, scaling the Rocky Mountains, and lost at last in the blue waters of the Pacific, I behold, in holy and patriotic vision, *one Union, one Constitution, one Destiny*. (Applause.) But this grand and magnificent destiny cannot be fulfilled by us, except as a united people. Clouds and darkness, indeed, rest now over us; we are in the midst of perils; rocks and quicksands are before us; strife and discord are all around us. How then, sir – mighty and momentous question, pregnant with the fate of an empire – shall we bring peace to this divided and distracted country? Sir, in my deliberate and most solemn judgment, there is but one way of escape; and that the immediate, absolute, unconditional disbandment of this sectional, anti-slavery, Republican party of yours. (Applause in the galleries.) If not, then upon your heads, and upon the heads of your children, be the blood of this Republic. You have organized a political party, based upon geographical discriminations, and for the purpose of administering this Government for the benefit of a part. You have neither strength, nor organization, nor existence even, in one half, nearly, of the States of this Union. Look around you. Behold upon this side of the House every section represented. Here are *the United States*. What do we see upon the left side of this Chamber? Not one solitary Representative of your faith or party from fifteen States of this Union. What does all this mean? It never was so before in the history of this Republic. What does it all tend to? Sir, there died, not many years ago, in New England, a man whom you all once idolized as approaching a little nearer in intellect to our notions of divinity than most men in any age. Died, did I say? No, he "still lives;" lives in history, lives in the public records, lives in his published works, lives in his public services, lives upon canvas, and in marble, and in bronze. Seven years ago, he wrote to a citizen of his native State:

> There are, in New Hampshire, many persons who call themselves Whigs, who are no Whigs at all; and no better than disunionists. Any man who hesitates in granting and securing to every part of the country its just and Constitutional rights, is *an enemy to the whole country*.

I know, gentlemen of the Republican party, that you profess, many of you, that you would not deny any Constitutional right to the States of the South. Admit it. But let me ask you by what rule of interpretation do you propose to ascertain these rights? I appeal to your platforms, to your speeches, to your acts. Like the learned doctor of Padua, you confess the bond; the Venetian law cannot impugn it; but you would give the exact pound of flesh, shedding no blood, cutting nor more nor less, under penalty of death and confiscation, than the just pound, not to be made light or heavy in the balance or the division of the twentieth part of one poor scruple, nor in the estimation of a hair. You well know that rights thus yielded are rights withheld; and withheld, too, with every aggravation of insult and wrong. Is that the spirit of the Constitutional compact? Is that the spirit which animated the great man and patriot whose ashes repose upon the banks of the Potomac, or of that other hero and patriot who finds a resting-place, in his long sleep, amid the shades of the Hermitage? How long, think you, can such a Union last? and what, above all, is it worth while it does last?

I have now finished what I desired to say upon the momentous subjects which have been introduced into this discussion. I have spoken freely of disunion. The time, most unhappily, has gone by when that melancholy theme can any longer be ignored or evaded. It must be met – met promptly, and met not with affected contempt, nor with real indifference. I have not spoken of it with any unmanly terror, but only with that sad and solemn alarm and apprehension which every patriot ought to feel in contemplating the overthrow of a Union so grand, a Constitution so admirable, a Government so vast, and institutions so noble, as these under and in the midst of which we are still permitted to live.

Sir, a Southern paper, not many miles from this capitol, has been pleased to say that there is no Southern State contemplating secession, in any possible contingency. No; they are only "coolly calculating the effect of disunion threats upon the nerves of the Northern and Western States." I do not believe it. Whoever utters it, libels the South and the North and the West. Idle threats and menaces will no longer frighten any one. Mutual interests and mutual fears do, indeed, bind us together still; but fraternal affection and good-will are the only bands which can keep us a united people. They are the silver cord and the golden bowl which are now so well-nigh broken at the fountain. If they be, indeed, snapped asunder, then neither threats, nor fears, nor interests, nor anything else can keep us together. My nerves, at least, are of the hardest and the toughest.

I am no more to be moved from my propriety by clamor and menace from the South, than by denunciation and fanaticism from the North or the West. Standing here – I repeat it – an armed neutral in the midst of this conflict of sections, I propose, in all humility, but in all justice, to hold even and impartial the scales between them. I have spoken freely and plainly, but have spoken justly and truly. I have not sought to conceal the evil which afflicts us – still less to exaggerate it, but only to exhibit it just as it is; for be assured – be assured there is no medicine nor surgery which can heal it without the utmost disclosure and knowledge of the true cause and character and extent of the disease. I have spoken briefly of the present evil state of public sentiment in the North and the West; in Ohio, my own native State. Yet, mother as she is, I have sought rather to imitate, not the rude and obscene behavior of Ham, but the filial piety and modesty of the elder sons of the Patriarch when mellowed with wine, and quietly, with averted eye, to cover her nakedness with the mantle of silence. Yet, as a Representative here in this Chamber, I have a duty to perform for the whole country, for the sake of the Constitution, for the perpetuity of the Union, and as its last hope.

I know well, indeed, that much that I have said to-day, will here, as elsewhere, be denounced as *pro-slavery*. Be it so. I have heard that too often, already, to feel the slightest apprehension or alarm; but I tell you, gentlemen, as a thousand times I have told those who sent me here, that: If to love my country, to revere the Constitution, to cherish the Union; if to abhor the madness and hate the treason which would lift up a sacrilegious hand against either; if to read that in the past, to behold it in the present, to foresee it in the future of this land, which is of more value to us and to the world, for ages to come, than all the multiplied millions who have inhabited Africa from the creation to this day – if this it is to be pro-slavery, then in every nerve, fiber, vein, bone, tendon, joint, and ligament, from the topmost hair of the head to the last extremity of the foot, I am all over and altogether a *proslavery man*. (Applause from the Democratic benches and the galleries.)

ABOLITION, THE UNION, AND THE CIVIL WAR

by
Clement Laird Vallandigham

THE CONFEDERATE
REPRINT COMPANY
☆ ☆ ☆ ☆
WWW.CONFEDERATEREPRINT.COM

CHAPTER THREE
How Shall the Union Be Preserved?
Speech Delivered in the House of Representatives, February 20, 1861

    This is that famous speech in which Mr. Vallandigham is said to have proposed to divide the Union into "four distinct nationalities." Such is the assertion repeatedly and persistently made by the Abolition press. The whole speech is here given: also, the proposed amendments to the Constitution. It is not easy to imagine a greater perversion of the plain and obvious meaning of language than has been exhibited in this case. A cause that requires the use of such means must be a bad one. The attention of the public has been repeatedly called to those misrepresentations; but thus far it has been found impossible to obtain a correction in the Abolition journals. So far from this, the leading papers of that class have continued to repeat the false statement, thus compelling the belief, that in making and circulating this declaration, those papers have been manufacturing and using a deliberate and intentional falsehood.

    But the people are pretty generally learning that the reports furnished by Abolition papers, pretending to give the sentiments of leading Democratic statesmen, are, almost invariably, caricatures or gross misrepresentations. They will not, therefore, be surprised to find that this speech, made in the hour of most imminent peril, when the greatest calamity any nation has ever endured was impending, so far from being, as has been so often and so falsely asserted, a proposition to divide the Union into "four distinct nationalities," was, in fact, a most wise and prudent suggestion, evincing the deepest political sagacity and foresight. If adopted, the country would have been saved that great waste and slaughter which have already wearied and sickened the heart of humanity, and of which the end is not yet. Even now, it may not be too late to make good use of some features of the plan here proposed.

The special order – namely, the Report of the Committee of Thirty-Three – being under consideration – Mr. Vallandigham addressed the House as follows:

> Mr. Speaker: It was my purpose, some three months ago, to speak solely upon the question of peace and war between the two great sections of the Union, and to defend, at length, the position which, in the very beginning of this crisis, and almost alone, I assumed against the employment of military force by the Federal Government to execute its laws and restore its authority within the States which might secede. Subsequent events have rendered this unnecessary. Within the three months, or more, since the Presidential election, so rapid has been the progress of events, and such the magnitude which the movement in the South has attained, that the country has been forced – as this House and the incoming Administration will at last be forced, in spite of their warlike purposes now – to regard it as no longer a mere casual and temporary rebellion of discontented individuals, but a great and terrible revolution, which threatens now to result in permanent dissolution of the Union, and division into two or more rival, if not hostile, confederacies. Before this dread reality, the atrocious and fruitless policy of a war of coercion to preserve or to restore the Union has, outside, at least, of these walls and of this capital, rapidly dissolved. The people have taken the subject up, and have reflected upon it, till, to-day, in the South, almost as one man, and by a very large majority, as I believe, in the North, and especially in the West, they are resolved, that, whatever else of calamity may befall us, that horrible scourge of civil war shall be averted. Sir, I rejoice that the hard Anglo-Saxon sense and pious and humane impulses of the American people have rejected the specious disguise of words without wisdom, which appealed to them to enforce the laws, collect the revenue, maintain the Union, and restore the Federal authority by the perilous edge of battle, and that thus early in the revolution they are resolved to compel us, their Representatives, belligerent as you of the Republican party here may now be, to the choice of peaceable disunion upon the one hand, or Union through adjustment and conciliation upon the other. Born, sir, upon the soil of the United States – attached to my country from earliest boyhood, loving and revering her with some part, at least, of the spirit of Greek and Ro-man patriotism – between these two alternatives, with all my mind, with all my heart, with all my strength of body and of soul, living or dying, at home or in exile, I am for the Union which made it what it is; and, therefore, I am also for such terms of peace and adjustment as will maintain that Union now and forever. This,

then, is the question which to-day I propose to discuss: How shall the Union of these States be restored and preserved?

Sir, it is with becoming modesty, and with something of awe, that I approach the discussion of a question which the ablest statesmen of the country have failed to solve. But the country expects even the humblest of her children to serve her in this, the hour of her sore trial. This is my apology.

Devoted as I am to the Union, I have yet no eulogies to pronounce upon it to-day. It needs none. Its highest eulogy is the history of this country for the last seventy years. The triumphs of war, and the arts of peace – science, civilization, wealth, population, commerce, trade, manufactures, literature, education, justice, tranquillity, security to life, to person, to property – material happiness, common defense, national renown, all that is implied in the "blessings of liberty" – these, and more, have been its fruits from the beginning to this hour. These have enshrined it in the hearts of the people; and, before God, I believe they will restore and preserve it. And, to-day, they demand of us, their embassadors and Representatives, to tell them how this great work is to be accomplished.

Sir, it has well been said that it is not to be done by eulogies. Eulogy is for times of peace. Neither is it to be done by lamentations over its decline and fall. These are for the poet and the historian, or for the exiled statesman who may chance to sit amid the ruins of desolated cities. Ours is a practical work, and it is the business of the wise and practical statesman to inquire first what the causes are of the evils for which he is required to devise a remedy.

Sir, the subjects of mere partisan controversy which have been chiefly discussed here and in the country, so far, are not the causes, but only the symptoms or developments of the malady which is to be healed. These causes are to be found in the nature of man, and in the peculiar nature of our system of governments. Thirst for power and place, or preeminence – in a word, ambition – is one of the strongest and earliest developed passions of man. It is as discernible in the school-boy as in the statesman. It belongs alike to the individual and to the masses of men, and is exhibited in every gradation of society, from the family up to the highest development of the State. In all voluntary associations of any kind, and in every ecclesiastical organization, also, it is equally manifested. It is the sin by which the angels fell. No form of government is exempt from it; for even the absolute monarch is obliged to execute his power through the instrumentality of agents; and ambition here courts one master instead of many masters. As between foreign States, it manifests itself in schemes of conquest and territorial aggrandizement. In despotisms it is shown in intrigues, assassinations, and revolts. In constitutional monarchies, and in aristocracies, it exhibits itself in contests among the different orders of society, and the several interests of agriculture, trade, commerce, and the professions. In democracies it is seen everywhere, and in its highest development; for here all the avenues to political place and preferment, and emolument, too, are open to every citizen; and all movements, and all interests of society, and every great question – moral, social, religious, scientific, no matter what – assumes, at some time or other, a political complexion, and forms a part of the election issues and legislation of the day. Here, when combined with interest, and where the action of the Government may be made a source of wealth, then honor, virtue, patriotism, religion, all perish before it. No restraints and no compacts can bind it.

In a federal republic all these evils are found in their amplest proportions, and take the form also of rivalries between the States; or more commonly, or finally, at least, especially where geographical and climatic divisions exist, or where several contiguous States are in the same interest, and sometimes where they are similar in institutions or modes of thought, or in habits and customs, of sectional jealousies and controversies, which end always, sooner or later, in either a dissolution of the union between them, or the destruction of the federal character of the government. But, however exhibited – whether in federative or in consolidated governments, or whatever the development may be – the great primary cause is always the same: the feeling that might makes right; that the strong ought to govern the weak; that the will of the mere and absolute majority of numbers ought always to control; that fifty men may do what they please with forty-nine; and that minorities have no rights, or at least that they shall have no means of enforcing their rights, and no remedy for the violation of them. And thus it is that the strong man oppresses the weak, and strong communities, states, and sections aggress upon the rights of weaker states, communities, and sections. This is the principle; but I propose to speak of it, to-day, only in its development in the political, and not in the personal or domestic relations.

Sir, it is to repress this principle that governments, with their complex machinery, are instituted among men; though in their abuse, indeed, governments may themselves become the worst engines of oppression. For this purpose treaties are entered into, and the law of nations acknowledged between foreign States. Constitutions and municipal laws and compacts are ordained, or enacted, or concluded to secure the same great end. No men understood this, the philosophy and aim of all just government, better than the framers of our Federal Constitution. No men tried more faithfully to secure the Government which they were instituting from this mischief; and, had the country over which it was established been circumscribed by nature to the limits which it then had, their work would have, perhaps, been perfect, enduring for ages. But the wisest among them did not foresee – who, indeed, that was less than omniscient, could have foreseen? – the amazing rapidity with which new settlements and new States have sprung up, as if by enchantment, in the wilderness; or that political necessity, or lust for territorial aggrandizement would, in sixty years, have given us new Territories and States equal in extent to the entire area of the country for which they were then framing a Government? They were not priests or prophets to that God of Manifest Destiny whom we now worship, and will continue to worship, whether united into one Confederacy still, or divided into many. And yet it is this very acquisition of territory which has given strength, though not birth, to that sectionalism which already has broken in pieces this, the noblest Government ever devised by the wit of man. Not foreseeing the evil, or the necessity, they did not guard against its results. Believing that the great danger to the system which they were about to inaugurate lay rather in the jealousy of the State Governments toward the power and authority delegated to the Federal Government, they defended diligently against that danger. Apprehending that the larger States might aggress upon the rights of the smaller States, they provided that no State should, without its consent, be deprived of its equal suffrage in the Senate. Lest the legislative department might encroach upon the executive, they gave to the President the self-protecting power of a qualified veto; and, in turn, made the President impeachable by the two Houses of Congress. Satisfied that the several State Governments were strong enough to protect themselves from Federal aggressions, if, indeed, not too strong for the efficiency of the General Government, they thus devised a system of internal checks and balances looking chiefly to the security of the several departments from aggression upon each other, and to prevent the system from being used to the oppression of individuals. I think, sir, that the debates in the Federal Convention, and in the conventions of the several States called to ratify the Constitution, as well as the cotemporaneous letters and publications of the time, will support me in the statement that the friends of the Constitution wholly under-estimated the power and influence of the Government which they were establishing. Certainly, sir, many of the ablest statesmen of that day earnestly desired a stronger Government; and it was the policy of Mr. Hamilton, and of the Federal party, which he created, to strengthen the General Government; and hence the funding and protective systems, the national bank, and other similar schemes of finance, along with the "general-welfare doctrine," and a liberal construction of the Constitution.

Sir, the framers of the Constitution – and I speak it reverently, but with the freedom of history – failed to foresee the strength and centralizing tendencies of the Federal Government. They mistook wholly the real danger to the system. They looked for it in the aggressions of the large States upon the small States, without regard to geographical position, and accordingly guarded jealously in that direction, giving, for this purpose, as I have said, the power of a self-protecting veto in the Senate to the small States, by means of their equal suffrage in that Chamber, and forbidding even amendment of the Constitution, in this particular, without the consent of every State. But, they seem wholly to have overlooked the danger of sectional combinations as against other sections, and to the injury and oppression of other sections, to secure possession of the several departments of the Federal Government, and of the vast powers and influence which belong to them. In like manner, too, they seem to have utterly under-estimated slavery as a disturbing element in the system, possibly because it existed still in almost every State, but chiefly because the growth and manufacture of cotton had scarce yet been commenced in the United States – because cotton was not yet crowned king. The vast extent of the patronage of the Executive, and the immense power and influence which it exerts, seem also to have been altogether under-estimated. And independent of all these, or rather, perhaps, in connection with them, there were inherent defects, incident to the nature of all governments; some of them peculiar to our system, and to the circumstances of the country, and the character of the people over which it was instituted, which no human sagacity could have foreseen, but which have led to evils, mischiefs, and abuses, which time and experience alone have disclosed. The men who made our Government were human; they were men, and they made it for men of like passions and infirmities with themselves.

I propose now, sir, to inquire into the practical workings of the system; the experiment – as the fathers themselves called it – after seventy years of trial.

No man will deny – no American, at least, and I speak to-day to, and for Americans – that in its results it has been the most successful of any similar Government ever established; and yet, in the very midst of its highest development and its perfect success, in the very hour of its might, while "towering in its pride of place," it has suddenly been stricken down by a revolution which it is powerless to control. Sir, if I could believe, as the gentlemen from Tennessee (Mr. Etheridge), would seem to have me believe, that for more than half a century the South has had all that she ever asked, and more than she ever deserved, and that now, at last, a few discontented spirits have been able to precipitate already seven States into insurrection and rebellion, because they are displeased with the results of a presidential election; or, if I could persuade myself, with the gentleman from Massachusetts (Mr. Adams), that thirteen States, or fifteen States, and eleven or twelve millions people have been already drawn, or may soon be drawn, into a revolt against the grandest and most beneficent Government, in form and in practice, that ever existed, from no other than the trivial and most frivolous causes which he has assigned, then I should, indeed, regard this revolution, in the midst of which we are, as the most extraordinary phenomenon ever recorded in history. But the muse of history will, I venture to say, not so write

How Shall the Union Be Preserved?

it down upon the scroll which she still holds in her hand, in that grand old Hall of Representatives, where, linked to time, solemnly and sadly she numbers out yet the fleeting hours of this perishing Republic. No; believe me, Representatives, the causes for these movements lie deeper, and are of longer duration, than all this. If not, then the malady needs no extreme medicine, no healing remedies, nothing, nothing. Time, patience, forbearance, quiet – these, these alone will restore the Union in a few months. But, sir, I have not so read the history of this country, especially for the last fourteen years. The causes, I repeat, are to be found in the practical workings of the system, and are to be removed only by remedies which go down to the very root of the evil; not, indeed, by eradicating the passions which give it birth and strength – for even religion fails to accomplish that impossible mission – but by checking or taking away the power with which these passions are armed for their work of evil and mischief.

I find, then, sir, the first or remote cause which, has led to the incipient dismemberment of the Union, in the infinite honors and emoluments, the immense, and continually increasing, power and patronage of the Federal Government. Every admission of new States, every acquisition of new territory, every increase of wealth, population, or resources of any kind; all moral, social intellectual, or inventive development; the press, the telegraph, the railroad, and the application of steam in every form – whatsoever there is of greatness at home, or of national honor and glory abroad – all, all has inured to the aggrandizement of this central Government. Part of this, certainly, is the result of causes which no constitutional restriction, no party policy, and no statesmanship can control; but much of it, nevertheless, from infringements of the Constitution, and from usurpations, abuses, corruptions, and mal-administration of the Government. In the very beginning, as I have said, a fixed policy of strengthening the General Government, in every department, was inaugurated by the Federal party; and this led to the bitter and vehement struggle, in the very first decade of the system, between the Democratic-Republicans and the Federalists; between the advocates of power, and the friends of liberty; those who leaned strongly toward the General Government, and those who were for State rights and State sovereignty – the followers of Hamilton and the disciples of Jefferson – which ended, in 1801, in the overthrow of the Federal party, and the inauguration of the Democratic policy, which demanded a simple Government, a strict construction of the Constitution, no public debt, no protective tariff, no system of internal improvements, no national bank, hard money for the public dues, and economical expenditures; and this policy, after a long and violent contest for more than forty years – a contest marked with various fortune, and occasional defeat, and sometimes temporary departure by its own friends – at last became the established policy of the Government, and so continued until this pestilent sectional question of slavery obliterated old party divisions, and obscured and hid over and covered up for a time – if, indeed, it has not removed utterly – some, at least, of the ancient landmarks of the Democratic party. And yet, in spite of the overthrow of the Federal party, in spite of the final defeat of its policy, looking especially and purposely to the strengthening of the General Government, partly from natural causes, as I have said, and partly because the Democratic party has sometimes been false to its professed principles – above all, to its great doctrine of State rights, and its true and wise policy of economy in expenditures, and decrease in executive patronage and influence – the Federal Government has gone on, steadily increasing in power and strength and honor and consideration and corruption, too, from the hour of its inauguration to this day; and when I speak of "corruption," I use the word in the sense in which British statesmen use it – men who understand the word, and who have, for a century and a half, reduced the thing itself to a science and a system, and have made it an element of very great strength in the British Government.

Nor, sir, is this mischief, if mischief indeed it be, confined wholly to any one department of the General Government? The Federal judiciary – to begin with it – here and in the States, dazzles the imagination and invites the ambition of the lawyers, that not most numerous but yet most powerful class of citizens, by its superior honors, its great emoluments, its life-tenure, its faith in precedents, and its settled forms and ancient practice, untouched by codes and unshaken by crude and reckless and hasty legislation. Here, in this venerable forum, where States at home and States and empires from abroad, and the Federal Government itself, are accustomed to contend for the judgment of the court, whatever there yet remains of ancient and black-letter law; whatever of veneration and regard for the names and memories, and the volumes of Littleton and Coke, and Croke, and Plowden, and the year books; or for silk gowns, and for all else, too, that is valuable in legal archaeology, has taken refuge, and stands intrenched. All that there was of form and ceremony and dignity and decorum, in the beginning of the Government, is still to be found here, and only here; all but the bench and bar of forty years ago – the Marshalls, and the Storys, the Harpers, the Pinckneys, the Wirts, and the Websters of an age gone by.

Still, the circle of honor through the judiciary is a narrow one, and it lies open to but few; and yet, in times past, the judiciary has done much to enlarge the powers and increase the consideration and importance of the central Government.

But it is the Senate and the House of Representatives which are the great objects of ambition, and the seats of power. All the legislative powers of this great and mighty Republic, whose name and authority and majesty are known and felt and feared, too, throughout the earth, are vested in the

How Shall the Union Be Preserved?

Congress of the United States. War, revenues, credit, disbursement, commerce, coinage, the postal system, the punishment of crimes upon the high seas, and against the law of nations, the admission of new States, the disposition of the public lands, armies, navies, the militia – all belong to it to control, together with an unnumbered, innumerable, and most indefinable host of implied or derivative powers: whence funding systems, banks, protective tariffs, internal improvements, distributions, surveys, explorations, railroads, land grants, submarine telegraphs, postal steam navigation and post roads upon the high seas, plunder schemes, speculations, and peculations, pensions, claims, the acquisition and government of Territories, and a long train of usurpations and abuses, all tending – legitimate powers and illegitimate assumptions of power alike – to aggrandize the central Government, and to make its possession and control the highest object of a corrupt, wicked, perverted, and peculating ambition, in any party or any section.

But great and imposing as the powers, honors, and consideration of Congress are, the executive department is scarce inferior in anything, and, in some things, is far superior to it. Your President stands in the place of a king. There is a divinity that doth hedge him in; it is the divinity of patronage. He is the god whose priests are a hundred and fifty thousand, and whose worshipers a host whom no man can number; and the sacrifices of these priests and worshipers are literally "a broken spirit." Sir, your President is commander-in-chief of your armies, your navies, and of the militia – four millions of men. He carries on war, concludes peace, and makes treaties of every sort. Through his qualified veto, he is a participant in the entire legislation of the Government, and it behooves the whole army of speculators, jobbers, contractors, and claimants, to propitiate him as well as Senators and Representatives. He calls the Congress together on extraordinary occasions, and adjourns them in case of disagreement. He appoints and receives embassadors and all other diplomatic agents; appoints judges of the Supreme Court, and of other judicial tribunals; cabinet ministers; collectors of customs, and post-masters, and controls the appointment of a hundred and fifty thousand other officers, of every grade, from Secretary of State down to the humblest tide-waiter. All that is implied in the word "patronage," and all that is meant by that other word, the "spoils" – *res detestabilis et caduca* – a word and a thing unknown to the fathers of the Republic, all belong to him to control. His power of appointment and removal at discretion makes him the master of every man who would look to the Executive for honor or emolument; and its tremendous influence is reflected back upon the Senate and this House, on every Senator or Representative who would reward his friends for their support at home, or secure new friends for a re-election. The Constitution forbids titles of nobility; yet your President is the fountain of honor. Sir, to pass by the utter and extraordinary perversion of the original purpose of the Constitution in the choice of electors for the President – a perversion the result of caucuses, national conventions, and other party machinery, and which has led to those violent and debauching presidential struggles, every four years, for possession of the immense spoils of the executive office – no department has, in other respects also, so utterly outstripped the estimate of the founders of the Government, except, indeed, of the few who, like Patrick Henry, were derided as ghost-seers and hypochondriacs.

When the elder Adams was President, the great east-room of the White House – where now, or lately, on gala days, are gathered the embassadors and ministers of a hundred courts, from Mexico to Japan, and the assembled wit and fashion and beauty and distinction of the thirty-three States of the Union – was then used by the excellent and patriotic wife of the President as a drying-room for – not the maids of honor – but the washerwoman of the palace.

Sir, there is an incident connected with the early settlement of this city – still the capital of the Republic, selected as the seat of Government, by Washington, the Father of the Republic, and bearing his honored name – an incident which shows how much he and the other great men who made the Constitution under-estimated the power and importance of the Executive. This capitol, within which we now deliberate, *fronts to the east*. There all your Presidents are inaugurated: and it was the design and the expectation of the founders of the city that it should extend to the eastward. There, sir – there, in that direction – was to be the future home of the American continent. The Executive mansion was meant to be in the rear, and to be kept in the rear of the Chambers of the Legislature. A long vista through the original forest trees – a sort of American mall – was to connect them together; and the President was expected to enter below stairs, and at the back door, into this capitol. But he was to be kept for the most part trans Tiberem – on the other side of the Tiber. The low, marshy ground to the westward, it was supposed, would forever forbid the building up of a city between the seats of legislative and executive magistracy; and the whole – if, indeed, ever laid out at all – might have become a great national park. But behold the strange perversity of man! The city has all gone to the westward. The rear of the capitol has now become its front. Pennsylvania Avenue, instead of a suburban drive, is now a grand thoroughfare, the chief artery which conveys the blood from that which is now the center or heart of the system – the President. The Executive mansion – that old castle, with bad fires and without bells, to the sore discomfort of Mistress Abigail Adams – is now, and has been for years, the great object of attraction; and whereas, in the beginning, the "taverns" – for that was the name given them sixty years ago – all clustered around this capitol, I observe that now the greatest, most flourishing, and best patronised "hotel" has established itself within bow-shot of the

White House. Sir, the power of executive gravitation has proved too strong for the framers of the Government and the founders of the city. Westward the course of architecture has taken its way; and certainly, sir – certainly – it is not because of any especial attraction about that most venerable of ancient marts – old Georgetown.

But to resume, sir. Nothing adds so much to the power and influence of the Executive as a large revenue and heavy expenditures; and if a public debt be added, so much the worse. Every dollar more borrowed or collected, and every dollar more spent, is just so much added to the power and value of the executive office. Nothing in the political history of the country has been so marked as the steady, but enormous, increase in the taxation and disbursement of the Federal Government. Fifteen years ago – to go back no further – just previous to the Mexican War, the receipts of the Treasury were $29,000,000, and the expenditures $27,000,000; while four years ago – only ten years later – the receipts had run up to $69,000,000, and the expenditures to $71,000,000 – the latter being always, or nearly always, a little in advance of the former. Nature, it is said, sir, abhors a vacuum; but government – our government, at least – would seem to abhor a plethoric treasury. There are always surgeons, volunteers too, at that, if need be, of a very famous school of surgery, who are ready to resort, upon all occasions, to financial phlebotomy. Verily, sir – verily these surgeons of the executive household have great faith in a low fiscal regimen.

The collection and disbursement of $80,000,000 a year, for four years, is a prize worth every sacrifice. The power of the sword, the command of armies and navies and the militia, is itself a tremendous power; and, from the signs around us, from all that everywhere meets the eye or falls upon the ear, at every step throughout this capital, I am afraid that now at length, and before the close of the last quarter of the first century of the Republic, it is about to assume a terrible significancy, and that the reign of military despotism is henceforth to be dated from this year. But, great as this power is, it is nothing – nothing as yet in this country – compared with the power of the purse. He who commands that unnumbered host of eager and hungry expectants whose eyes are fixed upon the Treasury, to say nothing of that other host of seekers of office, is mightier far than the commander of military legions. The gentleman from Tennessee (Mr. Etheridge) entertained us the other day with a glowing picture of the exodus of the present incumbents about the executive offices and elsewhere. Sir, I should be pleased, when he next addresses the House, to have his fine powers of "wit and eloquence tested by a description of the flight of the incoming locusts about the fourth of March. Certainly, sir – certainly – the departure of the army of fat, sleek, contented, well-fed and well-clad officeholders, whose natural habitat is the Treasury building, or some other of the same sort, is a picture melancholy enough to excite commiseration in even the hardest and the stoniest heart. But the ingress of that other mighty host of office-seekers, fifty to one – lean, lank, cadaverous, hungry, hollow-eyed, with bones bursting through their garments, and long, skinny fingers, eager to clutch the spoils; and stung, too, with the cestus of that practical sort of patriotism which loves the country for its material benefits, would require some part, at least, of the powers of those diabolical old painters of the Spanish or Italian school. The gentleman will pardon me, but I am sure that even he is not equal to it.

Such, Mr. Speaker, is the central Government of the United States, and such its powers and honors and emoluments; and every year adds strength to them. Against the centralizing tendencies and influences of such a Government, the States, separately, cannot contend. Neither ambition nor avarice, the love of honor or the love of gain, find anything to satisfy their large desires in the State governments. Sir, the State executives have no cabinets, no veto for the most part, no army, no navy, no militia, except upon the peace establishment, and that commonly despised; no foreign appointments, and no diplomatic intercourse; no treaties, no post-office, no land-office, no great revenues to disburse; small salaries, and no patronage – in short, sir, nothing to arouse ambition, or to excite avarice. The Legislature of the State have a most valuable, but not the most dignified, field of labor. They declare no war, levy no imports, regulate no external commerce, coin no money, establish no post-routes, oceanic or overland; make no land grants, emit no bills of credit of their own, publish no *Globe*, have no franking privilege, and their Senators and Representatives serve the State for a few hundred dollars a years. The State judiciaries, however important the litigation before them may be to the parties, attract commonly but small interest from the public; and, of late years, no great or splendid legal reputation is to be acquired, outside of a few of the larger cities at least, either upon the bench or at the bar of the State courts. Whatever, sir, the dignity or power or consideration of the United States may be, that of each State is but the one thirty-fourth part of it; and, indeed, for some years past, the control of the State governments has, to a great extent, been sought after chiefly as an instrumentality for securing control of legislative, executive, or judicial position in the Federal Government. And all this mischief – for mischief certainly I must regard it – has been steadily aggravated by the policy pursued in nearly all the States, of diminishing, in every way, in their constitutions, and by their laws, the dignity, power, and consideration of the several departments of their State governments. Short tenures, low salaries, biennial sessions, crude, hasty, and continually changing legislation, new constitutions every ten years, and whatever else may be classed under the head of reform, falsely so called, have been the bane of State sovereignty and importance. Indeed, for years past, State constitutions, laws, and institutions of every sort, seem to have been regarded as but so many subjects for rude and wanton experiments at the hands of reckless ideologists or demagogues. But, besides all this, the infinite subdivision of political power in the States, from the chief departments of State down through counties, townships, school-districts, cities, towns, and villages, all which certainly is very necessary and proper in a democratic Government, tends very much of itself to decrease the dignity and importance of the States. In short, sir, in nearly all the States, and especially in the new States, the great purpose of the politicians would seem to have been, to ascertain just how feeble and simple and insignificant their governments could be made – just how near to a pure and perfect democracy our representative form of republicanism can be carried. All this, sir, would have been well, and consistent enough, no doubt, if the States were totally disconnected, or if the Federal Government could have been kept down equally low, simple, and democratic. Certainly, this is the true idea of a strictly democratic form and administration of government; and the nearer it is approached, the purer and better the system – in theory, at least. But the experiment having been fairly tried, and the fact settled, that in a country so large, wealthy, populous, and enterprising as ours is, it is impossible to reduce down, or to keep down, the central Government to one of economy and simplicity, it is the true wisdom and policy of the States to see to it that their own separate governments are not rendered any more insignificant, at least, than they are already.

Such, sir, I repeat, then, is the central Government of the United States, and such its great and tremendous powers and honors and emoluments. With such powers, such honors, such patronage, and such revenues, is it any wonder, I ask, that everything, yes, even virtue, truth, justice, patriotism, and the Constitution itself, should be sacrificed to obtain possession of it? There is no such glittering prize to be contended for every four or two years anywhere throughout the whole earth; and accordingly, from the beginning, and every year more and more, it has been the object of the highest and lowest, the purest, and the most corrupt ambition known among men. Parties and combinations have existed from the first, and have been changed, and reorganized, and built up, and cast down, from the earliest period of our history to this day, all for the purpose of controlling the powers and honors and the moneys of the central Government. For a good many years parties were organized upon questions of finance or of political economy. Upon the subjects of a permanent public debt, a national bank, the public deposits, a protective tariff, internal improvements, the disposition of the public lands, and other questions of a similar character, all of them looking to the special interests of the moneyed classes, parties were, for a long while, divided. The different kinds of capitalists sometimes also disagreed among themselves – the manufacturer with the commercial men of the country; and, in this manner, party issues were occasionally made up. But the great dividing line, at last, was always between capital and labor – between the few who had money, and who wanted to use the Government to increase and "protect" it, as the phrase goes, and the many who had little, but wanted to keep it, and who only asked Government to let them alone. Money, money, sir, was at the bottom of the political contests of the times; and nothing so curiously demonstrates the immense power of money, as the fact, that in a country where there is no entailment of estates, no law of primogeniture, no means of keeping up vast accumulations of wealth in particular families, no exclusive privileges, and where universal suffrage prevails, these contests should have continued, with various fortune, for full half a century. But, at the last, the opponents of Democracy, known at different periods of the struggle by many different names, but around whom the moneyed interests always rallied, were overborne, and utterly dispersed. The Whig party, their last refuge, the last and ablest of the economic parties, died out; and the politicians who were not of the Democratic party, with a good many more, also, who had been of it, but who had deserted it, or whom it had deserted, were obliged to resort to some other and new element for an organization which might be made strong enough to conquer and to destroy the Democracy, and thus obtain control of the Federal Government. And most unfortunately for the peace of the country, and for the perpetuity, I fear, of the Union itself, they found the nucleus of such an organization ready formed to their hands – an organization odious, indeed, in name, but founded upon two of the most powerful passions of the human heart: *sectionalism,* which is only a narrow and localized patriotism, and *anti-slavery*, or love of freedom, which commonly is powerful just in proportion as it is very near coming home to one's own self, or very far off, so that either self-interest, or the imagination can have full power to act.

And here let me remark, that it had so happened that almost, if not quite, from the beginning of the Government, the South, or slaveholding section of the Union – partly because the people of the South are chiefly an agricultural and producing, a non-commercial and non-manufacturing people, and partly because there is no conflict, or little conflict, among them between labor and capital, inasmuch as to a considerable extent, capital owns a large class of their laborers not of the white race; and it may be also, because, as Mr. Burke said, many years ago, the holders of slaves are "by far the most proud and jealous of their freedom," and because the aristocracy of birth and family, and of talent, is more highly esteemed among them than the aristocracy of wealth – but no matter from what cause, the fact was that the South, for fifty years, was nearly always on the side of the Democratic party. It was the natural ally of the Democracy of the North, and especially of the West. Geographical partition and identity of interests bound us together; and till this sectional question of slavery arose, the South and the new States of the West were always together; and the latter, in the beginning, at least, always Democratic. Sir, there was not a triumph of the Democratic party in half a century, which was not won by the aid of the statesmen and the people of the South. I would not be understood, however, as intimating that the South was ever slow to appropriate her full share of the spoils – the *opima spolia* of victory, or especially that the politicians of that great and noble old Commonwealth of Virginia – God bless her – were ever remarkable for the grace of self-denial in this regard – not at all. But it was natural, sir, that they who had been so many times, and for so many years, baffled and defeated by the aid of the South, should entertain no very kindly feelings towards her. And here I must not omit to say, that all this time there was a powerful minority in the whole South, sometimes a majority in the whole South, and always in some of the States of the South, who belonged to the several parties which, at different times, contended with the Democracy for the possession and control of the Federal Government. Parties, in those days, were not sectional, but extended into every State, and every part of the Union. And, indeed, in the Convention of 1787, the possibility, or, at least, the probability, of sectional combinations, seems, as I have already said, to have been almost wholly overlooked. Washington, it is true, in his Farewell Address, warned us against them, but it was rather as a distant vision than as a near reality; and a few years later, Mr. Jefferson speaks of a possibility of the people of the Mississippi Valley seceding from the East; for even then a division of the Union, North and South, or by slave lines in the Union, or out of it, seems scarcely to have been contemplated. The letter of Mr. Jefferson upon this subject, dated in 1803, is a curious one; and I commend it to the attention of gentlemen upon both sides of the House.

So long, sir, as the South maintained its equality in the Senate, and something like equality in population, strength, and material resources in the country, there was little to invite aggression, while there were the means, also, to repel it. But, in the course of time, the South lost its equality in the other wing of the capitol, and every year the disparity between the two sections became greater and greater. Meantime, too, the anti-slavery sentiment, which had lain dormant at the North for many years after the inauguration of the Federal Government, began, just about the time of the emancipation in the British West Indies, to develop itself in great strength, and with wonderful rapidity. It had appeared, indeed, with much violence at the eriod of the admission of Missouri, and even then shook the Union to its foundation. And yet, how little a sectional controversy, based upon such a question, had been foreseen by the founders of the Government, may be learned from Mr. Jefferson's letter to Mr. Holmes, in 1820, where he speaks of it falling upon his ear like "a fire-bell in the night." Said he:

> I considered it, at once, as the death-knell of the Union. It is hushed, indeed, for the moment; but this is a reprieve only, not a final sentence. A geographical line, coinciding with a marked principle, moral and political –

Sir, it is this very coincidence of geographical line with the marked principle, moral and political, of slavery, which I propose to reach and to obliterate in the only way possible; by running other lines, coinciding with other and less dangerous principles, none of them moral, and, above all, with other and conflicting interests –

> A geographical line, coinciding with a marked principle, moral and political, once conceived and held up to the angry passions of men, will never be obliterated, and every new irritation will mark it deeper and deeper.... I regret that I am now to die in the belief that the useless sacrifice of themselves, by the generations of 1776, to acquire self-government and happiness to their country, is to be thrown away by the unwise and unworthy passions of their sons; and that my only consolation is to be that I shall not live to weep over it.

Fortunate man! He did not live to weep over it. To-day he sleeps quietly beneath the soil of his own Monticello, unconscious that the mighty fabric of government which he helped to rear – a government whose foundations were laid by the hands of so many patriots and sages, and cemented by the blood of so many martyrs and heroes – hastens now, day by day, to its fall. What recks he, or that other great man, his compeer, fortunate in life and opportune alike in death, whose dust they keep at Quincy, of those dreadful notes of preparation in every State for civil strife and fraternal carnage; or of that martial array which already has changed this once peaceful capital into a beleaguered city? Fortunate men! They died while the Constitution yet survived, while the Union survived, while the spirit of fraternal affection still lived, and the love of true American liberty lingered yet in the hearts of their descendants.

Sir, the antagonism of parties founded on money or questions of political economy having died out, and the balance of power between the North and the South being now lost, and the strength and dignity, and the revenues and disbursements – the patronage and spoils – of the Federal Government having grown to an enormous size, was anything more natural than the organization, *upon any basis peculiar to the stronger section,* of a sectional party, to secure so splendid and tempting a prize? Or was anything more inevitable than that the "marked principle, moral and political," of slavery, *coinciding with the very geographical line which divided the two sections,* and appealing so strongly to Northern sentiments and prejudices, and against which it was impossible for any man or any party long to contend, should be revived? Unhappily, too, just about this time, the acquisition of a very large territory from Mexico, not foreseen or provided for by the Missouri compromise, opened wide the door for this very question of slavery, in a form every way the most favorable to the agitators. The Wilmot Proviso, or Congressional prohibition – now, indeed, exploded, but which, nevertheless, received, in some form or other, the indorsement of every free State then in the Union – it was proposed to establish over the whole territory thus acquired, as well south of 36° 30' as north of that latitude. The proposition, upon the other hand, to extend the Missouri compromise line to the Pacific, was rejected by the votes of almost the entire Whig party, and of a large majority, I believe, of the Democratic party of the free States. That, sir, was the fatal mistake of the North; and in tribulation and anguish will she and the other sections of the Union, and our posterity, too, for ages, it may be, weep tears of bloody repentance and regret over it.

This controversy, however, sir, after having again shaken the Union to its center, was at last, though with great difficulty, adjusted through the compromise measures of 1850, by the last of the great statesmen of the second period of the Republic. But four years afterward, upon the bill to organize the Territories of Kansas and Nebraska, upon the principles of the legislation of 1850, the imprisoned winds – Eurus, Notusque, *creberque procellis Africus* – were all again let loose with more than the rage of a tropical hurricane. The Missouri restriction, which for years had been denounced as a wicked and atrocious concession to slavery, and which, some thirty years before, had consigned almost every free State Senator or Representative who supported it, to political oblivion, became now a most sacred compact, which it was sacrilege to touch. A distinguished Senator, late the Governor of Ohio, who had entitled his great speech against the adjustment measures of 1850, "Union and Freedom without Compromise," now put forth his elaborate defense, four years later, of the Missouri restriction, with the rubric or text, in ambitious characters, "Maintain Plighted Faith." But, right or wrong, wise or unwise, at the time, as the repeal of that restriction may have seemed, subsequent acts and events have made it both a delusion and a snare. Yes, sir, I confess it. I, who, as a private citizen, was one of its earliest defenders, make open confession of it here to-day. It was this which gave a new and terrible vitality to the languishing element of Abolitionism, and which precipitated, at least, a crisis which, I fear, was, nevertheless, sooner or later, inevitable. It is the crisis of which the President elect spoke three years ago. It is, indeed, reached. Would to God it were passed, also, in peace.

But, sir, whether the leaders of the movement against the repeal of the Missouri restriction were consistent or inconsistent, honest or dishonest, the great mass of the people of the free States were roused, for a time, to the highest indignation by it; and, inasmuch as the Whig party was just then falling to pieces, wicked, or reckless, or short-sighted men eagerly seized upon this unsettled condition of the public mind, to reorganize the Free Soil party of 1818, under a new and captivating name, but very nearly upon the principles of the Buffalo platform of that year, thus abandoning the extreme abolition sentiments of the Liberty party, and bringing up the great majority of the Whig party, and not a few of the Democratic party, also, to the Free Soil and non-slavery extension principle; and by this compromise, forming and consolidating that powerful party, which, for the first time in our history, by a mere sectional plurality – in a minority, in fact, by a million of votes – has obtained possession of the power and patronage of the central Government. Sir, if all this had happened solely by accident, and were likely never to be repeated, portentous as it might be of present evil, it would have caused, and ought to have caused, none of the disasters which have already followed. But the dread secret once disclosed, that the immense powers and revenues and honors and spoils of this great and mighty Republic may be easily won, by a mere sectional majority, upon a popular sectional issue, will never die; and new aggressions and new issues must continually spring from it. This is the philosophy and the justification of the alarm and consternation which have shaken the South from the Potomac to the Gulf. It is the philosophy, and the justification, too, of the amendment of the gentleman from Massachusetts (Mr. Adams), and of all the other propositions for new adjustments and new guarantees. Sir, the gentleman from New York (Mr. Sedgwick) was right when he said that there never was any great event which did not spring from some adequate cause. The South is afraid of your sectional majority, organized and consolidated upon the abstract principle of hostility to slavery generally, and the practical application of that principle to the exclusion of slavery from all the Territories, and its restriction, by the power of that sectional majority, to where it now exists. And if this be not the fundamental doctrine of the Republican party, I shall be greatly obliged to some gentleman of that party to tell me what its fundamental doctrine is.

But unjust and oppressive as the South feel their exclusion from the common Territories of the States to be, they know well, also, that the propelling power of a great moral and religious principle, as it is regarded in the North, added to the still more enduring, persistent, and prudent passion of ambition, of thirst for power and place, for the honors and emoluments of such a Government as ours, with its half a million of dependents and expectants, and its eighty millions of revenues and disbursements, all, all to be secured by the Aladdin's lamp of a sectional majority, cannot be arrested or extinguished by anything short of the suppression of the power which makes it potent for mischief. And nothing less than this, be assured, will satisfy any considerable number of even the more moderate of the people of the border slave States, and certainly without it there is not the slightest hope of the return of the States upon the Gulf, and thus of a restoration of the Union as it existed but three months ago. The statesmen and the people of all these States well know, also, that, by the civil law of every country, among individuals, and by the law of nations, as between sovereign and foreign States, the power to aggress, along with the threat and the preparation to aggress, is a good cause why an individual or a State should be required to give some adequate assurance that the power shall not be used to execute the threat; or, otherwise, that the power shall itself be taken away. Apply now, sir, these principles to the case in hand. The North has the power; that power is in the hands of the Republican party, and already they have resolved to use it for the exclusion of the South from all the Territories. There shall be no more extension of slavery. More than this: the leaders of the party – many of them leaders and founders of the old Liberty Guard, the original Abolition party of the North – the very men who brought the masses of the Whig party, and many of the Democratic party, from utter indifference and non-intervention years ago upon the question of slavery, up to the point of no more slavery extension, and persuaded them, in spite of the warning voice of Washington, in the very face of the appalling danger of disunion, to unite, for this purpose, in a powerful sectional party, for the first time in the history of the Government – these self-same leaders proclaim now, not indeed as present doctrines or purposes of the Republican party, but as solemn abstract truths, as fixed, existing facts, that there is a "higher law" than the Constitution, and an "irrepressible conflict" of principle and interest, between the dominant and the minority sections of the Union, and that one or the other must conquer in the conflict. Sir, in this contest with ballots, who is it that must conquer – the section of the minority, or the section of the majority?

And now, sir, when sentiments like these are held and proclaimed – deliberately, solemnly, repeatedly proclaimed – by men, one of whom is now the President elect, and the other the Secretary of State of the incoming Administration, is it at all surprising that the States of the South should be filled with excitement and alarm, or that they should demand, as almost with one voice they have demanded, adequate and complete guarantees for their rights, and security against aggression? Right or wrong, justifiably or without cause, they have done it; and I lament to say, that some of these States have even gone so far as to throw off wholly the authority of the Federal Government, and withdraw themselves from the Union. Sir, I will not discuss the right of secession. It is of no possible avail now, either to maintain or to condemn it; yet it is vain to tell me that States cannot secede. Seven States *have* seceded; they now refuse any longer to recognize the authority of this Government, and already have entered into a new confederacy, and set up a provisional government of their own. In three months their agents and commissioners will return from Europe with the recognition of Great Britain and France, and of the other great powers of the continent. Other States at home are preparing to unite with this new confederacy, if you do not grant to them their just and equitable demands. The question is no longer one of mere preservation of the Union. That was the question when we met in this Chamber some two months ago. Unhappily, that day has passed by; and while your "perilous Committee of Thirty-three" debated and deliberated to gain time – yes, to gain time – for that was the insane and most unstatesmanlike cry in the beginning of the session – star after star shot madly from our political firmament. The question to-day is: How shall we now keep the States we have, and restore those which are lost? Ay, sir, *restore,* till every wanderer shall have returned, and not one be missing from the "starry flock."

If, then, Mr. Speaker, I have justly and truly stated the causes which have led to those most disastrous results, if, indeed, the control of the immense powers, honors, and revenues – the spoils – of the Federal Government, in a word, if the possession of power, and the temptation to abuse it, be the primary cause of the present dismemberment of the United States, ought not every remedy proposed to reach at once the very seat of the disease? And why, sir, may not the malady be healed? Why cannot this controversy be adjusted? Has, indeed, the union of these States received the immedicable wound? I do not believe it. Never was there a political crisis for which wise, courageous, and disinterested statesmen could more speedily devise a remedy. British statesmen would have adjusted it in a few weeks. Twice, certainly, if not three times, in this century, they have healed troubles threatening a dissolution of the monarchy and civil war, and each time healed them by yielding promptly to the necessities which pressed upon them, giving up principles and measures to which they had every way for years been committed. They have learned wisdom from the obstinacy of the king who lost to Great Britain her thirteen colonies; and have been taught, by that memorable lesson, to concede and to compromise in time, and to do it radically; and history has pronounced it statesmanship, not weakness. In each case, too, they yielded up, not doctrines and a policy which they were seeking for the first time to establish, but the ancient and settled principles, usages, and institutions of the realm; and they yielded up these to save others yet more essential, and to maintain the integrity of the empire. They did save it, and did maintain it; and, to-day, Great Britain is stronger and more prosperous and more secure than any government on the globe.

Sir, no man had, for a longer time, or with a more inexorable firmness, opposed Catholic emancipation than the Duke of Wellington; yet, when the issue came, at last, between emancipation or civil war, the hero of a hundred battle-fields, the conqueror at Waterloo, the greatest military commander, except Napoleon, of modern times, yes, the Iron Duke lost not a moment, but yielded to the storm, and himself led the party which carried the great measure of peace and compromise through the very citadel of conservatism – the House of Lords. Sir, he sought no middle ground, no half-way measure, confessing weakness, promising something, doing nothing. And in that memorable debate he spoke words of wisdom, moderation, and true courage, which I commend to gentlemen in this House – to our Wellington outside of it, and to all others, anywhere, whose parched jaws seem ravenous for blood. He said:

> It has been my fortune to have seen much of war – more than most men. I have been constantly engaged in the active duties of the military profession from boyhood until I have grown gray. My life has been passed in familiarity with scenes of death and human suffering. Circumstances have placed me in countries where the war was internal – between opposite parties in the same nation; and, rather than a country I loved should be visited with the calamities which I have seen, with the unutterable horrors of civil war, I would run any risk – I would make any sacrifice – I would freely lay down my life. There is nothing which destroys property and prosperity, and demoralizes character, to the extent which civil war does. By it, the hand of man is raised against his neighbor, against his brother, and against his father; the servant betrays his master, and the master ruins his servant. Yet this is the resource to which we must have looked – these are the means which we must have applied, in order to have put an end to this state of things, if we had not embraced the option of bringing forward the measure for which I hold myself responsible.

Two years later, sir, in a yet more dangerous crisis upon the Reform Bill, which the Commons had rejected, and when civil commotion and discord, if not revolution, were again threatened, and it became necessary to dissolve the Parliament, and, for that purpose, to secure the consent of a king adverse to the dissolution, the Lord Chancellor of England, one of the most extraordinary men of the age – by, perhaps, the boldest and most hazardous experiment ever tried upon royalty – surprised the King into consent, assuring him that the further existence of the Parliament was incompatible with the peace and safety of the kingdom; and having, without the royal command, summoned the great officers of State, prepared the crown, the robes, the King's speech, and whatever else was needed, and, at the risk of the penalties of high treason, ordered, also, the attendance of the troops required by the usages of the ceremony, he hurried the King to the Chamber of the House of Lords, where, in the presence of the Commons, the Parliament was dissolved, while each House was still in high debate, and without other notice in advance than the sound of the cannon which announced his majesty's approach. Yet all this was done in the midst of threatened insurrection and rebellion; when the Duke of Wellington, the Duke of Cumberland, and other noblemen were assaulted in the streets, and their houses broken into and mobbed; when London itself was threatened with capture, and the dying Sir Walter Scott was hooted and reviled by ruffians at the polls. It was done while the kingdom was one vast mob; while the cry rang through all England, Ireland, and Scotland, that the Bill must be carried through Parliament or over Parliament – if possible, by peaceable means – if not possible, then by force; and when the Prime Minister declared, in the House of Commons that, by reason of its defeat, "much blood would be shed in the struggle between the contending parties, and that he was perfectly convinced that the British Constitution would perish in the conflict." And, sir, when all else failed, the King himself at last gave permission, in writing, to Earl Grey and the Lord Chancellor, to create as many new peers as might be necessary to secure a majority for the Reform Bill in the House of Lords.

Such, sir, is British statesmanship. They remember, but we have forgotten, the lessons which our fathers taught them. Sir, it will be the opprobrium of American statesmanship forever, that this controversy of ours shall be permitted to end in final and perpetual dismemberment of the Union.

I propose, now, sir, to consider, briefly, the several propositions before the House looking to the adjustment of our difficulties by Constitutional amendment, in connection, also, with those which I have myself had the honor to submit.

Philosophically or logically considered, there are two ways in which the work before us may be effected: the first, by removing the temptation to aggress; the second, by taking the power away. Now, sir, I am free to confess that I do not see how any amendment of the Constitution can diminish the powers, dignity, or patronage of the Federal Government, consistently with the just distribution of power between the several departments; or between the States and the General Government, consistently with its necessary strength and efficiency. The evil here lies rather in the administration than in the organization of the system; and a large part of it is inherent in the administration of every government. The virtue and intelligence of the people, and the capacity and honesty of their representatives, in every department, must be intrusted with the mitigation and correction of the mischief. The less the legislation of every kind, the smaller the revenues and fewer the disbursements; the less the Government shall have to do, every way, with debt, credit, moneyed influences, and jobs, and schemes of every sort, the longer peace can be maintained; and the more the number of the employees and dependents on Government can be reduced, the less will be the patronage and the corruption of the system, and the less, therefore, the motive to sacrifice truth and justice, and to overleap the Constitution to secure the control of it. In other words, the more you diminish temptation, the more you will deliver us from the evil.

But I pass this point by without further remark, inasmuch as none of the plans of adjustment proposed – either here or in the Senate – look to any change of the Constitution in this respect. They all aim – every one of them – at checking the power to aggress; and, except the amendment of the gentleman from Massachusetts (Mr. Adams), which goes much further than mine in giving a negative upon one subject to every slave State in the Union, they propose to effect their purpose by mere constitutional prohibitions. It is not my purpose, sir, to demand a vote upon the propositions which I have myself submitted. I have not the party position, nor the power behind me, nor with me, nor the age, nor the experience which would justify me in assuming the lead in any great measure of peace and conciliation; but I believe, and very respectfully I suggest it, that something similar, at least, to these propositions will form a part of any adequate and final adjustment which may restore all the States to the Federal Union. No, sir; I am able now only to follow where others may lead.

I shall vote for the amendment of the gentleman from Massachusetts (Mr. Adams) – though it does not go far enough – because it ignores and denies the moral or religious element of the anti-slavery agitation, and thus removes, so far, at least, its most dangerous sting – *fanaticism* – and, dealing with the question as one of mere policy and economy, of pure politics alone, proposes a new and most comprehensive guarantee for the peculiar institution of the States of the South. I shall vote, also, for the Crittenden propositions – as an experiment, and only as an experiment – because they proceed upon the same general idea which marks the Adams amendment; and whereas, for the sake of peace and the Union, the latter would give a new security to slavery in the States, the former, for the self-same great and paramount object of Union and peace, proposes to give a new security also to slavery in the Territories south of the latitude 36° 30'. If the Union is worth the price which the gentleman from Massachusetts volunteers to pay to maintain it, is it not richly worth the very small additional price which the Senator from Kentucky demands as the possible condition of preserving it? Sir, it is the old parable of the Roman Sibyl; and to-morrow she will return with fewer volumes, and, it may be, at a higher price.

I shall vote to try the Crittenden propositions, because, also, I believe that they are perhaps the least which even the more moderate of the slave States would, under any circumstances, be willing to accept; and because, North, South, and West, the people seem to have taken hold of them, and to demand them of us, as an experiment, at least. I am ready to try, also, if need be, the propositions of the Border State Committee, or of the Peace Congress; or any other fair, honorable, and reasonable terms of adjustment, which may so much as promise, even, to heal our present troubles, and to restore the Union of these States. Sir, I am ready and willing and anxious to try all things and to do all things "which may become a man," to secure that great object which is nearest to my heart.

But, judging all of these propositions, nevertheless, by the lights of philosophy and statesmanship, and as I believe they will be regarded by the historian who shall come after us, I find in them all two capital defects, which will, in the end, prove them to be both unsatisfactory to large numbers alike of the people of the free and the slave States, and wholly inadequate to the great purpose of the reconstruction and future preservation of the Union. None of them – except that of the gentleman from Massachusetts (Mr. Adams), and his in one particular only – proposes to give to the minority section any veto or self-protecting power against those aggressions, the temptation to which, and the danger from which, are the very cause or reason for the demand for any new guarantees at all. They who complain of violated faith in the past, are met only with new promises of good faith for the future; they who tell you that you have broken the Constitution heretofore, are answered with proposed additions to the Constitution, so that there may be more room for breaches hereafter. The only protection here offered against the aggressive spirit of the majority, is the simple pledge of power that it will not abuse itself, nor aggress, nor usurp, nor amplify itself to attain its ends. You place, in the distance, the highest honors, the largest emoluments, the most glittering of all prizes, and then you propose, as it were, to exact a promise from the race-horse that he will accommodate his speed to the slow-moving pace of the tortoise. Sir, if I meant terms of equality, I would give the tortoise a good ways the start in the race.

My point of objection, therefore, is that you do not allow to that very minority which, because it is a minority, and because it is afraid of your aggressions, is now about to secede and withdraw itself from your Government, and set up a separate confederacy of its own, you do not allow to it the power of self-protection within the Union. If, Representatives, you are sincere in your protestations that you do not mean to aggress upon the rights of this minority, you deny yourselves nothing by these new guarantees. If you do mean to aggress, then this minority has a right to demand self-protection and security.

But, sir, there remains yet another, and a still stronger objection to these several propositions. Every one of them proposes to recognize, and to embody in the Constitution, that very sort of sectionalism which is the immediate instrumentality of the present dismemberment of these States, and the existence of which is, in my judgment, utterly inconsistent with the peace and stability of the Union. Every one of them recognizes and perpetuates the division line between slave labor and free labor, that self-same "geographical line, coinciding with the marked principle, moral and political" of slavery, which so startled the prophetic ear of Jefferson, and which he foretold, forty years ago, every irritation would mark deeper and deeper, till, at last, it would destroy the Union itself. They, one and all, recognize slavery as an existing and paramount element in the politics of the country, and yet only promise that the non-slaveholding majority section, immensely in the majority, will not aggress upon the rights or trespass upon the interests of the slaveholding minority section, immensely in the minority. *Adeo senuerunt Jupiter et Mars?*

Sir, just so long as slavery is recognized as an element in politics at all – just so long as the dividing line between the slave labor and the free labor States is kept up as the only line, with the disparity between them growing every day greater and greater – just so long it will be impossible to keep the peace, and maintain a Federal Union between them. However sufficient any of these plans of adjustment might have been one year ago, or even in December last, when proposed, and prior to the secession of any of the States, I fear that they will be found utterly inadequate to restore the Union now. I do not believe that, alone, they will avail to bring back the States which have seceded, and, therefore, to withhold the other slave States from ultimate secession; for, surely, no man fit to be a statesman can fail to foresee that unless the cotton States can be returned to the Union, the border States must and will, sooner or later, follow them out of it. As between two confederacies – the one non-slaveholding, and the other slaveholding – all the States of the South must belong to the latter, except, possibly, Maryland and Delaware, and they, of course, could remain with the former only upon the understanding that, just as soon as practicable, slavery should be abolished within their limits. If fifteen slave States cannot protect themselves, and feel secure in a Union with eighteen anti-slavery States, how can eight slave States maintain their position and their rights in a Union with nineteen, or with thirty anti-slavery States? The question, therefore, is not merely, What will keep Virginia in the Union, but also, what will bring Georgia back? And here let me say, that I do not doubt that there is a large and powerful Union sentiment still surviving in all the States which have seceded, South Carolina alone, perhaps, excepted; and that if the people of those States can be assured that they shall have the power to protect themselves by their own action *within the Union,* they will gladly return to it, very greatly preferring protection within to security outside of it. Just now, indeed, the fear of danger, and your persistent and obstinate refusal to enable them to guard against it, have delivered the people of those States over into the hands, and under the control, of the real secessionists and disunionists among them; but give them security, and the means of enforcing it; above all, dry up this pestilent fountain of slavery agitation, as a political element, in both sections, and, my word for it, the ties of a common ancestry, a common kindred, and common language; the bonds of a common interest, common danger, and common safety; the recollections of the past, and of associations not yet dissolved, and the bright hopes of a future to all of us, more glorious and resplendent than any other country ever saw; ay, sir, and visions, too, of that old flag of the Union, and of the music of the Union, and precious memories of the statesmen and heroes of the dark days of the Revolution, will fill their souls yet again with desires and yearnings intense for the glories, the honors, and the material benefits, too, of that Union which their fathers and our fathers made; and they will return to it, not as the prodigal, but with songs and rejoicing, as the Hebrews returned from the captivity to the ancient city of their kings.

Proceeding, sir, upon the principles which I have already considered, and applying them to the causes which, step by step, have led to our present troubles, I have ventured, with great deference, to submit the propositions which are upon the table of the House. While not inconsistent with any of the other pending plans of adjustment, they are, in my judgment, and again I speak it with becoming deference, fully adequate to secure that protection from aggression, without which there can be no confidence, and, therefore, no peace and no restoration for the Union.

There are two maxims, sir, applicable to all constitutional reform, both of which it has been my purpose to follow. In the first place, not to amend more, or further, than is necessary for the mischief to be remedied; and next, to follow strictly the principles of the Constitution which is to be amended; and corollary to these, I might add, that in framing amendments, the words and phrases of the Constitution ought, so far as practicable, to be adopted.

I propose, then, sir, to do as all others in the Senate and the House have done, so far – to recognize the existence of sections as a fixed fact, which, lamentable as it is, can no longer be denied or suppressed; but, for the reasons I have already stated, I propose to establish four instead of two grand sections of the Union, all of them well known, or easily designated by marked, natural, or geographical lines and boundaries. I propose four sections instead of two; because, if two only are recognized, the natural and inevitable division will be into slaveholding and non-slaveholding sections; and it is this very division, either by constitutional enactment, or by common consent, as hitherto, which, in my deliberate judgment and deepest conviction, it concerns the peace and stability of the Union, should be forever hereafter ignored. Till then, there cannot be, and will not be, perfect union and peace between these United States; because, in the first place, the nature of the question is such that it stirs up, necessarily, as forty years of strife conclusively proves, the strongest and the bitterest passions and antagonism possible among men; and, in the next place, because the non-slaveholding section has now, and will have to the end, a steadily increasing majority, and enormously disproportioned weight and influence in the Government; thus combining that which never can be very long resisted in any Government – the temptation and the power to aggress.

Sir, it was not the mere geographical line which so startled Mr. Jefferson, in 1820; but the coincidence of that line with the marked principle, moral and political, of slavery. And now, sir, to remove this very mischief which he predicted, and which has already happened, it is essential that this coincidence should be obliterated; and the repeated failure, for years past, of all other compromises, based upon a recognition of this coincidence, has proved, beyond doubt, that it cannot be obliterated unless it be by other and conflicting lines of principle and interests. I propose, therefore, to multiply the sections, and thus efface the slave-labor and free-labor division, and, at the same time, and in this manner, to diminish the relative power of each section. And to prevent combinations among these different sections, I propose, also, to allow a vote in the Senate by sections, upon demand of one-third of the Senators of any section, and to require the concurrence of a majority of the Senators of each section in the passage of any measure, in which, by the Constitution, it is necessary that the House, and therefore, also, the President, should concur. All this, sir, is perfectly consistent with the principles of the Constitution, as shown in the division of the legislative department into the two Houses of Congress; the veto power; the two-thirds vote of both Houses necessary to pass a bill over the veto; the provisions in regard to the ratification of treaties, and amendments of the Constitution; but especially in the equal representation and suffrage of each State in the Senate, whereby the vote of Delaware, with a hundred thousand inhabitants, vetoes the vote of New York, with her population of nearly four millions. If the protection of the smaller States against the possible aggressions of the larger States required, in the judgment of the framers of the Constitution, this peculiar, and apparently inequitable provision, why shall not the protection, by a similar power of veto, of the smaller and weaker sections against the aggressions of the larger and stronger sections, not be now allowed, when time and experience have proved the necessity of just such a check upon the majority? Does any one doubt that, if the men who made the Constitution had foreseen that the real danger to the system lay not in aggression by the large upon the small States, but in geographical combinations of the strong sections against the weak, they would have guarded jealously against that mischief, just as they did against the danger to which they mistakenly believed the Government to be exposed? And if this protection, sir, be now demanded by the minority as the price of the Union, so just and reasonable a provision ought not for a moment to be denied. Far better this than secession and disruption. This would, indeed, enable the minority to fight for their rights in the Union, instead of breaking it to pieces to secure them outside of it.

Certainly, sir, it is in the nature of a veto power to each section in the Senate; but necessity requires it, secession demands it, just as twice in the history of the Roman Commonwealth secession demanded and received the power of the tribunitian veto as the price of a restoration of the Republic. The secession to the Sacred Mount secured, just as a second secession, half a century later, restored, the veto of tribunes of the people, and reinvigorated and preserved the Roman constitution for three hundred years. Vetoes, checks, balances, concurrent majorities – these, sir, are the true conservators of free Government.

But it is not in legislation alone that the danger or the temptation to aggress is to be found. Of the tremendous power and influence of the Executive I have already spoken. And, indeed, the present revolutionary movements are the result of the apprehension of executive usurpation and encroachments, to the injury of the rights of the South. But for secession because of this apprehended danger, the legislative department would have remained, for the present at least, in other and safer hands. Hence the necessity for equal protection and guarantee against sectional combinations and majorities to secure the election of the President, and to control him when elected. I propose, therefore, that a concurrent majority of the electors, or States, or Senators, as the case may require, of each section, shall be necessary to the choice of President and Vice-President; and lest, by reason of this increased complexity, there may be a failure of choice oftener than heretofore, I propose also a special election in such case, and an extension of the term, in all cases, to six years. This is the outline of the plan; the details may be learned in full from the joint resolution itself; and I will not detain the House by any further explanation now.

Sir, the natural and inevitable result of these amendments will be to preclude the possibility of sectional parties and combinations to obtain possession of either the legislative or the executive power and patronage of the Federal Government; and, if not to suppress totally, at least very greatly to diminish the evil results of national caucuses, conventions, and other similar party appliances. It will no longer be possible to elect a President by the votes of a mere dominant and majority section. Sectional issues must cease, as the basis, at least, of large party organizations. Ambition, or lust for power and place, must look no longer to its own section, but to the whole country; and he who would be President, or in any way the foremost among his countrymen, must consult, henceforth, the combined good, and the goodwill, too, of all the sections, and in this way, consistently with the Constitution, can the "general welfare" be best attained. Thus, indeed, will the result be, instead of a narrow, illiberal, and sectional policy, an enlarged patriotism and extended public spirit.

If it be urged that the plan is too complex, and, therefore, impracticable, I answer that that was the objection, in the beginning, to the whole Federal system, and to almost every part of it. It is the argument of the French Republicans against the division of the legislative department into two Chambers; and it was the argument especially urged at first against the entire plan or idea of the electoral colleges for the choice of a President. But, if complex, I answer again, it will prevent more evil than good. If it suspend some legislation for a time, I answer, the world is governed too much. If it cause delay, sometimes, in both legislation and the choice of President, I answer yet again, better, far better this, than disunion and the ten thousand complexities, peaceful and belligerent, which must attend it. Better, infinitely better this, in the Union, than separate confederacies outside of it, with either perpetual war or entangling and complicated alliances, offensive and defensive, from henceforth forever. To the South I say: If you are afraid of free State aggressions by Congress or the Executive, here is abundant protection for even the most timid. To the Republican party of the North and West I say: If you really tremble, as, for years past, you would have had us believe, over that terrible, but somewhat mythical monster – the Slave Power – here, too, is the utmost security for you against the possibility of its aggressions. And, from first to last, allow me to say that, being wholly negative in its provisions, this plan can only prevent evil, and not work any positive evil itself. It is a shield for defense, not a sword for aggression. In one word, let me add that the whole purpose and idea of this plan of adjustment which I propose, is to give to the several sections inside of the Union that power of self-protection which they are resolved, or will some day or other be resolved, to secure for themselves outside of the Union.

I propose further, sir, that neither Congress nor a Territorial Legislature shall have power to interfere with the equal right of migration, from all sections, into the Territories of the United States; and that neither shall have power to destroy or impair any rights of either person or property in these Territories; and, finally, that new States, either when annexed, or when formed out of any of the Territories, with the consent of Congress, shall be admitted into the Union with any constitution, republican in form, which the people of such States may ordain.

And now, gentlemen of the South, why cannot you accept it? The Federal Government has never yet, in any way, aggressed upon your rights. Hitherto, indeed, it has been in your own, or at least in friendly hands. You only fear, being in the minority, that it will aggress because it has now fallen under the control of those who, you believe, have the temptation, the will, and the power to aggress. But this plan of adjustment proposes to take away the power; and of what avail will the temptation or the will then be, without the power to execute? Both must soon perish.

And why cannot you of the Republican party accept it? There is not a word about slavery in it, from beginning to end – I mean in the amendments. It is silent upon the question. South of 36° 30', and east of the Rio Grande, there is scarce any territory which is not now within the limits of some existing State; and west of that river and of the Rocky Mountains, as well as north of 36° 30' and east of those mountains, though any new State should establish slavery, still her vote would be counted in the Senate and in the electoral colleges with the non-slaveholding section to which she would belong; just as if, within the limits of the South, any State should abolish slavery, or any new State not tolerating slavery should be admitted, the vote of such State would also be cast with the section of the South. However slavery might be extended, as a mere form of civilization or of labor, there could be no extension of it as a mere aggressive political element in the Government. If the South only demand that the Federal Government shall not be used aggressively to prohibit the extension of slavery; if she does not desire to use it herself, upon the other hand, positively to extend the institution, then she may well be satisfied; and if you of the Republican party do not really mean to aggress upon slavery where it now exists; if you are not, in fact, opposed to the admission of any more slave States; if, indeed, you do not any longer propose to use the powers of the Federal Government positively and aggressively to prohibit slavery in the Territories, but are satisfied to allow it to take its natural course, according to the laws of interest or of climate, then you, too, may well be content with this plan of adjustment, since it does not demand of you, openly and publicly, to deny, abjure, and renounce, in so many words, the more moderate principles and doctrines which you have this session professed. And yet candor obliges me to declare that this plan of settlement, and every other plan, whatsoever, which is of the slightest value – even the amendment of the gentleman from Massachusetts (Mr. Adams), is a virtual dissolution of the Republican party as a mere sectional and anti-slavery organization; and this, too, will, in my judgment, be equally the result, whether we compromise at all, and the Union be thus restored, or whether it be finally and forever dissolved. The people of the North and the West will never trust the destroyers – for destroyers, indeed, you will be, if you reject all fair terms of adjustment – the destroyers of our Government, and such a Government as this, with the administration and control of any other. You have now the executive department, as the result of the late election. Better, far better, reorganize and nationalize your party, and keep the Government for four years in peace, and with a Union of thirty-four States, than with the shadow and mockery of a broken and disjointed Union of sixteen or nineteen States, ending, at last, in total and hopeless dissolution.

    Having thus, sir, guarded diligently the rights of the several States and sections, and given to each section also the power to protect itself, inside of the Union, from aggression, I propose next to limit and to regulate the alleged right of secession, since this, from a dormant abstraction, has now become a practical question of tremendous import. As long, sir, as secession remained an untried and only menaced experiment, that confidence, without which no Government can be stable or efficient, was not shaken, because it was believed that actual secession would never be tried; or, if tried, that it must speedily and ingloriously fail. The popular faith, cherished for years, has been that the Union could not be dissolved. To that faith the Republican party was indebted for its success in the late election; and we who predicted its dissolution were smitten upon the cheek, and condemned to feed upon bread of affliction and water of affliction, like the prophet whom Ahab hated. But partial dissolution has already occurred. Secession has been tried, and has proved a speedy and a terrible success. The practicability of doing it, and the way to do it, have both been established. Sir, the experiment may readily be repeated – it will be repeated. And is it not madness and folly, then, to call back, by adjustment, the States which have seceded, or to hold back the States which are threatening to secede, without providing some safeguard against the renewal of this most simple and disastrous experiment? Can foreign nations have any confidence, hereafter, in the stability of a government which may so readily, speedily, and quietly be dissolved? Can we have any confidence among ourselves?

If it be said that it would have availed nothing to check secession in the gulf States, even had there been a Constitutional prohibition of it, I answer, perhaps not, if it had been total and absolute – for there would have been no alternative but submission or revolution; and, hence, I propose only to define and restrain and to regulate this alleged right. But I deny that, if a particular mode of secession had been prescribed by the Constitution, and thus every other mode prohibited, it would have been possible to have secured, in any of the seceding States – no, not even in South Carolina – a majority in favor of separate State secession, or secession in any other way than that provided in the Constitution. No, sir; it was the almost universal belief in the cotton States in the unlimited right of secession – a doctrine recognized by few in the free States, but held to by a great many, if not very generally, all over the slave States – which made secession so easy. It is hard to bring any considerable number of the people of the United States – suddenly, at least – up to the point of a palpable violation of the Constitution; but it is easy, very easy, to draw them into any act which seems to be only the exercise of one right for the purpose of securing and preserving the higher rights of life, liberty, person, and property for a whole State or a whole section. Sir, it is because of this very idea or notion among the people of the gulf States, that they were exercising a right reserved under the Constitution, that secession there, and the establishment of a new confederacy and provisional government, have been marked by so much rapidity, order, and method – all through the ballot-box, and not with the halter, or at the point of the bayonet, over oppressed minorities – and, for the most part, with so few of the excesses and irregularities which have characterized the progress of other revolutions. I would not prohibit totally the right of secession, lest violent revolutions should follow; for where laws and constitutions are to be overleaped, and they who make the revolution avow it to be a revolution, and claim no right except the universal rights of man, such revolutions are commonly violent and bloody within themselves; and, even if not, they cannot be resisted by the established authorities except at the cost of civil war; while, if submitted to in silence, they tend to demoralize all government. It is of vital importance, therefore, every way, in my judgment, that the exercise of this certainly quasi revolutionary right should be defined, limited, and restrained; and, accordingly, I propose that no State shall secede without the consent of the legislatures of all the States of the section to which the State proposing to secede may belong. This is, obviously, a most reasonable restraint; and yet, of its sufficiency no man can doubt, when he remembers that, in the present crisis of the country, had this provision existed, no State could have obtained the absolute consent, at least, of even one-half of the States of the South.

Such, Mr. Speaker, is the plan which, with great deference, and yet with great confidence, too, in its efficiency, I would propose for the adjustment of our controversies, and for the restoration and preservation of the Union which our fathers made. Like all human contrivances, certainly, it is imperfect, and subject to objection. But something searching, radical, extreme, going to the very foundations of government, and reaching the seat of the malady, must be done, and that right speedily, while the fracture is yet fresh and reunion is possible. Two months ago, when I last addressed the House, imploring you for immediate action, less, much less, would have sufficed; but we learned no wisdom from the lessons of the past – and now, indeed, not poppy, nor mandragora, nor other drowsy syrup is of any value to arrest that revolution, in the midst of which we are to-day – a revolution the grandest and the saddest of modern times.

The following are the amendments to the Constitution, proposed by Mr. Vallandigham, on the 7th of February, 1861, to the support of which the foregoing speech is devoted:

Joint Resolution

Whereas, the Constitution of the United States is a grant of specific powers delegated to the Federal Government by the people of the several

States, all powers not delegated to it nor prohibited to the States being reserved to the States, respectively, or to the people; and whereas it is the tendency of stronger governments to enlarge their powers and jurisdiction at the expense of weaker governments, and of majorities to usurp and abuse power and oppress minorities, to arrest and hold in check which tendency, compacts and Constitutions are made; and whereas the only effectual constitutional security for the rights of minorities – whether as people or as states – is the power expressly reserved in constitutions, of protecting those rights by their own action; and whereas this mode of protection, by checks and guarantees, is recognized in the Federal Constitution, as well in the case of the equality of the States in representation and in suffrage in the Senate, as in the provision for overruling the veto of the President and for amending the Constitution, not to enumerate other examples; and whereas, unhappily, because of the vast extent and diversified interests and institutions of the several States of the Union, sectional divisions can no longer be suppressed; and whereas it concerns the peace and stability of the Federal Union and Government, that a division of the States into mere slaveholding and non-slaveholding sections, causing, hitherto – and from the nature and necessity of the case – inflammatory and disastrous controversies, upon the subject of slavery, ending, already, in present disruption of the Union – should be forever hereafter ignored; and whereas this important end is best to be obtained by the recognition of other sections without regard to slavery, neither of which sections shall alone be strong enough to oppress or control the others, and each be vested with the power to protect itself from aggressions: Therefore,

Resolved, by the Senate and House of Representatives of the United States of America in Congress assembled (two-thirds of both Houses concurring), That the following articles be, and are hereby, proposed as amendments to the Constitution of the United States, which shall be valid, to all intents and purposes, as part of said Constitution, when ratified by conventions in three-fourths of the several States:

Article XIII.

Sec. 1. The United States are divided into four sections, as follows:

The States of Maine, New Hampshire, Vermont, Massachusetts, Rhode Island, Connecticut, New York, New Jersey, and Pennsylvania, and all new States annexed and admitted into the Union, or formed or erected within the jurisdiction of any of said States, or by the junction of two or more of the same, or of parts thereof, or out of territory acquired north of said States, shall constitute one section, to be known as the *North*.

The States of Ohio, Indiana, Illinois, Michigan, Wisconsin, Minnesota, Iowa, and Kansas, and all new States annexed or admitted into the Union, or erected within the jurisdiction of any of said States, or by the junction of two or more of the same, or of parts thereof, or out of territory now held or hereafter acquired north of latitude 36° 30', and east of the crest of the Rocky Mountains, shall constitute another section, to be known as the *West*.

The States of Oregon, and California, and all new States annexed and admitted into the Union, or formed or erected within the jurisdiction of any of said States, or by the junction of two or more of the same, or of parts thereof, or out of territory now held or hereafter acquired west of the crest of the Rocky Mountains and of the Rio Grande, shall constitute another section, to be known as the *Pacific*.

The States of Delaware, Maryland, Virginia, North Carolina, South Carolina, Georgia, Florida, Alabama, Mississippi, Louisiana, Texas, Arkansas, Tennessee, Kentucky, and Missouri, and all new States annexed and admitted into the Union, or formed or erected within the jurisdiction of any of said States, or by the junction of two or more of the same, or of parts thereof, or out of territory acquired east of the Rio Grande, and south of latitude 36° 30', shall constitute another section, to be known as the *South*.

Sec. 2. On demand of one-third of the Senators of any one of the sections on any bill, order, resolution, or vote, to which the concurrence of the House of Representatives may be necessary, except on a question of adjournment, a vote shall be had by sections, and a majority of the Senators from each section voting, shall be necessary to the passage of such bill, order, or resolution, and the validity of every such vote.

Sec. 3. Two of the electors for President and Vice-President shall be appointed by each State in such manner as the Legislature thereof may direct, for the State at large. The other electors to which each State may be entitled, shall be chosen in the respective congressional districts into which the State may, at the regular decennial period, have been divided, by the electors of each district, having the qualifications requisite for electors of the most numerous branch of the State legislature. A majority of all the electors in each of the four sections in this article established, shall be necessary to the choice of President and Vice-President; and the concurrence of a majority of the States of each section shall be necessary to the choice of President by the House of Representatives, and of the Senators from each section to the choice of Vice-President by the Senate, whenever the right of choice shall devolve upon them respectively.

Sec. 4. The President and Vice-President shall hold their office each during the term of six years; and neither shall be eligible to more than one term, except by the votes of two-thirds of all the electors of each section, or of the States of each section, whenever the right of choice of President shall devolve upon the House of Representatives, or of Senators from each section whenever the right of choice of Vice-President shall devolve upon the Senate.

Sec. 5. The Congress shall, by law, provide for the case of failure by the House of Representatives to choose a President, and of the Senate to choose a Vice-President, whenever the right of choice shall devolve upon them respectively, declaring what officer shall then act as President; and such officer shall act accordingly until a President shall be elected. The Congress shall also provide by law for a special election for President and Vice-President in such case to be held and completed within six months from the expiration of the term of office of the last preceding President, and to be conducted in all respects as provided for in the Constitution for regular elections of the same officer, except that if the House of Representatives shall not choose a President, should the right of choice devolve upon them, within twenty days from the opening of the certificates and counting of the electoral votes, then the Vice-President shall act as President, as in the case of the death or other constitutional disability of the President. The term of office of the President chosen under such special election shall continue six years from the fourth day of March preceding such election.

Article XIV.

No State shall secede without the consent of the Legislatures of the States of the section to which the State proposing to secede belongs. The President shall have power to adjust with seceding States all questions arising by reason of their secession; but the terms of adjustment shall be submitted to the Congress for their approval before the same shall be valid.

Article XV.

Neither the Congress nor a Territorial Legislature shall have power to interfere with the right of the citizens of any of the States within either of the sections to migrate upon equal terms with the citizens of the States within either of the other sections to the Territories of the United States: nor shall either the Congress or a Territorial Legislature have power to destroy or impair any rights of either person or property in the Territories.

New States annexed for admission into the Union, or formed or erected within the jurisdiction of other States, or by the junction of two or more States, or parts of States; and States formed, with the consent of the Congress, out of any territory of the United States, shall be entitled to admission upon an equal footing with the original States, under any constitution establishing a government republican in form which the people thereof may ordain, whenever such States, if formed out of any territory of the United States, shall contain, within an area of not less than sixty thousand square miles, a population equal to the then existing ratio of representation for one member of the House of Representatives.

A card, from which the following is extracted, was published by Mr. Vallandigham, in the Cincinnati *Enquirer*, on the 10th of November, 1860, a few days after the presidential election:

> And, now, let me add that I did say – not in Washington, not at a dinner-table, not in the presence of "fire-eaters," but in the city of New York, in a public assembly of Northern men, and in a public speech at the Cooper Institute, on the 2d of November, 1860 – that, "if any one or more of the States of this Union should, at any time, secede – for reasons of the sufficiency and justice of which, before God and the great tribunal of history, they alone may judge – much as I should deplore it, *I never would, as a Representative in the Congress of the United States, vote one dollar of money whereby one drop of American blood should be shed in a civil war.*" That sentiment, thus uttered in the presence of thousands of the merchants and solid men of the free and patriotic city of New York, was received with vehement and long-continued applause, the entire vast assemblage rising as one man, and cheering for some minutes. And I now deliberately repeat and reaffirm it, resolved, though I stand alone, though all others yield and fall away, to make it good to the last moment of my public life. No menace, no public clamor, no taunts, nor sneers, nor foul detraction, from any quarter, shall drive me from my firm purpose. Ours is a government of opinion, not of force – a Union of free will, not of arms; and coercion is civil war – a war of sections, a war of States, waged by a race compounded and made up of all other races, full of intellect, of courage, of will unconquerable, and, when set on fire by passion, the most belligerent and most ferocious on the globe – a civil war, full of horrors, which no imagination can conceive and no pen portray. If Abraham Lincoln is wise, looking truth and danger full in the face, he will take counsel of the "old men," the moderates of his party, and advise peace, negotiation, concession; but if, like the foolish son of the wise king, he reject these wholesome counsels, and hearken only to the madmen who threaten chastisement with scorpions, let him see to it, lest it be recorded at last that none remained to serve him "save the house of Judah only." At least, if he will forget the secession of the Ten Tribes, will he not remember and learn a lesson of wisdom from the secession of the Thirteen Colonies?

In answer to a gross telegraphic misrepresentation of this proposition, Mr. Vallandigham explained and defended it, in a card to the Cincinnati *Enquirer*, dated February 14, 1861, as follows:

> My proposition looks *solely to the restoration and maintenance of*

the Union forever, by suggesting a mode of voting in the United States Senate and the electoral colleges, by which the causes which have led to our present troubles may, in the future, be guarded against *without secession and disunion;* and, also, the agitation of the slavery question, as an element in our national politics, *be forever hereafter arrested.* My object – the sole motive by which I have been guided from the beginning of this most fatal revolution – is to *maintain the Union,* and not destroy it. When all possible hope is gone, and the Union irretrievably broken, then, but not till then, I will be for a Western confederacy.

One needs some familiarity with the persevering perversity of the Abolition press, not to feel a little surprised at finding the false statement, contradicted above, continually repeated and reaffirmed, as if made out of some grains of truth, at the first, and never denied. And yet a leading Abolition paper, in Cincinnati, so late as December 16, 1862, says:

> Mr. Vallandigham, by his propositions for a division of the Republic into *four distinct nationalities* – propositions as infamous in their design as ruinous in their consequences – did as much to rouse the people to a sense of their real danger, as the first shots of the insurrectionists at Charleston.

Referring to this statement, in a communication to the Cincinnati *Enquirer,* under date of Washington, D.C., December 18, 1862, Mr. Vallandigham says:

> Now, it is somewhat remarkable, certainly, that *after* the introduction, in February, 1861, of the propositions falsely thus described by that newspaper, it not only complimented the speech in which Mr. Vallandigham defended them, but actually so far failed to become aroused to a sense of danger, as to repeatedly and earnestly advocate the policy of letting the South go – a something that Mr. Vallandigham has never done, to this day. But let that pass.
>
> The deliberate and circumstantial repetition, at this time, and in its fullest form, of the misrepresentation of the nature of the propositions which I did introduce, is but another proof of the desperate fortunes of the Abolition party, and particularly of the press which has supported it. To the personal assaults of that press, and especially of the paper quoted from, I reply not. Pope and Pagan may now very calmly be allowed to sit at the mouth of the Abolition cave, and gnash their toothless gums at Democratic pilgrims as they pass by. "The effectual check and waning proportions" of this Administration, and its despotic and bloody policy, enable us to practice the more cheerfully now, a philosophy which hitherto may have been somewhat

compulsory. But false statements of recorded or historic facts do not come within the rule.

Now, Mr. Vallandigham never proposed to divide "the Republic into four distinct nationalities." So far as any such proposition has been suggested at all, it was by General Scott, who even went so far as to name the probable capitals of three of those "nationalities." My proposition, on the contrary, was to maintain the existing Union, or "nationality" forever, by dividing or arranging the States into sections *within the Union, under the Constitution,* for the purpose of voting in the Senate and electoral colleges.

CHAPTER FOUR
Executive Usurpation
Speech Delivered in the House of Representatives,
July 10, 1861

"After some time be past."

    If the sober and unerring review of history should demonstrate that the present Administration has, from the first, lent itself to the development and execution of a cunningly devised plot, whose object was to destroy the old Union, constituted by the suffrages of the States, and establish in its place a government under which civil rights would be held and enjoyed only at the pleasure of an absolute, centralized, and irresponsible despotism – should history, when it reviews the startling events of these times, and traces those events to their now hidden causes, convict the President, and those with whom and through whom he has been acting, of this great crime against God and their country, it will then be seen with what clear penetration that eminent statesman, to whose counsels we have been listening, described the most secret movings, the first and most cautious unfoldings of that infamous plot. Then, *"after some time be past"* the stern verdict of history will justify and vindicate the solemn warnings he gave, and it will be recorded that all who heeded those warnings, and rallied to the protection and defense of the Temple of Liberty, obeyed the dictates of prudence and wisdom. It has been said, a nation may lose its liberties in a day, and not discover the loss in a hundred years. Should this be the sad doom of our country, which once gloried in calling itself the land where civil freedom was most dearly cherished and widely enjoyed, there would still be a few whose names the historian would gather, and of whom record that they knew and noted the hour when liberty withdrew, heard the muffled death-knell, and sounded the alarm through the land. High on that scroll will be written the name of Vallandigham.

The speech that follows was delivered soon after the opening of the extra session of Congress, convened on the 4th of July, 1861. No speech was ever delivered in the midst of greater personal danger – not even Cicero's defense of Milo. The galleries were filled with an excited soldiery and infuriated partisans threatening assassination. A leading Abolition paper in New York had, two days before, declared that, if an attempt was made to speak for peace, "the aisles of the Hall would run with blood." Arbitrary arrests, for opinion and speech, had already been commenced. Almost without sympathy upon his own side of the House, and with a fierce, insolent, and overwhelming majority upon the other side, Mr. Vallandigham, calm and unawed, met every peril, and spoke as firmly, solemnly, and earnestly as under ordinary circumstances. The "motto" prefixed to the speech is from Lord Bacon's will, and is significant, interpreted, as it has now been, by the light of two years' experience. Some three hundred thousand copies of the speech, in various forms, were published and circulated in the United States. It was published, also, in England and on the Continent.

The House was in Committee of the Whole, the subject under consideration, *The State of the Union*, when Mr. Vallandigham, obtaining the floor, said:

> Mr. Chairman: In the Constitution of the United States, which the other day we swore to support, and by the authority of which we are here assembled now, it is written: "All legislative powers herein granted shall be vested in a Congress of the United States."
>
> It is further written, also, that the Congress to which all legislative powers granted, are thus committed: "Shall make no law abridging the freedom of speech or of the press."
>
> And, it is yet further written, in protection of Senators and Representatives, in that freedom of debate here, without which there can be no liberty, that: "For any speech or debate in either House they shall not be questioned in any other place."
>
> Holding up the shield of the Constitution, and standing here in the place, and with the manhood of a Representative of the people, I propose to myself, to-day, the ancient freedom of speech used within these walls, though with somewhat more, I trust, of decency and discretion than have sometimes been exhibited here. Sir, I do not propose to discuss the direct question of this civil war in which we are engaged. Its present prosecution is a foregone conclusion; and a wise man never wastes his strength on a fruitless enterprise. My position shall, at present, for the most part, be indicated by my

votes, and by the resolutions and motions which I may submit. But there are many questions incident to the war and to its prosecution, about which I have somewhat to say now.

Mr. Chairman, the President, in the message before us, demands the extraordinary loan of $400,000,000 – an amount nearly ten times greater than the entire public debt, State and Federal, at the close of the Revolution, in 1783, and four times as much as the total expenditures during the three years' war with Great Britain, in 1812.

Sir, that same Constitution which I again hold up, and to which I give my whole heart, and my utmost loyalty, commits to Congress alone the power to borrow money, and to fix the purposes to which it shall be applied, and expressly limits army appropriations to the term of two years. Each Senator and Representative, therefore, must judge for himself, upon his conscience and his oath, and before God and the country, of the justice and wisdom and policy of the President's demand; and whenever this House shall have become but a mere office wherein to register the decrees of the Executive, it will be high time to abolish it. But I have a right, I believe, sir, to say that, however, gentlemen upon this side of the Chamber may differ finally as to the war, we are yet firmly and inexorably united in one thing, at least, and that is in the determination that our own rights and dignities and privileges, as the Representatives of the people, shall be maintained in their spirit, and to the very letter. And, be this as it may, I do know that there are some here present who are resolved to assert, and to exercise these rights with becoming decency and moderation, certainly, but, at the same time, fully, freely, and at every hazard.

Sir, it is an ancient and wise practice of the English Commons, to precede all votes of supplies by an inquiry into abuses and grievances, and especially into any infractions of the Constitution and the laws by the Executive. Let us follow this safe practice. We are now in Committee of the Whole on the State of the Union; and in the exercise of my right and my duty as a Representative, and availing myself of the latitude of debate allowed here, I propose to consider *the present state of the Union,* and supply, also, some few of the many omissions of the President in the message before us. Sir, he has undertaken to give us information of the state of the Union, as the Constitution requires him to do; and it was his duty, as an honest Executive, to make that information full, impartial, and complete, instead of spreading before us a labored and lawyerly vindication of his own course of policy – a policy which has precipitated us into a terrible and bloody revolution. He admits the fact; he admits that, to-day, we are in the midst of a general civil war; not now a mere petty insurrection, to be suppressed in twenty days by a proclamation and a *posse comitatus* of three months' militia.

Sir, it has been the misfortune of the President, from the beginning, that he has totally and wholly under-estimated the magnitude and character of the revolution with which he had to deal, or surely he never would have ventured upon the wicked and hazardous experiment of calling thirty millions of people to arms among themselves, without the counsel and authority of Congress. But when, at last, he found himself hemmed in by the revolution, and this city in danger, as he declares, and waked up thus, as the proclamation of the 15th of April proves him to have waked up, to the reality and significance of the movement, why did he not forthwith assemble Congress, and throw himself upon the wisdom and patriotism of the Representatives of the States and of the people, instead of usurping powers which the Constitution has expressly conferred upon us? Ay, sir, and powers which Congress had but a little while before, repeatedly and emphatically refused to exercise, or to permit him to exercise? But I shall recur to this point again.

Sir, the President, in this message, has undertaken also to give us a summary of the causes which have led to the present revolution. He has made out a case – he might, in my judgment, have made out a much stronger case – against the secessionists and disunionists of the South. All this, sir, is very well, as far as it goes. But the President does not go back far enough, nor in the right direction. He forgets the still stronger case against the abolitionists and disunionists of the North and West. He omits to tell us that secession and disunion had a New England origin, and began in Massachusetts, in 1804, at the time of the Louisiana purchase; were revived by the Hartford convention, in 1814, and culminated, during the war with Great Britain, in sending commissioners to Washington to settle the terms for a peaceable separation of New England from the other States of the Union. He forgets to remind us and the country, that this present revolution began forty years ago, in the vehement, persistent, offensive, most irritating and unprovoked agitation of the slavery question in the North and West, from the time of the Missouri controversy, with some short intervals, down to the present hour. Sir, if his statement of the case be the whole truth, and wholly correct, then the Democratic party, and every member of it, and the Whig party, too, and its predecessors, have been guilty, for sixty years, of an unjust, unconstitutional, and most wicked policy in administering the affairs of the Government.

But, sir, the President ignores totally the violent and long-continued denunciation of slavery and slaveholders, and especially since 1835 – I appeal to Jackson's message for the date and proof – until at last a political anti-slavery organization was formed in the North and West, which continued to gain strength year after year, till, at length, it had destroyed and usurped the place of the Whig party, and finally obtained control of every free State in the Union, and elected himself, through free-State votes alone, to the Presidency of the United States. He chooses to pass over the fact that the party to which he thus owes his place and his present power of mischief, is wholly and totally a sectional organization; and, as such, condemned by Washington, by Jefferson, by Jackson, Webster, and Clay, and by all the founders and preservers of the Republic, and utterly inconsistent with the principles, or with the peace, the stability, or the existence even, of our Federal system. Sir, there never was an hour, from the organization of this sectional party, when it was not predicted by the wisest men and truest patriots, and when it ought not to have been known by every intelligent man in the country, that it must, sooner or later, precipitate a revolution, and the dissolution of the Union. The President forgets already that, on the 4th of March, he declared that the platform of that party was "a law unto him," by which he meant to be governed in his administration; and yet that platform announced that whereas there were two separate and distinct kinds of labor and forms of civilization in the two different sections of the Union, yet that the entire national domain, belonging in common to all the States, should be taken, possessed, and held by one section alone, and consecrated to that kind of labor and form of civilization alone which prevailed in that section which, by mere numerical superiority, had chosen the President, and now has, and for some years past has had, a majority in the Senate, as from the beginning of the Government it had also in the House. He omits, too, to tell the country and the world – for he speaks, and we all speak now, to the world, and to posterity – that he himself, and his prime minister, the Secretary of State, declared, three years ago, and have maintained ever since, that there was an "irrepressible conflict" between the two sections of this Union; that the Union could not endure part slave and part free; and that the whole power and influence of the Federal Government must henceforth be exerted to circumscribe and hem in slavery within its existing limits.

And now, sir, how comes it that the President has forgotten to remind us, also, that when the party thus committed to the principle of deadly hate and hostility to the slave institutions of the South, and the men who had proclaimed the doctrine of the irrepressible conflict, and who, in the dilemma or alternative of this conflict, were resolved that "the cotton and rice fields of South Carolina, and the sugar plantations of Louisiana, should ultimately be tilled by free labor," had obtained power and place in the common Government of the States, the South, except one State, chose first to demand solemn constitutional guarantees for protection against the abuse of the tremendous power and patronage and influence of the Federal Government, for the purpose of securing the great end of the sectional conflict, before resorting to secession or revolution at all? Did he not know – how could he be ignorant – that, at the last session of Congress, every substantive proposition for adjustment and compromise, except that offered by the gentleman from Illinois (Mr. Kellogg) – and we all know, how it was received – came from the South? Stop a moment, and let us see.

The Committee of Thirty-three was moved for in this House by a gentleman from Virginia, the second day of the session, and received the vote of every Southern Representative present, except only the members from South Carolina, who declined to vote. In the Senate, the Committee of Thirteen was proposed by a Senator from Kentucky (Mr. Powell), and received the silent acquiescence of every Southern Senator present. The Crittenden propositions, too, were submitted also by another Senator from Kentucky (Mr. Crittenden), now a member of this House; a man, venerable for his years, loved for his virtues, distinguished for his services, honored for his patriotism; for four and forty years a Senator, or in other public office; devoted from the first hour of his manhood to the Union of these States; and who, though he himself proved his courage fifty years ago, upon the battlefield against the foreign enemies of his country, is now, thank God, still for compromise at home, to-day. Fortunate in a long and well-spent life of public service and private worth, he is unfortunate only that he has survived a Union, and, I fear, a Constitution, younger than himself.

The border State propositions, also, were projected by a gentleman from Maryland, not now a member of this House, and presented by a gentleman from Tennessee (Mr. Etheridge), now the Clerk of this House. And yet all these propositions, coming thus from the South, were severally and repeatedly rejected by the almost united vote of the Republican party in the Senate and the House. The Crittenden propositions, with which Mr. Davis, now President of the Confederate States, and Mr. Toombs, his Secretary of State, both declared, in the Senate, that they would be satisfied, and for which every Southern Senator and Representative voted, never, on any occasion, received one solitary vote from the Republican party in either House.

The Adams or Corwin amendment, so-called – reported from the Committee of Thirty-three, and the only substantive amendment proposed from the Republican side – was but a bare promise that Congress should never be authorized to do what no sane man ever believed Congress would attempt to do – abolish slavery in the States where it exists; and yet, even this proposition, moderate as it was, and for which every Southern member present voted – except one – was carried through this House by but one majority, after long and tedious delay, and with the utmost difficulty – sixty-five Republican members, with the resolute and determined gentleman from Pennsylvania (Mr. Hickman) at their head, having voted against it and fought against it to the very last.

And not this, only, but, as a part of the history of the last session, let me remind you that bills were introduced into this House, proposing to abolish and close up certain Southern ports of entry; to authorize the President to blockade the Southern coast, and to call out the militia, and accept the services of volunteers – not for three years merely – but without any limit as to either numbers or time, for the very purpose of enforcing the laws, collecting the revenue, and protecting the public property – and were pressed, vehemently and earnestly, in this House, *prior to the arrival of the President in this city,* and were then – though seven States had seceded, and set up a government of their own – voted down, postponed, thrust aside, or in some other way disposed of, sometimes by large majorities in this House, till, at last, Congress adjourned without any action at all. Peace, then, seemed to be the policy of all parties.

Thus, sir, the case stood, at twelve o'clock on the 4th of March last, when, from the eastern portico of this capitol, and in the presence of twenty thousand of his countrymen, but enveloped in a cloud of soldiery, which no other American President ever saw, Abraham Lincoln took the oath of office to support the Constitution, and delivered his inaugural – a message, I regret to say, not written in the direct and straightforward language which becomes an American President and an American statesman, and which was expected from the plain, blunt, honest man of the North-west – but with the forked tongue and crooked counsel of the New York politician, leaving thirty millions of people in doubt whether it meant peace or war. But, whatever may have been the secret purpose and meaning of the inaugural, practically, for six weeks, the policy of peace prevailed; and they were weeks of happiness to the patriot, and prosperity to the country. Business revived; trade returned; commerce flourished. Never was there a fairer prospect before any people. Secession in the past, languished, and was spiritless, and harmless; secession in the future, was arrested, and perished. By overwhelming majorities, Virginia, Kentucky, North Carolina, Tennessee, and Missouri, all declared for the old Union, and every heart beat high with hope that, in due course of time, and through faith and patience and peace, and by ultimate and adequate compromise, every State would be restored to it. It is true, indeed, sir, that the Republican party, with great unanimity, and great earnestness and determination, had resolved against all conciliation and compromise. But, on the other hand, the whole Democratic party, and the whole Constitutional Union party, were equally resolved that there should be no civil war, upon any pretext: and both sides prepared for an appeal to that great and final arbiter of all disputes in a free country – the people.

Sir, I do not propose to inquire, now, whether the President and his Cabinet were sincere and in earnest, and meant, really, to persevere to the end in the policy of peace; or whether, from the first, they meant civil war, and only waited to gain time till they were fairly seated in power, and had disposed, too, of that prodigious horde of spoilsmen and office-seekers which came down, at the first, like an avalanche upon them. But I do know that the people believed them sincere, and cordially ratified and approved of the policy of peace – not as they subsequently responded to the policy of war, in a whirlwind of passion and madness – but calmly and soberly, and as the result of their deliberate and most solemn judgment; and believing that civil war was absolute and eternal disunion, while secession was but partial and temporary, they cordially indorsed, also, the proposed evacuation of Sumter, and the other forts and public property within the seceded States. Nor, sir, will I stop, now, to explore the several causes which either led to a change in the apparent policy, or an early development of the original and real purposes of the Administration. But there are two which I cannot pass by. And the first of these was party necessity, or the clamor of politicians, and especially of certain wicked, reckless, and unprincipled conductors of a partisan press. The peace policy was crushing out the Republican party. Under that policy, sir, it was melting away like snow before the sun. The general elections in Rhode Island and Connecticut, and municipal elections in New York and in the Western States, gave abundant evidence that the people were resolved upon the most ample and satisfactory Constitutional guarantees to the South, as the price of a restoration of the Union. And then it was, sir, that the long and agonizing howl of defeated and disappointed politicians came up before the Administration. The newspaper press teemed with appeals and threats to the President. The mails groaned under the weight of letters demanding a change of policy; while a secret conclave of the Governors of Massachusetts, New York, Ohio, and other States, assembled here, promised men and money to support the President in the irrepressible conflict which they now invoked. And thus it was, sir, that the necessities of a party in the pangs of dissolution, in the very hour and article of death, demanding vigorous measures, which could result in nothing but civil war, renewed secession, and absolute and eternal disunion were preferred and hearkened to before the peace and harmony and prosperity of the whole country.

But there was another and yet stronger impelling cause, without which this horrid calamity of civil war might have been postponed, and, perhaps, finally averted. One of the last and worst acts of a Congress which, born in bitterness and nurtured in convulsion, literally did those things which it ought not to have done, and left undone those things which it ought to have done, was the passage of an obscure, ill-considered, ill-digested, and unstatesmanlike high protective tariff act, commonly known as "the Morrill tariff." Just about the same time, too, the Confederate Congress, at Montgomery, adopted our old tariff of 1857, which we had rejected to make way for the Morrill act, fixing their rate of duties at five, fifteen, and twenty per cent. lower than ours. The result was as inevitable as the laws of trade are inexorable. Trade and commerce – and especially the trade and commerce of the West – began to look to the South. Turned out of their natural course, years ago, by the canals and railroads of Pennsylvania and New York, and diverted eastward at a heavy cost to the West, they threatened now to resume their ancient and accustomed channels – the water-courses – the Ohio and the Mississippi. And political association and union, it was well known, must soon follow the direction of trade and interest. The city of New York, the great commercial emporium of the Union, and the North-west, the chief granary of the Union – began to clamor now, loudly, for a repeal of the pernicious and ruinous tariff. Threatened thus with the loss of both political power and wealth, or the repeal of the tariff, and, at last, of both, New England – and Pennsylvania, too, the land of Penn, cradled in peace – demanded, now, coercion and civil war, with all its horrors, as the price of preserving either from destruction. Ay, sir, Pennsylvania, the great key-stone of the arch of the Union, was willing to lay the whole weight of her iron upon that sacred arch, and crush it beneath the load. The subjugation of the South – ay, sir, the subjugation of the South! – I am not talking to children or fools; for there is not a man in this House fit to be a Representative here, who does not know that the South cannot be forced to yield obedience to your laws and authority again, until you have conquered and subjugated her – the subjugation of the South, and the closing up of her ports – first, by force, in war, and afterward, by tariff laws, in peace – was deliberately resolved upon by the East. And, sir, when once this policy was begun, these self-same motives of waning commerce, and threatened loss of trade, impelled the great city of New York, and her merchants and her politicians and her press – with here and there an honorable exception – to place herself in the very front rank among the worshipers of Moloch. Much, indeed, of that outburst and uprising in the North, which followed the proclamation of the 15th of April, as well, perhaps, as the proclamation itself, was called forth, not so much by the fall of Sumter – an event long anticipated – as by the notion that the "insurrection," as it was called, might be crushed out in a few weeks, if not by the display, certainly, at least, by the presence of an overwhelming force.

  These, sir, were the chief causes which, along with others, led to a change in the policy of the Administration, and, instead of peace, forced us, headlong, into civil war, with all its accumulated horrors.

  But, whatever may have been the causes or the motives of the act, it is certain that there was a change in the policy which the Administration meant to adopt, or which, at least, they led the country to believe they intended to pursue. I will not venture, now, to assert, what may yet, some day, be made to appear, that the subsequent acts of the Administration, and its enormous and persistent infractions of the Constitution, its high-handed usurpations of power, formed any part of a deliberate conspiracy to overthrow the present form of Federal-republican government, and to establish a strong centralized Government in its stead. No, sir; whatever their purposes now, I rather think that, in the beginning, they rushed, heedlessly and headlong into the gulf, believing that, as the seat of war was then far distant and difficult of access, the display of vigor in re-enforcing Sumter and Pickens, and in calling out seventy-five thousand militia, upon the firing of the first gun, and above all, in that exceedingly happy and original conceit of commanding the insurgent States to "disperse in twenty days," would not, on the one hand, precipitate a crisis, while, upon the other, it would satisfy its own violent partisans, and thus revive and restore the falling fortunes of the Republican party.

I can hardly conceive, sir, that the President and his advisers could be guilty of the exceeding folly of expecting to carry on a general civil war by a mere *posse comitatus* of three-months militia. It may be, indeed, that, with wicked and most desperate cunning, the President meant all this as a mere entering-wedge to that which was to rive the oak asunder; or, possibly, as a test, to learn the public sentiment of the North and West. But however that may be, the rapid secession and movements of Virginia, North Carolina, Arkansas, and Tennessee, taking with them, as I have said, elsewhere, four millions and a half of people, immense wealth, inexhaustible resources, five hundred thousand fighting men, and the graves of Washington and Jackson, and bringing up, too, in one single day, the frontier from the Gulf to the Ohio and the Potomac, together with the abandonment, by the one side, and the occupation, by the other, of Harper's Ferry and the Norfolk navy-yard; and the fierce gust and whirlwind of passion in the North, compelled either a sudden waking-up of the President and his advisers to the frightful significancy of the act which they had committed, in heedlessly breaking the vase which imprisoned the slumbering demon of civil war, or else a premature but most rapid development of the daring plot to foster and promote secession, and then to set up a new and strong form of government in the States which might remain in the Union.

But, whatever may have been the purpose, I assert here, to-day, as a Representative, that every principal act of the Administration since has been a glaring usurpation of power, and a palpable and dangerous violation of that very Constitution which this civil war is professedly waged to support. Sir, I pass by the proclamation of the 15th of April, summoning the militia – not to defend this capital – there is not a word about the capital in the proclamation, and there was then no possible danger to it from any quarter, but to retake and occupy forts and property a thousand miles off – summoning, I say, the militia to suppress the so-called insurrection. I do not believe, indeed, and no man believed in February last, when Mr. Stanton, of Ohio, introduced his Bill to enlarge the act of 1795, that that act ever contemplated the case of a general revolution, and of resistance by an organized government. But no matter. The militia thus called out, with a shadow, at least, of authority, and for a period extending one mouth beyond the assembling of Congress, were amply sufficient to protect the capital against any force which was then likely to be sent against it – and the event has proved it – and ample enough, also, to suppress the outbreak in Maryland. Every other principal act of the Administration might well have been postponed, and ought to have been postponed, until the meeting of Congress; or, if the exigencies of the occasion demanded it. Congress should forthwith have been assembled. What if two or three States should not have been represented, although even this need not have happened; but better this, a thousand times, than that the Constitution should be repeatedly and flagrantly violated, and public liberty and private right trampled under foot. As for Harper's Ferry and the Norfolk navy-yard, they rather needed protection against the Administration, by whose orders millions of property were wantonly destroyed, which was not in the slightest danger from any quarter, at the date of the proclamation.

But, sir, Congress was not assembled at once, as Congress should have been, and the great question of civil war submitted to their deliberations. The Representatives of the States and of the people were not allowed the slightest voice in this, the most momentous question ever presented to any government. The entire responsibility of the whole work was boldly assumed by the Executive, and all the powers required for the purposes in hand were boldly usurped from either the States or the people, or from the legislative department; while the voice of the judiciary, that last refuge and hope of liberty, was turned away from with contempt.

Sir, the right of blockade – and I begin with it – is a belligerent right, incident to a state of war, and it cannot be exercised until war has been declared or recognized; and Congress alone can declare or recognize war. But Congress had not declared or recognized war. On the contrary, they had, but a little while before, expressly refused to declare it, or to arm the President with the power to make it. And thus the President, in declaring a blockade of certain ports in the States of the South, and in applying to it the rules governing blockades as between independent powers, violated the Constitution.

But if, on the other hand, he meant to deal with these States as still in the Union, and subject to Federal authority, then he usurped a power which belongs to Congress alone – the power to abolish and close up ports of entry; a power, too, which Congress had, also, but a few weeks before, refused to exercise. And yet, without the repeal or abolition of ports of entry, any attempt, by either Congress or the President, to blockade these ports, is a violation of the spirit, if not of the letter, of that clause of the Constitution which declares that "no preference shall be given, by any regulation of commerce or revenue, to the ports of one State over those of another."

Sir, upon this point I do not speak without the highest authority. In the very midst of the South Carolina nullification controversy, it was suggested, that in the recess of Congress, and without a law to govern him, the President, Andrew Jackson, meant to send down a fleet to Charleston and blockade the port. But the bare suggestion called forth the indignant protest of Daniel Webster, himself the arch enemy of nullification, and whose brightest laurels were won in the three years' conflict in the Senate Chamber, with its ablest champions. In an address, in October, 1832, at Worcester, Massachusetts, to a National Republican convention – it was before the birth, or christening, at least, of the Whig party – the great expounder of the Constitution, said:

> We are told, sir, that the President will immediately employ the military force, and at once blockade Charleston. A military remedy – a remedy by direct belligerent operation – has thus been suggested, and nothing else has been suggested, as the intended means of preserving the Union. Sir, there is no little reason to think that this suggestion is true. We can not be altogether unmindful of the past, and, therefore, we can not be altogether unapprehensive for the future. For one, sir, I raise my voice, beforehand, against the unauthorized employment of military power, and against superseding the authority of the laws, by an armed force, under pretense of putting down nullification. *The President has no authority to blockade Charleston.*

Jackson! Jackson, sir! the great Jackson! did not dare to do it without authority of Congress; but our Jackson of to-day, the little Jackson at the other end of the avenue, and the mimic Jacksons around him, do blockade, not only Charleston harbor, but the whole Southern coast, three thousand miles in extent, by a single stroke of the pen.

"The President has no authority to employ military force till he shall be duly required" – mark the word – *"required* so to do by law and the civil authorities. His duty is to cause the laws to be executed. His duty is to support the civil authority" – as in the Merryman case, forsooth; but I shall recur to that hereafter:

> His duty is, if the laws be resisted, to employ the military force of the country, if necessary, for their support and execution; *but to do all this in compliance only with law and with decisions of the tribunals.* If, by any ingenious devices, those who resist the laws escape from the reach of judicial authority, as it is now provided to be exercised, it is entirely competent to Congress to make such new provisions as the exigency of the case may demand.

Treason, sir, rank treason, all this to-day. And, yet, thirty years ago, it was true Union patriotism and sound constitutional law! Sir, I prefer the wisdom and stern fidelity to principle of the fathers.

Such was the voice of Webster, and such too, let me add, the voice, in his last great speech in the Senate, of the Douglas whose death the land now mourns.

Next after the blockade, sir, in the catalogue of daring executive usurpations, comes the proclamation of the 3d of May, and the orders of the War and Navy Departments in pursuance of it – a proclamation and usurpation which would have cost any English sovereign his head at any time within the last two hundred years. Sir, the Constitution not only confines to Congress the right to declare war, but expressly provides that "Congress (not the President) shall have power to raise and support armies;" and to "provide and maintain a navy." In pursuance of this authority, Congress, years ago, had fixed the number of officers, and of the regiments, of the different kinds of service; and also, the number of ships, officers, marines, and seamen which should compose the navy. Not only that, but Congress has repeatedly, within the last five years, refused to increase the regular army. More than that still: in February and March last, the House, upon several test votes, repeatedly and expressly refused to authorize the President to accept the service of volunteers for the very purpose of protecting the public property, enforcing the laws, and collecting the revenue. And, yet, the President, of his own mere will and authority, and without the shadow of right, has proceeded to increase, and has increased, the standing army by twenty-five thousand men; the navy by eighteen thousand; and has called for, and accepted the services of, forty regiments of volunteers for three years, numbering forty-two thousand men, and making thus a grand army, or military force, raised by executive proclamation alone, without the sanction of Congress, without warrant of law, and in direct violation of the Constitution, and of his oath of office, of eighty-five thousand soldiers enlisted for three and five years, and already in the field. And, yet, the President now asks us to support the army which he has thus raised, to ratify his usurpations by a law *ex post facto,* and thus to make ourselves parties to our own degradation, and to his infractions of the Constitution. Meanwhile, however, he has taken good care not only to enlist the men, organize the regiments, and muster them into service, but to provide, in advance, for a horde of forlorn, worn-out, and broken-down politicians of his own party, by appointing, either by himself, or through the Governors of the States, major-generals, brigadier-generals, colonels, lieutenant-colonels, majors, captains, lieutenants, adjutants, quarter-masters, and surgeons, without any limit as to numbers, and without so much as once saying to Congress, "By your leave, gentlemen."

Beginning with this wide breach of the Constitution, this enormous usurpation of the most dangerous of all powers – the power of the sword – other infractions and assumptions were easy; and after public liberty, private right soon fell. The privacy of the telegraph was invaded in the search after treason and traitors; although it turns out, significantly enough, that the only victim, so far, is one of the appointees and especial pets of the Administration. The telegraphic dispatches, preserved under every pledge of secrecy for the protection and safety of the telegraph companies, were seized and carried away without search-warrant, without probable cause, without oath, and without description of the places to be searched, or of the things to be seized, and in plain violation of the right of the people to be secure in their houses, persons, *papers,* and effects, against unreasonable searches and seizures. One step more, sir, will bring upon us search and seizure of the public mails; and, finally, as in the worst days of English oppression – as in the times of the Russells and the Sydneys of English martyrdom – of the drawers and secretaries of the private citizen; though even then tyrants had the grace to look to the forms of the law, and the execution was judicial murder, not military slaughter. But who shall say that the future Tiberius of America shall have the modesty of his Roman predecessor, in extenuation of whose character it is written by the great historian, *avertit occulos, jussitque scelera non spectavit.*

Sir, the rights of property having been thus wantonly violated, it needed but a little stretch of usurpation to invade the sanctity of the person; and a victim was not long wanting. A private citizen of Maryland, not subject to the rules and articles of war – not in a case arising in the land or naval forces, nor in the militia, when in actual service – is seized in his own house, in the dead hour of night, not by any civil officer, nor upon any civil process, but by a band of armed soldiers, under the verbal orders of a military chief, and is ruthlessly torn from his wife and his children, and hurried off to a fortress of the United States – and that fortress, as if in mockery, the very one over whose ramparts had floated that star-spangled banner immortalized in song by the patriot prisoner, who, "By the dawn's early light," saw its folds gleaming amid the wreck of battle, and invoked the blessings of heaven upon it, and prayed that it might long wave "O'er the *land of the free,* and the home of the brave."

And, sir, when the highest judicial officer of the land, the Chief Justice of the Supreme Court, upon whose shoulders, "when the judicial ermine fell, it touched nothing not as spotless as itself," the aged, the venerable, the gentle, and pure-minded Taney, who, but a little while before, had administered to the President the oath to support the Constitution, and to execute the laws, issued, as by law it was his sworn duty to issue, the high prerogative writ of *habeas corpus* – that great writ of right, that main bulwark of personal liberty, commanding the body of the accused to be brought before him, that justice and right might be done by due course of law, and without denial or delay, the gates of the fortress, its cannon turned towards, and in plain sight of the city, where the court sat, and frowning from the ram-

Executive Usurpation

parts, were closed against the officer of the law, and the answer returned that the officer in command has, by the authority of the President, *suspended* the writ of *habeas corpus*. And thus it is, sir, that the accused has ever since been held a prisoner without due process of law; without bail; without presentment by a grand jury; without speedy, or public trial by a petit jury, of his own State or district, or any trial at all; without information of the nature and cause of the accusation; without being confronted with the witnesses against him; without compulsory process to obtain witnesses in his favor; and without the assistance of counsel for his defense. And this is our boasted American liberty? And thus it is, too, sir, that here, here, in America, in the seventy-third year of the Republic, that great writ and security of personal freedom, which it cost the patriots and freemen of England six hundred years of labor and toil and blood to extort and to hold fast from venal judges and tyrant kings; written in the great charter at Runnymede by the iron barons, who made the simple Latin and uncouth words of the times, *nullus liber homo,* in the language of Chatham, worth all the classics; recovered and confirmed a hundred times afterward, as often as violated and stolen away, and finally, and firmly secured at last by the great act of Charles II, and transferred thence to our own Constitution and laws, has been wantonly and ruthlessly trampled in the dust. Ay, sir, that great writ, bearing, by a special command of Parliament, those other uncouth, but magic words, *per statutum tricessimo primo Caroli secundi regis,* which no English judge, no English minister, no king or queen of England, dare disobey; that writ, brought over by our fathers, and cherished by them, as a priceless inheritance of liberty, an American President has contemptuously set at defiance. Nay, more, he has ordered his subordinate military chiefs to suspend it at their discretion! And, yet, after all this, he coolly comes before this House and the Senate and the country, and pleads that he is only preserving and protecting the Constitution; and demands and expects of this House and of the Senate and the country their thanks for his usurpations; while, outside of this capitol, his myrmidons are clamoring for impeachment of the Chief Justice, as engaged in a conspiracy to break down the Federal Government.

Sir, however much necessity – the tyrant's plea – may be urged in extenuation of the usurpations and infractions of the President in regard to public liberty, there can be no such apology or defense for his invasions of private right. What overruling necessity required the violation of the sanctity of private property and private confidence? What great public danger demanded the arrest and imprisonment, without trial by common law, of one single private citizen, for an act done weeks before, openly, and by authority of his State? If guilty of treason, was not the judicial power ample enough and strong enough for his conviction and punishment? What, then, was needed in his case, but the precedent under which other men, in other places, might become the victims of executive suspicion and displeasure?

As to the pretense, sir, that the President has the Constitutional right to suspend the writ of *habeas corpus,* I will not waste time in arguing it. The case is as plain as words can make it. It is a legislative power; it is found only in the legislative article; it belongs to Congress only to do it. Subordinate officers have disobeyed it; General Wilkinson disobeyed it, but he sent his prisoners on for judicial trial; General Jackson disobeyed it, and was reprimanded by James Madison; but no President, nobody but Congress, ever before assumed the right to suspend it. And, sir, that other pretense of necessity, I repeat, cannot be allowed. It had no existence in fact. The Constitution cannot be preserved by violating it. It is an offense to the intelligence of this House, and of the country, to pretend that all this, and the other gross and multiplied infractions of the Constitution and usurpations of power were done by the President and his advisers out of pure love and devotion to the Constitution. But if so, sir, then they have but one step further to take, and declare, in the language of Sir Boyle Roche, in the Irish House of Commons, that such is the depth of their attachment to it, that they are prepared to give up, not merely a part, but the whole of the Constitution, *to preserve the remainder.* And yet, if indeed this pretext of necessity be well founded, then let me say, that a cause which demands the sacrifice of the Constitution and of the dearest securities of property, liberty, and life, cannot be just; at least, it is not worth the sacrifice.

Sir, I am obliged to pass by, for want of time, other grave and dangerous infractions and usurpations of the President since the 4th of March. I only allude casually to the quartering of soldiers in private houses without the consent of the owners, and without any manner having been prescribed by law; to the subversion in a part, at least, of Maryland of her own State Government and of the authorities under it; to the censorship over the telegraph, and the infringement, repeatedly, in one or more of the States, of the right of the people to keep and to bear arms for their defense. But if all these things, I ask, have been done in the first two months after the commencement of this war, and by men not military chieftains, and unused to arbitrary power, what may we not expect to see in three years, and by the successful heroes of the fight? Sir, the power and rights of the States and the people, and of their Representatives, have been usurped; the sanctity of the private house and of private property has been invaded; and the liberty of the person wantonly and wickedly stricken down; free speech, too, has been repeatedly denied; and all this under the plea of necessity. Sir, the right of petition will follow next – nay, it has already been shaken; the freedom of the press will soon fall after it; and let me whisper in your ear, that there will be few to mourn over its loss, unless, indeed, its ancient high and honorable character shall be rescued and redeemed from its present reckless mendacity and degradation. Freedom of religion will yield too, at last, amid the exultant shouts of millions, who have seen its holy temples defiled, and its white robes of a former innocency trampled now under the polluting hoofs of an ambitious and faithless or fanatical clergy. Meantime national banks, bankrupt laws, a vast and permanent public debt, high tariffs, heavy direct taxation, enormous expenditure, gigantic and stupendous peculation, anarchy first, and a strong government afterward, no more State lines, no more State governments, and a consolidated monarchy or vast centralized military despotism must all follow in the history of the future, as in the history of the past they have, centuries ago, been written. Sir, I have said nothing, and have time to say nothing now, of the immense indebtedness and the vast expenditures which have already accrued, nor of the folly and mismanagement of the war so far, nor of the atrocious and shameless peculations and frauds which have disgraced it in the State governments and the Federal Government from the beginning. The avenging hour for all these will come hereafter, and I pass them by now.

I have finished now, Mr. Chairman, what I proposed to say at this time upon the message of the President. As to my own position in regard to this most unhappy civil war, I have only to say that I stand to-day just where I stood upon the 4th of March last; where the whole Democratic party, and the whole Constitutional Union party, and a vast majority, as I believe, of the people of the United States stood too. I am for *peace,* speedy, immediate, honorable peace, with all its blessings. Others may have changed – I have not. I question not their motives nor quarrel with their course. It is vain and futile for them to question or to quarrel with mine. My duty shall be discharged – calmly, firmly, quietly, and regardless of consequences. The approving voice of a conscience void of offense, and the approving judgment which shall follow "after some time be past," these, God help me, are my trust and my support.

Sir, I have spoken freely and fearlessly to-day, as became an American Representative and an American citizen; one firmly resolved, come what may, not to lose his own Constitutional liberties, nor to surrender his own Constitutional rights in the vain effort to impose these rights and liberties upon ten millions of unwilling people. I have spoken earnestly, too, but yet not as one unmindful of the solemnity of the scenes which surround us upon every side to-day. Sir, when the Congress of the United States assembled here on the 3d of December, 1860, just seven months ago, the Senate was composed of sixty-six Senators, representing the thirty-three States of the Union, and this House of two hundred and thirty-seven members – every State being present. It was a grand and solemn spectacle – the embassadors of three and thirty sovereignties and thirty-one millions of people, the mightiest republic on earth, in general Congress assembled. In the Senate, too, and this House, were some of the ablest and most distinguished statesmen of the country; men whose names were familiar to the whole country – some of them destined to pass into history. The new wings of the capitol had then but just recently been finished, in all their gorgeous magnificence, and, except a hundred marines at the navy-yard, not a soldier was within forty miles of Washington.

Sir, the Congress of the United States meets here again to-day; but how changed the scene! Instead of thirty-four States, twenty-three only, one less than the number forty years ago, are here, or in the other wing of the capitol. Forty-six Senators and a hundred and seventy-three Representatives constitute the Congress of the now United States. And of these, eight Senators and twenty-four Representatives, from four States only, linger here yet as deputies from that great South which, from the beginning of the Government, contributed so much to mold its policy, to build up its greatness, and to control its destinies. All the other States of that South are gone. Twenty-two Senators and sixty-five Representatives no longer answer to their names. The vacant seats are, indeed, still here; and the escutcheons of their respective States look down now solemnly and sadly from these vaulted ceilings. But the Virginia of Washington and Henry and Madison, of Marshall and Jefferson, of Randolph and Monroe, the birthplace of Clay, the mother of States and of Presidents; the Carolinas of Pinckney and Sumter and Marion, of Calhoun and Macon; and Tennessee, the home and burial-place of Jackson; and other States, too, once most loyal and true, are no longer here. The voices and the footsteps of the great dead of the past two ages of the Republic linger still – it may be in echo – along the stately corridors of this capitol; but their descendants, from nearly one-half of the States of the Republic, will meet with us no more within these marble halls. But in the parks and lawns, and upon the broad avenues of this spacious city, seventy thousand soldiers have supplied their places; and the morning drum-beat from a score of encampments, within sight of this beleaguered capitol, give melancholy warning to the Representatives of the States and of the people, that *amid arms laws are silent*.

Sir, some years hence – I would fain hope some months hence, if I dare – the present generation will demand to know the cause of all this; and, some ages hereafter, the grand and impartial tribunal of history will make solemn and diligent inquest of the authors of this terrible revolution.

Addendum

In reply to a question by Mr. Holman, of Indiana, in regard to supporting the Government, Mr. Vallandigham said he would answer in the words of the following resolution, which he had prepared, and proposed to offer at a future time:

> *Resolved*, That the Federal Government is the agent of the people of the several States composing the Union; that it consists of three distinct departments – the legislative, the executive, and the judicial – each equally a part of the Government, and equally entitled to the confidence and support of the States and the people; and that it is the duty of every patriot to sustain the several departments of the Government in the exercise of all the Constitutional powers of each which may be necessary and proper for the preservation of the Government in its principles and in its vigor and integrity, and to stand by and defend to the utmost the flag which represents the Government, the Union, and the country.

CHAPTER FIVE
Charges of Disloyalty Triumphantly Repelled

It would not be easy to find a fair and honest Democrat who has not been denounced as a secessionist by the Abolition press. These denunciations have been more bitter and malignant, and involved a larger use of destructive epithets, in proportion to the power, influence, and consistency of the men against whom they have been directed. In Mr. Vallandigham's case, the whole vocabulary of Abolition Billingsgate has been brought into requisition. Of this "arch-traitor," "Southern sympathizer," "secessionist," the worst things that could be said by preachers, lecturers, and presses, gave but feeble expression to the intense and malignant hatred cherished against him. Those men who have been screeching for the Union, while plotting its destruction, have found Mr. Vallandigham always in their way. The piteous howlings of the Abolition demon have not been without provocation; for, in whatever direction that old devil would lay his course, he would be sure to find Mr. Vallandigham across his path. And no one has oftener dealt the old monster a square blow in the eye. But the demon has a wide circle of friends, among whom his sufferings have excited the deepest sympathy and commiseration.

Upon Congress there has been a strong outside pressure against Mr. Vallandigham, and, on the part of many members of that body, a great willingness to yield to that pressure. There has even been an intense and watchful anxiety to find something that would serve as a plausible excuse for making a hostile descent upon the special object of Abolition hatred. And yet – here is a most important and significant fact – no successful attempt to impeach, or even cast reproach upon, his loyalty, has ever been made. The efforts in that direction, made seven times in Congress, have not even attained to the dignity of decent failures, and have only been a mortifying and disgraceful reproach to the parties through whom they have been made.

When, on the 7th of January, 1862, Mr. Vallandigham denounced, in strong terms, the surrender of Mason and Slidell, under a threat, he was assailed, personally, as to his war record, by John Hutchins, of Ohio, the successor of Joshua R. Giddings. In reply, Mr. Vallandigham said:

> I do neither retract one sentiment that I have uttered, nor would I obliterate a single vote which I have given. I speak of the record as it will appear hereafter, and, indeed, stands now upon the Journals of this House and in the *Congressional Globe*. And there is no other record, thank God, and no act or word or thought of mine, and never has been from the beginning, in public or in private, of which any patriot ought to be ashamed. Sir, it is the record as I made it, and as it exists here to-day – and not as a mendacious and shameless press have attempted to make it up for me. Let us see who will grow tired of his record first. Consistency, firmness, and sanity, in the midst of general madness – these made up my offense. But "Time, the avenger," sets all things even: and I abide his leisure.
>
> To-day the magnitude and true character of the war stand confessed, and its real purposes begin to be revealed; and I am justified, or soon will be justified, by thousands, who, a little while ago, condemned me. But I appealed, in the beginning, as I appeal now, alike to the near and the distant future; and by the judgment of that impartial tribunal, even in the present generation, I will abide; or, if my name and memory shall fade away out of the record of these times, then will these calumnies perish with them.

But, of those attacks, the most important and serious was that made in the House of Representatives on the 19th of February, 1862, by Mr. Hickman, of Pennsylvania, who offered a resolution "Instructing the Committee on the Judiciary to inquire into the truth of certain charges of disloyalty made in the local columns of a Baltimore newspaper against C.L. Vallandigham, of Ohio."

The debate that ensued was racy and rare; contains some capital strokes. We give the full report, that all may see the extent and magnitude of the charges of disloyalty, as presented by one of the shrewdest and most cunning of the Abolition members.

The resolution above referred to having been offered, Mr. Vallandigham said:

> Mr. Speaker: I was just waiting for an opportunity to call the attention of the House to that statement myself, having received it from some unknown source a moment ago. I do not know, of course, what the motive just now of the gentleman from Pennsylvania may be, nor do I care. My purpose then was just what it is now, to give a plain, direct, emphatic contra-

diction – a flat denial to the infamous statement and insinuation contained in the newspaper paragraph just read. I never wrote a letter or a line upon political subjects, least of all, on the question of secession, to the Baltimore *South*, or to any other paper, or to any man south of Mason and Dixon's line, since this revolt began – never; and I defy the production of it. It is false, infamous, scandalous; and, it is beyond endurance, too, that a man's reputation shall be at the mercy of every scavenger employed to visit the haunts of vice in a great city, a mere local editor of an irresponsible newspaper, who may choose to parade before the country false and malicious libels like this. I avail myself of this opportunity, to say that I enter into no defense, and shall enter into none, until some letter shall be produced here which I have written, or authorized to be written, referring to "bleeding Dixie," or making any suggestion "how the Yankees might be defeated." If any such are in existence, I pronounce them, here and now, utter and impudent forgeries. I have said that I enter upon no defense. I deny that it is the duty or the right of any member to rise here and call for investigation founded upon statements like this; and I only regret that I did not have the opportunity to denounce this report before the chairman of the Committee on the Judiciary rose, and, in this formal manner, called the attention of the House to it – himself the accuser and the judge. Sir, I have been for five years a member of this House, and I never rose to a personal explanation but once, and that to correct a report of the proceedings of the House. I have always considered such mere personal explanations and controversies with the press as unbecoming the dignity of the House.

Nevertheless, I did intend to make this the first exception in my congressional career, and to say – and I wish my words reported, not only at the desk here officially, but in the gallery – that I denounce, in advance, this foul and infamous statement, that I have been in treasonable, or even suspicious correspondence with any one in that State – loyal though it is to the Union – or in any other State, or have ever uttered one sentiment inconsistent with my duty, not only as a member of this House, but as a citizen of the United States – one who has taken a solemn oath to support the Constitution, and who, thank God, has never tainted that oath in thought, or word, or deed. I have had the right, and have exercised it, and as God liveth and my soul liveth, and as He is my judge, I will exercise it still in this House, and out of it, of vindicating the rights of the American citizen; and beyond that I have never gone. My sentiments will be found in the records of the House, except as I have made them public otherwise, and they will be found nowhere else. There, sir, is their sole repository. And foreseeing, more than a year ago, but especially in the early part of December, 1860, the magnitude and true character of the revolution or rebellion into which this country was about to be plunged, I then resolved not to write, although your own mails still carried the letters, nor have I written, one solitary syllable or line – as to the gulf States months even before secession began – to any one residing in a seceded State. And yet, the gentleman avails himself now of this paragraph, to give dignity and importance to charges of the falsest and most infamous character. Had the letter been produced; had the charge come in any tangible or authentic shape; had any editor of any respectable newspaper, even, indorsed the accusation, and made it specific, there might have been some apology; but the gentleman knows well that this base insinuation was placed in the local columns of a vile newspaper, put there by some person who had never seen any such letter. Sir, I meet this first specific charge of disloyalty, made responsibly here – I meet it at the very threshold, as becomes a man and a Representative – by an emphatic but contemptuous denial. This is due to the House; it is due to myself.

Mr. Richardson. I hope the gentleman from Pennsylvania will allow me to make a single remark.

Mr. Hickman. Certainly.

Mr. Richardson. Mr. Speaker: I want to hear nothing about disloyalty on this side of the House while there is a class of members here upon the other side of the House who have declared that they will vote for no proposition to carry on the war, unless it is prosecuted in a particular line, and for the abolition of slavery. They would subvert the Constitution and the Government, and I denounce them as traitors, and they ought to be brought to trial, condemnation, and execution.

Mr. Hickman. Mr. Speaker: The motives which actuated me in introducing the resolution in question ought not to be doubted. The severe charge contained in the article in question is made against the gentleman from Ohio, a member of this House. Even a suspicion, a mere suspicion, would justify such an investigation as this resolution contemplates. But the gentleman from Ohio, as well as other members upon this floor, knows that the suspicions which have existed against him – I do not say whether justly or unjustly – have been numerous, and in circulation for a long time past. It is the duty of this House to purge itself of unworthy members. I do not assert whether the gentleman from Ohio occupies, properly or improperly, his seat upon this floor. By offering this resolution I do not prejudge him. If he were the most intimate friend I had on earth, accused as the gentleman from Ohio is in the paragraph in question, I should deem it my solemn duty to urge the investigation which is here suggested. But, sir, this charge does not come in a very questionable shape. It appears as an original article in the Baltimore *Clipper*, and is, therefore, presumed to be editorial, or at least under the supervision of the editor. It, to all appearances, emanates from a responsible source.

But, sir, I suggest further, that the suppression of the newspaper in question, the Baltimore *South*, and the seizure of its office of publication, was made under the direct authority of the Government, and it is to be presumed that the effects of the office are, at this time, in the custody of the Government, or of the agents of the Government, and, therefore, the information communicated in this paper must have come through the Government, or the agents of the Government. It is responsible in its origin, as far as we can judge. Now, sir, I refer the gentleman from Ohio, as my answer to the suggestion that I was not justified in offering this resolution under the circumstances, to page 69 of the last edition of the Manual. The first paragraph of section thirteen, headed "Examination of Witnesses," reads as follows: "Common fame is a good ground for the House to proceed to inquiry, and even to accusation." This, sir, is more than common fame. I repeat, that it is, so far as it appears, a direct charge by the editor of a responsible newspaper. The information comes, we must believe, through the Government, or the agents of the Government, and it is, therefore, more than common fame. It is good ground, at least, for instituting an inquiry.

Mr. Vallandigham. I desire to ask the gentleman from Pennsylvania whether he does not know that this is a mere local item, and that the author of it does not even pretend to have seen the letters.

Mr. Hickman. I do not understand what the gentleman means by saying that the author of the paragraph has not seen them.

Mr. Vallandigham. I say he does not profess to have seen them, and I know that he never did, for they never were written, do not now exist, and never did exist.

Mr. Hickman. Who never saw them?

Mr. Vallandigham. The author of that paragraph in the local columns of this newspaper.

Mr. Hickman. He never saw the letters!

Mr. Vallandigham. He does not profess even to have seen them.

Mr. Hickman. Whether it is a local item or not, it is an original article in a responsible newspaper, and is, therefore, presumed to have been inserted under the direct supervision of the editor, if not written by him.

Mr. Vallandigham. The gentleman from Pennsylvania has alluded to suspicions existing heretofore. Now, I desire to know of him, whether he ever heard of any specific item on which any such suspicions ever rested – anything other than words spoken in this House or made public over my own name?

Mr. Hickman. Yes, sir.

Mr. Vallandigham. Well, let us have it.

Mr. Hickman. I have heard a thousand.

Mr. Vallandigham. Name a single one.

Mr. Hickman. I do not desire to do any injustice to the gentleman from Ohio.

Mr. Vallandigham. I have asked the gentleman, and I demand a direct answer to my question, whether he can specify one single item?

Mr. Hickman. I will reply to it directly.

Mr. Vallandigham. Or does the gentleman mean merely the newspaper slanders that have been published against me, and which I have denounced as false, over and over again, in cards, and on the floor of this House?

Mr. Hickman. I know nothing about that, sir. I know that suspicions may well exist, and I know they do exist, where denials accompany them.

Mr. Vallandigham. Yes; I know that fact in the gentleman's own case.

Mr. Hickman. I have no controversy with the gentleman from Ohio, nor am I here to defend myself in the course which I have taken. Let him defend himself, and allow me to take care of myself, as I expect to be able to do.

Mr. Richardson. Will the gentleman from Pennsylvania allow me —

Mr. Hickman. I will not suffer any interruption except by the gentleman from Ohio. He has a right to interrupt me, and I am glad he does so, because I do not want to put the gentleman from Ohio in any false position any more than I would desire to be myself placed
in one; and I will not do it. I do say, most distinctly, that suspicions have existed against the loyalty of the gentleman from Ohio; and I would not have referred to them at all if I had not been satisfied that he himself knew of the existence of those suspicions as well as I did. Indeed, the remarks which preceded my rising on this floor indicated the fact, more clearly than I myself could indicate it by anything that I could say, that he was in possession of a knowledge of the existence of those suspicions, for he got up to repel them, not merely such as are contained in this article in question, but in general terms – general suspicions and imputations against his character. That was deemed right by him, sir. I have nothing to say against it.

Now, the gentleman asks for specifications. I am called upon by him to refresh my memory, and to give an instance. I will give him one or two. I may not be able to give more at this time. Perhaps, if he were to give me time, I would be able to refer him to many more instances.

Mr. Vallandigham. Mr. Speaker —

Mr. Hickman. The gentleman must allow me to answer his question, and then he may interrupt me. I must reply to one inquiry at a time. I am now on the witness-stand – brought to it by the gentleman from Ohio. I am on cross-examination, and he must allow me to answer one question before he propounds to me another. Now, sir, I refer to the fact of the Breckenridge meeting in the city of Baltimore, where the gentleman from Ohio attended, and which gave rise to very many suspicions, allow me to say; at least I have heard a great many expressed. Allow me again to refer to the fact of his attending a certain dinner in Kentucky, which was given, I believe, in his honor, or which was, at least, published as such in the papers.

 Mr. Vallandigham. Allow me, right there —

 Mr. Hickman. Allow me first —

 Mr. Vallandigham. That is a specific charge, which I wish to answer.

 Mr. Hickman. Not this moment.

 Mr. Vallandigham. I appeal to the gentleman's honor.

 Mr. Hickman. I will treat the gentleman from Ohio fairly. He must receive all my answer before he asks me another question,

 Mr. Vallandigham. Let him oblige me by replying to me specifically.

 Mr. Hickman. I am not done with my answer, and I refuse to yield the floor until I finish my answer. I am entitled to be treated here properly, as well as the gentleman from Ohio. I will extend to him all the courtesy that can possibly be demanded by any gentleman. That is my habit, I trust. There are many other items. There was the speech which the gentleman made at the July session in this House – a speech which was understood to be one of general accusation and crimination against the Government and against the party having the conduct of this war. It gave rise to a great many suspicions; and the gentleman from Ohio, with his intelligence, ought not to be ignorant of all these facts. Well, sir, will not conversation naturally arise in consequence of these facts? And I appeal to every member of this House whether they have not heard suspicion upon suspicion against the loyalty of the gentleman from Ohio. Is it not a common rumor, sir, that he is suspected? I allege that it is a common rumor in the Northern States, and among the loyal people of the loyal States, that the gentleman from Ohio is, at least, open to grave suspicion, if not to direct imputation. That is my answer. Now I will hear the gentleman.

 Mr. Vallandigham. In reply to the specification, and the only one, which the gentleman has been able to point out, relating to a public dinner in Kentucky, allow me to tell him that my foot has not pressed the soil of Kentucky since the 10th day of July, 1852, when, as a member of a committee appointed by the common council of the city where I reside, I followed the remains of that great and noble man, true patriot and Union man, Henry Clay, to their last resting-place. I have partaken of no dinners there, or elsewhere, of a political character, nor did I ever attend any Breckenridge meeting at Baltimore, or elsewhere, at any time. This is my answer to that, the only specification. And yet, the gentleman dares attempt to support that falsehood, which I here denounce as such, by alluding to suspicions which have been created and set afloat throughout the whole country, not merely against me, but against hundreds and thousands of others, in whose veins runs blood as patriotic and loyal as ever flowed since the world began. I tell the gentleman that, in years past, I have heard his loyalty to the Union questioned. I have known of things which would have justified me – had I relied on authority similar to that to which he has attempted to give dignity – in introducing similar resolutions to make inquiry into his purpose to disrupt this Union by the doctrines which he has held, and the opinions which he has expressed. And yet, opinions and sentiments, uttered here, are "the head and the front of my offending." It has "this extent, no more."

And, sir, I replied, some time ago, to two others, which, I doubt not, the gentleman would have dragged now out of the mire and slough into which they have fallen, but that they were answered, when thrust into debate by the gentleman before me (Mr. Hutchins). I refer to the charge that I had once uttered the absurd declaration that the soldiery of the North and West should pass over my dead body before they should invade the Southern States. I denied it then, and will not repeat the denial now.

Nor need I refer again to that other charge, that I had uttered, in debate, here or elsewhere, the sentiment that I preferred peace to the Union; I have heretofore met that charge with a prompt and emphatic contradiction, and no evidence has been found to sustain it. Referring to that and other charges and insinuations, on the 7th of January last, I said to my colleague: "As to my record here at the extra session, or during the present session, it remains, and will remain."

And just here, sir, in reference to the speech to which the gentleman alluded, delivered on this floor, in the exercise of my constitutional right as a member of this House, on the 10th of July last, I defy him – I hurl the defiance into his teeth – to point to one single disloyal sentiment or sentence in it. I proceeded to say, further, on the 7th of last month:

> I do neither retract one sentiment that I have uttered, nor would I obliterate a single vote which I have given. I speak of the record, as it will appear hereafter, and, indeed, stands now upon the Journals of this House and in the *Congressional Globe*. And there is no other record, thank God, and no act or word or thought of mine, and never has been from the beginning, in public or in private, of which any patriot ought to be ashamed. Sir, it is the record, as I made it, and as it exists here to-day; and not as a mendacious and shameless press have attempted to make it up for me. Let us see who will grow tired of his record first. Consistency, firmness, and sanity, in the midst of general madness – these made up my offense. But "Time, the avenger," sets all things even; and I abide his leisure.

And am I now to be told, that because of a speech made upon this floor, under the protection of the Constitution, in the exercise and discharge

Charges of Disloyalty Triumphantly Repelled 135

of my solemn right and duty, under the oath which I have taken, that I am today to be arraigned here, and the accusation supported by the addition of mere vague rumors and suspicions, which have been bruited over and over again, as I have said, against not myself only, but against hundreds and thousands, also, of other most patriotic and loyal men?

The gentleman from Pennsylvania makes the charge that I attended a certain dinner in the State of Kentucky. Sir, I was invited to that State, and have been frequently, by as true and loyal men as there are in that State today. I accepted no invitation, and never went at all. I have already named the last and only time when I stood upon the soil of Kentucky. But I know of nothing now – whatever there may have been in the past – certainly nothing to-day about Kentucky that should prevent a loyal and patriotic man from visiting a State which has given birth or residence to so many patriots, to so many statesman, and to orators of such renown.

Yet that is all, the grand aggregate of the charges, except this miserable falsehood which some wretched scavenger, prowling about the streets and alleys and gutters of the city of Baltimore, has seen fit to put forth in the local columns of a contemptible newspaper; so that the member from Pennsylvania may rise in his place and prefer charges against the loyalty and patriotism of a man who has never faltered in his devotion to the flag of his country – to that flag which hangs now upon the wall over against him; one who has bowed down and worshiped this holy emblem of the Constitution and of the old Union of these States, in his heart's core, ay, in his very heart of hearts, from the time he first knew aught to this hour; and who now would give life, and all that he is or hopes to be in the present or the future, to see that glorious banner of the Union – known and honored once over the whole earth and the whole sea – with no stripe erased, and not one star blotted out, floating forever over the free, united, harmonious old Union of every State once a part of it, and a hundred more yet unborn. *I am that man;* and yet he dares to demand that I shall be brought up before the secret tribunal of the Judiciary Committee – that committee of which he is chairman, and thus both judge and accuser – to answer to the charge of disloyalty to the Union!

Sir, I hurl back the insinuation. Bring forward the specific charge; wait till you have found something – and you will wait long – something which I have written, or something I have said, that would indicate anything in my bosom which he who loves his country ought not to read or hear. In every sentiment that I have expressed, in every vote that I have given, in my whole public life, outside this House, before I was a member of it, and since it has been my fortune to sit here, I have had but one motive, and that was the real, substantial, permanent good of my country. I have differed with the majority of the House, differed with the party in power, differed with the Administration, as, thank God, I do and have the right to differ, as to the best means of preserving the Union, and of maintaining the Constitution and securing the true interests of my country; and that is my offense, that the crime, and the only crime, of which I have been guilty.

Mr. Speaker, if, in the Thirty-fifth Congress, I or some other member had seen fit to seize upon the denunciations, long-continued, bitter, and persistent against that member (Mr. Hickman) – for he, too, has suffered, and he ought to have had the manhood to remember, in this, the hour of sore persecution, that he himself has been the victim of slanders and detraction, peradventure – for, sir, I would do him the justice which he denies to me – what, I say, if I had risen and made a vile paragraph in some paper published in his own town, or elsewhere, the subject of inquiry and investigation, and had attempted to cast yet further suspicion upon him, by reference to language uttered here in debate, which he had the right to utter, or by charges vague and false, and without the shadow of a foundation except the malignant breath of partisan suspicion and slander, what would have been his record, in the volumes of your reports, and the *Congressional Globe*, going down to his children after him? But, sir, it is not in the power of the gentleman to tarnish the honor of my name, or to blast the fair fame and character for loyalty which I have earned – dearly earned, with labor and patience and faith, from the beginning of my public career. From my boyhood, at all times and in every place, I have never looked to anything but the permanent, solid, and real interests of my country.

Beyond this, Mr. Speaker, I deem it unnecessary to extend what I have to say. I would have said not a word, but that I know this Committee will find nothing, and that they will be obliged, therefore, to report – a majority of them cheerfully, I doubt not – that nothing exists to justify any charge or suspicion such as the member from Pennsylvania has suggested here today. I avail myself of the occasion thus forced on me, to repel this foul and slanderous assault upon my loyalty, promptly, earnestly, indignantly, yea, scornfully, and upon the very threshold. Sir, I do not choose to delay week after week, until your partisan press shall have sounded the alarm; and till an organization shall have been effected for the purpose of dragooning two-thirds of this House into an outrage upon the rights of one of the Representatives of the people, which is without example except in the worst of times. I meet it and hurl it back defiantly here and now.

Why, sir, suppose that the course which the member from Pennsylvania now proposes, had been pursued in many cases which I could name in years past; suppose that his had been the standard of accusation, and irresponsible newspaper paragraphs had been regarded as evidence of disloyalty or want of attachment to the Constitution and the Union; nay, more, if a yet severer test had been applied, what would have been the fate of some members of this House, or of certain Senators at the other end of the capitol, some

Charges of Disloyalty Triumphantly Repelled 137

years ago? What punishment might not have been meted out to the predecessor (Mr. Giddings) of my colleague on the other side of the House? How long would he have occupied a seat here? Where would the Senator from Massachusetts (Mr. Sumner) have been? Where the other Senator from Massachusetts (Mr. Wilson)? Where the Senator from New Hampshire (Mr. Hale)? Where the three Senators – Mr. Seward, Mr. Chase, and Mr. Hale, two of them now in the Cabinet, and the other in the Senate still – who, in 1850, twelve years ago, on the 11th of February, voted to receive, refer, print, and consider a petition praying for the dissolution of the Union of these States? Yet I am to be singled out now by these very men, or their minions, for attack; and they who have waited and watched and prayed, by day and by night, with the vigilance of the hawk and the ferocity of the hyena, from the beginning of this great revolt, that they might catch some unguarded remark, some idle word spoken, something written carelessly or rashly, some secret thought graven yet upon the lineaments of my face, which they might torture into evidence of disloyalty, seize now upon the foul and infectious gleanings of an anonymous wretch who earns a precarious subsistence by feeding the local columns of a pestilent newspaper, and, while it is yet wet from the press, hurry it, reeking with falsehood, into this House, and seek to dignify it with an importance demanding the consideration of the House and of the country.

Sir, let the member from Pennsylvania go on. I challenge the inquiry, unworthy of notice as the charge is, but I scorn the spirit which has provoked it. Let it go on.

Mr. Hickman then replied briefly; and, in the course of his remarks, said: As the gentleman has called upon me, I will answer further. Does he not know of a camp in Kentucky having been called by his name – that disloyal men there called their camp Camp Vallandigham? That would not indicate that in Kentucky they regarded him as a man loyal to the Federal Union.

Mr. Vallandigham. Is there not a town – and it may be a camp, too – in Kentucky by the name of Hickman? (Laughter.)

Mr. Hickman. Thank God! disloyal men have never called one of their camps by my name. There are a great many Hickmans in Kentucky, but I have not the pleasure of their acquaintance. I have heard of but one Vallandigham.

Mr. Vallandigham. And there are a great many Vallandighams there, too.

Mr. Hickman, after a few words further, withdrew his resolutions; and there the matter ended.

A few other less formidable attempts have been made to extinguish Mr. Vallandigham. On the 21st of April, 1862, Benjamin F. Wade, of Ohio

– whom John A. Gurley declared to be "a good combination of Old Hickory and Zach Taylor" – attacked Mr. Vallandigham in the Senate, in the following language:

> I accuse them (the Democratic party) of deliberate purpose to assail, through the judicial tribunals and through the Senate and House of Representatives of the United States, and everywhere else, and to overawe, intimidate, and trample under foot, if they can, the men who boldly stand forth in defense of their country, now imperiled by this gigantic rebellion. I have watched it long. I have seen it in secret. I have seen its movements ever since that party got together, with a colleague of mine in the other House as chairman of the Committee on Resolutions – *a man who never had any sympathy with the Republic, but whose every breath is devoted to its destruction, just as far as his heart dare permit him to go.* – Congressional Globe, page 1735.

Quoting the foregoing extract, in the House, on the 21th of April, Mr. Vallandigham said:

> Now, sir, here in my place in the House, and as a Representative, I denounce – and I speak it advisedly – the author of that speech as a liar, a scoundrel, and a coward. His name is Benjamin F. Wade.

This had the effect to silence Wade's battery, and the "combination of Old Hickory and Zach Taylor" has not seen fit to renew hostile demonstrations.

The only other attack of this sort, worthy of notice – if, indeed, these we are mentioning are – was made in June 1862, by Shellabarger and Gurley, of Ohio, who presented printed petitions from citizens of their own Districts – none from Mr. Vallandigham's – asking for his expulsion from the House as "a traitor and a disgrace to the State of Ohio." The petitions were referred to the Committee on the Judiciary, consisting of the following members: John Hickman, chairman, John A. Bingham, William Kellogg, Albert G. Porter, Benjamin F. Thomas, Alexander S. Diven, James F. Wilson, George H. Pendleton, and Henry May – all of them Republicans except May and Pendleton. This Committee, on the very same day on which the petitions were presented, by a unanimous vote, ordered them to be reported back and laid upon the table; and, accordingly, on the first day that the Committee was called – July 3, 1862 – Mr. Bingham reported them back, and, *on his motion, they were laid on the table,* no evidence whatever of either "treason" or "disgrace" having been produced to the Committee. And there they "lie" now.

CHAPTER SIX
Columbus Democratic Convention
Speech Before the Democratic State Convention, July 4, 1862

The Convention that met in Columbus, on the 4th of July, 1862, was one of the largest, most enthusiastic and harmonious ever convened in Ohio. The delegation from Mr. Vallandigham's district alone numbered *five hundred and fifty*. The largest hall in the city, crowded to its utmost capacity, failed to accommodate more than one-fourth part of those in attendance. It was, therefore, determined, after a partial and temporary organization, to adjourn to the State-House grounds, in order that the thousands of Democrats present might be enabled to participate in, and witness the proceedings of the Convention. This order having been made known, the vast assemblage promptly reported themselves on the east side of the State-House, ready for business. Gov. Medary was elected President, and conducted to the chair amidst shouts of triumphant rejoicings.

The immediate object of the convention was to nominate candidates for the offices of Supreme Judge, Secretary of State, Attorney General, School Commissioner, and Board of Public Works. Candidates were soon agreed upon; those in the minority gracefully retired, or were withdrawn by their friends; and, in every case, the nominations were made unanimous. A platform and series of resolutions were then read and adopted, the latter quoting from the Constitution that important provision, "The trial of all crimes, except in cases of impeachment, shall be by jury, and such trial shall be held in the State where the said crimes shall have been committed." Also, from the Amendments, the 1st, 4th, 5th, 6th, and 10th articles, so clear, comprehensive, and specific, and designed as an absolute and perpetual guarantee to the people of this country against those very outrages and violations of their rights which they have been compelled to suffer under this Administration. The resolutions then say:

> We utterly condemn and denounce the repeated and gross violation, by the Executive of the United States, of the said rights, thus secured by the Constitution; and we also utterly repudiate and condemn the monstrous dogma that in time of war the Constitution is suspended, or its powers in any respect enlarged beyond the letter and true meaning of that instrument.

And close with the bold and solemn declaration –

> That we view, with indignation and alarm, the illegal and unconstitutional seizure and imprisonment, for alleged political offenses, of our citizens, without judicial process, in States where such process is unobstructed, but by Executive order, by telegraph or otherwise, and call upon all who uphold the Union, the Constitution, and the laws, to unite with us in denouncing and repelling such flagrant violation of the State and Federal Constitutions, and tyrannical infraction of the rights and liberties of American citizens; and that the people of this State cannot safely, and will not submit to have the freedom of speech and freedom of the press – the two great and essential bulwarks of civil liberty – put down by unwarranted and despotic exertion of power.

At this point of the proceedings, loud and continued calls were made for Vallandigham, who, when he ascended the platform, was greeted with rapturous applause. He spoke as follows:

> Mr. President and fellow Democrats of the State of Ohio: I am obliged again to regret that the lateness of the hour precludes me from addressing you either in the manner or upon the particular subjects which otherwise I should prefer. This is my misfortune again to-day, as last night; but speaking thus, without premeditation, and upon such matters chiefly as may occur to me at the moment, if I should happen to get fairly under headway, it may turn out to be your misfortune. (Laughter.) I congratulate the Democracy of Ohio, that, in the midst of great public trial and calamity, of persecution for devotion to the doctrines of the fathers who laid deep and strong the foundations of the Constitution and the Union under which this country has grown great and been prosperous – the fathers, by whose principles, one and all, the party to which we are proud to belong has always been guided – to-day we have assembled in numbers greater than at any former convention in Ohio. I congratulate you that, despite the threats which have been uttered, and the denunciations which have been poured out upon that time-honored and most patriotic organization, peaceably and in quiet,

with enthusiasm and earnestness of purpose, we are here met; and, in harmony, which is the secret of strength and the harbinger of success, have discharged the duties for which we were called together. There was a time when it was questionable if, in free America – in the United States, boasting of their liberties for more than eighty years – a party to which this country is indebted for all that is great and good and grand and glorious – would have been permitted peaceably to assemble to exercise its political rights, and perform its appropriate functions. Threats have even been made, in times more recent, that this most essential of all political rights, secured to us by the precious blood of our fathers, in a seven years' revolutionary war, should no longer be enjoyed. The Democrats of our noble sister State of Indiana, second-born daughter of the North-west, have been menaced, within the last ten days, with a military organization and the bayonet, to put down their party. I hold in my hand a telegraphic dispatch from the capital of that State, boasting of this infamous purpose. I will read it, gentlemen, because I know that the same dastardly menaces have been proclaimed against the Democrats of Ohio, and because I am here to-day to rebuke them, as becomes a freeborn man who is resolved to perish — (Great applause, in the midst of which the rest of the sentence was lost.)

Some months ago, a Democratic State Convention was held in Indiana. It was a Convention of the party founded by Thomas Jefferson, built up by a Madison and Monroe, and consolidated by an Andrew Jackson (applause) – a party under whose principles and policy, from thirteen States, we have grown to thirty-four, for thirty-four there were, true and loyal to this Union, before the Presidential election of 1860 – a party under whose wise and liberal policy the course of empire westward did take its way, until the symbol of American power – the stars and stripes – waved proudly from the Atlantic to the Pacific, over the breadth of a whole continent – a party which, by peace and compromise, and through harmony, wisdom, and sound policy, brought us up from feeble and impoverished colonies, struggling in the midst of defeat and disaster in the war of the Revolution, to a mighty empire, foremost among the powers of the earth, the foundations of whose greatness were laid, broad and firm, in that noble Constitution, and that grand old Union which the Democratic party has ever maintained and defended. The Democratic party, with such principles, and such a history and record to point to, held a State Convention, in pursuance of its usages for more than thirty years, and under the rights secured by a State and Federal Constitution, older still, in the capital of the State of Indiana. And yet, referring to this party and its Convention, the correspondent of a disloyal and pestilent, but influential newspaper, in the chief city of Ohio, dared to send over the telegraphic wires – wires wholly under the military control of the Administration, which permits nothing to be transmitted not acceptable to its censors

– a dispatch in these words: "The fellows are frightened, evidently not without cause."

Well, gentlemen, I know not how far Democrats of Indiana may be frightened – and a nobler and more fearless body of men never lived – but I see thousands of Democrats before me, to whom fear and reproach are alike unknown. Frightened at what? Frightened by whom? We are made of sterner stuff.

"The militia of the State," he adds, "will, probably, be put upon a war footing very poorly." And who, I pray, are the militia of the State? They are not made up of the leaders of the Republican party in Indiana or Ohio, I know. I never knew that sort of politicians to go into any such organization, in peace or in war. No men have ever been more bitter and unrelenting in their opposition to, and ridicule of, the militia, and none know it better than I, as my friend before me, by his smile, reminds me, that one of my own offenses is that I am a militia brigadier, in favor of the next foreign war.

But who are the militia? They are the freeborn, strong-armed, stout-hearted Democrats of Indiana, as they are of Ohio. Let them be put on a war footing. Good! We have hosts of them in the array already, and on a war footing, but who are as sound Democrats and as much devoted to the principles of the party, as they were the hour they enlisted. They have been in the South, and I have the authority of hundreds of officers and privates in that gallant army for saying, that not only are the original Democrats in it more devoted to the party to-day than ever before, but that hundreds, also, who went hence Republicans, have returned, or will return, cured of the disease. (Laughter and applause.) Sir, the army is, fortunately, most fortunately for the country, turning out to be a sort of political hospital or sanitary institution, and I only regret that there are not many more Republican patients in it. (Laughter.)

Well, put the militia upon a war footing. Put arms in their hands. They never can be made the butchers or jailers of their fellow-citizens, but the guardians rather of free speech and a free press, and of the ballot-box. Standing armies of mercenaries, not the militia of a country, are the customary instruments of tyranny and usurpation.

But this correspondent proceeds: "If the sympathizers with treason and traitors" – We sympathize with treason and traitors! We, who have stood by the Constitution and the Union from the organization of the party, in our fathers' day, and in our own day, in every hour of trial, in peace and in war, in victory and in defeat, amid disaster, and when prosperity beamed upon us – we to be branded as enemies to our country, by those whose traitor fathers burned blue lights as signals for a foreign foe, or met in Hartford Convention to plot treason and disunion fifty years ago! We false to the Constitution and to our Government, the bones of whose fathers lie buried on every battlefield of the war of 1812, from the massacre at the River Raisin to the splendid victory at New Orleans; we, who bore aloft the proud banner of the Republic, and planted it in triumph upon the palace of the Montezumas; we, by whose wisdom in council, and courage in the field, for seventy years, the Constitution and the Union, and the country which has grown great under them, have been preserved and defended; we to be denounced as sympathizing with treason and traitors, by the men who, for twenty years, have labored day and night for the success of those principles and of that policy and that party which are now destroying the grandest Union, the noblest Constitution and the fairest Country on the globe! Talk to me about sympathizing with disunion, with treason and with traitors! I tell you, men of Ohio, that in six months, in three months, in six weeks it may be, these very men, and their masters in Washington, whose bidding they do, will be the advocates of the eternal dissolution of this Union, and denounce all who oppose it, as enemies to the peace of the country. Foreign intervention and the repeated and most serious disasters which have lately befallen our arms, will speedily force the issue of separation and Southern independence – *disunion* – or of Union by negotiation and compromise. Between these two I am – and I here publicly proclaim it – for the Union, the whole Union, and nothing less, if, by any possibility, I can have it; if not, then for so much of it as can yet be rescued and preserved; and in any event, and under all circumstances, for the Union which God ordained, of the Mississippi Valley, and all which may cling to it, under the old name, the old Constitution, and the old flag, with all their precious memories, with the battlefields of the past, and the songs and the proud history of the past – with the birthplace and the burial place of Washington, the founder, and Jackson, the preserver of, the Constitution as it is, and of the Union as it was. (Great applause.)

But this correspondent again proceeds: "If the sympathizers with treason and traitors meditate to carry out their plans in this quarter" – What plans? Just such as to-day have been the business of this Convention; the plans of that old Union party, laying down a platform, and nominating Democrats to fill the offices and control the policy of the Government, to the end that the Constitution may be again maintained, the Union restored, and peace, prosperity, and happiness once more drop healing from their wings.

"Plans," the fellow proceeds, "in this quarter, they will doubtless find the work quite as hot as they bargained for." And I tell the cowardly miscreant who telegraphed the threat that, he, and those behind him, will find the work fifty-fold hotter when they begin it, than they had reckoned on, both here and in Indiana.

"Ten thousand stand of arms," he adds, "have been ordered for the State troops." For what? To put down the Democratic party? Sir, that is a work which cannot be done by ten, or twenty, or fifty thousand stand of arms in the hands of any such dastards, in office or out of it. If full of valor, and so thirsty for blood, let them enlist under the call just issued for troops in Ohio and Indiana. Let them go down and fight the armies of the "rebels" in the South, and let Democrats fight the unarmed, but more insidious and dangerous, Abolition rebels of the North and West, through the ballot-box.

Forty thousand additional troops, I estimate it, are called for, in the proclamation of yesterday, from the State of Ohio. Where are the forty thousand Wide Awakes of 1860, armed with their portable lamp posts, and drilled to the music of the Chicago platform? Sir, I propose that thirty-five thousand of them be conscripted forthwith. They will never enlist; they never do. They are "Home Guards." They "don't go," but stay vigorously at home to slander and abuse and threaten Democrats whose fathers or brothers or sons are in the Union armies, or have fallen in battle. I speak generally – certainly there are exceptions. But I will engage that if the records of the old Wide Awake clubs in the several cities and towns of Ohio shall be produced, and the Republicans will detail or draft thirty-five thousand from the lists, I will find five thousand strong-armed, stout-hearted, brave and loyal Democrats to go down and see that they don't run away at the first fire. (Great laughter.)

Sympathizers with treason and traitors! Secessionists! Sir, it is about time that we have heard the last of this. The Democracy of Ohio, and of the United States, are resolved that an end shall be put to this sort of slander and abuse. But I do not propose to discuss this particular subject further now. (Go on, go on.)

Well, then, from that which concerns the Democratic party, to a word, a single word, about what relates to myself; and I beg pardon for the digression. I am rejoiced that it has been permitted to me to be here present, to-day, in person before you. Had you believed the reports of the Republican press, you would, no doubt, have expected to see, probably, the most extraordinary compound of leprous and unsightly flesh and blood ever exhibited. (Laughter.) Well, my friends, you see that I am not quite "monstrous," at least, and bear no especial resemblance to the beast of the Apocalypse, either in heads or horns, but am a man of like fashion with yourselves. To the Republican party alone, and its press and its orators, I am indebted, no doubt, for a large part of the "curiosity" which, I am sorry to say, I seem to have excited, and which has brought out even some of them, as if to "see the elephant." They have never meant to be friendly toward me, I know; but as I see some of them now within my vision, let me whisper in their ears, that I never had better friends, and no man had, since the world began. They have advertised me free of cost, absolutely free of cost, for the last fifteen months; yes, I may say, for some five years past, all over the United States. Why, sir, a Republican editor, without "the undersigned" for a text, would be the most unhappy mortal in the world. Every little "printer's devil" in the office would be hallooing for copy, and no copy to be had. I know that they are friends, by the usual sign, "the remarks they make." Gentlemen, I have had my share of what Jefferson called the unction, the holy oil with which the Democratic priesthood has always been anointed – slander, detraction, and calumny without stint. Really, I am not sure that with me it has not reached "extreme unction," though I am by no means ready, and do not mean to depart yet. Well, I will not complain. It has cost me not a single night's loss of sleep from the beginning. My appetite, if you will pardon the reference – if you will allow me, as Lincoln would say, to "blab" upon so delicate a subject – has been in no degree impaired by it. Others before me, and with me, have endured the same. Here is my excellent friend near me (Mr. Medary). O, blessed martyr! (Great applause.) For one and sixty years the storms of partisan persecution, and malignity in every form, have beaten upon his head; but, though time and toil have made it gray, the heart beneath beats still, to-day, as sound and true to its instincts of Democracy and patriotism, and of humanity too, as when he laid his first offerings upon the altar of his country, just forty years ago. What others have heroically suffered in ages past, we, too, can endure.

We are all, indeed, still in the midst of trials. Here, before me, is the gentleman of whom I have just spoken, whom you have honored with the Presidency of this noble Convention, for forty years a Democratic editor – for forty years devoted to the Constitution and the Union of these States – a man who, through evil and through good report, has adhered, with the faith of a devotee and the firmness of a martyr, to the principles and policy of that grand old party of the Union; and now that the frosts of three-score years have descended and whitened his head, he, I say, has lived to see the paper to which he gives the labor and the wisdom of his declining years, prohibited from circulation through a part of the mails as "disloyal" to the Government! (Cries of no, no, shame!) Samuel Medary disloyal! and Wendell Phillips a patriot! Sir, it is not many months since, that in the city of Washington, in that magnificent building erected by the charity of an Englishman who loved America – I would there were more like him – that art and science might the more widely flourish in this country – the Smithsonian Institute – Wendell Phillips addressed an assemblage of men as false to the Union and the Constitution as himself. Upon the platform was the Speaker of the House of Representatives, the third officer in the Government; by his side the Vice-President of the United States, and between these two, in proportions long drawn out, the form of "Honest Old Abraham Lincoln." Am I mistaken, and was it at another and earlier abolition lecture by that other disunionist, Horace Greeley, in the same place – there have been many of them – that Lincoln attended? The Speaker and Vice-President, I know, were there; and with these two or three witnesses before him, and in presence of the priesthood of Abolitionism, the Sumners and Wilsons, the Lovejoys and the Wades of the House and Senate (great laughter), surrounded by these, the very architects of disunion, he proclaimed that "for nineteen years he had labored to take nineteen States out of the Union." And yet this most spotted traitor was pleading for disunion in the City of Washington, where women are arrested for the wearing of red, white, and red upon their bonnets, and babes of eighteen months are dragged from the little willow wagons drawn by their nurses, because certain colors, called seditious, are found upon their swaddling clothes! The next day, or soon after, this same Wendell Phillips did dine with, or was otherwise entertained, by his Excellency, the President of the United States, who related to him one of his choicest anecdotes. Yet Democratic editors, Democratic Senators and Representatives, and those holding other official positions by the grace of the States or of the people, are "traitors" forsooth, because they would adhere to the principles and organization of their noble and patriotic old party! Such are some of the exhibitions which Washington has witnessed during the past winter.

Congress, too, has been in session. Sir, I saw it announced in one of the disloyal papers of this city yesterday, that Jeff. Davis and Toombs and Yancey and Rhett and other secessionists of the South, would derive much comfort from this day's meeting. Well, sir, I have just come from a body of men which I would not, for a moment, pretend to compare for statesmanship, respectability, or patriotism with this Convention. That body has devoted its time and attention to doing more, in six months, for the cause of secessionism, than Beauregard and Lee and Johnson and all the Southern Generals combined have been able to accomplish in one year. Said a Senator from the South, the other day, a Union man: "Jeff. Davis is running two Congresses now, and is making a d—d sight more out of the Washington Congress than the one at Richmond." (Laughter, and many remarks of approval.)

Sir, the legislation of that body has been almost wholly for the "Almighty African." From the prayer in the morning – for, gentleman, we are a pious body, we are – making long faces, and sometimes wry faces, too (laughter) – we open with prayer, but there is not much of the Almighty Maker of heaven and earth in it – from the prayer to the motion to adjourn, it is negro in every shape and form in which he can, by any possibility, be served up. But it is not only the negro inside of the House and Senate, but, outside, also. The city of Washington has, within the past three weeks, been converted into one universal hospital; every church, except one for each denomination, has been seized for hospital purposes. But while the sanctuaries of the Ever-living God – the God of Abraham, Isaac, and Jacob

– not the new god of the Burlingames and Sumners and other Abolitionists, not that god whose gospel is written in the new bible of Abolition – but the ever-living Jehovah God, have been confiscated for hospitals, every theater, every concert saloon, every other place of amusement, from the highest to the lowest, from the spacious theater in which a Forrest exhibits to an enraptured audience his graphic renderings of the immortal creations of Shakespeare, down to the basest den of revelry and drunkenness, is open still. As in the Inferno of the great Italian poet, "The gates of hell stand open night and day."

Sir, if these places of amusement – innocent some of them, but not holy, certainly – had first been seized as hospitals for the comfort and cure of the thousands of brave and honest men who went forth believing in their hearts that they were to battle for the Constitution and the Union, but who now lie wasting away upon their lonely pallets, with no wife, or sister, or mother there to soothe, groaning in agony, with every description of wound which the devilish ingenuity of man can inflict by weapons whose invention would seem to have been inspired by the very spirit of the author of all human woe and suffering – wounds, too, rankling and festering for the want of surgical aid – if those places, I say, had first been seized, and then it had become necessary, for the comfort or life of the thousands of other sick and wounded who are borne in the city every day, to occupy the churches of Washington, I know of no better or holier purpose to which they could have been devoted. And now, sir, not far from that stately capitol, within whose marble walls Abolition treason now runs riot, is a building, "Green's Row" by name, *rented by the Government,* in which one thousand one hundred fugitive slaves – "contrabands," in the precious slang of the infamous Butler – daily receive the rations of the soldier, which are paid for out of the taxes levied upon the people. One hundred thousand dollars a day are taken from the public treasury for the support of fugitive slaves there and elsewhere; while the army of Shields, and other Union armies in the field, even so late as six weeks ago, marched barefooted, bareheaded, and in their drawers, for many weary miles, without so much as a cracker or a crust of bread with which to allay their hunger. Ay, sir, while many a gallant young soldier of Ohio, just blooming into manhood, who heard the cry that went up fifteen months ago: "Rally to defend the flag, and for the rescue of the capital," and went forth to battle, with honesty in his heart, his life in his hand, with courage in every fiber, and patriotism in every vein, lies wan and sad on his pallet in the hospital, your surgeons are forced to divide their time and care between the wounded soldiers and these vagabond fugitive slaves, who have been seduced or forced from the service of their masters. These things, and much more – I have told you not a tithe of all – are done in Washington. We know it there, though it is withheld from the people; and while every falsehood that the ingenuity of man can invent to delude and deceive, is transmitted or allowed by the telegraphic censors of the Administration – themselves usurpers unknown to the Constitution and laws – these facts are not permitted to reach the people of the United States.

Your newspapers, the natural watch-dogs of liberty, are threatened with suppression, if but the half or the hundredth part of the truth be told. And now, too, when but one other means remains for the redress of this and the hundred other political grievances under which the land groans – party organization and public assemblages of the people – even these, too, are threatened with suppression by armed force. Ay, sir, that very party, which, not many years ago, bore upon every banner the motto, "Free Speech and a Free Press," now, day by day, forbids the transmission through your mails of the papers from which you derive your knowledge of public events, and which advocate the principles you cherish. And Democratic editors, too, are seized, "kidnapped" in the midnight hour – torn from their families – gagged – their wives with officers over them menacing violence if they but ask one farewell grasp of the hand, one parting kiss – thrust into a close carriage, in the felon hour of midnight, and with violence dragged to this capital, and here forced upon an express train and hurried off to a military fortress of the United States. Yes, men of Ohio, to a fortress that bears the honored name of that first martyr to American liberty – the Warren of Bunker Hill; or, it may be, to that other bastile, desecrating that other name sacred in American history, and honored throughout the earth – the name of that man who forsook home and gave up rank and title, and, in the first flush of youth and manhood, came to our shores and linked his fortunes with the American cause – the prisoner of Olmutz, the brave and gallant Lafayette. Ay, freemen of the West, fortresses bearing these honored names, and meant for the defense of the country against foreign foes, and out of whose casemates bristle cannon planted to hurl death and destruction at armed invaders, echo now with the groans and are watered by the tears, not of men only from States seceded and in rebellion, or captured in war, but from the loyal States of the North and the West, and from that party which has contributed nearly three-fourths of the soldiers in the field to-day. Are these things to be borne? (Never; no, never.) If you have the spirit of freemen in you, bear them not! (Great applause, and cries of that's it, that's the talk). What is life worth? What are property and personal liberty and political liberty worth; of what value are all these things, if we, born of an ancestry of freemen, boasting, in the very first hours of our boyhood, of a more extended liberty than was ever vouchsafed to any other people, are to fail now in this the hour of sore trial, to demand and to defend them at every hazard? Freedom of the press! Is the man who sits in the White House at Washington, and who owes all his power to the press and the ballot, is he now to play the tyrant over us? (No; never,

never!) Shall the man who sits at one end of a telegraphic wire in the War Department, or the Department of State – a mere clerk, it may be, a servant of servants – sit down, and by one single click of the instrument, order some minion of his, a thousand miles off, to arrest Samuel Medary, or Judge Ranney, or Judge Thurman, and hurry them to a bastile? (No; it can't be done; we will never allow it.) The Constitution says: "No man shall be held to answer for crime except on due process of law." Our fathers, six hundred years ago, assembled upon the plains of Runnymede, in old England, and rescued from tyrant hands, by arms and firm resolve, the God-given right to be free. Our fathers, in the time of James I, and of Charles I, and James II, endured trial and persecution and loss of life and of liberty, rather than submit to oppression and wrong. John Hampden – glorious John Hampden! the first gentleman of England arrested upon an illegal executive warrant – went calmly and heroically to the cells of a prison rather than pay twenty shillings of an illegally-assessed tax, laid in defiance of the Constitution and laws of England, and of the rights and privileges of Englishmen. And all history is full of like examples. William Tell brooked the tyrant's frown in his day and generation, in defense of these same rights, in the noble Republic of the Swiss; and that gallant little people, he named in among the Alps, though surrounded on every side by despots whose legions numbered more than the whole population of Switzerland, have, by that same indomitable spirit of freedom, maintained their rights, their liberties, and their independence to this hour. And are Americans now to offer themselves up a servile sacrifice upon the altar of arbitrary power? Sir, I have misread the signs of the times, and the temper of the people, if there is not already a spirit in the land which is about to speak in thunder-tones to those who stretch forth still the strong arm of despotic power: "Thus far shalt thou come, and no farther. We made you; you are our servants." That, sir, was the language which I was taught to apply to men in office when I was a youth, or in first manhood and a private citizen, and afterward, when holding office as the gift of the people, to hear applied to me; and I bore the title proudly. And I asked then, as I ask now, no other or better reward than, "Well done, good and faithful servant." (Cries of "You shall have it; you deserve it.") But to-day, they who are our servants, creatures made out of nothing by the power of the people, whose little brief authority was breathed into their nostrils by the people, would now, forsooth, become the masters of the people; while the organs and instruments of the people – the press and public assemblages – are to be suppressed; and the Constitution, with its right of petition, and of due process of law, and trial by jury, and the laws, and all else which makes life worth possessing, are to be sacrificed now upon the tyrant's plea that it is necessary to save the Government, the Union. Sir, we did save the Union for years – yes, we did. We were the "Union savers," not eighteen months ago. Then there was not an epithet in the whole vocabulary of political Billingsgate so opprobrious in the eyes of a Republican, when applied to the Democratic party, as "Union shriekers," or "Union savers." I remember, in my own city, on the day of the Presidential election, in 1860 – I remember it well, for I had that day traveled several hundred miles to vote for Stephen A. Douglas for the Presidency – that, in a ward where the judges of election were all Democrats, your patriotic Wide-Awakes, strutting in unctuous uniform, came up, hour after hour, thrusting their Lincoln tickets twixt thumb and finger at the judges, with the taunt and sneer, *"Save the Union! Save the Union!"* And yet now, forsooth, we are "traitors" and "secessionists!" And old gray-bearded and gray-headed men, who lived and voted in the times of Jefferson and Madison and Monroe and Jackson – men who have fought and bled upon the battle-field, and who fondly indulged the delusion, for forty years, that they were patriots, wake up suddenly to-day to find themselves "traitors!" – sneered at, reviled and insulted by striplings "whose fathers they would have disdained to have set with the dogs of their flocks." Of all these things an inquisition, searching and terrible, will yet be made, as sure and as sudden, too, it may be, as the day of judgment. We of the loyal States – we of the loyal party of the country, the Democratic party – we, the loyal citizens of the United States, the editors of loyal newspapers – we, who gather together in loyal assemblages, like this, and are addressed by truly loyal and Union men, as I know you are to-day and at this moment (that's so; that's the truth) – we, forsooth, are to be now denied our privileges and our rights as Americans and as freemen; we are to be threatened with bayonets at the ballot-box, and bayonets to disperse Democratic meetings! Again I ask, why do they not take up their muskets and march to the South, and, like brave men, meet the embattled hosts of the Confederates in open arms, instead of threatening, craven like, to fight unarmed Democrats at home – possibly unarmed, and possibly not. (Laughter and applause, and a remark, "That was well put in.") If so belligerent, so eager to shed that last drop of blood, let them volunteer to re-enforce the broken and shattered columns of McClellan in front of Richmond, sacrificed as he has been by the devilish machinations of Abolition, and there mingle their blood with the blood of the thousands who have already perished on those fatal battle-fields. But no; the whistle of the bullet and the song of the shell are not the sort of music to fall pleasantly upon the ears of this Home Guard Republican soldiery.

With reason, therefore, fellow-citizens, I congratulate you to-day upon the victory which you have achieved. A great poet has said: "Peace hath her victories as well as War."

To-day the cause of free government has triumphed. A victory of the Constitution, a victory of the Union has been won, but is yet to be made complete by the men who go forth from this, the first political battle-field of the campaign, bearing upon their banners that noble legend, that grand inscription: *The Constitution as it is, and the Union as it was.* (Great cheering.) In that sign shall you conquer. Let it be inscribed upon every ballot, emblazoned upon every banner, flung abroad to every breeze, whispered in the zephyr, and thundered in the tempest, till its echoes shall rouse the fainting spirit of every patriot and freeman in the land. It is the creed of the truly loyal Democracy of the United States. In behalf of this great cause it is that we are now, if need be, to do and to suffer in political warfare whatever may be demanded of freemen who know their rights, and knowing, dare maintain them. Is there any one man, in all this vast assemblage, afraid to meet all the responsibilities which an earnest and inexorable discharge of duty may require at his hands in the canvass before us? (No, no, not one.) If but one, let him go home and hide his head for very shame:

> Who would be a traitor knave?
> Who could fill a coward's grave?
> Who so base as be a slave?
> Let him turn and flee.

It is no contest of arms to which you are invited. Your fathers, your brothers, your sons are already, by thousands and hundreds of thousands, on the battle-field. To-day their bones lie bleaching upon the soil of every Southern State, from South Carolina to Missouri. It is to another conflict, men of Ohio, that you are summoned, but a conflict, nevertheless, which will demand of you some portion, at least, of that same determined courage, that same unconquerable will, that same inexorable spirit of endurance, which make the hero upon the military battle-field. I have mistaken the temper of the men who are here to-day, I have misread the firm purpose that speaks in every eye and beams from every countenance, which stiffens every sinew and throbs in every breast; I have misread it all, if you are not resolved to go home and there maintain, at all hazards and by every sacrifice, the principles, the policy, and the organization of that party to which again, and yet again, I declare unto you, this Government and country are indebted for all that have made them grand, glorious, and great. (Cheers and great applause.)

The foregoing speech was received with shouts of applause, sometimes obliging the speaker to wait. In fact, the whole reception of Mr. Vallandigham, at Columbus, was one of the proudest and most gratifying that could have been given. He arrived from Washington on the 3d, and about midnight, on that evening, a crowd surrounded his hotel, and made it unmistakably evident that a speech must be forthcoming, or there would be no sleep for him or them that night. And, again, on the evening of the 4th, another speech was demanded, and given from the balcony of the hotel – *three speeches within twenty hours.*

Those exhibitions of deep interest and profound admiration, thus given in behalf of Mr. Vallandigham, were that spontaneous reaction which, sooner or later, was sure to return to the man who, in the hour of his country's most imminent peril, and when surrounded and pressed upon, from every direction, by the most malignant obloquy and reproach, still adhered, with unflinching integrity and firmness, to those great principles of political justice and truth wherein is involved the only hope for our country. This speech was made the subject of a long and complimentary review in the London *Times*.

CHAPTER SEVEN
State of the Country
Speech Delivered at Dayton, Ohio,
August 2, 1862

The reign of terror was at its height, and the most serious apprehensions were entertained for the personal safety of Mr. Vallandigham, when he announced his determination to address the public in Dayton. A bolder stroke was never made, nor a more fearless exhibition given, of high moral as well as physical courage. At the first intimation of the proposed meeting, a low, ugly growl, like the fretting of hungry but chained tigers, might have been heard in the purlieus of Abolition fanaticism, and those were the places where the edicts of the Abrahamic dynasty were kept, and whence they were issued. It has been said that fanaticism is one of the hounds who, when once they have tasted blood, never bolt their track. But this hound does sometimes bolt his track; at least, he cowers and hides himself, when he sees his prey is too large for his grapple. An exhibition of that sort was given in Dayton, on the 2d of August, 1862. Mr. Vallandigham had been selected as their next victim by the base minions of a corrupt and desperate Administration. As some blood-thirsty, but cowardly beast of prey watches for his victim, so had they been watching for him, and a good time to pounce upon him had come, if only the pounce could be made without danger to themselves. But as the hour for the meeting approached, the brave and true men of Montgomery and adjacent counties were seen coming in, until fully *seven thousand* were there. The men who had sworn that Vallandigham should never again speak in Dayton, very wisely concluded that discretion was better than valor; so gracefully retired behind each other, and kept that position till the speech was over. A few hours before the speaking commenced, the *Empire* of that day was distributed through the city, and contained a few words of prudent advice, which may have been of some service in bringing those men to the conclusion they came to. After stating the object of the meeting, and alluding to threats of disturbance, the *Empire* said:

> Political meetings, like churches, are open alike to saint and to sinner – all who conduct themselves in an orderly manner are invited, and all such are made welcome. We have no apprehension that the threats of a few shoulder-hitters, urged on by those who lack but the courage to do that which they urge others to do, will be carried out. The Democrats present will preserve the peace and the credit of our city, and will tolerate no disturbance of any kind. No affray, no disturbance, will be commenced by them, but they will promptly end all such summarily, and with as little disorder as the nature of the case will admit.

This advice was taken, and, without interruption, the speech was delivered to a vast assembly, on the south side of the Court-House. Of this speech, Gov. Medary, republishing it in the *Crisis*, said:

> It should be read by every voter in the United States. Nothing equal to it has been made during the past few years. Seldom has it ever been equaled for power, pathos, purity of diction, and truthfulness in point of facts. Elevated in tone, statesmanlike in conception, it thrills the reader as though fresh from a Roman Senate in the hour of Rome's most terrible trials for freedom and existence. It should be read in every school-house, to the assembled people, before the elections, on the second Tuesday of next October.

The following report is full in some parts, in others condensed:

Mr. Vallandigham began by an allusion to the fact that he had arranged to be absent from the city, on a visit to an aged and very near relative, but that, meantime, false charges, and rumors also as to intended arrests, were started. "My rule," said he, "is to always meet such things a little more than half way. Conscious of rectitude, I mean, face to face with every foe and every danger, to do all, and to bear all that may become a man; and, therefore, at much inconvenience, I have postponed my visit, and am here tonight, surrounded by thousands of such constituents and friends as no man ever had."

He then referred to the spring election and its result in this city, upon a direct issue against himself, presented to and accepted by his friends – the triumphant election of the whole Democratic city ticket; and observed that the lesson to our enemies was a severe one, and that they ought to learn from it that there was such a thing as abusing a man so persistently, wantonly, and wickedly, as to make him immensely popular.[1]

Mr. V. next gave a full and minute narrative of the infamous conspiracy just exploded, to procure his arrest as "implicated" with two clergymen from the "Border States," who had been guests at his house. Nothing had been found; both of them were promptly released, and the whole plot had failed. But those concerned in it, some of them "Christians," were known, and would be remembered. A telegraphic dispatch had been prepared by one of the conspirators, and sent off to the New York *Tribune*, from Dayton, though dated at Columbus, announcing his (Mr. V.'s) "arrest;" and it had never been contradicted to this day.[2]

> Democrats have never received any justice at the hand of the telegraph, and never will, till after the 4th of March, 1865, when, with everything else, it will be in Democratic hands. The Republican party are teaching us many things, and may find us apt scholars, possibly improving on their lessons, if they shall finally succeed in overthrowing all constitution, law, and order. But I trust that it will never come to this.
>
> I am for obedience to all laws and constitutions. No man can be a good democrat who is not in favor of law and order. No matter how distasteful constitutions and laws may be, they must be obeyed. I am opposed to all mobs, and opposed also – inexorably opposed above everything – to all violations of constitution and law by men in authority – public servants. The danger from usurpations and violations by them is fifty-fold greater than from any other quarter, because these violations and usurpations come clothed with the false semblance of authority. Those parts of our constitutions and laws which command or restrain the people must be obeyed; but still more must those also which limit and restrain public servants, from the President down. There are rights of the people, to secure which constitutions were ordained, and they must and will be exacted at all hazards; and among the most sacred of these rights, are free speech, a free press, public assemblages, political liberty, and above all, or at least, at the foundation of all, *personal liberty,* or freedom from illegal and arbitrary arrests. It was a right, secured in Greece, while she was free, and in Rome in her purer days. But it is peculiarly an Anglo-Saxon right; and it has cost more struggles in England to hold it fast than any other. The right is declared, in the strongest language, in the Great Charter, in the time of King John, six hundred years

---

1. "The City of Dayton repudiates Clement L. Vallandigham." – Dayton Republican Platform.

2. A full account of the infamous transaction here referred to, was published in the Dayton *Empire*, Aug. 5, 1862.

ago. Here is the pledge wrung from the tyrant by men, none of whom could read or write, but who were resolved to be free:

> No freeman shall be arrested, or imprisoned, or disseized (of property), or outlawed, or banished, or any ways injured, nor will we pass sentence upon him, nor send trial upon him, unless by the legal judgment of his peers, or by the law of the land.

This is the "keystone of English liberty," the pride and boast of every Englishman. The violation of it cost one English monarch his head, another his crown, and a third his most valuable colonies; and to-day, if Queen Victoria were to attempt to suspend it by telegraph, or by executive order, or order of privy council in any way, she would be a refugee in a foreign land before a fortnight.

Eighty years later, this sacred and invaluable right to be free from arrest, except by law, was confirmed; and in 1627, by the celebrated Petition of Right, drawn up by that great lawyer, Lord Coke, was again confirmed and extended, as follows:

> No man, of what estate or condition that he be, shall be put out of his land, or tenements, nor arrested, nor imprisoned, nor disinherited, nor put to death, without being brought to answer by due process of law.

And it was further provided that no commissioner should be appointed to try any one by "martial law," who was not in the array, "lest by color of them, any of his Majesty's subjects be destroyed, or put to death, contrary to the laws and franchises of the land."

Next came the Habeas Corpus Act of 1679, to secure the rights asserted by the Great Charter and its confirmations, a statute by virtue of which, says Lord Campbell – and with shame I confess now to the justice of the proud boast – "Personal liberty has been more effectually guarded in England than it has in any country in the world."

Next after this came the Bill of Rights of 1689, enacted by the profoundest statesmen and purest patriots which England ever had. These great and good men, after that, by arms, they had driven James II from the throne, for his repeated violations of the rights of Englishmen, declared that he had been guilty of an attempt to subvert the laws and liberties of the kingdom, among other things:

> 1. By assuming and exercising a power of dispensing with and suspending of laws and the execution of laws, without consent of Parliament.
>
> 2. By committing and prosecuting divers worthy prelates, for humbly petitioning to be excused from concurring to the said assumed power....

7. By violating the freedom of election of members to serve in Parliament.

"All which," say they, "are utterly and directly contrary to the known laws and statutes and freedom of this realm."

These, sir, are the "Liberties of Englishmen." They are the Liberties which were brought over by our ancestors from England, and embodied in all our constitutions and laws. In 1641, twenty years after the first settlement of Massachusetts, that infant colony declared, in her "Body of Liberties," that

> No man's life shall be taken away, no man's honor or good name shall be stained, *no man's person shall be arrested,* restrained, banished, dismembered, nor any ways punished, no man shall be deprived of his wife or children, no man's goods or estate shall be taken away from him, nor any way endamaged under color of law or countenance of authority, unless it be by virtue or equity of some express law of the country, warranting the same, etc.
>
> No man's person shall be restrained or imprisoned *by any authority whatsoever,* before the law hath sentenced him thereto, if he can put in sufficient security, bail, or mainprise," etc.

So, also, in the Declaration of Independence, July 4th, 1776, among the many grievances set forth against the king, are the following:

> He has affected to render the military independent of, and superior to, the civil power:
> For depriving us, in many cases, of the benefits of trial by jury:
> For transporting us beyond seas to be tried for pretended offenses.

In the Virginia "Bill of Rights" of 1776, written also by Jefferson, it is declared that:

> All power is vested in, and consequently derived from, the people; that magistrates are their trustees and servants, and at all times amenable to them.
>
> All power of suspending laws, or the execution of laws, by any authority, without consent of the representatives of the people, is injurious to their rights, and ought not to be exercised.
>
> In all cases the military should be under strict subordination to, and governed by, the civil power.
>
> Freedom of the press is one of the great bulwarks of liberty, and can never be restrained, but by despotic governments.

And yet again; in the "Declaration of Rights" of Massachusetts, in 1780, it is laid down that:

> No person shall be held to answer for any crime or offense, until the same is fully and plainly, substantially and formally described to him. And no person shall be arrested, imprisoned, or despoiled, or deprived of his property, immunities, or privileges, put out of the protection of the law, exiled or deprived of his life, liberty, or estate, but by the judgment of his peers, or the law of the land.
>
> Every person has a right to be secure from all unreasonable searches and seizures of his person, his houses, his papers, and all his possessions.
>
> The liberty of the press is essential to the security of freedom in a State.
>
> The people have a right to keep and bear arms for the common defense. The military power shall always be held in exact subordination to the civil authority, and be governed by it.
>
> The people have a right in an orderly and peaceable manner to assemble, to consult upon the common good.
>
> The power of suspending the laws ought never to be exercised but by the Legislature, or by authority derived from it, to be exercised in such particular cases only as the Legislature shall expressly provide for.
>
> No person can, in any case, be subjected to law martial, or to any penalties or pains, by virtue of that law (except those employed in the army or navy, and except the militia in actual service), but by authority of the Legislature.

Such were the liberties of Americans in the Revolutionary period of our history, and before it; and they have been embodied in all our constitutions ever since.

Let the present Constitution of Ohio speak. In our "Bill of Rights" we declare that:

> All political power is inherent in the people.
>
> The people have the right to assemble together in a peaceable manner, to consult for their common good; to instruct their representatives, and to petition the General Assembly for the redress of grievances.
>
> The people have the right to bear arms for their defense and security. The military shall be in *strict subordination* to the civil power.
>
> The privilege of the writ of *habeas corpus* shall not be suspended, unless, in cases of rebellion or invasion, the public safety require it. No power of suspending laws shall ever be exercised except by the General Assembly.
>
> In any trial, in any court, the party accused shall be allowed a speedy public trial, by an impartial jury of the county or district in which the offense is alleged to have been committed.
>
> Every citizen may freely speak, write, and publish his sentiments on all subjects, being responsible for the abuse of the right; and no law shall be passed to abridge the liberty of speech or of the press.

> The right of the people to be secure in their persons, houses, papers, and possessions, against unreasonable searches and seizures, shall not be violated.
>
> All courts shall be open, and justice administered without denial or delay.

Similar provisions exist in every State constitution in the United States, thus securing every citizen from State tyranny and oppression. Nor is the Federal Constitution less ample and explicit. Hear it:

> All legislative powers herein granted shall be vested in a Congress of the United States.
>
> The privilege of the writ of *habeas corpus* shall not be suspended, unless when, in cases of rebellion or invasion, the public safety require it.

Now, sir, from the beginning of the Government down to the year 1861, no lawyer, no jurist, no statesman, no writer upon the Constitution, ever pretended that the President, or any other authority, could suspend the privilege of this writ, except Congress alone.

But I read further:

> The judicial power shall extend to all cases in law and equity arising under this Constitution, the laws of the United States, and treaties made, or which shall be made, under their authority,
>
> The trial of all crimes, except in cases of impeachment, shall be by jury, and such trial shall be held in the State where the said crimes shall have been committed.
>
> Treason against the United States shall consist only in levying war against them, or in adhering to their enemies, giving them aid and comfort. No person shall be convicted of treason unless on the testimony of two witnesses to the same overt act, or on confession in open court.
>
> Congress shall make no law respecting an establishment of religion, or prohibiting the free exercise thereof; or abridging the freedom of speech, or of the press; or the right of the people peaceably to assemble, and to petition the government for a redress of grievances.
>
> The right of the people to keep and bear arms shall not be infringed.
>
> The right of the people to be secure in their persons, houses, papers, and effects, against unreasonable searches and seizures, shall not be violated; and no warrant shall issue but upon probable cause, supported by oath or affirmation, and particularly describing the place to be searched, and the persons and things to be seized.
>
> No person shall be held to answer for a capital or otherwise infamous crime, unless on a presentment or indictment of a grand jury, except in cases arising in the land and naval forces, or in the militia, when in actual service, in time of war and public danger; nor shall be deprived of life, liberty, or property, without due process of law; nor shall private prop-

erty be taken for public use without just compensation.

In all criminal prosecutions, the accused shall enjoy the right to a speedy and public trial by an impartial jury of the State and district wherein the crime shall have been committed, which district shall have been previously ascertained by law; and to be informed of the nature and cause of the accusation; to be confronted with the witnesses against him; to have compulsory process for obtaining witnesses in his favor, and to have the assistance of counsel for his defense.

The powers not delegated to the United States by the Constitution, nor prohibited by it to the States, are reserved to the States respectively, or to the people.

These, thus repeated and multiplied over and over again, are the Magna Charta of American freemen. They constitute the *Body of American Liberties*. They cost much blood and treasure, and are worth the most precious treasure and blood of the whole country.

Let them be maintained at every hazard and sacrifice. They are dearer in time of war and public danger, than in time of peace. They are secured by the Constitution, and can only be forfeited in accordance with the Constitution. I abhor and denounce the monstrous doctrine, so rife of late, that the Constitution is suspended in time of war; or that the powers under it are enlarged; or, at least, that there is a "war power" above and greater than the Constitution. Sir, that instrument was made for war as well as peace. It expressly gives to Congress the right to declare war, raise armies, provide navies, and call out the militia to execute the laws, suppress insurrection, put down rebellion, and repel invasion. Every power, the very utmost necessary and proper for carrying on any war, foreign or domestic, is explicitly given. The "tyrant's plea" of necessity, is false. No power that ought to be exercised is withheld, and every usurpation is utterly without excuse. Whoever maintains that the framers of the Constitution failed to make it good enough and strong enough for any crisis – for war and for peace – libels Washington and Madison and Hamilton, and the other patriots of '87. And the man who denounces "sticklers" for the Constitution, and declares that he can tell a "traitor" by his crying out for the Constitution, is himself a traitor or a fool. Keep an eye on him.

We have no hope for ourselves, or our children, except in the Constitution. The President, more than any other man, is bound to obey it. He takes a solemn oath to support it. It is his duty to act according to law. Among the personal rights under the Constitution is that of *habeas corpus*. The uniform testimony of courts and statesmen is that it can be suspended only by Congress. If the President can suspend it, it can only be by proclamation, declaring where, and for how long it is suspended. He has no right to send a dispatch for the arrest of any citizen of the United States, and to say that, by that act, his minions are authorized to suspend the writ. Better to live in Austria, in Turkey, or under any other admitted despotism, than where the President, the servant of the people, shall seize, without "due process of law," and carry off to prison any citizen under the pretence of treason.

These guarantees were not in the original Constitution, but demanded by the States and the people, and added afterwards. They were added for fear some President might be elected who would claim to have the power, if not expressly withheld by the Constitution. What are they? Freedom of speech, of the press, peaceable assemblages, the right to keep and bear arms, freedom from illegal arrest. Yet you have been told that we shall not be allowed to enjoy these rights – that "executive orders" shall be issued against us – that men who represent the voice of the people shall not be heard – that the press shall be muzzled, and men's mouths gagged, and no censure or criticism of the acts of the President, or of the officials under him, shall be permitted, under penalty of arrest and imprisonment; and, thus, that our personal and political liberties shall be disregarded, and the Constitution trampled under foot.

Well, sir, we shall see about it. "No person shall be deprived of life, liberty, or property, without due process of law." Every civil officer knows what "due process of law" is, and, when armed with such due process, it is the duty of every person to obey. But whoever comes with any other papers, or any pretence of authority, by telegraphic dispatch, or otherwise, from the Secretary of War, Commander-in-chief, or President, deserves to be met as a burglar. It is a desecration of the citizen. There is a statute against it. Let such persons be met by the law. Every house is a castle, the poor man's cottage as well as the rich man's palace, in which he may defy arbitrary power. Such is the law in England. In the language of Lord Chatham, in that noblest outburst of English eloquence, " The poorest man in his cottage may bid defiance to all the forces of the Crown. It may be frail; its roof may shake; the wind may blow through it; the storm may enter; the rain may enter; but the King of England cannot enter it. All his power dares not cross the threshold of that ruined tenement." (Tremendous cheering.)

This right is equally sacred and secured to us here in America, and we will never yield it up, least of all to our own public servants. The sooner it is made known to this Administration that the people who created it and put it in power will maintain their rights, the less trouble there will be. I but repeat the declaration of the two hundred thousand Democratic voters of Ohio – fifty thousand of them in the army from this State – that freedom cannot be violated by the Administration. Hear the resolution of that Democracy, in State Convention assembled, on the 4th of July last:

> That we view with indignation and alarm the illegal and unconstitutional seizure and imprisonment, for alleged political offenses, of our

citizens, without judicial process, in States where such process was unobstructed, but, by executive order, by telegraph or otherwise; and call upon all who uphold the Union, the Constitution, and the laws, to unite with us in denouncing and repelling such flagrant violation of the State and Federal Constitutions and tyrannical infraction of the rights and liberties of American citizens; and that the people of this State cannot safely, and will not submit to have the freedom of speech and the freedom of the press, the two great essential bulwarks of civil liberty, put down by unwarranted and despotic exertion of power.

Sir, the men who urge on these violations know not what they do. The title to your lands, to your personal property, the legal right to all you have, rests in obedience to constitution and laws. Let this terrible truth be proclaimed everywhere, that whenever, either through infraction and usurpation by the President, or by violence, the Constitution is no longer of binding force and the highest rule of action, then we are at the mercy of mere power, military power at last. This is despotism, absolute, unmixed, cruel despotism – a despotism enforcing its orders to-day by arbitrary imprisonments, and to-morrow by bloody executions. Let all men who love the peace, good order, and happiness of society, who desire that the rights of all classes, and that rights of all kinds shall be maintained, lift up their voices against the arbitrary and unconstitutional acts of the party in power. Men of the Republican party, it is your day now: to-morrow, it may be, it will be ours. Be warned in time. Stand by the Constitution – by law and order. Do nothing by usurpation or violence. It must react – it will react – and there is no raging flood, no mountain torrent, neither the whirlwind, the surging ocean, nor the avalanche, like the madness of an oppressed and outraged people. Do men who are inciting to mobs and acts of violence, or applauding usurpation and infraction of Constitution and law, not know that they are those who suffer most and worst in the end? Do they imagine that they whose nights, sacred, by God's appointment, to silence and rest, have been invaded without process of law, and their wives and children terror-stricken by arbitrary arrests of husbands and fathers – editors and public men of the loyal States, who have languished, for opinion's sake, within Bastiles for months – will have no day of reckoning for all these enormities? Sir, that great reaction has set in; it hastens on. O, that you may allow it to be under the Constitution and according to law – but come it will; and be assured – be assured – that when that great day of account does come, by the measure you have meted out to us, by *that* measure *shall it be meted out to you again*. Remember, remember, that wrongs like these burn deep into the innermost recesses of our souls, steeling them against atonement and mercy; and that when the inevitable change which already is hurrying on upon the wings of the wind, shall have arrived, that same power by virtue of which you imprison us, will be in our hands. Be warned in time. All history has been written in vain, if our day does not come, and come right speedily:

> For time at last sets all things even –
> And if we do but watch the hour,
> There never yet was human power
> Which could evade, if unforgiven,
> The patient search and vigil long
> Of him who treasures up a wrong.

I speak it not as a menace, but by way of entreaty, that your hereafter in this life depends upon your adherence to the laws and Constitution. And yet I am amazed to learn that men of wealth and position in this city – lawyers, clergy, merchants, and others – are proclaiming that those in authority have a right to disobey the Constitution and laws, and ought to disobey them, to secure objects which cannot be had without disregarding all law and the personal and political rights of the citizen. Do these men know what they do? Have they read history?

Mr. Vallandigham here referred, at length, to Greece, Rome, England, and the French Revolution for historic parallels, reading from the 10th and 14th chapters of Allison's *History of Europe*. He quoted the "Law of Suspected Persons," under which all France was divided into twelve classes liable to arrest; among them the following:

> 1. All those who, in the assemblies of the people, discourage their enthusiasm by cries, menaces, or crafty discourses.
> 2. All those who more prudently speak only of the misfortunes of the Republic, and are always ready to spread bad news with an affected air of sorrow.
> 3. All those who have changed their conduct and language according to the course of events, who were mute on the crimes of the Royalists, and loudly exclaimed against the slight faults of the Republicans....
> 10. Those who speak with contempt of the constituted authorities, the ensigns of the law, the popular societies, or the "defenders of liberty," etc.

Having read these passages, Mr. Vallandigham proceeded:

> Sir, fifty thousand "Revolutionary Committees" sprang up in France to execute this terrible decree. They numbered five hundred and forty thousand members, each one a special marshal or policeman to enforce it; and in a few weeks seven hundred thousand citizens were suspected of "disloyalty." The prisons were speedily loaded with victims in every part of France. "Let them quake in their cells," said Collot d' Herbois, in the Convention; "let the base traitors tremble at the successes of our enemies; let a mine be dug under their prisons, and at the approach of those whom they call their liberators,

let a spark blow them into the air."

Mr. Vallandigham then read a passage concluding as follows:

> Night came, but with it no diminution of the anxiety of the people. Every family early assembled its members; with trembling looks they gazed round the room, fearful that the very walls might harbor traitors. The sound of a foot, the stroke of a hammer, a voice in the streets, froze all hearts with horror. If a knock was heard at the door, every one, in agonized suspense, expected his fate. Unable to endure such protracted misery, numbers committed suicide.

Sir, all of these enormities sprang first from a disregard of law and right in little things, or in violations declared to be "necessary;" and advanced step by step, till they culminated in the bloody and accumulated atrocities of Marat, Danton, and Robespierre, when, by execution or massacre, tens of thousands perished. All history is but a repetition of itself; and what has been, may be. You of the Republican party did not believe me, two years and more ago, when I foretold that Abolition and sectionalism must and would produce civil war. And you do not believe me now. Neither did the ante-diluvians believe Noah; but the Flood came.

It is the history of the past, that, in times of great public danger, the provisions of the law will not be respected. It was that which made France go into such great excesses. They began with the savans and lawyers of France, who taught the multitude that constitutions and laws and personal rights did not stand in their way; and that men might be imprisoned or put to death without process of law. In such cases, power falls always, at last, into the hands of the worst of men.

Let the day of reckoning come, and these men will perish as they have done in all ages. Robespierre died horribly in atonement for his crimes; and, as the ax fell upon his neck, a woman exclaimed in tones of terrible exultation: "Murderer of my kindred, your agony fills me with joy; descend to hell, covered with the curses of every mother in France!"

Sirs, by the memories of the past, by the history of the tyrannies of Greece and Rome, and the terrors of the French Revolution, I call on all men to demand of the Administration that it obey the Constitution. If any man is a traitor, guilty of any act of treason – not for opinion's sake, not for political differences – let him be proceeded against according to law, and, if guilty, let him perish on a gallows as high as Haman's. It is because I would avoid these horrors that I call on the President to keep the exercise of the military law where the Constitution keeps it – in the army and navy – and to see to it that no man, not in the army and navy, shall be arrested without "due process of law."

Hear the Constitution again: "No person shall be deprived of life, liberty, or property without due process of law." "The accused shall enjoy the right to a speedy and public trial by an impartial jury." Was this, was either of these rights "enjoyed" by Flanders, of Malone, in New York, a Democratic editor, who was dragged from his family, imprisoned for months, and then released without charge against him, and without redress for the wrong? Were they enjoyed by General Charles Stone? Were they not flagrantly violated in the person of James W. Wall, the honored son of a patriot Senator of New Jersey? Have they been allowed to any one arrested by "Executive order?" Sir, this Administration has no Constitutional or legal authority to make these arrests. I have as good a right to arrest the President, or any one of his Cabinet, as he or they have to arrest me or any other citizen in this manner. The Constitution is broad enough and strong enough for any emergency. It points out the mode of arrest and trial wherever there is actual or suspected guilt. Let it be obeyed. I, too, have sworn to support that Constitution; and, more than that, I have done it. I demand that all men, from the humblest citizen up to the President, shall be made to obey it likewise. In no other way can we have liberty, order, security. I was born a freeman. I shall die a freeman. It is appointed to all men once to die; and death never comes too soon to one in the discharge of his duty. I have chosen my course – have pursued it – have adhered to it to this hour, and will to the end, regardless of consequences. My opinions are immovable; fire cannot melt them out of me. I scorn the mob. I defy arbitrary power. I may be imprisoned for opinion's sake – never for crime; never because false to the country of my birth, or disloyal to the Constitution which I worship. Other patriots, in other ages, have suffered before me. I may die for the cause; be it so; but the "immortal fire shall outlast the humble organ which conveys it, and the breath of liberty, like the word of the holy man, will not die with the prophet, but survive him." (Loud cheers.)

And, meantime, men of Dayton, the opinions which I entertain, the deep convictions that control me in that course which, before Almighty God, I believe can alone maintain the Constitution and restore the Union as our fathers made it, I never, never will yield up. Neither height nor depth, neither death nor life, nor principalities, nor powers, nor things present, nor things to come – no, nor the knife of the assassin – shall move me from my firm purpose. (Great and long-continued cheering.)

The President professes to think that the Union can be restored by arms. I do not. A Union founded on consent can never be cemented by force. This is the testimony of the Fathers. It was his own. He said, in his Inaugural, but sixteen months ago:

> Suppose you go to war, you cannot fight always; and when, after *much loss on both sides, and no gain on either,* you cease fighting, the old identical questions as to terms of intercourse are upon you.

I agree with him in that. But now we are in the midst of war, and they who really think that war will maintain the Constitution and restore the Union, ought to fight. I am for the Union in any event. It is an impelling necessity, it is manifest destiny, certainly in the Valley of the Mississippi, that we be one people. We never can fulfill the Great Mission appointed for us without it. But, under Providence, it can only be brought about through the wisdom, courage, and integrity of the people.

At a late "war meeting," so-called, in this city, it was charged by an ex-Governor of the State, of "tin-cup" memory, that I proposed to divide this country into four confederacies or republics. It is false, and he knew it. I proposed only to divide the Senate into four divisions, and to change the mode of electing the President. And this I did in order to preserve, not to destroy the Union. And still my heart's desire and prayer is to see it restored just as our fathers made it.

And now, men of Montgomery, I have somewhat to say upon what Mr. Lincoln, in his late proclamation, has most justly and truly called "this unnecessary and injurious civil war." I am for suppressing rebellion – I am. I always have been. Perhaps my mode is not that of other men; but I have the right – and mean to exercise it still – of judging for myself of the true and proper mode. I think mine would have prevented it at first; and even after it began, would have ended it long since. It must, it will be tried at last, if ever anything is to be accomplished. But I have had no power to try it. They who have the power have determined upon another way – with what success, judge ye – and, like a good citizen, I resist not, but stand by to see the result of the experiment. If it is successful in maintaining the Constitution and restoring the Union, I will make full, open, explicit confession that I was wrong, utterly, totally wrong, and will retire to private life the residue of my days. But if it fail – let the people judge then between me and my accusers.

I repeat it: I am for suppressing all rebellion – both rebellions. There are two – the Secession Rebellion South, and the Abolition Rebellion North and West. I am against both; for putting down both. Since you have resolved that there shall be war, I commit the armed Rebellion South, to the soldiers of the army, three-fourths of them Democrats, young Democrats. I commit it to Halleck and Buell and Burnside and others, and to that abused, persecuted, outraged general and patriot, George B. McClellan. (Great cheering.) If he cannot do it, it is because, in the nature of things, it is not possible that it be done in that way. The plan proposed by him was the only one which even so much as promised success. And it implied a restoration of the Union as it was, and, meantime, the maintenance of the Constitution as it is. That is the reason why he has been so persecuted by Abolition rebels and disunionists. But it is the proud boast of himself and his friends, that in spite of all their abuse and calumny, he has calmly and steadfastly pursued his policy. All our victories were the result of that policy; all our reverses followed his supersession. From that hour to this, there has been no victory. Defeat has not lost him the confidence of the people. He has the devoted and enthusiastic affection of his soldiers; and he has the calmness, the firmness, and the unshaken consistency and persistency of purpose which will enable him to triumph in the end, at least, over his enemies at home. To him, therefore, and to the army, I commit the Secession Rebellion of the South. I waste no breath in idle denunciation of an enemy a thousand miles off. Cursing will not put down men in arms, else there would have been an end to this armed rebellion long ago. As Governor Richardson suggested in Congress, the Jericho of Secession is not to be thrown down by the blowing of Abolition horns. Whoever among the Abolitionists would curse secession, let him enlist, and then he will show his faith by his works, and your armies will be full in a week. Let every man who would invite others to go, first go himself. I have never interfered with enlistments. While the war lasts, our armies, for many reasons, must not be disbanded; so I said in Congress more than a year ago. Without enlistments they cannot be kept up; and if any man, subject to military duty, really thinks that the Union can be restored by force and arms, and only in that way, let him enlist; it is his duty to enlist; he is "disloyal" if he does not enlist. (Cries of good, good; that's the talk.) Whoever shall be drafted, should a draft be ordered according to Constitution and law, is in duty bound, no matter what he thinks of the war, to either go, or find a substitute, or pay the fine which the law imposes; he has no right to resist, and none to run away.

I have said that, in my deliberate and solemn judgment, war cannot restore the Union, but, if continued long enough, must destroy it; and, it may be, our own liberties also. "War," said Douglas, "is disunion; war is final, eternal separation." The Administration do not seem to think so. The country, just now, does not think so. Mr. Lincoln says, that war is the right way to restore the Union. I think there is another, a better, the only way to do it. He has the power to try his; I have not. War is upon us; and from the beginning, believing as I did, and yet powerless for good, I laid down the rule for myself, and have faithfully adhered to it, and will to the end, neither to vote for or against any purely war measure of the Administration. Wherever I have voted upon any question, my course has been governed by other considerations than those having reference to my opinions on the war. Accordingly, I have not voted for any army bill, or navy bill, or army or navy appropriation bill, since the meeting of Congress on the 4th of July, 1861. Neither have I voted against any such bill from the beginning. I appeal to the *Globe*, and to the Journals of the House, for the proof.

These facts I refer to, because you are my constituents, and have a right to know them. One thing, however, we all must demand of the Administration: that the war be conducted according to the Constitution, and for a constitutional purpose.

But, men of Dayton, there is another and different, yet most desperate rebellion to be dealt with – the Abolition Rebellion of the North and West. It, too, must be put down; speedily and firmly put down, if we would save the country. In my judgment, you will never suppress the armed Secession Rebellion till you have crushed under foot the pestilent Abolition Rebellion first. Ask the officers and soldiers of the army, and they will tell you the same thing. A Representative, and exempt, therefore, from military service, I believe it my duty to stay at home and fight the Abolition rebels of the North and West. In the exercise of my constitutional rights, which cannot and shall not be taken away, I propose to do my part toward putting down this, the earliest and most desperate and malignant rebellion. It must be met by reason and appeals to the people, through the press and in public assemblages, and be put down at the ballot-box. But if the overt rebellion in Wisconsin and in Ohio, at Urbana, in 1857, and Cleveland, in 1859 (the one at Urbana an armed rebellion), had been promptly and severely punished as they ought to have been, we never would have had any other.

Here Mr. V. traced briefly the history of the slavery question from the beginning to the present day.

In 1787 it had been settled by the compromises of the Constitution, and all had been peace, quiet, and prosperity, till the terrible "Missouri Question," which struck upon the ear of Jefferson "like a fire-bell in the night." That had been settled by compromise, and we had quiet and peace again for fifteen years, till the systematic and organized anti-slavery agitation began, in 1835, at which time it was so bitterly denounced by President Jackson. But it continued gaining strength every year, till it ended, as every wise man foresaw it must end, in an "unnecessary and injurious civil war." Fifteen years ago there were Secession disunionists South, just as there were Abolition disunionists in the North and West. The former were in public places, State and Federal; but as soon as they proclaimed their disunion proclivities, or were even suspected of them, they were speedily ejected from office, even in South Carolina. In 1851, every Southern State, without exception, carried the Union ticket upon a direct issue; and for years no disunionist, in the South, could be elected to any office. How was it, meantime, in the North and West? From absolute odium and weakness, Abolitionism steadily increased in position and power, till the Senate began to be filled with Abolitionists, open or in disguise, and the House of Representatives also; and till every free State, in every branch of its government, fell into the hands of active and aggressive anti-slavery men; and, finally, a President was elected by a sectional anti-slavery party, on a sectional anti-slavery platform, who himself declared that this Union could not endure "part slave and part free." And yet, at the South, even after secession began, it was with difficulty that any State was induced to secede, except South Carolina. In every other cotton State, there was a large minority against secession; and up to April 15th, 1861, North Carolina, Virginia, Tennessee, and Arkansas refused, by large majorities, to secede, while Delaware, Maryland, Kentucky, and Missouri adhere to the Union to this day. In the very midst of secession, if any fair and adequate compromise had been proposed by Congress, especially if the "Crittenden propositions" of December, 1860, had been adopted, secession would have perished. Mr. Davis and Mr. Toombs both declared that they would be content. That is the statement of Mr. Pugh. It is the testimony of Mr. Douglas also. But those propositions never received a solitary Republican vote in either the Senate or the House. "Hence, the sole responsibility for our disagreement," said Douglas, on the 3d of January, 1861, "and the only difficulty in the way of our amicable adjustment, *is with the Republican party.*"

Sir, these are facts which it is useless to deny, and senseless to quarrel with; and they are part of the many circumstances upon which I found my immovable hope of a final restoration of the Union, in spite of the folly and madness and wickedness every day exhibited, uniting the South, and dividing the North and West,

The South is now well nigh united as one man; and for nearly three months we have met with little else than defeat. What united the South? What changed the fortunes of the war? In the beginning it was declared to be for the Union and the Constitution. These were noble objects, and success attended our arms. Before the battle of Bull Run, Mr. Crittenden sought to offer his now often quoted resolution, defining the objects of the war, and the Republicans did not allow it to be even so much as received. It was met with sneers and contempt. The day after the battle, when Washington was full of escaped soldiers, and fugacious Congressmen from the battle-field, it was offered again, and without objection. But two men, both Republicans, voted against that part of it. I voted for that part of it, but not for the first, because it did not speak the whole truth; because it did not denounce the Abolition disunionists of the North and West also, and hold them responsible too. Six hundred thousand men were soon afterward enlisted. The victories of Hatteras, Port Royal, Mill Springs, Donelson, Roanoke, Winchester, Newbern, Island Ten, New Orleans, Norfolk, and others all followed. Then was the hour for wisdom and sound policy. But, no; it was the exact time selected by Abolitionism for the very saturnalia of its folly and madness. Every scheme and project of emancipation, execution, and confiscation, Congressional and Executive, of the whole session, was pressed forward, and many of them consummated during this same period of victory. The war was everywhere to be perverted from the spirit of the "Crittenden resolution." And with what result? The South, before that time divided, was now united as one man. Even the border slave States were shaken to the center, and thousands of their citizens driven into the Confederate service. The armies of the South were rapidly filled up. A spirit was breathed into each man's breast which made him a host. It was these things, and such infamous orders as Butler's at New Orleans, which inspired their armies, making them invincible – and not overwhelming numbers. Victory everywhere was theirs. McDowell, The Seven Pines, Front Royal, Winchester, Cross Keys, Port Republic, James Island, Vicksburg, and the Great Seven Days Battle of Richmond all followed. The men, and the women, too, of the South said, "If indiscriminate execution, confiscation, and emancipation are to be the rule of the Federal Government, let us perish rather on the battle-field."

This is what Abolitionism has cost us already – an unnecessary and injurious civil war; a united South; a divided North and West; a diminished Federal army; an increased Confederate army; the one dispirited, the other confident; fifteen months of most vigorous war, with the largest army and most numerous navy of modern times; and yet not a single State restored; but a public debt of a thousand millions of dollars incurred, and two hundred and fifty thousand brave men lost to the army, no man knows how. For all this, Abolitionism is responsible. Let it answer at the bar of public opinion. Let the people judge. Let the inexorable sentence go forth, and just and speedy judgment be executed upon it.

These, men of Dayton, are my opinions. They are my convictions. And yet, for these I am denounced as "disloyal"! What is loyalty? Obedience, faithfulness to law, or, in Norman-French, to *loy*; and there is no higher law than the Constitution. Whoever obeys the laws is loyal; whoever breaks them, whether one in authority or a private citizen, is disloyal. There is no such thing yet in the United States, thank God, as loyalty to a President, or to any Administration. And yet, I have heard of loyalty to Abraham Lincoln, to a man, a public servant, whom the people made, and can unmake! Whoever talks thus is fit only to be a slave. If these men mean that I am opposed to the Administration and party in power, and to the doctrines and policy of Abolition, and think them false to the Constitution, and disastrous to the country; if they mean that I am a Democrat, devoted to the principles and policy, and faithful to the organization of that grand old party which made this country what it is, and am for the old Constitution and the old Union, then I am disloyal, and bless God for it. But if they mean that I am false to the Constitution, untrue to the Union, or disloyal to the country of my birth, in thought, or word, or deed, then, in the language of an eloquent citizen of Indiana (Mr. Voorhees), "they lie in their teeth, in their throats, and in their hearts." (Loud cheers.)

Who is an Abolitionist? Whoever is for indiscriminate confiscation, in order to strike at slavery, is an Abolitionist. Whoever is for emancipation and purchase of the slaves of the border States, and the pretended colonization of them abroad, but really their importation North and West, to compete with our own white labor, is an Abolitionist. Whoever would reduce the Southern States to Territories, in order to strike down slavery in them by Federal power, is an Abolitionist. Whoever is in favor of arming the slaves, or of declaring slavery abolished by executive or military proclamation, is an Abolitionist. And, finally, whoever is for converting the war, directly or indirectly, into a crusade for the abolition of slavery, is an Abolitionist of the worst sort; and he who votes for those who favor these things, is also an Abolitionist in practice, no matter what his professions or his party name may be. Whoever is opposed to these projects and votes accordingly, and is for the Constitution as it is, and the Union as it was, is a truly loyal citizen, whether he fights Secession rebels in the field, or Abolition rebels at the ballot-box.

And now, men of Montgomery, if you desire that the rebellion at the South shall be suppressed, that the Confederate armies shall be dissolved, and that the Constitution shall be maintained, the Union restored, and all laws obeyed, unite with me at the ballot-box in speedily and forever crushing out the execrable Abolition rebellion in the North and West. Whoever feels it his duty to fight armed rebels at the South, let him enlist at once; let him not buy up a substitute, but go himself. Whoever remains at home, it is his duty to join with me against Abolition rebels in our midst. This is loyalty; this is fidelity to the Union. The hour of trial and of vindication will soon come. The great hereafter is at hand. In six months – I repeat it – in three months, in six weeks, it may be – sooner or later, come meantime what may, the question will be, eternal separation, or *the Union through compromise*. Which will you then choose – not now, not yet; for amid arms reason, too, is silent – but when it does come? Come it will, and then you must choose between the Union which our fathers made, or a hopeless, cheerless, eternal, and belligerent disunion. I believe that the Administration will declare for separation. Then, as now and ever, I shall be for the Union and against separation. Sir, the choice must be made, and made soon. We have already an enormous debt. A thousand millions would not pay it. We spend three millions a day. How long can you stand that? Our army of six hundred and thirty-seven thousand last January, has melted away to four hundred thousand; and now three hundred thousand more volunteers are demanded, and will soon be in the field. Yet, only fifteen months ago, just seventy-five thousand militia were called out, and the "insurgents" officially commanded to disperse in twenty days! A government paper currency of hundreds of millions is upon us; and a taxation the most onerous and unjust ever levied upon any but a conquered people. A tariff, too, of from forty-one to one hundred and thirteen per cent., as if to heap up the utmost measure of the load, is now added. Stand in the doorway of your farm-house and behold and feel nothing, nothing not taxed, except the air you breathe, and the bright sun-light or star-light of heaven! And yet, you must pay it to the uttermost farthing. None but a madman or a traitor will talk of resistance or repudiation. It was not so in Democratic times. For sixty years that party governed this country in peace and prosperity, and with wisdom and sound policy. Try it again. I am a party man more from conviction than inclination. There must be parties under every free government, and if there are not good parties, there will be bad ones; and "when bad men combine," said Burke, "good men must associate." Why did the Democratic party always govern this country wisely and well and all other parties fail? Because our institutions are Democratic, and the principles and policy of the Democratic party are consistent with them; just as a piece of mechanism can only be made to work upon the principle or theory on which it is constructed. That is the philosophy of the historic fact. But the Democratic party could not conduct the British government three months without signal and disastrous failure. Let the people lay these things to heart. Let them restore the Democratic party to power, if they would be rescued at last. And, meantime, if the President would be sustained, let him resist fearlessly the spirit of Abolitionism; let him adhere to the Constitution; and himself obey all laws, and execute all laws; let him unmuzzle the press, and unfetter the tongue, and give freedom again to assemblages of the people and to elections; let him liberate his so-called prisoners of State, and henceforth arrest no man without due process of law; in a word, let him look to love, not fear; to law, not terror, as the support of his administration; and every true patriot in the land will rally round him; and then, in God's good time, our eyes shall yet be gladdened, dark as the hour now is, with the blessed vision of the Constitution maintained, the Union restored, and the old flag of our country known and honored once again in every land and upon every sea. (Great and long-continued cheering.)

CHAPTER EIGHT
Political Campaign of 1862

The Democratic Congressional Convention, composed of the counties of Butler, Montgomery, Preble, and Warren, met at Hamilton, in Butler Co., September 4th, and nominated Hon. C. L. Vallandigham, by acclamation. Mr. V. being informed of his nomination, and conducted to the stand, signified his acceptance by reading the following address:

> To the Democrats and other loyal Union men of the Third Congressional District of Ohio:
>
> Just after the congressional election in 1860, acknowledging my very many and great obligations to you for past favors, I declared my fixed purpose to decline another candidacy. In this mind I continued through all the extraordinary changes of the past two years. I learned, indeed, some time ago, from many sources, and upon unmistakable evidence, that it was the general desire of the Democracy of the District that I should be their candidate again, and I thanked them for the confidence implied. But recently circumstances have changed. The "reign of terror" has been renewed with more severity than ever before. Freedom of the press and of speech has been repeatedly and causelessly stricken down. Political and personal liberty has, over and over again, been assailed by illegal and arbitrary arrests; and thus a determined purpose evinced to break down the ancient, customary, and constitutional means of opposition to the political party in power, under the false and tyrannical pretence that it is "opposition to the Government." To shrink from a canvass pressed upon me by the unanimous voice of the Democracy of the District, would be cowardice now. You have never deserted me; I will not, in this hour of peculiar trial and peril, desert you. With many and most heartful thanks, therefore, I accept the unanimous nomination just tendered to me, content with your indorsement here to-day, and the ratification of it, by the Democrats and other loyal Union men of the District at the

polls, as of more value than an election purchased by the sacrifice of the party and the principles which my judgment and conscience approve, and which I have adhered to and maintained from my very boyhood to this day; a party, too, the success of which is so essential, at this moment, to the reunion of the States, and the peace and prosperity of the country; for, if there be any one fact proved now beyond a reasonable doubt, it is the utter incompetency of the party in power to successfully administer the Government. I know, indeed, that the District in which I have been three times honored with an election, has been changed by a "no party" partisan Legislature, and made heavily Republican, for the purpose of preventing the return of a Democrat; and that at the election last fall, the counties which now compose this District, gave the Republican or Fusion candidate for Governor a very large majority. But districts made for party purposes have more than once been changed by the people at the polls, and greater majorities than this many times overcome, as was, indeed, done last spring, even in the District as now constituted. In any event, the vindication of Democratic principles and the Democratic cause is, at this time especially, of far more importance than mere success in any election.

At your demand, therefore, men of the Third District, I accept the nomination, and present myself to the people for their suffrages, upon no other platform than *the Constitution as it is and the Union as it was*.

It is a platform broad enough for every patriot. Whoever is for it, I ask his support. Whenever is against it, I would not have his vote. Every faculty of body and mind which I possess shall be exerted unremittingly for the great purpose implied in this platform.

As a Representative, it is my duty to visit the constituency of the old District, still a part of the new, and to render to them an account of my stewardship as a public servant. As a candidate, I have a right to address the people upon all political questions, and they have a right to hear me.

Says the Constitution: "Members of the House of Representatives shall be chosen every second year by the people."

And again: "Congress shall make no law abridging the freedom of speech, or of the press; or the right of the people peaceably to assemble, and to petition the government for a redress of grievances."

Our State Constitution is still more explicit: "The people have the right to assemble together in a peaceable manner, to consult for their common good; to instruct their representatives, and to petition the General Assembly for the redress of grievances."

These high and essential constitutional rights the Democrats and other loyal Union men of this District everywhere, and I as their candidate, mean to exercise to the fullest extent. And it will tend much toward the quiet and good feeling of communities, if all idle talk, such as that the Democratic candidate shall not speak in this place or that place, be dispensed with: for let it be understood, once for all, that wherever in any part of any county in the District it is deemed convenient and proper to advertise a Democratic meeting, *it will be held; and, God willing, I will address it.*

After reading the foregoing, Mr. Vallandigham spoke an hour or more, with great force and effect, often interrupted by applauding responses. No report was made of the speech, beyond a few notes by the secretary, from which we learn that, in closing, he stated, that he had supported the Six Million Bill for paying the three months' volunteers; and had also prepared and reported a bill to pay a bounty of thirty dollars to these volunteers, in addition to their pay. This bill, he said, passed the House, but failed in the Senate.

Mr. V. then defined his position as to State defense, expressed in the following resolution, which he offered, and which was adopted by the meeting unanimously, amid great cheering:

> *Resolved*, That it is the highest duty of the citizen, whenever his country or State is invaded, to rush to its rescue, by arms, if he is capable of military service, and by money or otherwise every way, if he is not; and that the Democracy, as a part of the people of this district, laying aside all party feeling for that purpose, are ready with life and fortune to do their part in discharging this patriotic duty.

The way being thus opened, by receiving and accepting the nomination, Mr. Vallandigham entered upon a thorough and vigorous canvass of his district. To carry his old congressional district, and by a larger majority than ever before, after all denunciation, was the great point to be attained. But the Legislature, at its last session, had added to his district the county of Warren, one of the strongest Abolition counties in the State, and by this most unfair and disingenuous piece of gerrymandering, had provided against the possibility of his re-election. But this, with him, was no reason for faltering. It was due to his friends, and the cause, that he should demonstrate to them, and to all concerned, that he had lost none of his fitness for the high office in which they desired to continue him; and should publicly nail to the wall those base slanders and lies with which the Abolition press had been teeming. The occasion, also, furnished an opportunity not to be lost, for bringing clearly and boldly to the view of the people, those great and true principles of political practice and faith, for whose fearless and unwavering advocacy and defense he had continually suffered the most malignant assaults.

The occasion was improved; the six weeks preceding the day of election being spent in addressing large and enthusiastic assemblies, at prominent points in the district. And the result was a triumphant indorsement and vindication of Mr. Vallandigham. His old district, which he has represented for the last six years, gave him a majority four times larger than ever before.

The Cincinnati *Times*, an Abolition paper, in its issue the day after election, said:

> Vallandigham, though his district, in the new apportionment, was arranged especially to defeat him, is barely defeated, and that is all. In his old district, where, a year ago, he scarcely dare attempt to address a popular assemblage, he has a majority of about 700, and is defeated only from the fact that a very strong Republican county has been added to the district. These facts are given as an illustration of the political revolution that has undoubtedly begun in the North-western States.

The Cincinnati *Enquirer*, referring to this statement, the next day, said:

> The *Times* is correct in its facts. The Hon. C.L. Vallandigham has obtained the greatest personal and political triumph ever won by any public man in the United States. In the face of a storm of abuse, obloquy, slander, and denunciation, from every Abolition print, and every Abolition orator, from Maine to California, which, in fury, was probably never equaled, Mr. Vallandigham has been indorsed by the constituents whom he represents in Congress, by a majority of 800 votes, an increase of 700 since his last election, in 1860. Denounced as a traitor, as a secessionist, as an enemy of his country, by the fawning parasites of power, by vindictive political partisans, who have sought to make his name synonymous with treason, his life and liberty threatened by those who were ignorant of his political record, he has appealed to the people of his district, and he has been triumphantly sustained.
>
> It was a spectacle that challenged admiration, to see an able, a bold and brave man standing up for what he deemed right, unawed by power, and unseduced by his personal advantages, which lay upon the other side. The American people are a generous people, and love to see fairness and honesty displayed.
>
> After the indorsement of the people of his district – after 10,000 American citizens have honored him with their votes – the slanderers of Mr. Vallandigham had better, for shame's sake, cease their abuse. If they do not, there is no knowing to what position of prominence he may advance. If Mr. Vallandigham has been beaten, it is owing to the rascality of an Abolition

legislature, which made a district with especial view to his defeat. He has carried his own district, but he could hardly be expected to carry Tom Corwin's in addition, which was saddled upon him.

The haters and slanderers of Mr. Vallandigham were thus despoiled of the triumph they had hoped to secure, and had nothing to boast of beyond what they obtained by unfair legislation and fraud.

A most corrupt and infamous Abolition sheet, the most deadly, persistent, and mendacious slanderer of Mr. Vallandigham, on the morning of the election, thus put in its last word:

> Vallandigham. – It will be enough to beat the cowardly, impudent, and malignant traitor Vallandigham in his district as it stands. In the name of the honor of Ohio, beat him in the old district. The new district – we explain for the public at large – is the old one, with Warren county attached. It is discreditable that Vallandigham can have the support of even a faction in Ohio. The disgrace will be black, burning, and infinitely shameful, if he is not beaten overwhelmingly.

Then, surely, the disgrace was "black, burning, and infinitely shameful," for, as the *Empire* remarked, referring to the above declaration:

> Mr. Vallandigham has not been beaten in the old district; on the contrary, he triumphantly carries it, by four times as large a majority as ever before. And, better still, he is indorsed in his own county, which he never carried before, by a majority of near four hundred.

The *Empire* says, also:

> And, further, he has not only been indorsed by the people of his own district, but by the Democracy of the whole State. Does the *Commercial* remember anything about the Fourth of July Convention, of which it said Vallandigham and Medary were the "ruling spirits"; that convention of "Butternuts," if you please, over which Sam Medary presided, and at which Vallandigham was the principal speaker? Well, the ticket which the "Vallandighammers" that day nominated has been elected, ratified, and indorsed by the people of the State. Montgomery county has a representative on that ticket, in the person of Professor C. W. H. Cathcart.

But the fact that Mr. Vallandigham's non-election was secured by adding to his district a piece of strong Abolition territory, has been studiously ignored, and even lied out of view, by the Abolition press. Referring to this subject, the Hon. J. W. Wall, lately elected United States Senator from

New Jersey, said, in a letter to the New York *World*, in October, 1862:

> If I am correctly informed, at the last session of the Ohio Legislature, over three thousand Republican votes were transferred bodily to the district, for the purpose, as was avowed, of preventing his return to Congress. Besides all this, resort was had to the base means that corruption and misrepresentation understand so well how to wield.
>
> There is no public man in the State of Ohio who wields the personal influence, and has a stronger hold upon the popular heart, than the fearless, incorruptible, and talented Representative from the Dayton district. Knowing him, as I do, and the fierce, malignant opposition against which he has had to contend, led on by the remorseless energies of fanaticism, I may say, as was said of Hector, *"Si Pergema dextra defendi possent, etiam hac defensa fuissent."* But Hector's arm was not strong enough to save the city.
>
> There is no more patriotic heart beats in any man's bosom than his. No man, either in Congress or out of it, has exhibited more wisdom and remarkable forecast in reference to this war and its results. No man has been more disinterested, devoted himself to his country's best interests, and labored more assiduously to stay the disastrous legislation of the last Congress, which he declared was pregnant with manifold mischief to the country. Any man familiar with his speeches, will be struck with the prophetic sagacity they manifest. He saw the "end from the beginning," and predicted the present ruined, disastrous condition of the country.

In every part of the Union the defeat of Mr. Vallandigham was deeply regretted, especially as he had been so well sustained by his own district, and was beaten only by a part of Corwin's old district being turned over unto him. The tone of the Democratic press was like this, from the Mount Vernon (Ohio) *Banner*:

> The defeat of the gallant Clement L. Vallandigham, in the Third District, is greatly lamented by all good Union-loving Democrats. The Republicans purposely formed a district to defeat him, and they have been successful by a small majority. But they cannot put Mr. Vallandigham down. Although slandered more than any living man, he has come out of the "fiery ordeal" like pure gold. Higher honors yet await him.

The Syracuse (N.Y.) *Courier* said:

> In this State the malignants and radicals crow lustily over the defeat of the brave, gifted, and patriotic Vallandigham. A high and independent spirit, such as the times require, has, perhaps, fallen there, but not sacrificed by the people whom he had represented. If victimized at all, he is a victim of

the same kind of radical gerrymandering of his district as sacrificed Biddle in Pennsylvania. A strong Republican county was added to his district, and it was so constituted that the counties composing the district gave last fall over 3,000 majority against the Democratic ticket. If defeated by 800 majority, he has every reason to be proud of the result, and of the confidence evinced by this diminished majority against him.

In Hamilton, where Mr. Vallandigham was nominated, a meeting, held soon after the election, indorsed him in a series of resolutions, among which are the following:

> *Whereas,* A recent act of the Ohio Legislature remapped the territory of the Third Congressional District, including within its well-known boundary the county of Warren; and, whereas, such remapping was executed by the enemies of the Democratic party, with the intent to prevent a return to Congress of the chosen tribune of the ancient district; and, whereas, by such partisan legislation we have been temporarily deprived of the services of our faithful public servant, Hon. C.L. Vallandigham, therefore,
>
> *Resolved,* By the Democracy of Butler county, in mass meeting assembled, That we reaffirm our confidence in the patriotism of our Representative, and again record an entire satisfaction of his management of our trust.
>
> *Resolved,* That to his fortitude and consummate policy as much as to any single existence, we attribute the recently disclosed sober second thought of the people.
>
> *Resolved,* That for his earnest deprecation of the calamities of these States; for his attempt to appease the wrath of the contending people of both sections of the Union; for his endeavor to invoke reason, and call back the blessings of happier days; for his marvelous perception of the consequences of this "unnatural civil war," and for his unequaled exertions in its repression; for this catalogue of crimes, which has excited the ire of fanatics, which has furnished the weapons of destruction to an Abolition press, and which has made his name synonymous with traitor, the constituents of Hon. Clement L. Vallandigham demand the judgment of history.

The closing resolution ends with a quotation which it will not always be treason to repeat, nor is it now treason against Heaven:

> Blessed are the peace-makers, for they shall be called the children of God.

CHAPTER NINE
Democratic Jubilees

After the election of October 14, 1862, which exhibited the gratifying results of the most important and remarkable political revolution ever witnessed in Ohio, it was determined to have some general jubilee celebrations. Those meetings were started, and went with a rush all over the State. For several weeks the "Democratic jubilees" were the order of the day, and were attended by immense multitudes. Indiana, also, took a part in those jubilees.

Mr. Vallandigham attended a large number of those meetings. One of the first at which he was present was held at Centreville, Indiana, on the 20th of October, where he spoke two hours to an audience of two thousand or more, who heard and applauded his speech with unbounded enthusiasm. One of that crowd ends a report of the doings with the remark that "Not only have the people of his district indorsed him, but the people of Indiana, Ohio, and Pennsylvania have spoken in thunder tones in favor of Vallandigham, the Constitution, and the Union."

On the 22d of October, two days later, Mr. Vallandigham was at the "grand jollification" in Hillsborough, Ohio, held in honor of "the great Democratic victories in Ohio, Indiana, and Pennsylvania." The Hillsborough *Gazette* says:

> Never was the truth of that old adage, "Truth is mighty and will prevail," more fully verified than on this occasion. Many who had come to hear the speaker, with opinions altogether biased against him, having never been Democrats in their lives, went away from the meeting impressed with the belief that he was the most powerful, forcible, and truthful speaker they had ever heard, and with a fixed determination to vote for him in case he shall ever be a candidate for any office that will give them an opportunity to

do so. We do not hesitate to say that Mr. Vallandigham is, to-day, the most popular man in the State of Ohio; and, as a rebuke for the shameful manner in which he was gerrymandered out of his seat in Congress by an Abolition legislature, the people of Ohio would now be willing to bestow upon him any office within their gift.

Three days later, October 25th, Mr. Vallandigham was at Mt. Vernon, Ohio, in midst of the Democracy of "Old Knox." The day was stormy and very unpleasant, but the city had no room large enough for the crowd; so they took a stand in the open air, and, defying the weather, listened to Mr. Vallandigham with the most earnest attention for three full hours. The Mt. Vernon *Banner* says:

> The audience would have heard him speak a whole day with the greatest pleasure. His speech was certainly the ablest and best ever delivered in this city; and men who have heard many of the most eminent speakers in the Union, declare Mr. Vallandigham equal, if not superior, to any of them. The speech, from beginning to end, was characteristic of the statesman, the patriot, and the Christian. It comprehended the situation and crisis of our affairs. The course and tendency of events were well told, and the condition of the country truly depicted. The designs of the factious demagogues, conspiring fanatics, and unfaithful public men, who now, unfortunately, sit in the high places of power and trust, were laid bare and reprobated with, crushing truth, reason, and common sense. Would that every honest and really patriotic citizen could hear and heed Mr. Vallandigham's words of truth and wisdom; the base schemes of wicked men would soon be exploded or frustrated, their authors punished, or, at least, deprived of power to ruin, and the country restored to peace, harmony, and prosperity.

The next of these meetings at which we find Mr. Vallandigham was held on the 1st of November, at his old home in New Lisbon, Columbiana county, Ohio. The Ohio *Patriot* of that place, describing the meeting, says:

> Word had circulated that Vallandigham, the friend of the Constitution and the Union – which, by Republican interpretation, means the traitor and secessionist – was to speak, and the old men of the county, who used to listen to his father's preaching, and the young men who admired his valor and his patriotism, came in, by hundreds, to get the political gospel from the son. Never in New Lisbon did there assemble so many of the sober and pious people of the county.

In another editorial the *Patriot* says:

Mr. Vallandigham was born and raised in New Lisbon, and was well known to the people of this county previous to his removal to Dayton. When a young man, fully confiding in his ability and integrity, they elected him to the legislature of the State; and their confidence in his patriotism and statesmanship has been increased by every act of his life. He has been the subject of much abuse from the Republicans; but they cannot show one word he has ever uttered that was disloyal: while it would be very easy to establish, that, if every man in the North had pursued the same course for the last ten years, we would have had no war, no Federal tax, no draft, no stricken people mourning for their dead kindred, victims of battle. Mr. Vallandigham is immensely popular.

On the 5th of November, Mr. Vallandigham was at that immense Democratic celebration in Newark, Ohio. A correspondent of the Cincinnati *Enquirer*, describing the meeting, says:

Such demonstrations as the one we had here yesterday should convince the most skeptical of the lively, healthy, vigorous existence of the Democracy. It is affirmed by those who ought to know, that it was the largest political meeting in this city since the year 1840. And certainly it could not well be exceeded in earnestness and zeal. About ten thousand people convened in the court-house square, between one and two o'clock, P.M. Many came from the adjoining counties. Hon. C.L. Vallandigham made the first speech. His introduction was accompanied by an enthusiastic outburst of applause from the whole multitude. Mr. Vallandigham began by referring to and narrating the incidents and revealing the motives of the recent causeless and most foul murder, at Dayton, of one of his best friends, J. F. Bollmeyer, editor of the Dayton *Empire*, by an Abolition assassin. He had, the day before, attended the funeral of his martyred friend, a victim of Abolition vindictiveness. He spoke most feelingly on this subject; he characterized the murder very truly and properly as one of the sad results of the Gospel of Hate, which has been for years persistently preached by so many of the clergy, and diffused and instilled by the Abolition press of the land. He scouted and exposed the false and miserable pretence which the lying telegraph and the Abolition papers had alleged, that it was the issue of a rencounter about a dog. The fact of the Grand Jury having indicted the assassin for murder in the first degree, showed the real character of the affair. It was a cowardly Abolition murder of a noble, talented, and courageous man, for no other reason than that he was an able and prominent Democrat.

Although, Mr. Vallandigham said, he sometimes felt like harboring a spirit of revenge for the many persecutions and outrages, even to the shedding of blood and loss of life, which had been inflicted upon Democrats by the Abolitionists, yet he counseled charity toward them, and would seek for redress, at least in the first place, at the hands of the law and through the ballot-box. His rebuke at our hypocritical opponents, who profess to be such pure Christians and moralists, was most scathing. He contrasted their conduct and practice with that of the Democracy, as to who had manifested the greater regard for the precepts of Christianity, which, as he understands it, is the Gospel of Love. The Abolitionists had preached and practiced the Gospel of Hate – hate toward everybody except the negro, and even with respect to him, they were more actuated by hate for the negro's master than by love for the negro.

On the 13th of November, Mr. Vallandigham spoke at the mass meeting in Circleville; and the next day at Lancaster. He then suddenly disappeared from the State; but, on the day following, was heard of at Cambridge, Ind., where a grand Democratic jubilee was that day to be held.

The "Butternuts" came in by car-loads, while wagons and horses, by thousands, brought up the rear. Mr. Vallandigham was there, as a part of the programme. He had visited the same district on the 20th of October, and spoken at Centreville, as we have said. Being, of course, a suspicious character, he was dogged by the United States Marshal for Indiana, named Garland Rose, under orders from Governor Morton, of that State. Referring to his former visit and its adventures, Mr. Vallandigham began his speech thus:

> Is the Marshal of Indiana here to-day? Are his minions about? Is his committee here again? Why liest thou hid now, O, sweet-scented Rose? Lift up thy delicate head, thou daughter of a mild sky. *"Quid lates dudum, Rosa?"*
>
> Why has not Morton threatened to deck me this time, also, with a garland of roses? Ah! I remember me, elections have been held, and the people have spoken. Their voice, as the voice of many waters, has been heard. It has reached the palaces at Washington and Indianapolis and Columbus, and penetrated even their darkened and deaf recesses. Lincoln and Morton have heard it, and their knees have smitten together. Tod heard it. The "Democratic thunder" reached his ears; he knew it, and his "back-bone" softened and shriveled and shrunk before it. *Sic semper tyrannis.* Let us rejoice. The people are once more masters, and henceforth, no more shall the rights of the citizen and the courtesies and hospitalities of States be violated. The occupation of marshals and detectives and spies and informers and affidavit-makers, is gone, never to return; and their offices, at least the official existence of them, one and all, will soon cease. "Teach me the measure of my days," says the Psalmist; and I commend the pious reflection to Lincoln and Morton and Tod, and all others under and around, or like them, who

have abused power, and outraged the people. The 4th of March, 1864, will end their days. *Habeas corpus* is here. Arbitrary arrests are at an end. The people of New York had restored the great charter of liberty on the 6th of November, and the people of Ohio and Indiana on the 14th day of October. In the midst of a despotism worse than that of Austria, the people of these great States have risen in their might, and pulled down the temple of Abolitionism, never to rise again. Not a vestige of it will be left. Its site will be plowed over, and salt sowed, after the custom of the Romans, upon the spot where it stood.

In the contest just closed, while the sky was dark, and the storm was gathering – when the old Democratic ship was struggling with the billows – men who had professed to be leaders, who had been foremost when the sky was bright and the wind blew fair, had deserted their posts. It was always so. Some were terrified, and fled; others, ambitious men, who would secure power dishonorably, fled; but the people, always true to themselves, retired to their homes, to their farms and their workshops and their offices, in the hour of trial, to commune with their sober thoughts, and they came forth at the appointed time, and righted the floundering ship. They achieved a victory surprising even to themselves, and perfectly astounding to the Abolitionists.

The railroads, the banks, the telegraph lines, the express companies, and another element, that had of late defiled itself in the land – the Churches – were all arrayed against the people. The pure altars of Christianity were defiled, and the disciples had huckstered in the political markets. The Churches had departed from the doctrines of Christ and him crucified, and taken up the negro and him glorified! There will be no Union, no peace, no hope, no country, until you drive out those who have defiled the temple of the Savior of mankind, and restore the gospel in its purity. It is time to abandon the Abolition churches. Refuse them support. It is time to speak out.

Mr. Vallandigham said he was the son of a clergyman, but of one who did not disgrace his calling. He had of late quoted freely from the Scriptures, in his speeches. Some of his friends remarked it, and he told them he had not attended church lately, and consequently he had time to examine the Bible. In his closet he could find its teachings, but not in the pulpit.

Proscription had been another means used. Men were proscribed in every way. His advice was to meet proscription with proscription. We have as much money as they have – at least, honestly. We have not as many contractors, nor as heavy amounts of stealings hoarded up, but we consume as much as they do, eat as much, wear as much, and, by honest toil, can pay for as much. Proscription is a game that two can play at, and they will be the first to tire of it.

Over all these means, freely and unscrupulously used, we behold the sublime spectacle of twenty millions of freemen making their voices heard, even in the White House. Abraham has heard it, the Cabinet have heard it, and the governors of States have heard it.

Mr. Vallandigham then counseled his Democratic friends to stand by the laws, to seek redress through the courts, and administer that rebuke to the corrupt – "exclusion from office." We will get satisfaction for our wrongs through the law. He called upon every man who had been unlawfully imprisoned in the walls of a Bastile, to seek for redress through the forms of law, as he valued himself and the liberties of his countrymen. England has given us examples of illegal arrest – these usurpers cannot even claim the merit of originality for their tyranny – she has also given us examples of the punishment of the offenders. In England, the person of a subject is inviolate. An Englishman's house or home is his castle. We have a notable instance of what an Englishman's liberty for one hour is considered worth by an English jury. A secretary of state arrested a British subject, and imprisoned him for one hour. At the end of that time he was released. He brought suit against "my Lord," and recovered a verdict for $5,000. Lord Chief Justice Pratt, afterward Lord Camden – the advocate of the cause of the Colonies, the friend of America in its youth – made the memorable declaration in this case: "None but an English jury can estimate the value of an Englishman's liberty for one hour." An Indiana jury may be able to make a like estimate. That is the way we should and will have satisfaction. The people have spoken – they must be heard, and will be heard. "We will have the Union as it was, the Constitution as it is, and the negroes where they are."

Mr. Vallandigham said that the campaign had only just begun. It must be kept up. We have a wily and unscrupulous antagonism to contend with. The good old times will return. He did believe in the possibility, nay, the probability, of the restoration of the Union as it was. We have commenced the work here, with the ballot-box; with it we have smitten the Philistines hip and thigh. The people of the South, after a little while, will, by the same instrumentality, put down the Secessionists there, as we have the Abolitionists here, and peace and union will once more smile upon the land. That is the sentiment in the ranks of both armies, and if you would to-day put ballots in the hands of the private soldiers of the North and South, the agitators and leaders, who are forcing streams of blood to flow, would be effectually put down. He related several instances of this feeling in the army, and concluded with an elegant peroration, which was received – as the main parts of his speech had been, throughout – by thunders of applause.

On the 21st of November, at the residence of Judge Morse, near Dayton, Mr. Vallandigham was presented with an elegant gold-headed cane, a gift from ladies of that city. Mr. Thomas O. Lowe, who, on behalf of the ladies, made the presentation speech, alluding to the sentiments of those for whom he was commissioned to speak, said:

> There are yet some who, from their very natures, have deprecated this war, who desired, as you did, that it should be averted, and who now pray that the Ruler of heaven and earth, who is the Prince of Peace and God of Love, will turn the hearts of men from all bitterness and strife, so that bloodshed may be known among us no more forever. And if there be a prayer which the "ministering angels" round about us more gladly hear, and more quickly bear to the ear of heaven, than any other, it must be theirs. The Savior of men said "Blessed are the peacemakers," and
>
> > Gave his life
> > To bend man's stubborn will;
> > When elements were fierce with strife,
> > Said to them "Peace; be still."

And, describing the estimation those ladies had placed upon the services of him to whom this elegant gift was offered, Mr. Lowe said:

> They desire to express to you their belief that if all the men of the North and South had but loved this Union as well, and had struggled as wisely for the best interests of the country as you, this war would have been averted; and that, even now, if the combatants could but be imbued with a patriotism as true as yours, this struggle would speedily cease, our Union be restored as it was, and everything which has, in days gone by, made Americans proud of their country, would come back to us again. They believe, too, that when the historian shall come to write of the causes of the downfall of this great Republic – if, in the providence of God, it be doomed to fall – if he write with an unprejudiced pen, "nothing extenuating, naught setting down in malice," he will have this to say of you: You hated and resisted the fell spirit of Abolitionism, which you knew to be
>
> > False, deceitful.
> > Sudden, malicious, smacking of every sin
> > That has a name,
>
> which, invigorated by the blood and carnage of the rebellion, you saw endeavoring, under various pretexts, to destroy our dearest liberties, and for this cause, and this alone, you were made the object of a persecution which, for malignity and persistency, has few parallels in history.

Mr. Lowe closed by saying:

> And we all think, sir, that it is not among the least of the services you have rendered to your country, that you have shown that there is such

a thing as unconquerable devotion to principle – that there is one statesman among us who is not to be moved from his conviction of right by any danger or threatenings – that if one obeys the exhortations of Woolsey, and makes his aims "his country's, his God's and truth's," he need not fear. Though storms may be raging all around him, he will be "sustained by an unfaltering trust," and have "that peace which is above all earthly dignities, a still and quiet conscience."

Accepting the beautiful gift, Mr. Vallandigham said:

> Mr. Lowe: With a grateful heart I receive this cane from the ladies for whom you have just spoken. Valuable in itself, it is to me far more valuable because of the kindly motives which have induced its presentation; but especially as a testimony of their approbation of my conduct as a public man, in the recent and present perilous times of the country. From them I accept it as a large recompense for whatever of calumny and reproach I have endured for the last eighteen months, because of my adherence to principle and a course of public policy which, in my conscience and judgment, I believed essential to the restoration of the Union and the best interests of my country. Such honors are bestowed commonly upon the heroes of military warfare. But if I merit any part of the praise which you have so eloquently expressed, it is moral heroism which, tonight, is honored by these ceremonies. It is the victories of peace which you here celebrate. Her triumphs are, indeed, grander, and her conquests nobler than any achieved by the military hero upon the battle-field. And it is especially fitting that these honors should be paid to the cause – though I, myself, may deserve them not – by the women of the country; and, while I lament that so many among them should have forgotten the softness of their sex, and the mild teachings of a religion, essential, indeed, to man, but especially congenial to woman's nature, yet I rejoice that so many, also, have laid not aside the ornament of a meek and quiet spirit, but remembered and clung yet the more steadfastly to the gospel of peace and love, even amid the phrensy of a desolating and demoralizing civil war. True to woman's mission, they are, or will be, the wives, mothers, daughters, and sisters, who, by precept, example, or association, shall bring back yet the present, or educate a new generation which shall restore peace, the Union, and constitutional liberty, with all their virtues and their blessings, once more to this bleeding and distracted country. If, indeed, sir, I have exhibited any part of the high qualities of courage, fortitude, and immovable devotion to the good and the right, which, on behalf of these ladies, you have so kindly attributed to me, it is to one of their own sex, more than to any other human agency, that I am indebted for them – my mother. In childhood, in boyhood, and in youth, in the midst of many trials, from her teachings, and by her example, I learned those lessons, and formed the character and habits

– if it be so – which fitted me, with courage and endurance, and unfaltering faith, to struggle with the terrible times in the midst of which we live.

Congratulating the ladies on the selection of yourself as their representative upon this occasion, and thanking you cordially for the many kind things you have been pleased to say, I accept this beautiful present, with my most grateful acknowledgments to one and all here assembled.

The next day Mr. Vallandigham addressed, at length, a very large Democratic meeting at Springfield, Clark county, Ohio. The Democrat of that city, speaking of it, said:

We would like to give a synopsis of his great speech, but will not attempt it. We but quote the words of hundred of others when we say that for beauty, simplicity, and strength many of the passages of the speech were equal to the best periods of Webster. Would to God that all his revilers could have heard him!

On the 26th of November Mr. Vallandigham attended another of those Democratic jubilees, held at Chillicothe, Ohio. The day was cold and unpleasant, and yet not less than four thousand were there. Mr. Vallandigham followed Hon. Wm. Allen, and spoke until near dark. The Chillicothe *Advertiser* says:

It was a remarkable circumstance – a thing almost unparalleled – that so many men and women should stand out there in the cold fully four hours after an election, and listen to two political speeches. Mr. Vallandigham spoke free from all restraint – free from the restraint that weighed many speakers down before the election – and yet no one could find in that speech either open or covert treason, unless the unvailing of the Republican Mohkanna is obnoxious to that charge.

He believed it possible, since the rendition of the verdict of the people through the ballot-box at the late elections, that the Union might be restored; he believed it would be in time – that when the Abolitionists were put down through the ballot-box, then the people of the South would put down secession there, and then would commence the work of restoration. His conviction, from the first, had been that the Union could not be restored through the agency of arms; he believed so now more firmly than ever.

Mr. Vallandigham closed amidst a profusion of bouquets thrown to him by the ladies, who, in addition, presented him a very beautiful wreath.

But the unbounded enthusiasm of the people was not satisfied by a four hours' meeting in the open air. They met again, at the courthouse, in the evening. Mr, Vallandigham, not expecting to speak again, came in late, but was "so earnestly called for," says the *Advertiser*, "that he felt constrained to respond, and did respond in a speech of two hours," which is described as fully equal to his effort of the afternoon.

The *Advertiser* expresses the belief that "the seed thus sown will undoubtedly, ripen into a 'butternut' crop by next fall far larger than the one that blessed the Democratic husbandmen this last fall."

This is the man whom some people call a "traitor;" and such were the proud and triumphant receptions with which the people of Ohio were delighted to honor a "defeated candidate."

Immediately after the meeting in Chillicothe, Mr. Vallandigham left for Washington city, the day for the reassembling of Congress being at hand.

CHAPTER TEN
The Great Civil War in America
Speech Delivered in the House of Representatives, January 14, 1863

No speech ever heard in the Halls of Congress has made a deeper impression on the mind of the American people than the one delivered by Mr. Vallandigham on the 14th of January, 1863. From the day Congress assembled, public expectation had been turned toward him, and many were waiting to hear what counsels he would give in this most perilous hour of our country's history. The highest hopes of his friends, and the worst fears of his enemies were realized; for he spoke like a statesman, a patriot, an American.

Already that speech has found a million of readers, but we will repeat it here, revised and corrected, for this purpose, by the author. Those who have read it will be glad to have it in a permanent form, while they and others will value it more highly in this connection, the last of a series of speeches, which, in the aggregate, furnish a thorough and complete exposition of the growth, progress, development, and culmination of a most pernicious, deadly, and destructive fanaticism.

It is right to call attention to the fact that the estimate we have formed of this speech is fully sustained by the opinions of the press, true index and exponent of popular sentiment.

The Washington correspondent of the Cincinnati *Gazette*, a bitter and malignant political opponent of Mr. Vallandigham, describing the speech, and the effect of its delivery, relates that the most busy and active members, such as Colfax, Wickliffe, Lovejoy, Olin, and others dropped everything else, and obtained the best positions for hearing. An effort was making to get a joint session of the military and naval committees to consider a matter to which attention had been called by the Secretary of War. Only three out of fourteen members could be got to the committee-room in the course of an hour. Even the reporters in the galleries wake up; the ladies cease their eternal chattering, and lean forward to catch every word.

Such are some of the indications, of deep and unusual interest, as described by the correspondent referred to, who says:

> This man is the hero of our Northern rebels; the most respectable in talents, the most honest in declaring his positions, the bravest in maintaining them against whatever storm of opposition and obloquy.

Describing his manner of commencing, the same writer says:

> He begins boldly, defiantly, even; and is speedily preaching the very doctrine of devils. "You can never subdue the seceded States. Two years of fearful experience have taught you that. Why carry on the war? If you persist, it can only end in final separation between the North and South. And in that case, believe it now, as you did not my former warnings, the whole North-west will go with the South!"
>
> He waxes more earnest as he approaches this key-note of his harangues, and with an energy and force that makes every hearer – as his moral nature revolts from the bribe – acknowledge, all the more, the splendid force with which the tempter urges his cause, with flashing eye and livid features and extended hand, trembling with the passion of his utterance, he hurls the climax of his threatening argument again upon the Republican side of the House: "Believe me, as you did not the solemn warning of years past, *the day which divides the North from the South, the self-same day decrees eternal divorce between the West and the East!*"

These solemn warnings have, at last, caught the ear of leading Republicans. Will they heed them?

The group of Republicans standing in the open space before the Clerk's desk, increases; they crowd down the aisles among the Opposition and cluster around the Speaker.

Mr. Vallandigham tells them:

> There is not one drop of rain that falls over the whole vast expanse of the North-west that does not find its home in the bosom of the Gulf. We must and we will follow it, with travel and trade; not by treaty, but by right; freely, peaceably, and without restriction or tribute, under the same Government and flag.

> The correspondent, whose unwilling testimony we are quoting, says of the above declaration:

It is eloquently spoken, and none are more willing to concede it than his opponents.

The strongest testimony to Mr. Vallandigham's power as a speaker, and to the resistless force of the great truths he was uttering, is given by this writer, in saying:

He has spoken over an hour and a quarter, and accomplished the rare feat of compelling the closest attention of the most disorderly deliberative body in the world, from the beginning to the end.

The speech being ended, the *Gazette's* correspondent adds:

There is a gradual relaxation, a sudden humming of conversation again on the floor and through the galleries. The Democrats and Border-State men, with faces wreathed in smiles, crowd around their champion with their congratulations. At a single step, the shunned and execrated Vallandigham has risen to the leadership of their party. Deny it, as some of them still may, henceforth it is accomplished.

The Washington correspondent of the New York *Herald* said:

The speech of Mr. Vallandigham in the House, to-day, produced a profound sensation. It was bold and able. The Republican side, also, listened intently to it.

The correspondent of the New York *Journal of Commerce* wrote:

Mr. Vallandigham's speech of to-day commanded marked attention, and those who do not agree with him in policy, give him credit for great abilities. He declared himself for the Union as it was, wanted Massachusetts to come back where she was in other days, and in the event of a final separation, prophesied that the North-west would go with the South, leaving the North-east "in the cold" – but still he battled, with great force, for a united country.

The correspondent of the Boston *Herald*, describing the speech and the effect of its delivery, says:

The long-expected speech of Vallandigham was delivered in the presence of a large audience in the galleries, and an unusual attendance on the floor. As soon as he arose to address the House, a large number of members of all parties gathered about him. His method of speaking is very attractive. Added to fine appearance of person, he has a good voice and gesture, and always speaks without notes. To-day he was bold and determined; and while his views may be regarded "as words of brilliant and polished treason," it was universally admitted to have been a most able speech from that stand-point. He spoke for an hour without interruption of any kind, and had most attentive listeners. I might add, that Vallandigham's great coolness amid the most heated discussions, is one of his peculiarities, and gives him decided advantages over more impassioned antagonists.

Of a similar character is the notice of the Washington correspondent of the St. Louis *Republican*, who writes:

> The peace speech of this Ohio Congressman, in the House, yesterday, was received with remarkable and respectful attention by the Republicans; and it is significant, as the first occasion when that party in Congress calmly listened to the semi-secession doctrines of Vallandigham, or any other peace man. It also attracts attention from every other quarter, and, to-day, is the general subject of comment in the city.

The Boston *Courier*, one of the ablest and most reliable of the Eastern papers, thus certifies its worth:

> This is an extremely able and a very honest speech. No one can read it and help believing that Mr. Vallandigham is a brave and honest man; and the speech itself affords irresistible evidence that it is his unfaltering devotion to the Union and the Constitution which has led those less loyal to stigmatize him as a secessionist and a traitor. His opinions will answer for themselves; but for its historical value and its strong grasp of the future, the speech ought to have the widest circulation.

The Philadelphia *Constitutional Union* has a bold, full, and unequivocal indorsement:

> The speech of this distinguished statesman and heroic defender of the Constitution, which we present in full to-day, is the crowning effort of his public life. It rises above the mere cant and humbug of present popularity, into the clear and comprehensive realm of unselfish statesmanship, and discusses the exciting and momentous topics of the day with that measure of candor which their importance demands. While proclaiming that peace is the only road which can lead to a satisfactory settlement of this vexed question, Mr. Vallandigham at the same time points out the principles upon which peace must rest, in order to make it permanent. He traces with a master hand the causes which have produced our national estrangement, shows how the difficulties have grown to their present gigantic proportions, and then appeals to the good sense of the nation to apply the remedy before it be too late. The speech should be read by every man in the country.

The above are fair specimens of the opinions of leading newspapers. Even the Republican press has limited its denunciations to the sentiments of the speech; and no paper whose opinions the public respect, has denied its great power and merit as a production of eloquence and logical skill. Even Forney, in the Washington *Chronicle*, says it is a *"logical and powerful speech."*

A few quotations will indicate the general tone of the Democratic press of Ohio. The Cincinnati *Enquirer* says:

> No speech has been made in Congress for years that has produced so great an effect in political circles, has been so universally admired for surpassing ability, for genuine and manly patriotism, for its wise statesmanship, as that of Mr. Vallandigham. It is a valuable and undying contribution to American Congressional eloquence, and will raise its author to a high place among the greatest men of the country. We do not know of a speech made by any of our eminent statesmen that has received higher praise or been more sought for.

The Columbus *Crisis*, edited by Gov. Medary, says:

> This is no ordinary speech – made by no ordinary man, and under circumstances the most remarkable which ever overtook any nation or people. It will be well if this nation ponders seriously and with judgment over the words of wisdom and burning eloquence which run through every paragraph, sentence, and line.
>
> The speech of Cato, in the Roman Senate, warning the people against the designs of Cæsar upon the liberties of the Roman people, contained not more truthful and thrilling interest to that great people about to be sacrificed at the shrine of ambition, than does this speech of the member from the Dayton district, but the true representative of the whole people, of all the States, and the nation as it was, collectively.

The Newark *Advocate* calls it "the ablest speech Mr. Vallandigham has ever made," and says: "No higher praise need be desired." The Bucyrus *Forum* says: "Every Democratic paper that comes, contains the great master-speech of Vallandigham," whom the *Forum* calls the "coming man." The Marion *Mirror* pronounces it "the greatest effort of the age," and says "it reflects undying credit upon its author." The Ohio *Democrat* calls it "the most able speech delivered in Congress during the war." The Stark County *Democrat* says: "This speech is in favor of stopping the war, and looking to other means for restoring the Union," and adds: "That is the right talk." With general agreement, the Democratic press everywhere, but especially in Ohio and other Western States, has bestowed higher commendations than upon any other speech delivered during the late Congressional session. And this is the estimate the public, also, are forming of the speech that here follows, and which is destined to find a prominent place in the literature these perilous times have created.

Mr. Vallandigham said:

> Mr. Speaker: Indorsed at the recent election, within the same district for which I still hold a seat on this floor, by a majority four times greater than ever before, I speak to-day in the name and by the authority of the people who, for six years, have intrusted me with the Office of a Representative. Loyal, in the true and highest sense of the word, to the Constitution and the Union, they have proved themselves devotedly attached to, and worthy of, the liberties to secure which the Union and the Constitution were established. With candor and freedom, therefore, as their Representative, and much plainness of speech, but with the dignity and decency due to this presence, I propose to consider the State of the Union to-day, and to inquire what the duty is of every public man and every citizen in this the very crisis of the Great Revolution.
>
> It is now two years, sir, since Congress assembled soon after the Presidential election. A sectional anti-slavery party had then just succeeded through the forms of the Constitution. For the first time a President had been chosen upon a platform of avowed hostility to an institution peculiar to nearly one half of the States of the Union, and who had himself proclaimed that there was an irrepressible conflict, because of that institution, between the States; and that the Union could not endure "part slave and part free." Congress met, therefore, in the midst of the profoundest agitation, not here only, but throughout the entire South. Revolution glared upon us. Repeated efforts for conciliation and compromise were attempted, in Congress and out of it. All were rejected by the party just coming into power, except only the promise in the last hours of the session, and that, too, against the consent of a majority of that party both in the Senate and House: that Congress – not the Executive – should never be authorized to abolish or interfere with slavery in the States where it existed. South Carolina seceded; Georgia, Alabama, Florida, Mississippi, Louisiana, and Texas speedily followed. The Confederate Government was established. The other slave States held back. Virginia demanded a peace congress. The commissioners met, and, after some time, agreed upon terms of final adjustment. But neither in the Senate nor the House were they allowed even a respectful consideration. The President elect left his home in February, and journeyed towards this capital, jesting as he came; proclaiming that the crisis was only artificial, and that "nobody was hurt." He entered this city under cover of night and in disguise.

On the 4th of March he was inaugurated, surrounded by soldiery; and, swearing to support the Constitution of the United States, announced in the same breath that the platform of his party should be the law unto him. From that moment all hope of peaceable adjustment fled. But for a little while, either with unsteadfast sincerity or in premeditated deceit, the policy of peace was proclaimed, even to the evacuation of Sumpter and the other Federal forts and arsenals in the seceded States. Why that policy was suddenly abandoned, time will fully disclose. But just after the spring elections, and the secret meeting in this city of the Governors of several Northern and Western States, a fleet carrying a large number of men was sent down ostensibly to provision Fort Sumpter. The authorities of South Carolina eagerly accepted the challenge, and bombarded the fort into surrender, while the fleet fired not a gun, but, just as soon as the flag was struck, bore away and returned to the North. It was Sunday, the 14th of April, 1861; and that day the President, in fatal haste, and without the advice or consent of Congress, issued his proclamation, dated the next day, calling out seventy-five thousand militia for three months, to repossess the forts, places, and property seized from the United States, and commanding the insurgents to disperse in twenty days. Again the gage was taken up by the South, and thus the flames of a civil war, the grandest, bloodiest, and saddest in history, lighted up the whole heavens. Virginia forthwith seceded. North Carolina, Tennessee, and Arkansas, followed; Delaware, Maryland, Kentucky, and Missouri were in a blaze of agitation, and within a week from the proclamation, the line of the Confederate States was transferred from the cotton States to the Potomac, and almost to the Ohio and the Missouri, and their population and fighting men doubled.

In the North and West, too, the storm raged with the fury of a hurricane. Never in history was anything equal to it. Men, women, and children, native and foreign born. Church and State, clergy and laymen, were all swept along with the current. Distinction of age, sex, station, party, perished in an instant. Thousands bent before the tempest; and here and there only was one found bold enough, foolhardy enough it may have been, to bend not, and him it smote as a consuming fire. The spirit of persecution for opinion's sake, almost extinct in the old world, now, by some mysterious transmigration, appeared incarnate in the new. Social relations were dissolved; friendships broken up; the ties of family and kindred snapped asunder. Stripes and hanging were every where threatened, sometimes executed. Assassination was invoked; slander sharpened his tooth; falsehood crushed truth to the earth; reason fled; madness reigned. Not justice only escaped to the skies, but peace returned to the bosom of God, whence she came. The gospel of love perished; hate sat enthroned, and the sacrifices of blood smoked upon every altar.

But the reign of the mob was inaugurated only to be supplanted by the iron domination of arbitrary power. Constitutional limitation was broken down; *habeas corpus* fell; liberty of the press, of speech, of the person, of the mails, of travel, of one's own house, and of religion; the right to bear arms, due process of law, judicial trial, trial by jury, trial at all; every badge and muniment of freedom in republican government or kingly government – all went down at a blow; and the chief law officer of the crown – I beg pardon, sir, but it is easy now to fall into this courtly language – the Attorney-General, first of all men, proclaimed in the United States the maxim of Roman servility: *Whatever pleases the President, that is law!* Prisoners of State were then first heard of here. Midnight and arbitrary arrests commenced; travel was interdicted; trade embargoed; passports demanded; bastiles were introduced; strange oaths invented; a secret police organized; "piping" began; informers multiplied; spies now first appeared in America. The right to declare war, to raise and support armies, and to provide and maintain a navy, was usurped by the Executive; and in a little more than two months a land and naval force of over three hundred thousand men was in the field or upon the sea. An army of public plunderers followed, and corruption struggled with power in friendly strife for the mastery at home.

On the 4th of July Congress met, not to seek peace; not to rebuke usurpation nor to restrain power; not certainly to deliberate; not even to legislate, but to register and ratify the edicts and acts of the Executive; and in your language, sir, upon the first day of the session, to invoke a universal baptism of fire and blood amid the roar of cannon and the din of battle. Free speech was had only at the risk of a prison; possibly of life. Opposition was silenced by the fierce clamor of "disloyalty." All business not of war was voted out of order. Five hundred thousand men, an immense navy, and two hundred and fifty millions of money were speedily granted. In twenty, at most in sixty days, the rebellion was to be crushed out. To doubt it was treason. Abject submission was demanded. Lay down your arms, sue for peace, surrender your leaders – forfeiture, death – this was the only language heard on this floor. The galleries responded; the corridors echoed; and contractors and place-men and other venal patriots everywhere gnashed upon the friends of peace as they passed by. In five weeks seventy-eight public and private acts and joint resolutions, with declaratory resolutions, in the Senate and House, quite as numerous, all full of slaughter, were hurried through without delay and almost without debate.

Thus was *civil war* inaugurated in America. Can any man to-day see the end of it?

And now pardon me, sir, if I pause here a moment to define my own position at that time upon this great question.

Sir, I am one of that number who have opposed abolitionism; or the political development of the anti-slavery sentiment of the North and West, from the beginning. In school, at college, at the bar, in public assemblies, in the Legislature, in Congress, boy and man, as a private citizen and in public life, in time of peace and in time of war, at all times and at every sacrifice, I have fought against it. It cost me ten years' exclusion from office and honor, at that period of life when honors are sweetest. No matter: I learned early to do right and to wait. Sir, it is but the development of the spirit of intermeddling, whose children are strife and murder. Cain troubled himself about the sacrifices of Abel, and slew him. Most of the wars, contentions, litigation, and bloodshed, from the beginning of time, have been its fruits. The spirit of non-intervention is the very spirit of peace and concord. I do not believe that if slavery had never existed here we would have had no sectional controversies. This very civil war might have happened fifty, perhaps a hundred years later. Other and stronger causes of discontent and of disunion, it may be, have existed between other States and sections, and are now being developed every day into maturity. The spirit of intervention assumed the form of Abolitionism because slavery was odious in name, and by association to the Northern mind, and because it was that which most obviously marks the different civilizations of the two sections. The South herself, in her early and later efforts to rid herself of it, had exposed the weak and offensive parts of slavery to the world. Abolition intermeddling taught her at last to search for and defend the assumed social, economic, and political merit and values of the institution. But there never was an hour from the beginning when it did not seem to me as clear as the sun at broad noon, that the agitation in any form, in the North and West, of the slavery question, must sooner or later end in disunion and civil war.

This was the opinion and prediction for years of Whig and Democratic statesmen alike; and after the unfortunate dissolution of the Whig party, in 1854, and the organization of the present Republican party upon an exclusively anti-slavery and sectional basis, the event was inevitable; because, in the then existing temper of the public mind, and after the education through the press, and by the pulpit, the lecture and the political canvass for twenty years, of a generation, taught to hate slavery and the South, the success of that party, possessed, as it was, of every engine of political, business, social, and religious influence, was certain. It was only a question of time, and short time. Such was its strength, indeed, that I do not believe that the union of the Democratic party, in 1860, on any candidate, even though he had been supported also by the entire so-called conservative or anti-Lincoln vote of the country, would have availed to defeat it; and if it had, the success of the Abolition party would only have been postponed four years longer. The disease had fastened too strongly upon the system to be healed until it had run its course. The doctrine of the "irrepressible conflict" had been taught too long, and accepted too widely and earnestly, to die out until it should culminate in secession and disunion; and, if coercion were resorted to, then in civil war. I believed from the first that it was the purpose of some of the apostles of that doctrine to force a collision between the North and the South, either to bring about a separation, or to find a vain, but bloody pretext for abolishing slavery in the States. In any event, I knew, or I thought I knew, that the end was certain collision, and death to the Union.

Believing thus, I have for years past denounced those who taught that doctrine with all the vehemence, the bitterness, if you choose – I thought it a righteous, a patriotic bitterness – of an earnest and impassioned nature. Thinking thus, I forewarned all who believed the doctrine, or followed the party which taught it, with a sincerity and a depth of conviction as profound as ever penetrated the heart of man. And when, for eight years past, over and over again, I have proclaimed to the people that the success of a sectional anti-slavery party would be the beginning of disunion and civil war in America, I believed it. I did. I had read history, and studied human nature, and meditated for years upon the character of our institutions and form of government, and of the people South as well as North; and I could not doubt the event. But the people did not believe me, nor those older and wiser and greater than I. They rejected the prophesy, and stoned the prophets. The candidate of the Republican party was chosen President. Secession began. Civil war was imminent. It was no petty insurrection; no temporary combination to obstruct the execution of the laws in certain States; but a revolution, systematic, deliberate, determined, and with the consent of a majority of the people of each State which seceded. Causeless it may have been; wicked it may have been; but there it was; not to be railed at, still less to be laughed at, but to be dealt with by statesmen as a fact. No display of vigor or force alone, however sudden or great, could have arrested it, even at the outset. It was disunion at last. The wolf had come. But civil war had not yet followed. In my deliberate and most solemn judgment, there was but one wise and masterly mode of dealing with it. Non-coercion would avert civil war, and compromise crush out both Abolitionism and Secession. The parent and the child would thus both perish. But a resort to force would at once precipitate war, hasten secession, extend disunion, and, while it lasted, utterly cut off all hope of compromise. I believe, that war, if long enough continued, would be final, eternal disunion. I said it; I meant it; and, accordingly, to the utmost of my ability and influence, I exerted myself in behalf of the policy of non-coercion. It was adopted by Mr. Buchanan's Administration, with the almost unanimous consent of the Democratic and Constitutional Union parties in and out of Congress; and, in February, with the concurrence of a majority of the Republican party in the Senate and this House. But that party, most disastrously for the country, refused all compromise. How, indeed, could they accept any? That which the South demanded, and the Democratic and conservative parties of the North and West were willing to grant, and which alone could avail to keep the peace and save the Union, implied a surrender of the sole vital element of the party and its platform – of the very principle, in fact, upon which it had just won the contest for the Presidency; not, indeed, by a majority of the popular vote – the majority was nearly a million against it – but under the forms of the Constitution. Sir, the crime, the "high crime" of the Republican party was not so much its refusal to compromise, as its original organization upon a basis and doctrine wholly inconsistent with the stability of the Constitution and the peace of the Union.

But to resume: the session of Congress expired. The President elect was inaugurated; and now, if only the policy of non-coercion could be maintained, and war thus averted, time would do its work in the North and the South, and final peaceable adjustment and reunion be secured. Some time in March it was announced that the President had resolved to continue the policy of his predecessor, and even go a step further, and evacuate Sumter and the other Federal forts and arsenals in the seceded States. His own party acquiesced; the whole country rejoiced. The policy of non-coercion had triumphed, and for once, sir, in my life, I found myself in an immense majority. No man then pretended that a Union founded in consent, could be cemented by force. Nay, more, the President and the Secretary of State went further. Said Mr. Seward, in an official diplomatic letter to Mr. Adams:

> For these reasons, he [the President] would not be disposed to reject a cardinal dogma of theirs [the Secessionists], namely, that the Federal Government could not reduce the seceding States to obedience by conquest, although he were disposed to question that proposition. *But in fact the President willingly accepts it as true. Only an imperial or despotic Government could subjugate thoroughly disaffected and insurrectionary members of the State.*

Pardon me, sir, but I beg to know whether this conviction of the President and his Secretary, is not the philosophy of the persistent and most vigorous efforts made by this Administration, and first of all through this same Secretary, the moment war broke out, and ever since till the late elections, to convert the United States into an imperial or despotic Government? But Mr. Seward adds, and I agree with him:

> This Federal Republican system of ours is, of all forms of government, the very one which is most unfitted for such a labor.

This, sir, was on the 10th of April, and yet that very day the fleet was under sail for Charleston. The policy of peace had been abandoned. Collision followed; the militia were ordered out; civil war began.

Now, sir, on the 14th of April, I believed that coercion would bring on war, and war disunion. More than that, I believed, what you all in your hearts believe to-day, that the South could never be conquered – never. And not that only, but I was satisfied – and you of the Abolition party have now proved it to the world – that the secret but real purpose of the war was to abolish slavery in the States. In any event, I did not doubt that, whatever might be the momentary impulses of those in power, and whatever pledges they might make, in the midst of the fury, for the Constitution, the Union, and the flag, yet the natural and inexorable logic of revolutions would, sooner or later, drive them into that policy, and with it to its final but inevitable result, the change of our present democratical form of government into an imperial despotism.

These were my convictions on the 14th of April. Had I changed them on the 15th, when I read the President's proclamation, and become convinced that I had been wrong all my life, and that all history was a fable, and all human nature false in its development from the beginning of time, I would have changed my public conduct also. But my convictions did not change. I thought that, if war was disunion on the 14th of April, it was equally disunion on the 15th, and at all times. Believing this, I could not, as an honest man, a Union man, and a patriot, lend an active support to the war; and I did not. I had rather my right arm were plucked from its socket and cast into eternal burnings than, with my convictions, to have thus defiled my soul with the guilt of moral perjury. Sir, I was not taught in that school which proclaims that "all is fair in politics." I loathe, abhor and detest the execrable maxim. I stamp upon it. No State can endure a single generation whose public men practice it. Whoever teaches it is a corrupter of youth. What we most want in these times, and at all times, is honest and independent public men. That man who is dishonest in politics, is not honest at heart in anything; and sometimes moral cowardice is dishonesty. Do right; and trust to God, and truth, and the people. Perish office, perish honors, perish life itself – but do the thing that is right, and do it like a man. I did it. Certainly, sir, I could not doubt what he must suffer who dare defy the opinions and the passions, not to say the madness, of twenty millions of people. Had I not read history? Did I not know human nature? But I appealed to Time; and right nobly hath the Avenger answered me.

I did not support the war; and to-day I bless God, that not the smell of so much as one drop of its blood is upon my garments. Sir, I censure no brave man who rushed patriotically into this war; neither will I quarrel with any one, here or elsewhere, who gave to it an honest support. Had their convictions been mine, I, too, would doubtless have done as they did. With my convictions I could not.

But I was a Representative. War existed – by whose act no matter

– not mine. The President, the Senate, the House, and the country, all said that there should be war – war for the Union; a union of consent and goodwill. Our Southern brethren were to be whipped back into love and fellowship at the point of the bayonet. O, monstrous delusion! I can comprehend a war to compel a people to accept a master; to change a form of government; to give up territory; to abolish a domestic institution – in short, a war of conquest and subjugation; but a war for union! Was the Union thus made? Was it ever thus preserved? Sir, history will record that, after nearly six thousand years of folly and wickedness in every form and administration of government – theocratic, democratic, monarchic, oligarchic, despotic and mixed – it was reserved to American statesmanship, in the nineteenth century of the Christian era, to try the grand experiment, on a scale the most costly and gigantic in its proportions, of creating love by force, and developing fraternal affection by war! And history will record, too, on the same page, the utter, disastrous, and most bloody failure of the experiment.

But to return: the country was at war; and I belonged to that school of politics which teaches that when we are at war, the Government – I do not mean the Executive alone, but the Government – is entitled to demand and have, without resistance, such number of men, and such amount of money and supplies generally, as may be necessary for the war, until an appeal can be had to the people. Before that tribunal alone, in the first instance, must the question of the continuance of the war be tried. This was Mr. Calhoun's opinion, and he laid it down very broadly and strongly in a speech on the loan bill, in 1841. Speaking of supplies, he said:

> I hold that there is a distinction in this respect between a state of peace and war. In the latter, the right of withholding supplies ought ever to be held subordinate to the energetic and successful prosecution of the war. I go further, and regard the withholding supplies, *with a view of forcing the country into a dishonorable peace,* as not only to be what it has been called, moral treason, but very little short of actual treason itself.

Upon this principle, sir, he acted afterward in the Mexican War. Speaking of that war, in 1847, he said:

> Every Senator knows that I was opposed to the war; but none knows but myself the depth of that opposition. With my conception of its character and consequences, it was impossible for me to vote for it.

And again, in 1848:

> But, after the war was declared, by authority of the Government, *I acquiesced in what I could not prevent, and which it was impossible for me to arrest;* and I then felt it to be my duty to limit my efforts to *give such direction to the war as would, as far as possible, prevent the evils and dan-*

gers with which it threatened the country and its institutions.

Sir, I adopt all this as my own position and my defense; though, perhaps, in a civil war I might fairly go further in opposition. I could not, with my convictions, vote men and money for this war, and I would not, as a Representative, vote against them. I meant that, without opposition, the President might take all the men and all the money he should demand, and then to hold him to a strict accountability before the people for the results. Not believing the soldiers responsible for the war, or its purposes, or its consequences, I have never withheld my vote where their separate interests were concerned. But I have denounced, from the beginning, the usurpations and the infractions, one and all, of law and Constitution, by the President and those under him; their repeated and persistent arbitrary arrests, the suspension of *habeas corpus,* the violation of freedom of the mails, of the private house, of the press and of speech, and all the other multiplied wrongs and outrages upon public liberty and private right, which have made this country one of the worst despotisms on earth for the past twenty months; and I will continue to rebuke and denounce them to the end; and the people, thank God! have at last heard and heeded, and rebuked them, too. To the record and to time I appeal again for my justification.

And now, sir, I recur to the state of the Union to-day. What is it? Sir, twenty months have elapsed, but the rebellion is not crushed out; its military power has not been broken; the insurgents have not dispersed. The Union is not restored; nor the Constitution maintained; nor the laws enforced. Twenty, sixty, ninety, three hundred, six hundred days have passed; a thousand millions been expended; and three hundred thousand lives lost or bodies mangled; and to-day the Confederate flag is still near the Potomac and the Ohio, and the Confederate Government stronger, many times, than at the beginning. Not a State has been restored, not any part of any State has voluntarily returned to the Union. And has anything been wanting that Congress, or the States, or the people in their most generous enthusiasm, their most impassionate patriotism, could bestow? Was it power? And did not the party of the Executive control the entire Federal Government, every State government, every county, every city, town and village in the North and West? Was it patronage? All belonged to it. Was it influence? What more? Did not the school, the college, the church, the press, the secret orders, the municipality, the corporation, railroads, telegraphs, express companies, the voluntary association, all, all yield it to the utmost? Was it unanimity? Never was an Administration so supported in England or America. Five men and half a score of newspapers made up the Opposition. Was it enthusiasm? The enthusiasm was fanatical. There has been nothing like it since the Crusades. Was it confidence? Sir, the faith of the people exceeded that of the patriarch.

They gave up Constitution, law, right, liberty, all at your demand for arbitrary power that the rebellion might, as you promised, be crushed out in three months, and the Union restored. Was credit needed? You took control of a country, young, vigorous, and inexhaustible in wealth and resources, and of a Government almost free from public debt, and whose good faith had never been tarnished. Your great national loan bubble failed miserably, as it deserved to fail; but the bankers and merchants of Philadelphia, New York and Boston lent you more than their entire banking capital. And when that failed too, you forced credit by declaring your paper promises to pay, a legal tender for all debts. Was money wanted? You had all the revenues of the United States, diminished indeed, but still in gold. The whole wealth of the country, to the last dollar, lay at your feet. Private individuals, municipal corporations, the State governments, all, in their frenzy, gave you money or means with reckless prodigality. The great Eastern cities lent you $150,000,000. Congress voted, first, $250,000,000, and next $500,000,000 more in loans; and then, first $50,000,000, next $10,000,000, then $90,000,000, and, in July last, $150,000,000 in Treasury notes; and the Secretary has issued also a paper "postage currency," in sums as low as five cents, limited in amount only by his discretion. Nay, more: already since the 4th of July, 1861, this House has appropriated $2,017,864,000, almost every dollar without debate, and without a recorded vote. A thousand millions have been expended since the 15th of April, 1861; and a public debt or liability of $1,500,000,000 already incurred. And to support all this stupendous outlay and indebtedness, a system of taxation, direct and indirect, has been inaugurated, the most onerous and unjust ever imposed upon any but a conquered people.

Money and credit, then, you have had in prodigal profusion. And were men wanted? More than a million rushed to arms! Seventy-five thousand first (and the country stood aghast at the multitude), then eighty-three thousand more were demanded; and three hundred and ten thousand responded to the call. The President next asked for four hundred thousand, and Congress, in their generous confidence, gave him five hundred thousand; and, not to be outdone, he took six hundred and thirty-seven thousand. Half of these melted away in their first campaign; and the President demanded three hundred thousand more for the war, and then drafted yet another three hundred thousand for nine months. The fabled hosts of Xerxes have been out-numbered. And yet victory, strangely, follows the standard of the foe. From Great Bethel to Vicksburg, the battle has not been to the strong. Yet every disaster, except the last, has been followed by a call for more troops, and every time, so far, they have been promptly furnished. From the beginning the war has been conducted like a political campaign, and it has been the folly of the party in power that they have assumed, that numbers alone would win the field in a contest not with ballots but with musket and sword.

But numbers, you have had almost without number – the largest, best appointed, best armed, fed, and clad host of brave men, well organized and well disciplined, ever marshaled. A Navy, too, not the most formidable perhaps, but the most numerous and gallant, and the costliest in the world, and against a foe, almost without a navy at all. Thus, with twenty millions of people, and every element of strength and force at command – power, patronage, influence, unanimity, enthusiasm, confidence, credit, money, men, an Army and a Navy the largest and the noblest ever set in the field, or afloat upon the sea; with the support, almost servile, of every State, county, and municipality in the North and West, with a Congress swift to do the bidding of the Executive; without opposition anywhere at home; and with an arbitrary power which neither the Czar of Russia, nor the Emperor of Austria dare exercise; yet after nearly two years of more vigorous prosecution of war than ever recorded in history; after more skirmishes, combats and battles than Alexander, Cæsar, or the first Napoleon ever fought in any five years of their military career, you have utterly, signally, disastrously – I will not say ignominiously – failed to subdue ten millions of "rebels," whom you had taught the people of the North and West not only to hate, but to despise. Rebels, did I say? Yes, your fathers were rebels, or your grandfathers. He, who now before me on canvas looks down so sadly upon us, the false, degenerate, and imbecile guardians of the great Republic which he founded, was a rebel. And yet we, cradled ourselves in rebellion, and who have fostered and fraternized with every insurrection in the nineteenth century everywhere throughout the globe, would now, forsooth, make the word "rebel" a reproach. Rebels certainly they are; but all the persistent and stupendous efforts of the most gigantic warfare of modern times have, through your incompetency and folly, availed nothing to crush them out, cut off though they have been, by your blockade, from all the world, and dependent only upon their own courage and resources. And yet, they were to be utterly conquered and subdued in six weeks, or three months! Sir, my judgment was made up, and expressed from the first. I learned it from Chatham: "My lords, you cannot conquer America." And you have not conquered the South. You never will. It is not in the nature of things possible; much less under your auspices. But money you have expended without limit, and blood poured out like water. Defeat, debt, taxation, sepulchers, these are your trophies. In vain, the people gave you treasure, and the soldier yielded up his life. "Fight, tax, emancipate, let these," said the gentleman from Maine (Mr. Pike), at the last session, "be the trinity of our salvation." Sir, they have become the trinity of your deep damnation. The war for the Union is, in your hands, a most bloody and costly failure. The President confessed it on the 22d of September, solemnly, officially, and under the broad seal of the United States. And he has now repeated the confession. The priests and rabbis of Abolition taught him that

God would not prosper such a cause. War for the Union was abandoned; war for the negro openly begun, and with stronger battalions than before. With what success? Let the dead at Fredericksburg and Vicksburg answer.

And now, sir, can this war continue? Whence the money to carry it on? Where the men? Can you borrow? From whom? Can you tax more? Will the people bear it? Wait till you have collected what is already levied. How many millions more of "legal tender" – to-day forty-seven per cent. below the par of gold – can you float? Will men enlist now at any price? Ah, sir, it is easier to die at home. I beg pardon; but I trust I am not "discouraging enlistments." If I am, then first arrest Lincoln, Stanton, Halleck, and some of your other generals, and I will retract; yes, I will recant. But can you draft again? Ask New England – New York. Ask Massachusetts. Where are the nine hundred thousand? Ask not Ohio – the Northwest. She thought you in earnest, and gave you all, all – more than you demanded.

> The wife whose babe first smiled that day,
> The fair, fond bride of yester eve,
> And aged sire and matron gray,
> Saw the loved warriors haste away,
> And deemed it sin to grieve.

Sir, in blood she has atoned for her credulity; and now there is mourning in every house, and distress and sadness in every heart. Shall she give you any more?

But ought this war to continue? I answer, no – not a day, not an hour. What then? Shall we separate? Again I answer, no, no, no! What then? And now, sir, I come to the grandest and most solemn problem of statesmanship from the beginning of time; and to the God of heaven, illuminer of hearts and minds, I would humbly appeal for some measure, at least, of light and wisdom and strength to explore and reveal the dark but possible future of this land.

Can the Union of these States be restored? How shall it be done?

And why not? Is it historically impossible? Sir, the frequent civil wars and conflicts between the States of Greece did not prevent their cordial union to resist the Persian invasion; nor did even the thirty years Peloponnesian war, springing, in part, from the abduction of slaves, and embittered and disastrous as it was – let Thucidides speak – wholly destroy the fellowship of those States. The wise Romans ended the three years Social War, after many bloody battles and much atrocity, by admitting the States of Italy to all the rights and privileges of Roman citizenship – the very object to secure which those States had taken up arms. The border wars between Scotland and England, running through centuries, did not prevent the final union, in peace and by adjustment, of the two kingdoms under one monarch.

Compromise did at last what ages of coercion and attempted conquest had failed to effect. England kept the crown, while Scotland gave the king to wear it; and the memories of Wallace, and the Bruce of Bannockburn, became part of the glories of British history. I pass by the union of Ireland with England – a union of force, which God and just men abhor; and yet precisely "the Union as it should be" of the Abolitionists of America. Sir, the rivalries of the houses of York and Lancaster, filled all England with cruelty and slaughter; yet compromise and intermarriage ended the strife at last, and the white rose and the red were blended in one. Who dreamed a month before the death of Cromwell that in two years the people of England, after twenty years of civil war and usurpation, would, with great unanimity, restore the house of Stuart, in the person of its most worthless prince, whose father, but eleven years before, they had beheaded? And who could have foretold, in the beginning of 1812, that within some three years, Napoleon would be in exile upon a desert island, and the Bourbons restored? Armed foreign intervention did it; but it is a strange history. Or who then expected to see a nephew of Napoleon, thirty-five years later, with the consent of the people, supplant the Bourbon, and reign Emperor of France? Sir, many States and people, once separate, have become united in the course of ages, through natural causes, and without conquest; but I remember a single instance only, in history, of States or peoples once united, and speaking the same language, who have been forced permanently asunder by civil strife or war, unless they were separated by distance or vast natural boundaries. The secession of the Ten Tribes is the exception: these parted without actual war; and their subsequent history is not encouraging to secession. But when Moses, the greatest of all statesmen, would secure a distinct nationality and government to the Hebrews, he left Egypt, and established his people in a distant country. In modern times, the Netherlands, three centuries ago, won their independence by the sword; but France and the English channel separated them from Spain. So did our Thirteen Colonies; but the Atlantic ocean divided us from England. So did Mexico, and other Spanish colonies in America, but the same ocean divided them from Spain. Cuba and the Canadas still adhere to the parent Governments. And who now, North or South, in Europe or America, looking into history, shall presumptuously say, that because of civil war the reunion of these States is impossible? War, indeed, while it lasts, is disunion, and, if it lasts long enough, will be final, eternal separation first, and anarchy and despotism afterward. Hence, I would hasten peace now, to-day, by every honorable appliance.

    Are there physical causes which reader reunion impracticable? None. Where other causes do not control, rivers unite; but mountains, deserts, and great bodies of water – *oceani dissociabiles* – separate a people. Vast forests originally, and the lakes now also, divide us – not very widely or wholly – from the Canadas, though we speak the same language, and are similar in manners, laws, and institutions. Our chief navigable rivers run from North to South. Most of our bays and arms of the sea take the same direction. So do our ranges of mountains. Natural causes all tend to Union, except as between the Pacific coast and the country east of the Rocky mountains to the Atlantic. It is "manifest destiny." Union is empire. Hence, hitherto we have continually extended our territory, and the Union with it, South and West. The Louisiana purchase, Florida, and Texas all attest it. We passed desert and forest, and scaled even the Rocky mountains, to extend the Union to the Pacific. Sir, there is no natural boundary between the North and the South, and no line of latitude upon which to separate; and if ever a line of longitude shall be established it will be east of the Mississippi valley. The Alleghanies are no longer a barrier. Highways ascend them everywhere, and the railroad now climbs their summits, and spans their chasms, or penetrates their rockiest sides. The electric telegraph follows, and, stretching its connecting wires along the clouds, there mingles its vocal lightnings with the fires of heaven.

But if disunionists in the East will force a separation of any of these States, and a boundary, purely conventional, is at last to be marked out, it must, and it will be either from Lake Erie upon the shortest line to the Ohio river, or from Manhattan to the Canadas.

And now, sir, is there any difference of race here so radical as to forbid reunion? I do not refer to the negro race, styled now, in unctuous official phrase, by the President, "Americans of African descent." Certainly, sir, there are two white races in the United States, both from the same common stock, and yet so distinct – one of them so peculiar – that they develop different forms of civilization, and might belong, almost, to different types of mankind. But the boundary of these two races is not at all marked by the line which divides the slaveholding from the non-slaveholding States. If race is to be the geographical limit of disunion, then Mason and Dixon's can never be the line.

Next, sir, do not the causes which, in the beginning, impelled to Union, still exist in their utmost force and extent? What were they?

First, the common descent – and, therefore, consanguinity – of the great mass of the people from the Anglo-Saxon stock. Had the Canadas been settled, originally, by the English, they would, doubtless, have followed the fortunes of the Thirteen Colonies. Next, a common language, one of the strongest of the ligaments which bind a people. Had we been contiguous to Great Britain, either the causes which led to a separation would have never existed, or else been speedily removed; or, afterward, we would long since have been reunited as equals, and with all the rights of Englishmen. And along with these were similar, at least not essentially dissimilar, manners, habits, laws, religion, and institutions of all kinds, except one. The common defense was another powerful incentive, and is named in the Constitution as one among the objects of the "more perfect Union" of 1787. Stronger yet than all these, perhaps, but made up of all of them, was a common interest. Variety of climate and soil, and, therefore, of production, implying, also, extent of country, is not an element of separation, but, added to contiguity, becomes a part of the ligament of interest, and is one of its toughest strands. Variety of production is the parent of the earliest commerce and trade; and these, in their full development, are, as between foreign nations, hostages for peace; and between States and people united, they are the firmest bonds of union. But, after all, the strongest of the many original impelling causes to the Union was the securing of domestic tranquillity. The statesmen of 1787 well knew that between thirteen independent but contiguous States, without a natural boundary, and with nothing to separate them, except the machinery of similar governments, there must be a perpetual, in fact, an "irrepressible conflict" of jurisdiction and interest, which, there being no other common arbiter, could only be terminated by the conflict of the sword. And the statesmen of 1863 ought to know that two or more confederate governments, made up of similar States, having no natural boundary either, and separated only by different governments, cannot endure long together in peace, unless one or more of them be either too pusillanimous for rivalry, or too insignificant to provoke it, or too weak to resist aggression.

These, sir, along with the establishment of justice, and the securing of the general welfare, and of the blessings of liberty to themselves and their posterity, made up the causes and, motives which impelled our fathers to the Union at first.

And now, sir, what one of them is wanting? What one diminished? On the contrary, many of them are stronger to-day than in the beginning. Migration and intermarriage have strengthened the ties of consanguinity. Commerce, trade, and production have immensely multiplied. Cotton, almost unknown here in 1787, is now the chief product and export of the country. It has set in motion three-fourths of the spindles of New England, and given employment, directly or remotely, to full half the shipping, trade, and commerce of the United States. More than that: cotton has kept the peace between England and America for thirty years; and, had the people of the North been as wise and practical as the statesmen of Great Britain, it would have maintained union and peace here. But we are being taught in our first century, and at our own cost, the lessons which England learned through the long and bloody experience of eight hundred years. We shall be wiser next time. Let not cotton be king, but peace-maker, and inherit the blessing.

A common interest, then, still remains to us. And union for the common defense, at the end of this war, taxed, indebted, impoverished, exhausted, as both sections must be, and with foreign fleets and armies around us, will be fifty-fold more essential than ever before. And finally, sir, without union, our domestic tranquillity must forever remain unsettled. If it cannot be maintained within the Union, how, then, outside of it, without an exodus or colonization of the people of one section or the other to a distant country? Sir, I repeat, that two governments so interlinked and bound together every way, by physical and social ligaments, cannot exist in peace without a common arbiter. Will treaties bind us? What better treaty than the Constitution? What more solemn, more durable? Shall we settle our disputes then by arbitration and compromise? Sir, let us arbitrate and compromise now, inside of the Union. Certainly it will be quite as easy.

And now, sir, to all these original causes and motives which impelled to Union at first, must be added certain artificial ligaments, which eighty years of association under a common Government have most fully developed. Chief among these are canals, steam navigation, railroads, express companies, the post-office, the newspaper press, and that terrible agent of good and evil mixed – "spirit of health, and yet goblin damned," if free, the gentlest minister of truth and liberty, when enslaved, the supplest instrument of falsehood and tyranny – the magnetic telegraph. All these have multiplied the speed or the quantity of trade, travel, communication, migration, and intercourse of all kinds, between the different States and sections; and thus, so long as a healthy condition of the body-politic continued, they became powerful cementing agencies of union. The numerous voluntary associations, artistic, literary, charitable, social, and scientific, until corrupted and made fanatical; the various ecclesiastical organizations, until they divided; and the political parties, so long as they remained all national, and not sectional, were also among the strong ties which bound us together. And yet all of these, perverted and abused for some years in the hands of bad or fanatical men, became still more powerful instrumentalities in the fatal work of disunion; just as the veins and arteries of the human body, designed to convey the vitalizing fluid through every part of it, will carry also, and with increased rapidity it may be, the subtle poison which takes life away. Nor is this all. It was through their agency that the imprisoned winds of civil war were all let loose at first with such sudden and appalling fury; and, kept in motion by political power, they have ministered to that fury ever since. But, potent alike for good and evil, they may yet, under the control of the people, and in the hands of wise, good, and patriotic men, be made the most effective agencies, under Providence, in the reunion of these States.

Other ties, also, less material in their nature, but hardly less persuasive in their influence, have grown up under the Union. Long association, a common history, national reputation, treaties and diplomatic intercourse abroad, admission of new States, a common jurisprudence, great men whose names and fame are the patrimony of the whole country, patriotic music and songs, common battle-fields, and glory won under the same flag. These make up the poetry of the Union; and yet, as in the marriage relation, and the family, with similar influences, they are stronger than hooks of steel. He was a wise statesman, though he may never have held an office, who said: "Let me write the songs of a people, and I care not who makes their laws." Why is the "Marseillaise" prohibited in France? Sir, "Hail Columbia" and the "Star-Spangled Banner" – Pennsylvania gave us one, and Maryland the other – have done more for the Union than all the legislation and all the debates in this capitol for forty years; and they will do more yet again than all your armies, though you call out another million of men into the field. Sir, I would add "Yankee Doodle;" but first let me be assured that Yankee Doodle loves the Union more than he hates the slaveholder.[1]

And now, sir, I propose to briefly consider the causes which led to disunion and the present civil war; and to inquire whether they are eternal and ineradicable in their nature, and at the same time powerful enough to overcome all the causes and considerations which impel to reunion.

Having, two years ago, discussed fully and elaborately the more abstruse and remote causes whence civil commotions in all Governments, and those also which are peculiar to our complex and Federal system, such as the consolidating tendencies of the General Government, because of executive power and patronage, and of the tariff, and taxation and disbursement generally, all unjust and burdensome to the West equally with the South, I pass them by now.

What then, I ask, is the immediate, direct cause of disunion and this civil war? Slavery, it is answered. Sir, that is the philosophy of the rustic in the play – "that a great cause of the night, is lack of the sun." Certainly slavery was in one sense – very obscure, indeed – the cause of the war. Had there been no slavery here, this particular war about slavery would never have been waged. In a like sense, the Holy Sepulcher was the cause of the war of the Crusades, and had Troy or Carthage never existed, there never would have been Trojan or Carthaginian war, and no such personages as Hector and Hannibal; and no *Iliad* or *Æneid* would ever have been written. But far better say that the negro is the cause of the war; for had there been no negro here, there would be no war just now. What then? Exterminate him? Who demands it? Colonize him? How? Where? When? At whose cost? Sir, let us have an end of this folly.

But slavery is the cause of the war. Why? Because the South obstinately and wickedly refused to restrict or abolish it at the demand of the

---

1. In truth, the song was written in derision by a British officer, and not by an American.

philosophers or fanatics and demagogues of the North and West. Then, sir, it was abolition, the purpose to abolish or interfere with and hem in slavery, which caused disunion and war. Slavery is only the *subject,* but Abolition the cause of this civil war. It was the persistent and determined agitation in the free States of the question of abolishing slavery in the South, because of the alleged "irrepressible conflict" between the forms of labor in the two sections, or in the false and mischievous cant of the day, between freedom and slavery, that forced a collision of arms at last. Sir, that conflict was not confined to the Territories. It was expressly proclaimed by its apostles, as between the States also – against the institution of domestic slavery everywhere. But, assuming the platforms of the Republican party as a standard, and stating the case most strongly in favor of that party, it was the refusal of the South to consent that slavery should be excluded from the Territories, that led to the continued agitation, North and South, of that question, and finally to disunion and civil war. Sir, I will not be answered now by the old clamor about "the aggressions of the slave power." That miserable specter, that unreal mockery, has been exorcised and expelled by debt and taxation and blood. If that power did govern this country for the sixty years preceding this terrible revolution, then the sooner this Administration and Government return to the principles and policy of Southern statesmanship, the better for the country; and that, sir, is already, or soon will be, the judgment of the people. But I deny that it was the "slave power" that governed for so many years, and so wisely and well. It was the Democratic party, and its principles and policy, molded and controlled, indeed, largely by Southern statesmen. Neither will I be stopped by that other cry of mingled fanaticism and hypocrisy, about the sin and barbarism of African slavery. Sir, I see more of barbarism and sin, a thousand times, in the continuance of this war, the dissolution of the Union, the breaking up of this Government, and the enslavement of the white race, by debt and taxes and arbitrary power. The day of fanatics and sophists and enthusiasts, thank God, is gone at last; and though the age of chivalry may not, the age of practical statesmanship is about to return. Sir, I accept the language and intent of the Indiana resolution, to the full – "that in considering terms of settlement, we will look only to the welfare, peace, and safety of the white race, without reference to the effect that settlement may have upon the condition of the African." And when we have done this, my word for it, the safety, peace, and welfare of the African will have been best secured. Sir, there is fifty-fold less of anti-slavery sentiment to-day in the West than there was two years ago; and if this war be continued, there will be still less a year hence. The people there begin, at last, to comprehend, that domestic slavery in the South is a question, not of morals, or religion, or humanity, but a form of labor, perfectly compatible with the dignity of free white labor in the same community, and with national vigor, power, and prosperity, and especially with military strength. They have learned, or begin to learn, that the evils of the system affect the master alone, or the community and State in which it exists; and that we of the free States partake of all the material benefits of the institution, unmixed with any part of its mischief. They believe, also, in the subordination of the negro race to the white, where they both exist together, and that the condition of subordination, as established in the South, is far better every way, for the negro, than the hard servitude of poverty, degradation, and crime, to which he is subjected in the free States. All this, sir, may be "pro-slaveryism," if there be such a word. Perhaps it is; but the people of the West begin now to think it wisdom and good sense. We will not establish slavery in our own midst; neither will we abolish it, or interfere with it outside of our own limits.

Sir, an anti-slavery paper in New York [the *Tribune*], the most influential, and therefore most dangerous, of all of that class – it would exhibit more of dignity, and command more of influence, if it were always to discuss public questions and public men with a decent respect – laying aside now the epithets of "secessionist" and "traitor," has returned to its ancient political nomenclature, and calls certain members of this House "pro-slavery." Well, sir, in the old sense of the term, as applied to the Democratic party, I will not object. I said years ago, and it is a fitting time now to repeat it:

> If to love my country; to cherish the Union; to revere the Constitution; if to abhor the madness and hate the treason, which would lift up a sacrilegious hand against either; if to read that in the past, to behold it in the present, to foresee it in the future of this land, which is of more value to us, and to the world, for ages to come, than all the multiplied millions who have inhabited Africa from the creation to this day! – if this it is to be pro-slavery, then in every nerve, fiber, vein, bone, tendon, joint, and ligament, from the topmost hair of the head to the last extremity of the foot, I am all over and altogether a pro-slavery man.

And now, sir, I come to the great and controlling question within which the whole issue of union or disunion is bound up: Is there "an irrepressible conflict" between the slaveholding and non-slave-holding States? Must "the cotton and rice fields of South Carolina, and the sugar plantations of Louisiana," in the language of Mr. Seward, "be ultimately tilled by free labor, and Charleston and New Orleans become marts for legitimate merchandise alone, or else the rye fields and wheat fields of Massachusetts and New York again be surrendered by their farmers to slave culture and the production of slaves, and Boston and New York become, once more markets for trade in the bodies and souls of men?" If so, then there is an end of all union, and forever. You cannot abolish slavery by the sword; still less by proclamations, though the President were to "proclaim" every month. Of what possible avail was his proclamation of September? Did the South submit? Was she even alarmed? And yet, he has now fulmined another "bull against the comet" – *brutum fulmen* – and, threatening servile insurrection with all its horrors, has yet coolly appealed to the judgment of mankind, and invoked the blessing of the God of peace and love! But declaring it a military necessity, an essential measure of war to subdue the rebels, yet, with admirable wisdom, he expressly exempts from its operation the only States, and parts of States, in the South, where he has the military power to execute it.

Neither, sir, can you abolish slavery by argument. As well attempt to abolish marriage, or the relation of paternity. The South is resolved to maintain it at every hazard, and by every sacrifice; and if "this Union cannot endure, part slave and part free," then it is already and finally dissolved. Talk not to me of "West Virginia." Tell me not of Missouri, trampled under the feet of your soldiery. As well talk to me of Ireland. Sir, the destiny of those States must abide the issue of the war. But Kentucky you may find tougher. And Maryland – "E'en in her ashes live their wonted fires." Nor will Delaware be found wanting in the day of trial.

But I deny the doctrine. It is full of disunion and civil war. It is disunion itself. Whoever first taught it ought to be dealt with as not only hostile to the Union, but an enemy of the human race. Sir, the fundamental idea of the Constitution is the perfect and eternal compatibility of a union of States "part slave and part free;" else the Constitution never would have been framed, nor the Union founded; and seventy years of successful experiment have approved the wisdom of the plan. In my deliberate judgment, a confederacy made up of slaveholding and non-slaveholding States, is, in the nature of things, the strongest of all popular governments. African slavery has been, and is, eminently conservative. It makes the absolute political equality of the white race everywhere practicable. It dispenses with the English order of nobility, and leaves every white man, North and South, owning slaves or owning none, the equal of every other white man. It has reconciled universal suffrage, throughout the free States, with the stability of government. I speak not now of its material benefits to the North and West, which are many and more obvious. But the South, too, has profited many ways by a union with the non-slaveholding States. Enterprise, industry, self-reliance, perseverance, and the other hardy virtues of a people living in a higher latitude, and without hereditary servants, she has learned or received from the North. Sir, it is easy, I know, to denounce all this, and to revile him who utters it. Be it so. The English is, of all languages, the most copious in words of bitterness and reproach. "Pour on: I will endure."

Then, sir, there is not an "irrepressible conflict" between slave labor and free labor. There is no conflict at all. Both exist together in perfect harmony in the South. The master and the slave, the white laborer and the black, work together in the same field, or the same shop, and without the slightest sense of degradation. They are not equals, either socially or politically. And why, then, cannot Ohio, having only free labor, live in harmony with Kentucky, which has both slave and free? Above all, why cannot Massachusetts allow the same right of choice to South Carolina, separated as they are a thousand miles, by other States, who would keep the peace, and live in good will? Why this civil war? Whence disunion? Not from slavery – not because the South chooses to have two kinds of labor instead of one – but from *sectionalism,* always and every where a disintegrating principle. Sectional jealousy and hate – these, sir, are the only elements of conflict between these States; and, though powerful, they are yet not at all irrepressible. They exist between families, communities, towns, cities, counties, and States; and if not repressed, would dissolve all society and government. They exist, also, between other sections than the North and South. Sectionalism East, many years ago saw the South and West united by the ties of geographical position, migration, intermarriage, and interest, and thus strong enough to control the power and policy of the Union. It found us divided only by different forms of labor, and, with consummate, but most guilty sagacity, it seized upon the question of slavery as the surest and most powerful instrumentality by which to separate the West from the South, and bind her wholly to the North. Encouraged every way, from abroad, by those who were jealous of our prosperity and greatness, and who knew the secret of our strength, it proclaimed the "irrepressible conflict" between slave labor and free labor. It taught the people of the North to forget both their duty and their interests; and, aided by the artificial ligaments and influences which money and enterprise had created between the seaboard and the North-west, it persuaded the people of that section, also, to yield up every tie which binds them to the great valley of the Mississippi, and to join, their political fortunes especially, wholly with the East. It resisted the fugitive slave law, and demanded the exclusion of slavery from all the Territories, and from this District, and clamored against the admission of any more slave States into the Union. It organized a sectional anti-slavery party, and thus drew to its aid as well political ambition and interest as fanaticism; and, after twenty-five years of incessant and vehement agitation, it obtained possession, finally, and upon that issue, of the Federal Government, and of every State government North and West. And, to-day, we are in the midst of the greatest, most cruel, most destructive civil war ever waged. But two years, sir, of blood and debt and taxation, and incipient commercial ruin are teaching the people of the West, and, I trust, of the North, also the folly and madness of this crusade against African slavery, and the wisdom and necessity of a union of the States, as our fathers made it, "part slave and part free."

What then, sir, with so many causes impelling to reunion, keeps us apart to-day? Hate, passion, antagonism, revenge – all heated seven times hotter by war. Sir, these, while they last, are the most powerful of all motives with a people, and with the individual man; but, fortunately, they are the least durable. They hold a divided sway in the same bosoms with the nobler qualities of love, justice, reason, placability; and, except when at their height, are weaker than the sense of interest, and always, in States, at least give way to it at last. No statesman who yields himself up to them can govern wisely or well; and no State whose policy is controlled by them can either prosper or endure. But war is both their offspring and their aliment, and, while it lasts, all other motives are subordinate. The virtues of peace cannot flourish, cannot even find development in the midst of fighting; and this civil war keeps in motion all the centrifugal forces of the Union, and gives to them increased strength and activity every day. But such, and so many and powerful, in my judgment, are the cementing or centripetal agencies impelling us together, that nothing but perpetual war and strife can keep us always divided.

Sir, I do not under-estimate the power of the prejudices of section, or, what is much stronger, of race. Prejudice is colder, and, therefore, more durable than the passions of hate and revenge, or the spirit of antagonism. But, as I have already said, its boundary in the United States is not Mason and Dixon's line. The long standing mutual jealousies of New England and the South do not primarily grow out of slavery. They are deeper, and will always be the chief obstacle in the way of full and absolute reunion. They are founded in difference of manners, habits, and social life, and different notions about politics, morals, and religion. Sir, after all, this whole war is not so much one of sections – least of all, between the slaveholding and non-slaveholding sections – as of races, representing not difference in blood, but mind and its development, and different types of civilization. It is the old conflict of the Cavalier and the Roundhead, the Liberalist and the Puritan; or, rather, it is a conflict, upon new issues, of the ideas and elements represented by those names. It is a war of the Yankee and the Southron. Said a Boston writer, the other day, eulogizing a New England officer who fell at Fredericksburg: "This is Massachusetts' war; Massachusetts and South Carolina made it." But, in the beginning, the Roundhead outwitted the Cavalier, and, by a skillful use of slavery and the negro, united all New England first, and afterwards the entire North and West, and finally sent out to battle against him Celt and Saxon, German and Knickerbocker, Catholic and Episcopalian, and even a part of his own household, and of the descendants of his own stock. Said Mr. Jefferson, when New England threatened secession, some sixty years ago: "No, let us keep the Yankees to quarrel with." Ah, sir, he forgot that quarreling is always a hazardous experiment; and, after some time, the countrymen of Adams proved themselves too sharp at that work for the countrymen of Jefferson. But every day the contest now tends again to its natural and original elements. In many parts of the North-west – I might add, of Pennsylvania, New Jersey, and New York city – the prejudice against the "Yankee" has always been almost as bitter as in the South. Suppressed for a little while by the anti-slavery sentiment and the war, it threatens now to break forth in one of those great, but unfortunate, popular uprisings, in the midst of which reason and justice are, for the time, utterly silenced. I speak advisedly, and let New England heed, else she, and the whole East, too, in their struggle for power, may learn yet, from the West, the same lesson which civil war taught to Rome, that *evulgato imperii arcano, posse principem alibi, quam Ronæ fieri*. The people of the West demand peace, and they begin to more than suspect that New England is in the way. The storm rages; and they believe that she, not slavery, is the cause. The ship is sore tried; and passengers and crew are now almost ready to propitiate the waves, by throwing the ill-omened prophet overboard. In plain English – not very classic, but most expressive – they threaten to "set New England out in the cold."

And now, sir, I, who have not a drop of New England blood in my veins, but was born in Ohio, and am wholly of Southern ancestry – with a slight cross of Pennsylvania Scotch-Irish – would speak a word to the men of the West and the South, in behalf of New England. Sir, some years ago, in the midst of high sectional controversies, and speaking as a Western man, I said some things harsh of the North, which now, in a more catholic spirit, as a United States man, and for the sake of reunion, I would recall. My prejudices, indeed, upon this subject, are as strong as any man's; but in this, the day of great national humiliation and calamity, let the voice of prejudice be hushed.

Sir, they who would exclude New England in any reconstruction of the Union, assume that all New Englanders are "Yankees" and Puritans; and that the Puritan or pragmatical element, or type of civilization, has always held undisputed sway. Well, sir, Yankees, certainly, they are, in one sense; and so to Old England we are all Yankees, North and South; and to the South just now, or a little while ago, we, of the middle and Western States, also, are, or were, Yankees, too. But there is really a very large, and most liberal and conservative non-Puritan element in the population of New England, which, for many years, struggled for the mastery, and sometimes held it. It divided Maine, New Hampshire, and Connecticut, and once controlled Rhode Island wholly. It held the sway during the Revolution, and at the period when the Constitution was founded, and for some years afterwards. Mr. Calhoun said, very justly, in 1847, that to the wisdom and enlarged patriotism of Sherman and Ellsworth, on the slavery question, we were indebted for this admirable Government; and that, along with Paterson, of New Jersey, "their names ought to be engraven on brass, and live forever." And Mr. Webster, in 1830, in one of those grand historic word-paintings, in which he was so great a master, said of Massachusetts and South Carolina: "Hand in hand they stood around the Administration of Washington, and felt his own great arm lean on them for support." Indeed, sir, it was not till some thirty years ago that the narrow, presumptuous, intermeddling, and fanatical spirit of the old Puritan element began to reappear in a form very much more aggressive and destructive than at first, and threatened to obtain absolute mastery in Church, and School, and State. A little earlier it had struggled hard, but the conservatives proved too strong for it; and so long as the great statesmen and jurists of the Whig and Democratic parties survived, it made small progress, though John Quincy Adams gave to it the strength of his great name. But after their death, it broke in as a flood, and swept away the last vestige of the ancient, liberal, and tolerating conservatism. Then every form and development of fanaticism sprang up in rank and most luxuriant growth, till Abolitionism, the chief fungus of all, overspread the whole of New England first, and then the middle States, and finally every State in the North-west.

Certainly, sir, the more liberal or non-Puritan element was mainly, though not altogether, from the old Puritan stock, or largely crossed with it. But even within the first ten years after the landing of the Pilgrims, a more enlarged and tolerating civilization was introduced. Roger Williams, not of the *Mayflower*, though a Puritan himself, and thoroughly imbued with all its peculiarities of cant and creed and form of worship, seems yet to have had naturally a more liberal spirit; and, first, perhaps, of all men, some three or more years before the Ark and the Dove touched the shores of the St. Mary's, in Maryland, taught the sublime doctrine of freedom of opinion and practice in religion. Threatened first with banishment to England, so as to "remove, as far as possible, the infection of his principles," and, afterward, actually banished beyond the jurisdiction of Massachusetts, because, in the language of the sentence of the General Court, "he broached and divulged divers new and strange doctrines against the authority of magistrates," over the religious opinions of men, thereby disturbing the peace of the colony, he became the founder of Rhode Island, and, indeed, of a large part of New England society. And, whether from his teachings and example, and in the persons of his descendants and those of his associates, or from other causes and another stock, there has always been a large infusion throughout New England of what may be called the *Roger Williams element,* as distinguished from the extreme Puritan or *Mayflower* and *Plymouth Rock* type of the New Englander; and, its influence, till late years, has always been powerful.

The Speaker. The gentleman's hour has expired.

Mr. Vallandigham. I ask for a short time longer.

Mr. Potter. I hope there will be no objection from this side of the House.

The Speaker. If there be no objection, the gentleman will be allowed further time.

There was no objection, and it was ordered accordingly.

Mr. Vallandigham. Sir, I would not deny or disparage the austere virtues of the old Puritans of England or America. But I do believe that, in the very nature of things, no community could exist long in peace, and no government endure long alone, or become great, where that element, in its earliest or its more recent form, holds supreme control. And, it is my solemn conviction, that there can be no possible or durable reunion of these States, until it shall have been again subordinated to other and more liberal and conservative elements, and, above all, until its worst and most mischievous development, Abolitionism, has been utterly extinguished. Sir, the peace of the Union and of this continent demands it. But, fortunately, those very elements exist abundantly in New England herself; and to her I look with confidence to secure to them the mastery within her limits. In fact, sir, the true voice of New England has, for some years past, been but rarely heard, here or elsewhere, in public affairs. Men now control her politics, and are in high places, State and Federal, who, twenty years ago, could not have been chosen selectmen in old Massachusetts. But, let her remember, at last, her ancient renown; let her turn from vain-glorious admiration of the stone monuments of her heroes and patriots of a former age, to generous emulation of the noble and manly virtues which they were designed to commemorate. Let us hear less from her of the Pilgrim Fathers and the *Mayflower* and of Plymouth Rock, and more of Roger Williams and his compatriots, and his toleration. Let her banish, now and forever, her dreamers and her sophists and her fanatics, and call back again into her State administration, and into the national councils, "her men of might, her grand in soul" – some of them still live – and she will yet escape the dangers which now threaten her with isolation.

Then, sir, while I am inexorably hostile to Puritan domination in religion or morals or literature or politics, I am not in favor of the proposed exclusion of New England. I would have the Union as it was, and, first, New England as she was. But if New England will have no union with slaveholders, if she is not content with "the Union as it was," then, upon her own head be the responsibility for secession; and there will be no more coercion now; I, at least, will be exactly consistent.

And now, sir, can the central States, New York, New Jersey, and Pennsylvania, consent to separation? Can New York city? Sir, the trade of the South made her largely what she is. She was the factor and banker of the

South. Cotton filled her harbor with shipping, and her banks with gold. But in an evil hour, the foolish, I will not say bad "men of Gotham" persuaded her merchant princes – against their first lesson in business – that she could retain or force back the Southern trade by war. War, indeed, has given her, just now, a new business and trade, greater and more profitable than the old; but with disunion, that, too, must perish. And let not Wall street, or any other great interest, mercantile, manufacturing, or commercial, imagine that it shall have power enough, or wealth enough, to stand in the way of reunion through peace. Let them learn, one and all, that a public man, who has the people as his support, is stronger than they, though he may not be worth a million, nor even one dollar. A little while ago the banks said that they were king, but President Jackson speedily taught them their mistake. Next, railroads assumed to be king; and cotton once vaunted largely his kingship. Sir, these are only of the royal family – princes of the blood. There is but one king on earth. Politics is king.

But to return: New Jersey, too, is bound closely to the South, and the South to her; and more and longer than any other State, she remembered both her duty to the Constitution and her interest in the Union. And Pennsylvania, a sort of middle ground, just between the North and the South, and extending, also, to the West, is united by nearer, if not stronger ties to every section than any other one State, unless it be Ohio. She was – she is yet – the keystone in the great but now crumbling arch of the Union. She is a border State; and, more than that, she has less within her of the fanatical or disturbing element than any of the States. The people of Pennsylvania are quiet, peaceable, practical, and enterprising, without being aggressive. They have more of the honest old English and German thrift than any other. No people mind more diligently their own business. They have but one idiosyncrasy or specialty – the tariff; and even that is really far more a matter of tradition than of substantial interest. The industry, enterprise, and thrift of Pennsylvania are abundantly able to take care of themselves against any competition. In any event, the Union is of more value, many times, to her, than any local interest.

But other ties also bind these States – Pennsylvania and New Jersey, especially – to the South, and the South to them. Only an imaginary line separates the former from Delaware and Maryland. The Delaware river, common to both Pennsylvania and New Jersey, flows into Delaware Bay. The Susquehanna empties its waters, through Pennsylvania and Maryland, into the Chesapeake. And that great watershed itself, extending to Norfolk, and, therefore, almost to the North Carolina line, does belong, and must ever belong, in common, to the central and Southern States, under one government; or else the line of separation will be the Potomac to its head waters. All of Delaware and Maryland, and the counties of Accomac and Northampton, in Virginia, would, in that event, follow the fortunes of the Northern confederacy. In fact, sir, disagreeable as the idea may be to many within their limits, on both sides, no man who looks at the map and then reflects upon history and the force of natural causes, and considers the present actual and the future probable position of the hostile armies and navies at the end of this war, ought for a moment to doubt that either the States and counties which I have named, must go with the North, or Pennsylvania and New Jersey with the South. Military force on either side cannot control the destiny of the States lying between the mouth of the Chesapeake and the Hudson. And if that bay were itself made the line, Delaware, and the eastern shore of Maryland and Virginia, would belong to the North; while Norfolk, the only capacious harbor on the south-eastern coast, must be commanded by the guns of some new fortress upon Cape Charles; and Baltimore, the now queenly city, seated then upon the very boundary of two rival, yes, hostile, confederacies, would rapidly fall into decay.

And now, sir, I will not ask whether the North-west can consent to separation from the South. Never. Nature forbids. We are only a part of the great valley of the Mississippi. There is no line of latitude upon which to separate. Neither party would desire the old line of 36° 30' on both sides of the river; and there is no natural boundary east and west. The nearest to it are the Ohio and Missouri rivers. But that line would leave Cincinnati and St. Louis, as border cities, like Baltimore, to decay, and, extending fifteen hundred miles in length, would become the scene of an eternal border warfare, without example even in the worst of times. Sir, we cannot, ought not, will not, separate from the South. And if you of the East who have found this war against the South, and for the negro, gratifying to your hate or profitable to your purse, will continue it till a separation be forced between the slaveholding and your non-slaveholding States, then, believe me, and accept it, as you did not the other solemn warnings of years past, *the day which divides the North from the South, that selfsame day decrees eternal divorce between the West and the East.*

Sir, our destiny is fixed. There is not one drop of rain which, descending from the heavens and fertilizing our soil, causes it to yield an abundant harvest, but flows into the Mississippi, and there mingling with the waters of that mighty river, finds its way, at last, to the Gulf of Mexico. And we must and will follow it with travel and trade – not by treaty, but by right – freely, peaceably, and without restriction or tribute, under the same government and flag, to its home in the bosom of that gulf. Sir, we will not remain, after separation from the South, a province or appanage of the East, to bear her burdens and pay her taxes; nor, hemmed in and isolated as we are, and without a sea-coast, could we long remain a distinct confederacy. But wherever we go, married to the South or the East, we bring with us three-fourths of the territories of that valley to the Rocky Mountains, and it may be to the Pacific – the grandest and most magnificent dowry that bride ever had to bestow.

Then, sir, New England, freed at last from the domination of her sophisters, dreamers, and bigots, and restored to the control once more of her former liberal, tolerant, and conservative civilization, will not stand in the way of the reunion of these States upon terms of fair and honorable adjustment. And in this great work the central free and border slave States, too, will unite heart and hand. To the West it is a necessity, and she demands it. And let not the States now called Confederate insist upon separation and independence. What did they demand at first? Security against Abolitionism within the Union: protection from the "irrepressible conflict," and the domination of the absolute numerical majority: a change of public opinion, and consequently of political parties in the North and West, so that their local institutions and domestic peace should no longer be endangered. And now, sir, after two years of persistent and most gigantic effort on part of this Administration to compel them to submit, but with utter and signal failure, the people of the free States are now, or are fast becoming, satisfied that the price of the Union is the utter suppression of Abolitionism or anti-slavery as a political element, and the complete subordination of the spirit of fanaticism and intermeddling which gave it birth. In any event, they are ready now, if I have not greatly misread the signs of the times, to return to the old Constitutional and actual basis of fifty years ago: three-fifths rule of representation, speedy rendition of fugitives from labor, equal rights in the Territories, no more slavery agitation anywhere, and transit and temporary sojourn with slaves, without molestation, in the free States. Without all these there could be neither peace nor permanence to a restored union of States "part slave and part free." With it, the South, in addition to all the other great and multiplied benefits of union, would be far more secure in her slave property, her domestic institutions, than under a separate government. Sir, let no man, North or West, tell me that this would perpetuate African slavery. I know it. But so does the Constitution. I repeat, sir, it is the price of the Union. Whoever hates negro slavery more than he loves the Union must demand separation at last. I think that you can never abolish slavery by fighting. Certainly you never can till you have first destroyed the South, and then, in the language, first of Mr. Douglas and afterward of Mr. Seward, converted this Government into an imperial despotism. And, sir, whenever I am forced to a choice between the loss, to my own country and race, of personal and political liberty, with all its blessings, and the involuntary domestic servitude of the negro, I shall not hesitate one moment to choose the latter alternative. The sole question, to-day, is between the Union, with slavery, or final disunion, and, I think, anarchy and despotism. I am for the

Union. It was good enough for my fathers. It is good enough for us, and our children after us.

And, sir, let no man in the South tell me that she has been invaded, and that all the horrors implied in those most terrible of words, civil war, have been visited upon her. I know that, too. But we, also, of the North and West, in every State, and by thousands, who have dared so much as to question the principles and policy, or doubt the honesty, of this Administration and its party, have suffered everything that the worst despotism could inflict, except only loss of life itself upon the scaffold. Some even have died for the cause, by the hand of the assassin. And can we forget? Never, never. Time will but burn the memory of these wrongs deeper into our hearts. But shall we break up the Union? Shall we destroy the Government, because usurping tyrants have held possession, and perverted it to the most cruel of oppressions? Was it ever so done in any other country? In Athens? Rome? England? Anywhere? No, sir; let us expel the usurper, and restore the Constitution and laws, the rights of the States, and the liberties of the people; and then, in the country of our fathers, under the Union of our fathers, and the old flag – the symbol once again of the free and the brave – let us fulfill the grand mission which Providence has appointed for us among the nations of the earth.

And now, sir, if it be the will of all sections to unite, then upon what terms? Sir, between the South and most of the States of the North, and all of the West, there is but one subject in controversy – slavery. It is the only question, said Mr. Calhoun, twenty-five years ago, of sufficient magnitude and potency to divide this Union; and divide it it will, he added, or drench the country in blood, if not arrested. It has done both. But settle it on the original basis of the Constitution, and give to each section the power to protect itself within the Union, and now, after the terrible lessons of the past two years, the Union will be stronger than before, and, indeed, endure for ages. Woe to the man, North or South, who, to the third or fourth generation, should teach men disunion.

And now the way to reunion: what so easy? Behold to-day two separate governments in one country, and without a natural dividing line; with two presidents and cabinets, and a double Congress; and yet, each under a Constitution so exactly similar, the one to the other, that a stranger could scarce discern the difference. Was ever folly and madness like this? Sir, it is not in the nature of things that it should so continue long.

But why speak of ways or terms of reunion now? The will is yet wanting in both sections. Union is consent, and good will, and fraternal affection. War is force, hate, revenge. Is the country tired at last of war? Has the experiment been tried long enough? Has sufficient blood been shed, treasure expended, and misery inflicted in both the North and the South?

What then? Stop fighting. Make an armistice – no formal treaty. Withdraw your army from the seceded States. Reduce both armies to a fair and sufficient peace establishment. Declare absolute free trade between the North and South. Buy and sell. Agree upon a zollverein. Recall your fleets. Break up your blockade. Reduce your navy. Restore travel. Open up railroads. Re-establish the telegraph. Reunite your express companies. No more Monitors and iron-clads, but set your friendly steamers and steamships again in motion. Visit the North and West. Visit the South. Exchange newspapers. Migrate. Intermarry. Let slavery alone. Hold elections at the appointed times. Let us choose a new President in sixty-four. And when the gospel of peace shall have descended again from heaven into their hearts, and the gospel of Abolition and of hate been expelled, let your clergy and the churches meet again in Christian intercourse, North and South. Let the secret orders and voluntary associations everywhere reunite as brethren once more. In short, give to all the natural, and all the artificial causes which impel us together, their fullest sway. Let time do his office – drying tears, dispelling sorrows, mellowing passion, and making herb and grass and tree to grow again upon the hundred battle-fields of this terrible war.

"But this is recognition." It is not formal recognition, to which I will not consent. Recognition now, and attempted permanent treaties about boundary, travel, and trade, and partition of Territories would end in a war fiercer and more disastrous than before. Recognition is absolute disunion; and not between the slave and the free States, but with Delaware and Maryland as part of the North, and Kentucky and Missouri part of the West. But wherever the actual line, every evil and mischief of disunion is implied in it. And, for similar reasons, sir, I would not, at this time, press hastily a convention of the States. The men who now would hold seats in such a convention, would, upon both sides, if both agreed to attend, come together full of the hate and bitterness inseparable from a civil war. No, sir; let passion have time to cool, and reason to resume its sway. It cost thirty years of desperate and most wicked patience and industry to destroy or impair the magnificent temple of this Union. Let us be content if, within three years, we shall be able to restore it.

But, certainly, what I propose is informal, practical recognition. And that is precisely what exists to-day, and has existed, more or less defined, from the first. Flags of truce, exchange of prisoners, and all your other observances of the laws, forms, and courtesies of war, are acts of recognition. Sir, does any man doubt, to-day, that there is a Confederate Government at Richmond, and that it is a "belligerent"? Even the Secretary of State has discovered it at last, though he has written ponderous folios of polished rhetoric to prove that it is not. Will continual war then, without extended and substantial success, make the Confederate States any the less a government in fact?

"But it confesses disunion." Yes, just as the surgeon, who sets your fractured limb in splints, in order that it may be healed, admits that it is broken. "But the Government will have failed to crush out the rebellion." Sir, it has failed. You went to war to prove that we had a Government. With what result? To the people of the loyal States it has, in your hands, been the Government of King Stork, but to the Confederate States, of King Log. "But the rebellion will have triumphed." Better triumph to-day then ten years hence. But I deny it. The rebellion will, at last, be crushed out, in the only way in which it ever was possible. "But no one will be hung at the end of war." Neither will there be, though the war should last half a century, except by the mob or the hand of arbitrary power. But, really, sir, if there is to be no hanging, let this Administration, and all who have done its bidding everywhere, rejoice and be exceeding glad.

And now, sir, allow me a word upon a subject of very great interest at this moment, and most important, it may be, in its influence upon the future – *foreign mediation*. I speak not of armed and hostile intervention, which I would resist as long as but one man was left to strike a blow at the invader. But friendly mediation – the kindly offer of an impartial power to stand as a daysman between the contending parties in this most bloody and exhausting strife – ought to be met in a spirit as cordial and ready as that in which it is proffered. It would be churlish to refuse. Certainly, it is not consistent with the former dignity of this Government to ask for mediation, neither, sir, would it befit its ancient magnanimity to reject it. As proposed by the Emperor of France, I would accept it at once. Now is the auspicious moment. It is the speediest, easiest, most graceful mode of suspending hostilities. Let us hear no more of the mediation of the cannon and the sword. The day for all that has gone by. Let us be statesmen at last. Sir, I give thanks, that some, at least, among the Republican party, seem ready now to lift themselves up to the height of this great argument, and to deal with it in the spirit of the patriots and great men of other countries and ages, and of the better days of the United States.

And now, sir, whatever may have been the motives of England, France, and the other great powers of Europe, in withholding recognition so long from the Confederate States, the South and the North are both indebted to them for an immense public service. The South has proved her ability to maintain herself by her own strength and resources, without foreign aid, moral or material. And the North and West – the whole country, indeed – these great powers have served incalculably, by holding back a solemn proclamation to the world that the Union of these States was finally and formally dissolved. They have left to us every motive and every chance for reunion; and if that has been the purpose of England especially – our rival so long, interested more than any other in disunion, and the consequent weakening of our great naval and commercial power, and suffering, too, as she has suffered, so long and severely because of this war – I do not hesitate to say that she has performed an act of unselfish heroism without example in history. Was such, indeed, her purpose? Let her answer before the impartial tribunal of posterity. In any event, after the great reaction in public sentiment in the North and West, to be followed, after some time, by a like reaction in the South, foreign recognition now of the Confederate States could avail little to delay or prevent final reunion, if, as I firmly believe, reunion be not only possible, but inevitable.

Sir, I have not spoken of foreign arbitration. That is quite another question. I think it impracticable, and fear it as dangerous. The very powers – or any other power – which have hesitated to aid disunion directly or by force, might, as authorized arbiters, most readily pronounce for it at last. Very grand, indeed, would be the tribunal before which the great question of the Union of these States, and the final destiny of this continent, for ages, should be heard, and historic, through all time, the ambassadors who should argue it. And, if both belligerents consent, let the subjects in controversy be referred to Switzerland, or Russia, or any other impartial and incorruptible power or state in Europe. But, at last, sir, the people of these several States here, at home, must be the final arbiters of this great quarrel in America; and the people and States of the Northwest, the mediators who shall stand, like the prophet, betwixt the living and the dead, that the plague of disunion may be stayed.

Sir, this war, horrible as it is, has taught us all some of the most important and salutary lessons which a people ever learned.

First, it has annihilated, in twenty months, all the false and pernicious theories and teachings of Abolitionism for thirty years, and which a mere appeal to facts and arguments could not have untaught in half a century. We have learned that the South is not weak, dependent, unenterprising, or corrupted by slavery, luxury, and idleness; but powerful, earnest, warlike, enduring, self-supporting, full of energy, and inexhaustible in resources. We have been taught, and now confess it openly, that African slavery, instead of being a source of weakness to the South, is one of her main elements of strength; and hence the "military necessity," we are told, of abolishing slavery in order to suppress the rebellion. We have learned, also, that the non-slaveholding white men of the South, millions in number, are immovably attached to the institution, and are its chief support; and Abolitionists have found out, to their infinite surprise and disgust, that the slave is not "panting for freedom," nor pining in silent, but, revengeful grief over cruelty and oppression inflicted upon him, but happy, contented, attached deeply to his master, and unwilling – at least not eager – to accept the precious boon of freedom, which they have proffered him. I appeal to the President for the proof. I appeal to the fact, that fewer slaves have escaped, even from Virginia, in now yearly two years, than Arnold and Cornwallis carried away in six months of invasion, in 1781. Finally, sir, we have learned, and the South, too, what the history of the world ages ago, and our own history might have taught us, that servile insurrection is the least of the dangers to which she is exposed. Hence, in my deliberate judgment, African slavery, as an institution, will come out of this conflict fifty-fold stronger than when the war began.

The South, too, sir, has learned most important lessons; and among them, that personal courage is a quality common to all sections, and that in battle, the men of the North, and especially of the West, are their equals. Hitherto there has been a mutual, and most mischievous mistake upon both sides. The men of the South over-valued their own personal courage, and under-valued ours, and we, too, readily consented; but at the same time they exaggerated our aggregate strength and resources, and under-estimated their own; and we fell into the same error; and hence, the original and fatal mistake, or vice, of the military policy of the North, and which has already broken down the war by its own weight – the belief that we could bring overwhelming numbers and power into the field, and upon the sea, and crush out the South at a blow. But twenty months of terrible warfare have corrected many errors, and taught us the wisdom of a century. And now, sir, every one of these lessons will profit us all for ages to come; and if we do but reunite, will bind us in a closer, firmer, more durable union than ever before.

I have finished now, Mr. Speaker, what I desired to say at this time, upon the great question of the reunion of these States. I have spoken freely and boldly – not wisely, it may be, for the present, or for myself personally, but most wisely for the future and for my country. Not courting censure, I yet do not shrink from it. My own immediate personal interests, and my chances just now for the more material rewards of ambition, I again surrender as hostages to that great hereafter, the echo of whose footsteps already I hear along the highway of time. Whoever, here or elsewhere, believes that war can restore the Union of these States; whoever would have a war for the abolition of slavery, or disunion; and he who demands Southern independence and final separation – let him speak, for him I have offended. Devoted to the Union from the beginning, I will not desert it now in this the hour of its sorest trial.

Sir, it was the day-dream of my boyhood, the cherished desire of my heart in youth, that I might live to see the hundredth anniversary of our national independence, and, as orator of the day, exult in the expanding glories and greatness of the still United States. That vision lingers yet before my eyes, obscured, indeed, by the clouds and thick darkness and the blood of civil war. But, sir, if the men of this generation are wise enough to profit by the hard experience of the past two years, and will turn their hearts now from bloody intents to the words and arts of peace, that day will find us again the United States. And if not earlier, as I would desire and believe, at least upon that day let the great work of reunion be consummated; that thenceforth, for ages, the States and the people who shall fill up this mighty continent, united under one Constitution, and in one Union, and the same destiny, shall celebrate it as the birthday both of Independence and of the Great Restoration.

Sir, I repeat it, we are in the midst of the very crisis of this revolution. If, to-day, we secure peace, and begin the work of reunion, we shall yet escape; if not, I see nothing before us but universal political and social revolution, anarchy, and bloodshed, compared with which, the Reign of Terror in France was a merciful visitation.

CHAPTER ELEVEN
The Conscription Bill
Speech Delivered in the House of Representatives,
February 23, 1863

In the last days of the late Congress, a law was enacted which gives the President power to call into the military service every man between the ages of eighteen and forty-five. No exceptions on the ground of color; and only a few special exemptions, at the head of which is the President. The bill virtually admits that the war is no longer one to which the people give, freely, themselves and their substance; but a war whose further prosecution must be enforced by arbitrary power. The Constitution makes a distinction between the army and the militia; to the States, it reserves the right to control, officer, and discipline the latter, until mustered into the service of the United States. This reserved right of the States the Conscription Bill disregards, and clothes the President with power to convert the entire militia into a Federal army, under his immediate direction and command; leaving out those who are able and willing to commute by paying three hundred dollars.

The bill passed the Senate without much opposition: went through at midnight, when Democrats and Conservatives were not there to oppose it, or even record their votes against it. On coming to the House, the Chairman of the Military Committee gave notice of their intention to bring the bill to a final vote, without debate. Its opponents could not muster more than thirty fighting men, but had such men as Vallandigham and Voorhees for leaders, and determined to give all the resistance parliamentary rules would permit. By perseverance and management, they brought the majority to a discussion of the bill, and the war opened in earnest. A debate ensued which, for power, eloquence, strength of argument, and bold defense of constitutional rights, has not often been equaled. Inspired with the courage always given to those who are right, Vallandigham, Vorhees, Pendleton, and the others, standing unmoved against the strong current of despotism, boldly assailed the most dangerous and vulnerable features of the bill. Its friends faltered, relaxed their hold upon one after another of their favorite despotic measures. They had determined to give the provost marshals power to arrest and hold civilians, but were compelled to insert a provision that persons arrested should be handed over to the civil authorities for trial. All that related to "treasonable practices" was stricken out, though retained in the "Indemnity Bill." Other important concessions were made; thus, by fearless, and manly courage, a few sacred constitutional rights were wrested from the hard grasp of despotism. At the most exciting moment of the conflict, Mr. V. addressed the House. Bingham, of Ohio, thought his "assumptions unworthy of any man who had grown to man's estate under the shelter of the Constitution." Voorhees replied he "had held the House spell-bound with one of the ablest arguments he had ever heard." Mr. Vallandigham said:

> Mr. Speaker: I do not propose to discuss this bill at any great length in this House. I am satisfied that there is a settled purpose to enact it into a law, so far as it is possible for the action of the Senate and House, and the President, to make it such. I appeal, therefore, from you, from them, directly to the country; to a forum where there is no military committee, no previous question, no hour rule, and where the people themselves are the masters. I commend the spirit in which this discussion was commenced by the chairman of the military committee (Mr. Olin), and I do it the more cheerfully because, unfortunately, he is not always in so good a temper as he was to-day; and I trust, that throughout the debate, and on its close, he will exhibit that same disposition which characterized his opening remarks. Only let me caution him that he cannot dictate to the minority here what course they shall pursue. But, sir, I regret that I cannot extend the commendation to the gentleman from Pennsylvania (Mr. Campbell), who addressed the House a little while ago. His speech was extremely offensive, and calculated to stir up a spirit of bitterness and strife, not at all consistent with that in which debates in this House should be conducted. If he, or any other gentleman of the majority, imagines that any one here is to be deterred by threats, from the expression of his opinions, or from giving such votes as he may see fit to give, he has utterly misapprehended the temper and determination of those who sit on this side of the Chamber. His threat I hurl back with defiance into his teeth. I spurn it. I spit upon it. That is not the argument to be addressed to equals here; and I, therefore, most respectfully suggest, that hereafter, all such be dispensed with, and that we shall be spared personal denunciation, and insinuations against the loyalty of men who sit with me here; men whose devotion

to the Constitution, and attachment to the Union of these States is as ardent and immoveable as yours, and who only differ from you as to the mode of securing the great object nearest their hearts.

Mr. Campbell. The gentleman will allow me –

Mr. Vallandigham. I yield for explanation.

Mr. Campbell. Mr. Speaker: It is a significant fact, that the gentleman from Ohio has applied my remarks to himself, and others on his side of the House. Why was this done? I was denouncing traitors here, and I will denounce them while I have a place upon this floor. It is my duty and my privilege to do so. And if the gentleman from Ohio chooses to give my remarks a personal application, he can so apply them.

Mr. Vallandigham. That is enough.

Mr. Campbell. One moment.

Mr. Vallandigham. Not another moment after that. I yielded the floor in the spirit of a gentleman, and not to be met in the manner of a blackguard. (Applause and hisses in the galleries.)

Mr. Campbell. The member from Ohio is a blackguard. (Renewed hisses and applause in the galleries.)

Mr. Robinson. I rise to a question of order. I demand that the galleries be cleared. We have been insulted time and again by contractors and plunderers of the Government, in these galleries, and I ask that they be now cleared.

Mr. Cox. I hope my friend from Illinois will not insist on that. Only a very small portion of those in the galleries take part in these disturbances. The fool killer will take care of them.

The Speaker *pro tem*. The chair will have to submit the question to the House.

Mr. Cox. I hope the demand will be withdrawn.

The Speaker *pro tem*. The Chair will state, that if disorder is repeated, whether by applause or expressions of disapprobation, he will feel called upon himself to order the galleries to be cleared, trusting that the House will sustain him in so doing.

Mr. Robinson. I desire the order to be enforced now, and the galleries to be cleared, excepting the ladies' gallery.

Mr. Roscoe Conkling. I was going to say that I hoped the order would not be extended to that portion of the galleries.

Mr. Robinson. The galleries were cautioned this afternoon.

Mr. Johnson. And it is the same men who have been making this disturbance now. I know their faces well.

Mr. Vallandigham. I think, Mr. Speaker, that this lesson has not been lost; and that it is sufficiently impressed now upon the minds of the audience that this is a legislative, and is supposed to be a deliberative, assembly, and that no breach of decorum or order should occur among them, whatever may be the conduct of any of us on the floor. I trust, therefore, that my friends on this side will withdraw the demand for the enforcement of the rule of the House.

Mr. Robinson. I withdraw the demand.

Mr. Verree. I raise the point of order, that members here, in debating questions before the House, are not at liberty to use language that is unparliamentary, and unworthy of a member.

The Speaker. That is the rule of the House.

Mr. Verree. I hope it will be enforced.

Mr. Vallandigham. And I hope that it will be enforced, also, against members on the other side of the Chamber. We have borne enough, more than enough of such language, for two years past.

The Speaker. The gentleman from Illinois withdraws his demand to have the galleries cleared. The Chair desires to say to gentlemen in the galleries, that this being a deliberative body, it is not becoming this House, or the character of American citizens, to disturb its deliberations by any expression of approval or disapproval.

Mr. Vallandigham. The member from Pennsylvania (Mr. Campbell) alluded to-day, generally, to gentlemen on this side of the House. There was no mistaking the application. The language and gesture were both plain enough. He ventured also, approvingly, to call our attention to the opinions and course of conduct of some Democrats in the State of New York, as if we were to learn our lessons in Democracy, or in anything else, from that quarter. I do not know, certainly, to whom he alluded. Perhaps it was to a gentleman who spoke, not long since, in the city of New York, and advocated on that occasion, what is called in stereotype phrase "the vigorous prosecution of the war," and who, but two months previously, addressed assemblages in the same State and city, in which he proposed only to take Richmond, and then let the "wayward sisters depart in peace." Now I know of no one on this side of the Chamber occupying such a position; and I, certainly, will not go to that quarter to learn lessons in patriotism or Democracy.

I have already said, that it is not my purpose to debate the general merits of this bill at large, and for the reason, that I am satisfied that argument is of no avail here. I appeal, therefore, to the people. Before them, I propose to try this great question – the question of constitutional power, and of the unwise and injudicious exercise of it in this bill. We have been compelled, repeatedly, since the 4th of March, 1861, to appeal to the same tribunal. We appealed to it at the recent election. And the people did pronounce judgment upon our appeal. The member from Pennsylvania ought to have heard their sentence, and I venture to say that he did hear it, on the night of the election. In Ohio they spoke as with the voice of many waters. The very question, of summary and arbitrary arrests, now sanctioned in this bill, was submitted, as a direct issue, to the people of that State, as also of other States, and their verdict was rendered upon it. The Democratic Convention of Ohio, assembled on the 4th of July, in the city of Columbus, the largest and best, ever held in the State, among other resolutions, of the same temper and spirit, adopted this without a dissenting voice:

> And we utterly condemn and denounce the repeated and gross violation, by the Executive of the United States, of the rights thus scoured by the Constitution; and we also utterly repudiate and condemn the monstrous dogma, that in time of war the Constitution is suspended, or its power in any respect enlarged beyond the letter and true meaning of that instrument.
>
> And we view, also, with indignation and alarm, the illegal and unconstitutional seizure and imprisonment, for alleged political offenses, of our citizens, without judicial process, in States where such process is unobstructed, but by Executive order by telegraph, or otherwise, and call upon all who uphold the Union, the Constitution and the laws, to unite with us, in denouncing and repelling such flagrant violation of the State and Federal Constitutions, and tyrannical infraction of the rights and liberties of American citizens; and that the people of this State cannot safely, and will not, submit to have the freedom of speech and freedom of the press, the two great and essential bulwarks of civil liberty, put down by unwarranted and despotic exertion of power.

On that, the judgment of the people was given at the October elections, and the party candidates nominated by the convention which adopted that resolution, were triumphantly elected. So, too, with the candidates of the same party in the States of Wisconsin, Illinois, Indiana, Pennsylvania, New Jersey, and New York. And, sir, that "healthy re-action," recently, of which the member from Pennsylvania (Mr. Campbell) affected to boast, has escaped my keenest sense of vision. I see only that hand-writing on the wall which the fingers of the people wrote against him and his party, and this whole Administration, at the ballot-box, in October and November last. Talk to me, indeed, of the leniency of the Executive! too few arrests! too much forbearance by those in power! Sir, it is the people who have been too lenient. They have submitted to your oppressions and wrongs as no free people ought ever to submit. But the day of patient endurance has gone by at last. Mistake them not. They will be lenient no longer. Abide by the Constitution, stand by the laws, restore the Union, if *you* can restore it – not by force – you have tried that and failed. Try some other method now – the ancient, the approved, the reasonable way – the way in which the Union was first made. Surrender it not now – not yet – never. But unity is not Union; and attempt not, at your peril – I warn you – to coerce unity by the utter destruction of the Constitution and of the rights of the States and the liberties of the people. Union is liberty and consent: unity is despotism and force. For what was the Union ordained? As a splendid edifice, to attract the gaze and admiration of the world? As a magnificent temple – a stupendous superstructure of marble and iron, like this Capitol, upon whose lofty dome the bronzed image – hollow and inanimate – of Freedom is soon to stand erect in colossal mockery, while the true spirit, the living Goddess of Liberty, veils her eyes and turns away her face in sorrow, because, upon the altar established here, and dedicated by our fathers to her worship – you, a false and most disloyal priesthood, offer up, night and morning, the mingled sacrifices of servitude and despotism? No, sir. It was for the sake of the altar, the service, the religion, the devotees, that the temple of the Union was first erected; and when these are all gone, let the edifice itself perish. Never – never – never – will the people consent to lose their own personal and political rights and liberties, to the end that you may delude and mock them with the splendid unity of despotism.

Sir, what are the bills which have passed, or are still before the House? The bill to give the President entire control of the currency – the purse – of the country. A tax-bill to clothe him with power over the whole property of the country. A bill to put all power in his hands over the personal liberties of the people. A bill to indemnify him, and all under him, for every act of oppression and outrage already consummated. A bill to enable him to suspend the writ of *habeas corpus,* in order to justify or protect him, and every minion of his, in the arrests which he or they may choose to make – arrests, too, for mere opinions' sake. Sir, some two hundred years ago, men were burned at the stake, subjected to the horrors of the Inquisition, to all the tortures that the devilish ingenuity of man could invent – for what? For opinions on questions of religion – of man's duty and relation to his God. And now, to-day, for opinions on questions political, under a free government, in a country whose liberties were purchased by our fathers by seven years' out-pouring of blood, and expenditure of treasure – we have lived to see men, the born heirs of this precious inheritance, subjected to arrest and cruel imprisonment at the caprice of a President, or a secretary, or a constable. And, as if that were not enough, a bill is introduced here, to-day, and pressed forward to a vote, with the right of debate, indeed – extorted from you by the minority – but without the right to amend, with no more than the mere privilege of protest – a bill which enables the President to bring under his power, as commander-in-chief, every man in the United States between the ages of twenty and forty-five – three millions of men. And, as if not satisfied with that, this bill provides, further, that every other citizen, man, woman, and child, under twenty years of age and over forty-five, including those that may be exempt between these ages, shall be also, at the mercy –

so far as his personal liberty is concerned – of some miserable "provost marshal" with the rank of a captain of cavalry, who is never to see service in the field; and every Congressional district in the United States is to be governed – yes, governed – by this petty satrap – this military eunuch – this Baba – and he even may be black – who is to do the bidding of your Sultan, or his Grand Vizier. Sir, you have but one step further to go – give him the symbols of his office – the Turkish bow-string and the sack.

What is it, sir, but a bill to abrogate the Constitution, to repeal all existing laws, to destroy all rights, to strike down the judiciary, and erect, upon the ruins of civil and political liberty, a stupendous superstructure of despotism. And for what? To enforce law? No, sir. It is admitted now, by the legislation of Congress, and by the two proclamations of the President; it is admitted by common consent, that the war is for the abolition of negro slavery, to secure freedom to the black man. You tell me, some of you, I know, that it is so prosecuted because this is the only way to restore the Union; but others openly and candidly confess that the purpose of the prosecution of the war is to abolish slavery. And thus, sir, it is that the freedom of the negro is to be purchased, under this bill, at the sacrifice of every right of the white men of the United States.

Sir, I am opposed – earnestly, inexorably opposed – to this measure. If there were not another man in this House to vote against it – if there were none to raise his voice against it – I, at least, dare stand here alone in my place, as a Representative, undismayed, unseduced, unterrified, and heedless of the miserable cry of "disloyalty," of sympathy with the rebellion, and with rebels, to denounce it as the very consummation of the conspiracy against the Constitution and the liberties of my country.

Sir, I yield to no man in devotion to the Union. I am for maintaining it upon the principles on which it was first formed; and I would have it, at every sacrifice, except of honor, which is "the life of the nation." I have stood by it in boyhood and in manhood, to this hour; and I will not now consent to yield it up; nor am I to be driven from an earnest and persistent support of the only means by which it can be restored, either by the threats of the party of the Administration here, or because of affected sneers and contemptuous refusals to listen, now, to re-union, by the party of the Administration at Richmond. I never was weak enough to cower before the reign of terror inaugurated by the men in power here, nor vain enough to expect favorable responses now, or terms of settlement, from the men in power, or the presses under their control, in the South. Neither will ever compromise this great quarrel, nor agree to peace on the basis of re-union: but I repeat it – stop fighting, and let time and natural causes operate – uncontrolled by military influences – and the ballot there, as the ballot here, will do its work. I am for the Union of these States; and but for my profound conviction that it can never be restored by force and arms; or, if so restored, could not be maintained, and would not be worth maintaining, I would have united, at first – even now would unite, cordially – in giving, as I have acquiesced, silently, in your taking, all the men and all the money you have demanded. But I did not believe, and do not now believe, that the war could end in anything but final defeat; and if it should last long enough, then in disunion; or, if successful upon the principles now proclaimed, that it must and would end in the establishment of an imperial military despotism – not only in the South – but in the North and West. And to that I never will submit. No, rather, first I am ready to yield up property, and liberty – nay, life itself.

Sir, I do not propose to discuss now the question of the constitutionality of this measure. The gentleman from Ohio, who preceded me (Mr. White), has spared me the necessity of an argument on that point. He has shown that, between the army of the United States, of which, by the Constitution, the President of the United States is the commander-in-chief, and the militia, belonging to the States, there is a wide, and clearly marked line of distinction. The distinction is fully and strongly defined in the Constitution; and has been recognized in the entire legislation and practice of the Government from the beginning. The States have the right, and have always exercised it, of appointing the officers of their militia, and you have no power to take it away. Sir, this bill was originally introduced in the Senate as a militia bill, and as such, it recognized the right of the States to appoint the officers; but finding it impossible, upon that basis, to give to the Executive of the United States the entire control of the millions thus organized into a military force, as the conspirators against State rights and popular liberty desire, the original bill was abandoned; and to-day behold here a stupendous Conscription Bill, for a standing army of more than three millions of men, forced from their homes, their families, their fields, and their workshops – an army organized, officered, and commanded by the servant President, now the master Dictator, of the United States. And for what? Foreign war? Home defense? No; but for coercion, invasion, and the abolition of negro slavery by force. Sir, the conscription of Russia is mild and merciful and just, compared with this. And yet, the enforcement of that conscription has just stirred again the slumbering spirit of insurrection in Poland, though the heel of despotic power has trodden upon the necks of her people for a century.

Where now are your taunts and denunciations, heaped upon the Confederate Government for its conscription, when you, yourselves, become the humble imitators of that government, and bring in here a Conscription Act, more odious even than that passed by the Confederate Congress at Richmond? Sir, the chairman of the military committee rejoiced that for the last two years the army had been filled up by voluntary enlistments. Yes, your army has hitherto been thus filled up by the men of the North and West.

One million two hundred and thirty-seven thousand men – for most of the drafted men enlisted, or procured substitutes – have voluntarily surrendered their civil rights, subjected themselves to military law, and thus passed under the command and within the control of the President of the United States. It is not for me to complain of that. It was their own act – done of their own free will and accord – unless bounties, promises, and persuasion may be regarded as coercion. The work you proposed was gigantic, and your means proportionate to it. And what has been the result? What do you propose now? What is this bill? A confession that the people are no longer ready to enlist: that they are not willing to carry on this war longer, until some effort has been made to settle this great controversy in some other way than by the sword. And yet, in addition to the 1,237,000 men who have voluntarily enlisted, you propose now to force the entire body of the people, between the ages of twenty and forty-five, under military law, and within the control of the President, as commander-in-chief of the army, for three years, or during the war – which is to say "for life;" aye, sir, for life, and half your army has already found, or will yet find, that their enlistment was for life too.

I repeat it, sir, this bill is a confession that the people of the country are against this war. It is a solemn admission, upon the record in the legislation of Congress, that they will not voluntarily consent to wage it any longer. And yet, ignoring every principle upon which the Government was founded, this measure is an attempt, by compulsion, to carry it on against the will of the people. Sir, what does all this mean? You were a majority at first; the people were almost unanimously with you, and they were generous and enthusiastic in your support. You abused your power, and your trust, and you failed to do the work which you promised. You have lost the confidence, lost the hearts of the people. You are now in a minority at home. And yet, what a spectacle is exhibited here tonight! You, an accidental, temporary majority, condemned and repudiated by the people, are exhausting the few remaining hours of your political life, in attempting to defeat the popular will, and to compel, by the most desperate and despotic of expedients ever resorted to, the submission of the majority of the people, at home, to the minority, their servants, here. Sir, this experiment has been tried before, in other ages and countries, and its issue always, among a people born free, or fit to be free, has been expulsion or death to the conspirators and tyrants.

I make no threats. They are not arguments fit to be addressed to equals in a legislative assembly; but there is truth, solemn, alarming truth, in what has been said, to-day, by gentlemen on this side of the Chamber. Have a care, have a care, I entreat you, that you do not press these measures too far. I shall do nothing to stir up an already excited people – not because of any fear of your contemptible petty provost marshals, but because I desire to see no violence or revolution in the North or West. But I warn you now, that whenever, against the will of the people, and to perpetuate power and office in a popular government which they have taken from you, you undertake to enforce this bill, and, like the destroying angel in Egypt, enter every house for the first-born sons of the people – remember Poland. You cannot, and will not be permitted to, establish a military despotism. Be not encouraged by the submission of other nations. The people of Austria, of Russia, of Spain, of Italy, have never known the independence and liberty of freemen. France, in seventy years, has witnessed seven principal revolutions – the last brought about in a single day, by the arbitrary attempt of the king to suppress freedom of speech and of the press, and next the free assembling of the people; and when he would have retraced his steps and restored these liberties, a voice from the galleries, not filled with clerks and plunderers and place-men, uttered the sentiments and will of the people of France, in words now historic: "It is too late." The people of England never submitted, and would not now submit, for a moment, to the despotism which you propose to inaugurate in America. England cannot, to-day, fill up her standing armies by conscription. Even the "press gang," unknown to her laws, but for a time acquiesced in, has long since been declared illegal; and a sweeping conscription like this now, would hurl not only the ministry from power, but the queen from her throne.

Sir, so far as this bill is a mere military measure, I might have been content to have given a silent vote against it; but there are two provisions in it hostile, both to the letter and spirit of the Constitution, and inconsistent with the avowed scope and purpose of the bill itself; and, certainly, as I read them in the light of events which have occurred in the past two years, of a character which demands that the majority of this House shall strike them out. There is nothing in the argument, that we have no time to send the bill back to the Senate, lest it should be lost. The presiding officers of both Houses are friends of the bill, and will constitute committees of conference of men favorable to it. They will agree at once, and can at any moment, between this and the 4th of March, present their report as a question of the highest privilege; and you have a two-thirds majority in both branches to adopt it.

With these provisions of the bill stricken out, leaving it simply as a military measure, to be tested by the great question of peace or war, I would be willing that the majority of the House should take the responsibility of passing it without further debate; although, even then, you would place every man in the United States, between the ages of twenty and forty-five, under military law, and within the control, everywhere, of the President, except the very few who are exempt; but you would leave the shadow, at least, of liberty to all men not between these ages, or not subject to draft under this bill, and to the women and children of the country too.

Sir, these two provisions propose to go a step further, and include every one, man, woman and child, and to place him or her under the arbitrary power, not only of the President and his cabinet, but of some two hundred and fifty other petty officers, captains of cavalry, appointed by him. There is no distinction of sex, and none of age. These provisions, sir, are contained in the seventh and twenty-fifth sections of the bill. What are they? I comment not on the appointment of a general provost marshal of the United States, and provost marshals in every Congressional District. Let that pass. But what do you propose to make the duty of each provost marshal in carrying out the draft? Among other things, that he shall "inquire into, and report to the provost marshal general" – what? Treason? No. Felony? No. Breach of the peace, or violation of law of any kind? No; but "treasonable practices;" yes, *treasonable practices*. What mean you by these strange, ominous words? Whence come they? Sir, they are no more new or original than any other of the cast-off rags filched by this Administration from the lumber-house of other and more antiquated despotisms. The history of European tyranny has taught us somewhat of this doctrine of constructive treason. Treasonable practices! Sir, the very language is borrowed from the old proclamations of the British monarchs, some hundreds of years ago. It brings up the old, identical quarrel of the fourteenth century. Treasonable practices! It was this that called forth that English Act of Parliament of twenty-fifth Edward III. from which we have borrowed the noble provision against constructive treason, in the Constitution of the United States. Arbitrary arrests, for no crime known, defined or limited by law, but for pretended offenses, herded together under the general and most comprehensive name of "treasonable practices," had been so frequent, in the worst periods of English history, that in the language of the act of Henry the Fourth, "no man knew how to behave himself, or what to do or say, for doubt of the pains of treason." The statute of Edward the Third, had cut all these fungous, toadstool treasons up by the root; and yet, so prompt is arbitrary power to denounce all opposition to it as treasonable, that, as Lord Hale observes:

> Things were so carried by parties and factions, in the succeeding reign of Richard the Second, that this statute was but little observed, but as this or that party got the better. So the crime of high treason was, in a manner, arbitrarily imposed and adjudged *to the disadvantage of the party which was to be judged;* which by various vicissitudes and revolutions, mischiefed all parties, first and last, and left a great unsettledness and unquietness in the minds of the people, and was one of the occasions of the unhappiness of the king.

And he adds that:

It came to pass that almost every offense that was, or seemed to he, a breach of the faith and allegiance due to the king, was, by construction, consequence, and interpretation, raised into the offense of high treason.

Richard the Second, procured an Act of Parliament – even he did not pretend to have power to do it by proclamation – declaring that the bare purpose to depose the king, and to place another in his stead, without any overt act, was treason; and yet, as Blackstone remarks, so little effect have over-violent laws to prevent crime, that within two years afterward this very prince was both deposed and put to death. Still the struggle for arbitrary and despotic power continued; and up to the time of Charles the First, at various periods, almost every conceivable offense relating to the government, and every form of opposition to the king, was declared high treason. Among these were execrations against the king; calling him opprobrious names by public writing; refusing to abjure the Pope; marrying without license, certain of the king's near relatives; derogating from his royal style or title; impugning his supremacy, or assembling riotously to the number of twelve, and refusing to disperse on proclamation. But steadily, in better times, the people and the Parliament of England returned to the spirit and letter of the act of Edward the Third, passed by a Parliament which now, for five hundred years, has been known and honored as *parliamentum benedictum,* the "blessed Parliament" – just as this Congress will be known, for ages to come, as "the accursed Congress" – and among many other acts, it was declared by a statute, in the first year of the Fourth Henry's reign, that "in no time to come any treason be judged, otherwise than as ordained by the statute of king Edward the Third." And for nearly two hundred years, it has been the aim of the lawyers and judges of England to adhere to the plain letter, spirit, and intent of that act, "to be extended," in the language of Erskine, in his noble defense of Hardy, "by no new or occasional constructions – to be strained by no fancied analogies – to be measured by no rules of political expediency – to be judged of by no theory – to be determined by the wisdom of no individual, however wise – but to be expounded by the simple, genuine letter of the law."

Such, sir, is the law of treason in England to-day; and so much of the just and admirable statute of Edward as is applicable to our form of government, was embodied in the Constitution of the United States. The men of 1787 were well read in history and in English constitutional law. They knew that monarchs and governments, in all ages, had struggled to extend the limits of treason, so as to include all opposition to those in power. They had learned the maxim that, miserable is the servitude where the law is either uncertain or unknown, and had studied and valued the profound declaration of Montesquieu, that "if the crime of treason be indeterminate, that alone is sufficient to make any government degenerate into arbitrary power." Hear Madison, in the *Federalist*:

> As new-fangled and artificial treasons have been the great engines by which violent factions, the natural offspring of free governments, have usually wreaked their alternate malignity on each other, the convention have, with great judgment, opposed a barrier to this peculiar danger, by inserting a constitutional definition of the crime, fixing the proof necessary for conviction of it, and restraining the Congress, even in punishing it, from extending the consequences of guilt beyond the person of its author.

And Story, not foreseeing the possibility of such a party or Administration as is now in power, declared it *"an impassable barrier* against arbitrary constructions, either by the courts or by Congress, upon the crime of treason." "Congress" – that, sir, is the word, for he never dreamed that the President, or, still less, his clerks, the cabinet ministers, would attempt to declare and punish treasons. And yet, what have we lived to hear in America daily, not in political harangues, or the press only, but in official proclamations and in bills in Congress! Yes, your high officials talk now of "treasonable practices," as glibly "as girls of thirteen do of puppy dogs." Treasonable practices! Disloyalty! Who imported these precious phrases, and gave them a legal settlement here? Your Secretary of War. He it was who by command of our most noble President, authorized every marshal, every sheriff, every township constable, or city policeman, in every State in the Union, to fix, in his own imagination, what he might choose to call a treasonable or disloyal practice, and then to arrest any citizen at his discretion, without any accusing oath, and without due process, or any process of law. And now, sir, all this monstrous tyranny, against the whole spirit and the very letter of the Constitution, is to be deliberately embodied in an Act of Congress! Your petty provost marshals are to determine what treasonable practices are, and "inquire into," detect, spy out, eavesdrop, ensnare, and then inform, report to the chief spy at Washington. These, sir, are now to be our American liberties under your Administration. There is not a crowned head in Europe who dare venture on such an experiment. How long think you this people will submit? But words, too – conversation or public speech – are to be adjudged "treasonable practices." Men, women, and children are to be haled to prison for free speech. Whoever shall denounce or oppose this Administration – whoever may affirm that war will not restore the Union, and teach men the gospel of peace, may be reported and arrested, upon some old grudge, and by some ancient enemy, it may be, and imprisoned as guilty of a treasonable practice.

Sir, there can be but one treasonable practice, under the Constitution, in the United States. Admonished by the lessons of English history, the framers of that instrument defined what treason is. It is the only offense defined in the Constitution. We know what it is. Every man can tell whether he has committed treason. He has only to look into the Constitution, and he knows whether he had been guilty of the offense. But neither the Executive, nor Congress, nor both combined, nor the courts, have a right to declare, either by pretended law, or by construction, that any other offense shall be treason, except that defined and limited in this instrument. What is treason? It is the highest offense known to the law – the most execrable crime known to the human heart – the crime of *læsæ majestatis*; of the parricide who lifts his hand against the country of his birth or his adoption. "Treason against the United States," says the Constitution, "shall consist *only* in levying war against them, or in adhering to their enemies, giving them aid and comfort." (Here a Republican member nodded several times and smiled, and Mr. V. said.) Ah, sir, I understand you. But was Lord Chatham guilty of legal treason, treasonable aid and comfort, when he denounced the war against the Colonies, and rejoiced that America had resisted? Was Burke, or Fox, or Barre guilty, when defending the Americans, in the British Parliament, and demanding conciliation and peace? Were even the Federalists guilty of treason, as defined in the Constitution, for "giving aid and comfort" to the enemy, in the war of 1812? Were the Whigs in 1846? Was the Ohio Senator liable to punishment, under the Constitution, and by law, who said, sixteen years ago, in the Senate Chamber, when we were at war in Mexico, "If I were a Mexican as I am an American, I would greet your volunteers with bloody hands, and welcome them to hospitable graves?" Was Abraham Lincoln guilty, because he denounced that same war, while a Representative on the floor of this House? Was all this "adhering to the enemy, giving him aid and comfort," within the meaning of this provision?

A Member. The Democratic papers said so.

Mr. Vallandigham. Sir, I am speaking now as a lawyer, and as a legislator, to legislators and lawyers acting under oath and the other special and solemn sanctions of this Chamber, and not in the loose language of the political canvass. And I repeat, sir, that if such had been the intent of the Constitution, the whole Federal party, and the whole Whig party, and their Representatives in this and the other Chamber, might have been indicted and punished as traitors. Yet, not one of them was ever arrested. And shall they, or their descendants, undertake now to denounce and to punish, as guilty of treason, every man who opposes the policy of this Administration, or is against this civil war, and for peace upon honorable terms? I hope, in spite of the hundreds of your provost marshals, and all your threats, that there will be so much of opposition to the war as will compel the Administration to show a decent respect for, and yield some sort of obedience to, the Constitution and laws, and to the rights and liberties of the States and of the people.

But to return; the Constitution not only defines the crime of treason, but, in its jealous care to guard against the abuses of tyrannic power, it expressly ascertains the character of the proof, and the number of witnesses necessary for conviction, and limits the punishment to the person of the offender, thus going beyond both the statute of Edward, and the common law. And yet every one of these provisions is ignored or violated by this bill.

"No person," says the Constitution, "shall be convicted of treason" – as just defined – "unless on the testimony of two witnesses." Where, and when, and by whom, sir, are the two witnesses to be examined, and under what oath? By your provost marshals, your captains of cavalry? By the jailors of your military bastiles, and inside of forts Warren and Lafayette? Before arrest, upon arrest, while in prison, when discharged, or at any time at all? Has any witness ever been examined in any case heretofore? What means the Constitution by declaring that no person shall be convicted of treason "unless on the testimony of two witnesses"? Clearly, conviction in a judicial court, upon testimony openly given under oath, with all the sanctions and safeguards of a judicial trial to the party accused. And if any doubt there could be upon this point, it is removed by the sixth article of the amendments.

But the Constitution proceeds: "Unless on the testimony of two witnesses *to the same overt act.*" But words, and still less, thoughts or opinions, sir, are not acts; and yet, nearly every case of arbitrary arrest and imprisonment, in the wholly loyal States, at least, has been for words spoken or written, or for thoughts, or opinions supposed to be entertained by the party arrested. And that, too, sir, is precisely what is intended by this bill.

But further: "The testimony of two witnesses to the same overt act, or *confession in open court.*" What, court? The court of some deputy provost marshal at home, or of your provost marshal general, or Judge Advocate General, here in Washington? The court of a military bastile, whose gates are shut day and night against every officer of the law, and whose very casemates are closed to the light and air of heaven? Call you that "open court"? Not so the Constitution. It means judicial court, law court, with judge and jury and witnesses and counsel; and to speak of it as anything else, is a confusion of language, and an insult to intelligence and common sense. Yet, tonight, you deliberately propose to enact the illegal and unconstitutional executive orders, or proclamations, of last summer, into the semblance and form of law.

"To inquire into treasonable practices," says the bill. So, then, your provost-marshals are to be deputy spies to the grand spy, holding his secret inquisitions here in Washington, upon secret reports, sent by telegraph perhaps, or through the mails, both under the control of the Executive. What right has he to arrest and hold me without a hearing, because some deputy spy of his chooses to report me guilty of "disloyalty," or of "treasonable practices"? Is this the liberty secured by the Constitution? Sir, let me tell you, that if the purpose of this bill be to crush out all opposition to the Administration and the party in power, you have no constitutional right to enact it, and not force enough to compel the people, your masters, to submit.

But the enormity of the measure does not stop here. Says the Constitution: "Congress shall make no law abridging the freedom of speech, or of the press." And yet speech – mere words, derogatory to the President, or in opposition to his Administration, and his party and policy, have, over and over again, been reported by the spies and informers and shadows, or other minions, of the men in power, to be "disloyal practices," for which hundreds of free American citizens, of American, not African, descent, have been arrested and imprisoned for months, without public accusation, and without trial by jury, or trial at all. Even upon pretence of guilt of that most vague and indefinite, but most comprehensive of all offenses, "discouraging enlistments," men have been seized at midnight, and dragged from their beds, their homes, and their families, to be shut up in the stone casemates of your military fortresses, as felons. And now, by this bill, you propose to declare, in the form and semblance of law, that whoever "counsels or dissuades" any one from the performance of the military duty required under this conscription, shall be summarily arrested by your provost marshals, and held, without trial, till the draft shall have been completed. Sir, even the "Sedition Law" of '98 was constitutional, merciful and just, compared with this execrable enactment. Wisely did Hamilton ask, in the *Federalist*, "What signifies a declaration that the liberty of the press [or of speech] shall be inviolably preserved, when its security must altogether depend on public opinion, and *on the general spirit of the people,* and of the Government."

But this extraordinary bill does not stop here. "No person," says the Constitution, "no person shall be held to answer for a capital or otherwise infamous crime, unless on a presentment or indictment of a grand jury, except in cases arising in the land and naval force, or in the militia when in actual service in time of war or public danger; nor be deprived of life, liberty, or property, without due process of law." Note the exception. Every man not in the military service, is exempt from arrest, except by due process of law; or, being arrested without it, is entitled to demand immediate inquiry and discharge, or bail; and if held, then presentment or indictment by a grand jury in a civil court, and according to the law of the land. And yet you now propose, by this bill, in addition to the 1,237,000 men who have voluntarily surrendered that great right of freemen, second only to the ballot – and, indeed, essential to it – to take it away forcibly, and against their consent, from three millions more, whose only crime is that they happen to have been so born as to be now between the ages of twenty and forty-five. Do it, if you can, under the Constitution; and when you have thus forced them into the military service, they will be subject to military law, and not entitled to arrest only upon due process of law, nor to indictment by a grand jury in a civil court. But you cannot, you shall not – because the Constitution forbids it – deprive the whole people, also, of the United States, of these rights, "inestimable to them, and formidable to tyrants only," under "the war power," or upon pretense of "military necessity," and by virtue of an act of Congress creating and defining new treasons, new offenses, not only unknown to the Constitution, but expressly excluded by it.

But again: "In all criminal prosecutions," – and wherever a penalty is to be imposed, imprisonment or fine inflicted, it is a criminal prosecution – "In all criminal prosecutions," says the Constitution, "the accused shall enjoy the right to a speedy and public trial, by an impartial jury of the State and district wherein the crime shall have been committed, which district shall have been previously ascertained by law; and to be informed of the nature and cause of the accusation; to be confronted with the witnesses against him; to have compulsory process for obtaining witnesses in his favor, and to have the assistance of counsel, for his defense." Do you propose to allow any of these rights? No, sir – none – not one; but, in the twenty-fifth section, you empower these provost marshals of yours to arrest any man – men not under military law – whom he may charge, or any one else may charge before him, with "counseling or dissuading" from military service, and to hold him in confinement indefinitely, until the draft has been completed. Sir, has it been completed in Connecticut yet? Is it complete in New York? Has it been given up? If so now, nevertheless it was in process of pretended execution for months. In any event, you propose, now, to leave to the discretion of the Executive the time during which all persons arrested, under the provisions of this bill, shall be held in confinement upon that summary and arbitrary arrest; and when he sees fit, and then only, shall the accused be delivered over to the civil authorities for trial. And is this the speedy and public trial by jury, which the Constitution secures to every citizen not in the military service?

"The State and district wherein the crime" – Yes, crime, for crime it must be known to and defined by law, to justify the arrest – "Shall have been committed, which district shall have been previously ascertained by law." Do you mean to obey that, and to observe State lines, or district lines, in arrests and imprisonments? Has it ever been done? Were not Keyes, and Olds, and Mahony, and Steward, and my friend here to the left (Mr. Allen, of Illinois), and my other friend from Maryland (Mr. May), dragged from their several States and districts, to New York, or Masssachusetts, or to this city? The pirate, the murderer, the counterfeiter, the thief – you would have seized by due and sworn process of law, and tried forthwith, by jury, at home;

but honorable and guiltless citizens, members of this House, your peers upon this floor, were thrust, and may, again, under this bill, be thrust into distant dungeons and bastiles, upon the pretence of some crawling, verminous spy and informer, that they have "dissuaded" some one from obedience to the draft, or are otherwise guilty of some "treasonable practice."

"And to be informed of the nature and cause of the accusation." How? By presentment or indictment of a grand jury. When? "Speedily," says the Constitution. "When the draft is completed," says this bill; and the President shall determine that. But who is to limit and define "counseling or dissuading" from military service? Who shall ascertain and inform the accused of the "nature and cause" of a "treasonable practice"? Who, of all the thousand victims of arbitrary arrests, within the last twenty-two months, even to this day, has been informed of the charge against him, although long since released? Yet even the Roman pro-consul, in a conquered province, refused to send up a prisoner, without signifying the crimes with which he was charged.

"To be confronted with the witnesses against him." Witnesses, indeed! Fortunate will be the accused if there be any witnesses against him. But is your deputy provost marshal to call them? O, no; he is only to "inquire into, and report." Is your provost marshal general? What! call witnesses from the remotest parts of the Union, to a secret inquisition here in Washington. Has any "prisoner of State," hitherto, been confronted with witnesses, at any time? Has he even been allowed to know so much as the names of his accusers? Yet, Festus could boast, that it was not the manner of the Romans, to punish any man, "before that he, which is accused, have the accusers face to face."

"To have compulsory process for obtaining witnesses in his favor." Sir, the compulsory process will be, under this bill, as it has been from the first, to compel the absence rather, of not only the witnesses, but the friends and nearest relatives of the accused; even the wife of his bosom, and his children – the inmates of his own household. Newspapers, the Bible, letters from home, except under surveillance, a breath of air, a sight of the waves of the sea, or of the mild, blue sky, the song of birds, whatever was denied to the prisoner of Chillon, and more too; yes, even a solitary lamp in the casemate, where a dying prisoner struggled with death, all have been refused to the American citizen accused of disloyal speech or opinions, by this most just and merciful Administration.

And, finally, says the Constitution: "To have the assistance of counsel for his defense." And yet your Secretary of State, the "conservative" Seward – the confederate of Weed, that treacherous, dissembling foe to constitutional liberty, and the true interests of his country – forbade his prisoners to employ counsel, under penalty of prolonged imprisonment. Yes, charged with treasonable practices, yet the demand for counsel was to be dealt with as equal to treason itself. Here is an order, signed by a minion of Mr. Seward, and read to the prisoners at Fort Lafayette, on the 3d of December, 1861:

> I am instructed, by the Secretary of State, to inform you, that the Department of State, of the United States, *will not recognize any one as an attorney for political prisoners,* and will look with distrust upon all applications for release through such channels; and that such applications *will be regarded as additional reasons for declining to release the prisoners.*

And here is another order to the same effect, dated "Department of State, Washington, November 27, 1861," signed by William H. Seward himself, and read to the prisoners at Fort Warren, on the 29th of November, 1861: "Discountenancing and repudiating all such practices." The disloyal practice, forsooth, of employing counsel:

> The Secretary of State desires that all the State prisoners may understand that they are expected to revoke all such engagements now existing, and avoid any hereafter, as they can only lead to new complications and embarrassments to the cases of prisoners, on whose behalf the Government might be disposed to act with liberality.

Most magnanimous Secretary! Liberality toward men guilty of no crime, but who, though they had been murderers or pirates, were entitled, by the plain letter of the Constitution, to have "the assistance of counsel for their defense." Sir, there was but one step further possible, and that short step was taken some months later, when the prisoners of State were required to make oath, as the condition of their discharge, that they would not seek their constitutional and legal remedy in Court, for the wrongs and outrages inflicted upon them.

Sir, incredible as all this will seem some years hence, it has happened, all of it, and more yet untold, within the last twenty months, in the United States. Under executive usurpation, and by virtue of presidential proclamations and cabinet orders, it has been done without law and against Constitution; and now it is proposed, I repeat, to sanction and authorize it all, by an equally unconstitutional and void act of Congress. Sir, legislative tyranny is no more tolerable than executive tyranny. It is a vain thing to seek to cloak all this under the false semblance of law. Liberty is no more guarded or secured, and arbitrary power no more hedged in and limited here, than under the executive orders of last summer. We know what has already been done, and we will submit to it no longer. Away, then, with your vain clamor about disloyalty, your miserable mockery of treasonable practices. We have read, with virtuous indignation, in history, ages ago, of an Englishman executed for treason, in saying that he would make his son heir to the crown, meaning of his own tavern-house, which bore the sign of the crown; and of that other Englishman, whose favorite buck the king had killed, and who suffered death as a traitor, for wishing, in a fit of vexation, that the buck, horns and all, were emboweled in the body of the king. But what have we not lived to see in our own time? Sir, not many months ago, this Administration, in its great and tender mercy toward the six hundred and forty prisoners of State, confined, for treasonable practices, at Camp Chase, near the capital of Ohio, appointed a commissioner, an extra-judicial functionary, unknown to the Constitution and laws, to hear and determine the cases of the several parties accused, and with power to discharge at his discretion, or to banish to Bull's Island, in Lake Erie. Among the political prisoners called before him, was a lad of fifteen, a newsboy upon the Ohio river, whose only offense proved, upon inquiry, to be, that he owed fifteen cents, the unpaid balance of a debt due to his washer-woman – possibly a woman of color – who had him arrested by the provost marshal, as guilty of "disloyal practices." And yet, for four weary months the lad had lain in that foul and most loathsome prison, under military charge, lest, peradventure, he should overturn the Government of the United States; or, at least, the Administration of Abraham Lincoln!

Several Members on the Democratic side of the House. Oh no: the case cannot be possible.

Mr. Vallandigham. It is absolutely true, and it is one only among many such cases. Why, sir, was not the hump-back carrier of the New York *Daily News*, a paper edited by a member of this House, arrested in Connecticut, for selling that paper, and hurried off out of the State, and imprisoned in Fort Lafayette? And yet, Senators and Representatives, catching up the brutal cry of a blood-thirsty but infatuated partisan press, exclaim "the Government has been too lenient, there ought to have been more arrests!"

Well did Hamilton remark, that "arbitrary imprisonments have been, in all ages, the favorite and most formidable instruments of tyranny;" and not less truly, Blackstone declares, that they are "a less public, a less striking, and therefore a more dangerous engine of arbitrary government," than executions upon the scaffold. And yet, tonight, you seek here, under cloak of an act of Congress, to authorize these arrests and imprisonments, and thus to renew again that reign of terror which smote the hearts of the stoutest among us, last summer, as "the pestilence which walketh in darkness."

But the Constitution provides further, that: "The right of the people to be secure in their persons, houses, papers, and effects, against unreasonable searches and seizures, shall not be violated, and no warrants shall issue, but upon probable cause, supported by oath or affirmation, and particularly describing the place to be searched, and the persons or things to be seized."

Sir, every line, letter, and syllable of this provision has been repeatedly violated, under pretence of securing evidence of disloyal or treasonable practices; and now you propose, by this bill, to sanction the past violations, and authorize new and continued infractions in future. Your provost marshals, your captains of cavalry, are to "inquire into treasonable practices." How? In any way, sir, that they may see fit; and of course, by search and seizure of person, house, papers or effects; for, sworn and appointed spies and informers as they are, they will be and can be of no higher character, and no more scrupulous of law, or right, or decency, than their predecessors of last summer, appointed under executive proclamations of no more or less validity than this bill, which you seek now to pass into a law. Sir, there is but one step further to take. Put down the peaceable assembling of the people; the right of petition for redress of grievances; the "right of the people to keep and bear arms;" and finally, the right of suffrage and elections, and then these United States, this Republic of ours, will have ceased to exist. And that short step you will soon take, if the States and the people do not firmly and speedily check you in your headlong plunge into despotism.

What yet remains? The Constitution declares that: "The enumeration in the Constitution, of certain rights, shall not be construed to deny or disparage others retained by the people." And again: "The powers not delegated to the United States by the Constitution, nor prohibited by it to the States, are reserved to the States respectively, or to the people." And yet, under the monstrous doctrine, that in war the Constitution is suspended, and that the President as commander-in-chief, not of the military forces only, but of the whole people of the United States, may, under "the war power," do whatever he shall think necessary and proper to be done, in any State or part of any State, however remote from the scene of warfare, every right of the people is violated or threatened, and every power of the States usurped. Their last bulwark, the militia, belonging solely to the States, when not called, as such, into the actual service of the United States, you now deliberately propose, by this bill, to sweep away, and to constitute the President supreme military dictator, with a standing army of three millions and more at his command. And for what purpose are the militia to be thus taken from the power and custody of the States? Sir, the opponents of the Constitution anticipated all this, and were denounced as raving incendiaries or distempered enthusiasts. The Federal Government, said Patrick Henry, in the Virginia Convention:

> Squints towards monarchy. Your President may easily become a king. If ever he violates the laws, *will not the recollection of his crimes teach him to make one bold push for the American throne?* Will not the immense difference between being master of everything, and being ignominiously tried and punished, powerfully excite him to make this bold push? But, sir, where is the existing force to punish him? Can he not, at

the head of his army, beat down all opposition? What then will become of you and your rights? Will not absolute despotism ensue?[1]

And yet, for these apprehensions, Henry has been the subject of laughter and pity for seventy years. Sir, the instinctive love of Liberty is wiser and more far-seeing than any philosophy.

Hear, now, Alexander Hamilton, in the *Federalist*. Summing up what he calls the exaggerated and improbable suggestions respecting the power of calling for the services of the militia, urged by the opponents of the Constitution, whose writings he compares to some ill-written tale, or romance full of frightful and distorted shapes, he says:

> The militia of New Hampshire (they allege) is to be marched to Georgia; of Georgia to New Hampshire; of New York to Kentucky; and of Kentucky to Lake Champlain. Nay, the debts due to the French and Dutch, are to be paid in militia-men, instead of Louis d'ors and ducats. At one moment, there is to be a large army to lay prostrate the liberties of the people; at another moment, the militia of Virginia are to be dragged from their homes, five or six hundred miles, to tame the republican contumacy of Massachusetts; *and that of Massachusetts is to be transported an equal distance, to subdue the refractory haughtiness of the aristocratic Virginians*. Do persons who rave at this rate, imagine that their eloquence can impose any conceits or absurdities upon the people of America, for infallible truths?

And yet, sir, just three-quarters of a century later, we have lived to see these raving conceits and absurdities practiced, or attempted, as calmly and deliberately as though the power and the right had been expressly conferred.

And now, sir, listen to the answer of Hamilton to all this – himself the friend of a strong government, a Senate for life, and an Executive for life, with the sole and exclusive power over the militia, to be held by the National Government; and the Executive of each State to be appointed by that Government:

> If there should be an army to be made use of as the engine of despotism, what need of the militia? If there should be no army, *whither would the militia, irritated at being required to undertake a distant and distressing expedition, for the purpose of riveting the chains of slavery upon a part of their countrymen, direct their course,* but to the seats of the tyrants who had meditated so foolish, as well as so wicked, a project; to

---

1. And the reporter, unable to follow the vehement orator of the Revolution, adds: "Here, Mr. Henry strongly and pathetically expatiated on the probability of the President's enslaving America, and the horrid consequences that must result."

crush them in their imagined intrenchments of power, and make them an example of the vengeance of an abused and incensed people? Is this the way in which usurpers stride to dominion over a numerous and enlightened nations?

Sir, Mr. Hamilton was an earnest, sincere man, and, doubtless, wrote what he believed: he was an able man also, and a philosopher; and yet how little did he foresee, that just seventy-five years later, that same Government, which he was striving to establish, would, in desperate hands, attempt to seize the whole militia of the Union, and convert them into a standing army, indefinite as to the time of its service, and for the very purpose of not only beating down State sovereignties, but of abolishing even the domestic and social institutions of the States.

Sir, if your objects are constitutional, you have power abundantly under the Constitution, without infraction or usurpation. The men who framed that instrument, made it both for war and peace. Nay, more, they expressly provide for the cases of insurrection and rebellion. You have ample power to do all that of right you ought to do – all that the people, your masters, permit under their supreme will, the Constitution. Confine, then, yourselves within these limits, and the rising storm of popular discontent will be hushed.

But I return, now, again, to the arbitrary arrests sanctioned by this bill, and by that other consummation of despotism, the Indemnity and Suspension Bill, now in the Senate. Sir, this is the very question which, as I said a little while ago, we made a chief issue before the people in the late elections. You did, then, distinctly claim – and you found an Attorney-General and a few other venal or very venerable lawyers to defend the monstrous claim – that the President had the right to suspend the writ of *habeas corpus;* and that every one of these arrests was legal and justifiable. We went before the people with the Constitution and the laws in our hands, and the love of liberty in our hearts; and the verdict of the people was rendered against you. We insisted that Congress alone could suspend the writ of *habeas corpus* when, in cases of rebellion or invasion, the public safety might require it. And to-day, sir, that is beginning to be again the acknowledged doctrine. The Chief Justice of the Supreme Court of the United States so ruled in the *Merryman* case; and the Supreme Court of Wisconsin, I rejoice to say, has rendered a like decision; and if the question be ever brought before the Supreme Court of the United States, undoubtedly it will be so decided, finally and forever. You yourselves now admit it; and at this moment, your "Indemnity Bill," a measure more execrable than even this Conscription, and liable to every objection which I have urged against it, undertakes to authorize the President to suspend the writ all over, or in any part of, the United States. Sir, I deny that you can thus delegate your right to the Executive. Even your own power is conditional. You cannot suspend the writ except where the public safety requires it, and then only in cases of rebellion or invasion. A foreign war, not brought home by invasion, to our own soil, does not authorize the suspension, in any case. And who is to judge whether and where there is rebellion or invasion, and whether and when the public safety requires that the writ be suspended? Congress alone, and they cannot substitute the judgment of the President for their own. Such, too, is the opinion of Story: "The right to judge," says he, "whether exigency has arisen, must exclusively belong to that body." But not so under the bill which passed this House the other day.

Nor is this all. Congress alone can suspend the writ. When and where? In cases of rebellion or invasion. Where rebellion? Where invasion? Am I to be told, that because there is rebellion in South Carolina, the writ of *habeas corpus* can be suspended in Pennsylvania and Massachusetts where there is none? Is that the meaning of the Constitution? No, sir; the writ can be suspended only where the rebellion or invasion exists – in States, or parts of States alone, where the enemy, foreign or domestic, is found in arms; and moreover, the public safety can require its suspension only where there is rebellion or invasion. Outside of these conditions, Congress has no more authority to suspend the writ, than the President – and least of all, to suspend it without limitation as to time, and generally all over the Union, and in States not invaded or in rebellion. Such an act of Congress is of no more validity, and no more entitled to obedience, than an Executive proclamation; and in any just and impartial court, I venture to affirm that it will be so decided.

But, again, sir, even though the writ be constitutionally suspended, there is no more power in the President to make arbitrary arrests than without it. The gentleman from Rhode Island (Mr. Sheffield), said, very justly – and I am sorry to see him lend any support to this bill – that the suspension of the writ of *habeas corpus* does not authorize arrests, except upon sworn warrant, charging some offence known to the law, and dangerous to the public safety. He is right. It does not; and this was so admitted in the bill which passed the Senate, in 1807. The suspension only denies release upon bail, or a discharge without trial, to parties thus arrested. It suspends no other right or privilege under the Constitution – certainly not the right to a speedy public trial, by jury, in a civil Court. It dispenses with no "due process of law," except only that particular writ. It does not take away the claim for damages to which a party illegally arrested, or legally arrested, but without probable cause, is entitled.

And yet, everywhere, it has been assumed, that a suspension of the writ of *habeas corpus*, is a suspension of the entire Constitution, and of all laws, so far as the personal rights of the citizen are concerned, and that, therefore, the moment it is suspended, either by the President, as heretofore asserted, or by Congress, as now about to be authorized, arbitrary arrests, without sworn warrant, or other due process of law, may be made at the sole pleasure or discretion of the Executive. I tell you no; and that, although we may not be able to take the body of the party arrested from the provost marshal by writ of *habeas corpus*, every other right and privilege of the Constitution and of the common law remains intact, including the right to resist the wrong-doer or trespasser, who, without due authority, would violate your person, or enter your house, which is your castle; and, after all this, the right also to prosecute on indictment, or for damages, as the nature or aggravation of the case may demand. And yet, as claimed by you of the party in power, the suspension of this writ is a total abrogation of the Constitution and of the liberties of the citizen, and the rights of the States. Why, then, sir, stop with arbitrary arrests and imprisonments? Does any man believe that it will end here? Not so have I learned history. The guillotine! the guillotine! the guillotine follows next.

Sir, when one of those earliest confined in Fort Lafayette – I had it from his own lips – made complaint to the Secretary of State of the injustice of his arrest, and the severity of the treatment to which he had been subjected in the exercise of arbitrary power, no offence being alleged against him, "Why, sir," said the Secretary, with a smile of most significant complacency, "my dear, sir, you ought not to complain; *we might have gone further.*" Light flashed upon the mind of the gentleman, and he replied: "Ah! that is true, sir; you had just the same right to behead, as to arrest and imprison me." And shall it come to this? Then, sir, let us see who is beheaded first. It is horrible enough to be imprisoned without crime, but when it becomes a question of life or death, remember the words of the book of Job: "All that a man hath will he give for his life."

Sir, it is this which makes revolutions. A gentleman upon the other side asked, this afternoon, which party was to rise now in revolution. The answer of the able and gallant gentleman from Pennsylvania (Mr. Biddle), was pertinent and just: "No party, but an outraged people." It is not, let me tell you, the leaders of parties who begin revolutions. Never. Did any one of the distinguished characters of the Revolution of 1776, participate in the throwing of the tea into Boston harbor? Who was it? Who, to-day, can name the actors in that now historic scene? It was not Hancock, nor Samuel Adams, nor John Adams, nor Patrick Henry, nor Washington; but men unknown to fame. Good men agitate; obscure men begin real revolutions; great men finally direct and control them. And if, indeed, we are about to pass through the usual stages of revolution, it will not be the leaders of the Democratic party – not I, not the men with me here, tonight – but some man among the people, now unknown and unnoted, who will hurl your tea into the harbor; and it may even be in Boston once again; for the love of liberty, I would fain believe, lingers still under the shadow of the monument on Bunker Hill. But sir, we seek no revolution – except through the ballot-box. The conflict to which we challenge you, is not of arms but of argument. Do you believe in the virtue and intelligence of the people? Do you admit their capacity for self-government? Have they not intelligence enough to understand the right, and virtue enough to pursue it? Come then: meet us through the press, and with free speech, and before the assemblages of the people, and we will argue these questions, as we and our fathers have done from the beginning of the Government: "Are we right, or you right, we wrong or you wrong?" And by the judgment of the people, we will, one and all, abide.

Sir, I have done now with my objections to this bill. I have spoken as though the Constitution survived, and was still the supreme law of the land. But if, indeed, there be no Constitution any longer, limiting and restraining the men in power, then there is none binding upon the States or the people. God forbid. We have a Constitution yet, and laws yet. To them I appeal. Give us our rights; give us known and fixed laws; give us the judiciary; arrest us only upon due process of law; give us presentment or indictment by grand juries; speedy and public trial; trial by jury and at home; tell us the nature and cause of the accusation; confront us with witnesses; allow us witnesses in our behalf, and the assistance of counsel for our defense; secure us in our persons, our houses, our papers, and our effects; leave us arms, not for resistance to law or against rightful authority, but to defend ourselves from outrage and violence; give us free speech and a free press; the right peaceably to assemble; and above all, free and undisturbed elections and the ballot – take our sons, take our money, our property, take all else, and we will wait a little, till at the time and in the manner appointed by Constitution and law, we shall eject you from the trusts you have abused, and the seats of power you have dishonored, and other and better men shall reign in your stead.

SUPPLEMENT

Under this head, we add some passages and items of historical value and interest. The collection, as will be seen, is gathered from the whole public life of Mr. Vallandigham. The design is, to add to the foregoing Speeches, as much as our space will admit of, matter best calculated to give a fair and full understanding of what Mr. Vallandigham has said, written, and done, bearing upon *"Abolition, Slavery, and the Civil War."* These questions are now before the people, and, in some of their varied aspects, determine the estimation of every man, who occupies any public position. By this ordeal every man's record must be tried. And it helps to assure us of the strength and endurance of a man's devotion to the principles held to-day, if, on examining his record, we find that the same principles have been consistently held and advocated through a long series of years.

A brief statement in relation to Mr. Vallandigham's parentage and education, may gratify a reasonable curiosity on the part of the public.

Clement Laird Vallandigham was born in New Lisbon, Columbiana county, Ohio, July 29th, 1820. His father, a Presbyterian clergyman, was a native of Virginia. His grandfather was also a Virginian, born near the now classic fields of "Bull Run." The name, originally, was Van Landeghem; the family came from French Flanders.

Mr. Vallandigham was educated at Jefferson College, Pennsylvania. After leaving college, he was for some time principal of an academy on the Eastern Shore of Maryland. Thence, he returned to his native county, where, in December, 1842, at the early age of twenty-two years, he was admitted to the practice of law. Three years later, he was chosen a representative from that county, in the Ohio Legislature of 1845-6-7. This was the opening of his political record. Additions have been continually made, and the record is not closed. A few interesting facts and items here follow, numbered for convenience.

No. I. Opposition to the Wilmot Proviso. – The present evil condition of the country began more directly with the renewal of the "Missouri controversy," by the introduction of the "Wilmot Proviso," in the summer of 1846. Mr. Vallandigham, while a member of the Ohio Legislature, distinguished himself by his opposition to that measure, and to all the schemes of the Abolitionists and semi-Abolitionists, then beginning to lift their hydra head throughout the country.

On the 16th of January, 1847, Harrison G. Blake, now a Republican member of Congress, moved a joint resolution, in the Ohio House of Representatives, requesting our Senators and Representatives to vote for "the exclusion of slavery from the territory of Oregon, and also from any other territory that now is, or may hereafter be, annexed to the United States."

Mr. Vallandigham moved the resolution be laid on the table, which motion prevailed. On the 18th of January, it came up again, and, on motion of Mr. Trimble, of Highland, it was again laid on the table, Mr. Vallandigham voting in the affirmative. On the 21st of January, it was brought up again, and after a long parliamentary fight, running late into the night, it passed. Mr. Vallandigham opposed it strongly (*House Journal,* 1846-7, pp. 241, 254, 288, 291, 295). During the struggle, the following debate took place, which we transcribe from the Ohio *Statesman,* of January 22, 1847:

> Mr. Ellison, of Brown, moved to add these words:
> "Excepting in those cases where the welfare and safety of the Union may otherwise require."
> Mr. Franklin T. Backus, of Cuyahoga [late Republican nominee for Supreme Judge], moved to amend, by inserting after the word "Union," the words "in the opinion of the chivalry." (A laugh.)
> Mr. Vallandigham rose, and began by rebuking the laughter, and laughing gentlemen, and asked them, if they had forgotten the great Missouri Compromise? That compromise – the principle of concession which was now (1847) laughed at – had saved the Union in 1820. But for the respect which our fathers felt for this principle, and which was then manifested by none more worthily than by Mr. Clay himself, *this Union would have then been dissolved.* Mr. V. declared, for himself, that whenever any question might arise, involving the Union in the alternative, *he would go with his might on that side* – on the side of the Union, "now and forever, one and inseparable." Would any gentleman relinquish the Union rather than tolerate the existence of slavery in the South?
> Mr. Backus also believed the compromise (1820) to have been necessary to the perpetuity of the Union. But such an issue was not likely again

to occur. *The slaveholding States would be the last to secede and dissolve the Union.* With what face could gentlemen give out their fears on this subject, when they remember the treatment which John Quincy Adams received at their hands, *at the time when he stood up in Congress for a considerate and rational report upon a petition to dissolve the Union.* What a bluster they made, and they were going to expel the old man from the House! Mr. B. affirmed again that we had all been deceived – the slaveholders themselves, by their acts had manifested the fact, that the very salvation of their system depends upon their remaining in the Union. We had heard enough of these threats to know how to regard them.

    Mr. Vallandigham. The gentleman says that such a portentous issue as that involved in the Missouri question was not likely again to arise. Let him not lay to his soul that flattering unction. But the gentleman from Cuyahoga seems o'er familiar with this talk of dissolving the Union. That gentleman (Mr. B.), resided in a district *claiming that there now existed cause for dissolving the Union.* He belonged to the district of Joshua R. Giddings, who declared of them, that they were dissolved from all political connection with the Southern States, on account of the annexation of Texas. But the mind of the House was not to be drawn off from this question by raising a dispute, whether Mr. Clay ever acted as an honest man. The question was, whether such an exigency as that developed in the Missouri question may not happen again. *What had once happened might happen again;* and let us not become wise above what comes to us as the lessons of the past. The gentleman from Cuyahoga had not answered the question. If he were to decide between the exclusion of slavery, with the dissolution of the Union, and the perpetuation of the Union, in connection with that institution, *whether he would prefer to go for dissolution?* He (Mr. V.) trusted the amendment would carry without the mutilation proposed by the gentleman from Cuyahoga. *If we were to throw a firebrand toward the South – if we must needs throw down the gauntlet before them, in the shape of these resolutions, they should, at least, be shaped so as not to endanger the Union; they should, by all means, be put in such a guarded form as not to endanger our favored institutions.* Mr. V. felt that, perhaps, he had been too felt that, perhaps, he had been too much in earnest upon this question. He had spoken from impulse, and, perhaps, with too much freedom and feeling, *because he felt called upon as a patriot and citizen to resist and expose every measure which might work incalculable mischief, not only to ourselves, but to generations yet unborn.*

    Mr. Backus moved to amend the first resolution, by adding thereto the following: "And strenuously to resist all attempts that may hereafter be made to introduce into this Union *any new State, by the Constitution of which slavery is not forever excluded from the territory of such State;*"

which motion was lost. Yeas 23, nays 37. Among the yeas, Backus, Blake, W.P. Cutler, etc.; among the nays, Vallandigham, etc.

No. II. Petitions to Dissolve the Union. – At the same session, on the 25th of January, 1847, in the House of Representatives:

> Mr. Truesdale, of Trumbull, presented the memorial of thirty-eight inhabitants of Lowell, and vicinity, in relation to the annexation of Texas, and *asking the Legislature to declare the Union dissolved, and to withdraw our Senators and Representatives in Congress.*
> Mr. Truesdale moved that said petition be laid upon the table.
> Mr. Smith, of Hamilton, moved that said petition be rejected.
> Upon which motion the yeas and nays being demanded and ordered, resulted – yeas 41, nays 24. – *House Journal*, 1846-7, p. 321.

Mr. Vallandigham, of course, denounced the petition, and those who supported it. He and every other Democrat in the House, except one, also several Whigs, voted to reject the petition. Those who voted to lay it on the table were: Beatty, Bennett, Blake, Breck, Clark of Franklin, Cotton, Harsh, Hibberd, Hogue, Horton, Johnston, Kiler, Matthews, Moore, McGrew, Owen, Park, Poor, Potter, Tallman, Truesdale, White, Wilson, and the Speaker, Wm. P. Cutler.

We venture to say that nearly every man among those twenty-four, if alive, is to-day supporting the Abolition party. And those traitors are now denouncing Mr. Vallandigham for his faithful adherence to the Constitution and laws of our country. He is still standing where he then did, contending for the Union of our fathers, while they are battling to destroy it.

Again, at the same session, on the 1st day of February, 1847, in the House of Representatives:

> Mr. Hogue presented the petition of Lot Holmes, and fifty-nine other citizens, of Fairfield township, Columbiana county, asking, as a consequence of the annexation of Texas, *that the Legislature may declare the Union dissolved, and the recall of our Senators and Representatives in Congress.*
> Mr. Hogue moved to lay said petition on the table.
> Mr. Smith, of Hamilton, moved that said petition be rejected.
> Upon which motion the yeas and nays being demanded and ordered, resulted – yeas 33, nays 21. – *House Journal*, 1846-7, p. 428.

Among the yeas, for rejection, were Vallandigham, and every other

Democrat in the House, and several Whigs; among the nays were the same members as upon the former vote, with two or three exceptions, and the additional names of Backus, Franklin, Corwin, Curtiss, and Trimble of Muskingum.

In that same Winter, of 1847, Massachusetts passed a secession resolution, which, to this day, remains unrescinded upon its official records.

No. III. The Mexican War, 1846-7. – On the 15th of December, 1846, in the Ohio House of Representatives, Mr. Vallandigham offered the following resolutions, which he supported in two speeches, boldly advocating the "vigorous prosecution" of that foreign war to an honorable peace:

> That the war thus brought about and commenced by the aggressions and act of Mexico herself, having been recognized by Congress, according to the forms of the Constitution, is a constitutional war, and a war of the *whole people* of the United States, begun (on our part), and *carried on in pursuance of the constitution and laws of the Union.*
>
> That this General Assembly has full confidence in the wisdom and the ability of the Executive of the United States to prosecute the war to a successful and speedy termination by *an honorable peace;* and that we hereby tender the cordial sympathies and support of this commonwealth, to the said Executive, in the further prosecution of the war.

These resolutions were smothered in committee, and never received a single Whig vote.

No. IV. As Editor of the Dayton *Empire*. – At the conclusion of his term in the Legislature of Ohio, Mr. Vallandigham removed to Dayton, and on the 2d of September, 1847, assumed the editorial control of the Dayton *Empire*. In that position, he distinguished himself as a vigorous and able journalist, and as a patriot, who sought to preserve the principles of constitutional liberty which were born of our Revolution. He took a prominent part, among the friends of the Union in Ohio, in favor of the compromise measures of 1850, the work of Clay and Webster, and other true men and patriots, who then saved the ship of state from splitting on the rock of Abolitionism.

The following, from his "Introductory Address," will give an idea of the principles to whose advocacy and defense his labors, as editor, were devoted:

We will support the Constitution of the United States, in its whole integrity, as it came to us from "the Fathers," believing it to establish, in principle, the very best form of government which the wisdom of man ever devised.

We will protect and defend, according to our opportunities and abilities, the Union of these States, as in very deed the "Palladium of our political prosperity," "the only rock of our safety," less sacred only than Liberty herself; *and we will pander to the sectional prejudices, or the fanaticism, or wounded pride, or disappointed ambition, of no man or set of men, whereby that Union shall be put in jeopardy.*

To the present Administration (James K. Polk's) we will lend that support (whatever it is worth) which an honest and independent man may and ought to extend to the administration of the party to which he belongs. Above all, and to the very uttermost of our energy and abilities, we will defend and support it in the war now waged against Mexico, till it shall have been terminated by *an honorable peace*.

On the 27th of June, 1849, Mr. Vallandigham's connection with the *Empire*, terminated. In his "Valedictory" is the following. Referring to the principles announced by him in his Introductory, he says:

We would stand or fall by them now as then, and *throughout life*. Of the vital importance to the welfare of the whole country in general, and the Democratic party in particular, of two, in an especial manner, to these principles, every hour has added to our deep conviction. And we would write them as in the rock, upon the hearts of our friends forever:

First, that *which is really and most valuable in our American liberties, depends upon the preservation and vigor of the Union of these States;* and therefore, all and every agitation in one section, necessarily generating counter-agitation in the other, ought, *from what quarter soever it may come*, by every patriot and well-wisher of his country, to be "indignantly frowned upon," and *arrested ere it be "too late."*

No. V. Compromise Measures of 1850. – On the 19th of October, 1850, a public meeting was held in the City Hall, Dayton, Ohio, to denounce the "Compromise Measures" of 1850. The following is one of the resolutions:

Resolved, That the Congress which could be so far frightened from its propriety, by the insolent bluster and bravado of a few slave-holders, as to pass an act (the Fugitive Slave Act) so fraught with injustice, and so odious, deserves the rebuke of the people of these United States.

From the official proceedings, we quote the following:

> C.L. Vallandigham, Esq., replied in opposition to the resolutions, and *in favor of the compromise policy* which gave birth to the law.

From the Dayton *Journal* (Whig), editorial, we quote the following:

> C.L. Vallandigham, Esq., followed in opposition to the resolutions. His speech was ingenuous and eloquent. His objection to the course proposed by the resolutions was, that it would lead to further agitation, and tend to endanger the Union.

The *Empire* noticed Mr. Vallandigham's speech as follows:

> C. L. Vallandigham, Esq. – The speech of this gentleman, at the meeting on Saturday night, is universally spoken of as a most eloquent and patriotic effort; and the positions he took in favor of such measures as would tend to restrain undue excitement and agitation, rather than increase them, cannot but receive the approbation of every cool and reflecting mind.
>
> His remarks were earnest, dignified, and appropriate. He strongly deprecated every new attempt to inflame the public mind, while he enforced, in strains of lofty and impassioned eloquence, *the duty of every good citizen to observe and maintain the sanction of law as the only way to secure the peace, order, and happiness of society anywhere.* The sentiments he uttered were warmly and enthusiastically applauded at the time, and are such, we doubt not, as will be approved and sustained by our citizens generally.

The Second "Compromise Meeting." – On the 26th of October, 1850, a very large meeting, composed of the first citizens of Dayton, assembled at the City Hall. From the committee, Mr. Vallandigham, as chairman, reported the following resolutions. In the first will be found the counterpart of the now celebrated motto of the Democratic party: *"The Constitution as it is, and the Union as it was."*

> 1. *That we are for the Union as it is, and the Constitution as it is,* and that we will preserve, maintain, and defend both at every hazard, observing, with scrupulous and uncalculating fidelity, every article, requirement, and compromise of the constitutional compact between these States, to the letter, and in its utmost spirit, and recognizing no "higher law," between which and the Constitution we know of any conflict.
>
> 2. That the Constitution was "the result of a spirit of amity, and of that mutual deference and concession which the peculiarity of our political

situation rendered indispensable," that by amity, conciliation and compromise alone can it, and the Union which it established, be preserved; and that it is the duty of all good citizens to frown indignantly upon every attempt, wheresoever or by whomsoever made, to array one section of the Union against the other; to foment jealousies and heart-burnings between them, by systematic and organized misrepresentation, denunciation and calumny, and thereby, to render them in feeling and affection the inheritors of so noble a common patrimony purchased by our fathers at so great expense of blood and treasure.

3. That as the friends of peace and concord, as lovers of the Union, and foes, sworn upon the horns of the altar of our common country, to all who seek, and all that tends to its dissolution, we have viewed with anxiety and alarm the perilous crisis brought upon us by years of ceaseless and persevering agitation of the slavery question in its various forms; and that the Executive and Congress of the United States have deserved well of the Republic, for their patriotic efforts so to compromise and adjust this vexed question, as to leave no good cause for clamor or offense by any portion of the Union.

4. That a strict adherence in all its parts, to the compromise thus deliberately and solemnly affected, is essential to the restoration and maintenance of peace, harmony, and fraternal affection between the different sections of the Union, and thereby to the preservation of the Union itself; and that good faith imperatively demands that adherence at the hands of all good citizens, whether of the North or of the South.

5. That, believing this compromise the very best which, in view of the circumstances and temper of the times, could have been attained, we are for it as it is, and opposed to all agitation, looking to a repeal or essential modification of any of its parts, and that we will lend no aid or comfort to those who, for any purpose, seek further to agitate and embroil the country upon these questions.

6. That "all obstructions to the execution of the laws, all combinations and associations, under whatever plausible character, with the real design to direct, control, counteract, or awe the regular deliberation and action of the constituted authorities, are destructive of the fundamental principle of our institutions and of fatal tendency; that all such efforts, wherever made or by whomsoever advised, find no answering sympathy in our breast – nothing but loathing and contempt – and that we hereby pledge ourselves to the country, that, so far as in us lies, *the Union, the Constitution and the Laws,* must and shall be maintained."

No. VI. Nominated for Congress. – In 1852, Mr. Vallandigham was first put in nomination, by the Democracy of the Third District of Ohio, composed of the counties of Montgomery, Butler, and Preble. His competitor was Hon. Lewis D. Campbell, the candidate of the anti-compromise or Abolition party. Mr. Campbell was elected, which so rejoiced the old "Liberty party" of Ohio, which ran John P. Hale, for President, and George W. Julian, for Vice-President, that their State committee issued a circular, in which they said of Mr. Vallandigham:

> In opposition to Mr. Campbell, the Democratic party had nominated C.L. Vallandigham, a lawyer of high standing, an eloquent and ready debater, of gentlemanly deportment and unblemished private character, and untiring industry and energy. But he was known, to all, to be an ultra pro-slavery man (anti-Abolitionist), he undertook, with a relish, to carry the load of the Compromise Measures, the Fugitive-Slave Law included, and he broke down under the burden.

No. VII. Election to Congress – Commencement of Congressional labors. – In 1854, Mr Vallandigham was unanimously re-nominated by the democracy against Mr. Campbell, but *was beaten by two thousand five hundred and sixty-five votes,* his competitor being carried triumphantly through on the "Know Nothing" flood.

In 1856, Mr. Vallandigham was again, by acclamation, the Democratic candidate against Mr. Campbell. His friends went into the canvas with "Vall and the Union" on their banners, while his opponents bore flags, with only sixteen stars on them – ensigns of disunion. The canvas was intensely exciting a hand to hand struggle. Scarcely a voter in the district but was secured by one party or the other. The returns showed nineteen majority against Mr Vallandigham. He contested the election on the ground that the majority was made up of negro votes, and, after a tedious and annoying contest, obtained the seat. On the 22d of May, 1858, arguing the contest before the House of Representatives, and speaking of negro suffrage and equality, Mr. Vallandigham said:

> It is enough to know that Ohio has chosen to make *citizenship of the United States* a qualification for her electors. The language of the Constitution of 1851 is: "Every *white* male citizen of the United States." Two qualifications are here prescribed – color and citizenship of the United States. Were these mulattoes and persons of color *"white,"* within the meaning of the Constitution? That, sir, is a term of ancient and established signification, in constitutional language. It needs no gloss; it has no synonym; it admits of no definition. It means *white – pure white!* and not any shade, or any variety of

shades, between white and black. Such it is in philology, and in the arts. White and black are the two extremes, between which there is a large variety of colors. No artist ever confounds these terms; no man in ordinary conversation confounds them. He may speak of a dark blue, or a light brown, or a bright yellow; but never of a dark white, or a light black.

But the term "white," in constitutions, is a designation of race rather than color; and it is used in this country to distinguish primarily between the African race and all others – between a servile race and races which are free. Strictly, indeed, it may refer to the several varieties of the Caucasian race. But in constitutions, and in popular language in the United States, it is a word of exclusion against the whole negro race, in every degree. Whoever has a distinct and visible admixture of the blood of that race is not white; and it is an utter confusion of language to call him white. Sir, it is a question of vision, of autopsy; it is to be resolved upon actual view, and by personal inspection rather than by pedigree. And the Almighty has marked the distinguishing characteristics of the race so strong, he has furrowed them so deep, that they are not eradicated in several generations. The Constitution of North Carolina has fixed the degree at the sixteenth; and this corresponds, in fact, with the rule adopted generally by courts, North and South, that by distinct and visible admixture of negro blood, without reference to the exact proportions, degrades to the class of persons of color.

But, apart from all this, the reason of the rule applies, equally, to all of the African race, no matter how they may have come to our shores. No negro emigrant could be naturalized. It is not alone his descent from slaves, in this country, that degrades him in the scale of social and political being. It is his color and his blood. It is because he is the descendant of a servile and degraded race almost from the beginning of time. The curse of Ham pursues him in every age, and all over the globe. Bayard Taylor – no apologist for slavery – speaks but the testimony of history, when he writes from Nubia, in upper Egypt, that:

> The only *negro features* represented in Egyptian sculpture are those of slaves and captives taken in Ethiopian wars of the Pharaohs; and that the temples and pyramids throughout Nubia, as far as Daref and Abyssinia, all bear the hieroglyphy of monarchs; and that there is no evidence, in all the valley of the Nile, that the negro race ever attained a higher degree of civilization than is at present exhibited in Congo and Ashantee.

Sir, no wise people will ever, in any manner, encourage the attempt to elevate such a race to social and political equality. And if the question of law were here doubtful, I might well demand, upon those high motives of public policy, that the doubt should be resolved against the race. Above all, I would urge these great considerations now, and in future, against this same spurious and mongrel issue, in whose behalf a relaxation of the policy is demanded. Look to Spanish America. Look at Mexico. The blood of the conquerors was lost in the veins of inferior and outcast races, and Mexico has no "people" to-day. With no tyrant strong enough to bind her down, and no yeomanry fit for self-government, she is the sport of faction, and the prey of anarchy and bloodshed; and, to-day, the spirit of the murdered Guatemozin, wandering three centuries through the halls of the Montezumas, gluts itself with revenge.

Sir, it is this same spurious and mongrel race who constitute your "free negroes," North and South. They will not be slaves, and they are not fit for freemen. And when this Government shall be broken up, and the fanaticism of the age shall have culminated in the North in red Republicanism and negro equality, and the South shall have driven out her free negroes upon you, and you shall have stolen away her slaves, then your troubles with this race, which already has plagued America for a century, will but have begun. They are your petty thieves now; they rob your larders and your sheep-cotes; they do fill up your penitentiaries, and they would fill up your hospitals and your alms-houses, *if you would let them*. Then they will be your highwaymen, your banditti; they will make up your mobs. With just enough of intelligence, derived from a white ancestry, to know, and enough of brutishness, inherited from the old African stock, to avenge, in any form, the ignominy and degradations of four thousand years; with fetish ideas of religion, and fanatic notions of politics, they are the *sans culotte*, who, led on by the worst of white men, will make your revolutions, and overturn your governments. Sir, such things have already occurred in history. They are not the baseless fabrics of a vision. No wonder the States of the Northwest have begun to erect Constitutional barriers, stronger than ever, against a negro population. In all this there is eminent wisdom, and a statesmanlike foresight.

Mr. Vallandigham was admitted to a seat, in the House of Representatives, on the 25th of May, 1858, and soon after, Congress adjourned. At the subsequent session, of 1858-9, he replied to, and refuted, a charge made by a Southern member, of having voted for the repeal of the "Black Laws" of Ohio. He spoke, also, upon the tariff, on the 24th of February, 1859.

No. VIII. The Ohio Rebellion – 1857. – In the year 1857, the deputies of the United States Marshal for the Southern District of Ohio were resisted in the execution of regular judicial writs issued under the Fugitive-Slave Act. They were pursued by a body of armed men, more than fifty in number, from Champaign county, through Clarke, into Greene, and there overpowered, and their prisoners rescued. They were, also, themselves arrested on State process. To discharge them from imprisonment, a *habeas corpus* was issued by Judge Leavitt, of the United States District Court. It was heard at Cincinnati, on the 25th of June, 1857. Salmon P. Chase, now Secretary of the Treasury, but then the Governor of Ohio, sent the Attorney-General of the State, C. P. Wolcott, now Assistant Secretary of War, to argue against their discharge. Mr. Vallandigham, along with Mr. Pugh and Mr. Stanley Matthews, argued the case for the Marshals. Maintaining the vital doctrine of State Rights to their fullest extent, Mr. V. asserted and upheld the absolute supremacy of the Federal authority, within its Constitutional limits. He also denounced Abolitionism and "personal liberty bills," in language severe indeed, but most just. The following are extracts from his argument:

> For sixty-eight years, also, the people of Ohio lived happily, freely, prosperously, and in neighborly intercourse with her sister States and Territories. Without slavery in her own limits, she yet had no quarrel, and waged no war, with those who had. Slaves repeatedly escaped into her territory, and were always peaceably and quietly, and oftentimes without officer or warrant, recaptured and remanded. Ohio herself, not many years ago, volunteered to enact a "Fugitive-Slave Law," not less stringent, and certainly more odious, than the now accursed Act of 1850. But times have changed, and we are changed with them. Men, wise above what is written – wiser than the fathers, men of more capacity, and a wisdom and sagacity more than ordinary – more than human, or of intellects narrowed and beclouded by ignorance, and fanaticism, or seduced by a corrupt and most wicked ambition, have discovered that the Constitution is all wrong, and its compacts all wrong, or, rather, that there is a higher law than the Constitution, and that discord is piety, and sedition patriotism. They have resolved to annul, and set at naught, an important and most essential part of the Constitution and its compacts, and to compel the Government of the United States to succumb to their resolves, or to bring the authorities of the State and of the Union into deadly and most destructive conflict.
>
> I concur with the Attorney-General in all that he has said, of the vast importance of the case now and hereafter, and the more especially, if the menaces which he, the law officer of the State, and her representative in this forum, has seen fit to more than insinuate, in case of an adverse decision by this tribunal, are, in the hour of madness, to be carried out by her authorities, as they are now constituted. But I am confident that this Court is prepared that the whole Government of the United States is prepared; and I tell Mr. Attorney-General, and through him the Executive of the State, whose vain

defiance he has this day borne here to this presence, that it is not to be awed by threats, not to be put down by denunciation, nor to be turned aside from its firm purpose to enforce its laws, and the process of its courts, in any event, at all hazards, and without respect to persons or to States, whether those States be Rhode Island or Ohio.

The writ was sustained and the defendants discharged.

No. IX. The "John Brown Raid" – 1859. – Returning from a visit to Washington City, in October, 1859, it was Mr. Vallandigham's ill-fortune to witness the first shedding of blood in the great quarrel between the North and the South. Passing through Harper's Ferry a few hours after the capture of "old Ossawattamie Brown," he saw that "first martyr," and asked him a few questions about the raid and its purpose, which, being duly reported, with the answers, in the New York *Herald*, Mr. V. was persistently and bitterly assailed and abused for it, by the Abolition orators and press. The abuse was of the same quality, and came from the same dark fountain with that which has been poured upon him for the last two years.

No. X. Suppressing Newspapers in the Post-Office. – In December, 1859, a postmaster, in Hardy county, Virginia, having suppressed the *Religious Telescope*, of Dayton, Ohio, at his office, as an Abolition paper, Mr. Vallandigham, at the request of the editor, addressed a letter to the Post-Office Department remonstrating against the act. The Virginia postmaster was immediately commanded to obey the law, and the *Telescope* had no further trouble. The following is an extract from Mr. V.'s letter:

> They, at least, whom I have the honor to represent, have always obeyed and respected, and ever will respect and obey, every requirement and obligation of the Constitutional compact. The vast majority of them, certainly, regard none of its obligations and requirements as either odious or onerous; and they ask only that their rights also, under that compact, shall be, in like manner and fully, protected and enjoyed.

Publishing the correspondence, the *Telescope* said:

> We thank Mr. Vallandigham, and our readers, especially those in Virginia, Kentucky, Tennessee, and other slave States, will thank him, for the prompt attention which he has given to this matter.

No. XI. Campaign of 1860.– On the 19th of May, 1860, Mr. Vallandigham returned home, on a brief visit, from Washington, and addressed the people in front of the Dayton Court-House. The following are extracts from a condensed report of the speech:

> He was not for the North, nor for the South, *but for the whole country;* and yet, in a conflict of sectional interests, he was for the West all the time. In a little while – even after the present year, men east of the mountains would learn that there was a West, which to them has heretofore been an "undiscovered country." *He hoped fervently to see the day when we should hear no more of sections;* but as long as men elsewhere demanded a "united North," and a "united South," he wanted to see a "united West." Still the "United States" was a better term, more patriotic, more constitutional, and more glorious than any of them.

Referring to Mr. Lincoln's "irrepressible conflict" speech of 1858:

> Mr. Vallandigham proceeded for some time to denounce the sentiment of the speech in a vehement and impassionate manner, as revolutionary, disorganizing, subversive of the government, *and ending necessarily in disunion.* Our fathers had founded a government expressly upon the compatibility and harmony of a Union of States, "part slave, and part free," and whoever affirmed the contrary, laid the ax at the very root of the Union.

On the 30th of June, 1860, Mr. Vallandigham returned home from Congress, and again addressed the people in front of the Court-House. The following is an extract from the speech:

> There are now two extreme sectional parties. Six years ago the Abolition sentiments of the free States culminated in the Republican organization. In the course of time *it has brought forth its inevitable fruit,* in the organization, especially in the Gulf or Cotton States, of an extreme Southern or pro-slavery party, the offspring, but the very antipode of the Republican party. If either of these is suffered to prevail, the Union is at an end. Even now it is in peril from mere conflict between them. But the death of the parent will be the death of the child. Kill the Northern and Western anti-slavery organization, the Republican party, and the extreme Southern pro-slavery, "fire-eating" organization of the Cotton States, will expire in three months. Continue the Republican party – above all, put it in power – and the antagonism, will grow till the whole South will become a unit. It is our mission here in Ohio, as one of the free States, to conquer and crush out Northern and Western sectionalism, as this is the especial enemy in our midst.

Supplement

On the 1st of August, 1860, Mr. Vallandigham addressed the Democracy of Detroit, Michigan. The following is an extract:

> For twenty years the country has been agitated by this subject of slavery. Men of the North and West have been taught to hate the men of the South, and Southerners have been taught to hate the men of the North and West. This Northern sectionalism and fanaticism has been approaching nearer and nearer to Mason and Dixon's line, while the Southern fanaticism, starting in the Cotton States, has been creeping northwardly, until the two factions have nearly met. What will be the inevitable result of the conflict that must ensue? They must meet, if the floods of fanaticism be not checked. When they meet on the plains of Southern Illinois, Indiana, and Ohio, how long, in God's name, can the country endure? *Human nature has been misread, from the time of Cain to this day, if blood, blood, human blood is not the result.* But, thank God, between the two sections there is a band of national men, patriots, who love their country more than sectionalism, ready to stay this conflict. Our mission is to drive this sectionalism of the North back to Canada, whence it sprung; and that of the South back to the Gulf of Mexico.

No. XII. After the Election of 1860. – On the 10th of November, 1860, four days after the Presidential election, Mr. Vallandigham published the card in reply to an attack by a Republican paper, which see on page 104, On the 22d of December, 1860, at a serenade in Washington, at which the Hon. John J. Crittenden spoke – also, given to Senator Pugh, of Ohio, for his noble anti-coercion and compromise speech in the Senate – Mr. Vallandigham, among other similar things, said:

> Tonight you are here to indorse the great policy of conciliation, not force; peace, not civil war. The desire nearest the heart of every patriot, in this crisis, is the preservation of the Union of these States, as our fathers made it. (Applause.) But the Union can be preserved only by maintaining the Constitution and the constitutional rights, and above all, the perfect equality of every State and every section of this Confederacy. (Cheers.) That Constitution was made in peace; it has, for now more than seventy years, been preserved by the policy of peace at home, and it can alone be maintained for our children, and their children after them, by that same peace policy.
>
> We mean to stand by it. Public sentiment may, indeed, at first be against us; the tide may run heavily the other way for a little while; but, thank God, we all have nerve enough, and will enough, and faith enough in the people, to know that, at last, it will turn for peace; and though we may

be prostrated for a time by the storm, yet, upon the gravestone of every patriot who shall die now in the cause of peace and humanity and the country, shall be written: *"Resurgam"* – I shall rise again. And it will be a glorious resurrection (Loud and continued applause).

Fellow-citizens, *I am all over, and altogether a Union man.* I would preserve the Union in all its integrity and worth. But, I repeat that this cannot be done by coercion – by the sword.

No. XIII. The Anti-Compromise and Secession Winter of 1860-61. – The Presidential election of 1860, having resulted in the choice of Abraham Lincoln, the whole South was, forthwith, stirred with the most violent excitement. Secession of some – if not all – of the Southern States, became imminent. Immediately upon the assembling of Congress, on the 3d of December, 1860, various propositions looking to compromise and settlement, were introduced. One of those propositions was the measure introduced by Mr. Boteler, of Virginia, who proposed, "That so much of the Message as relates to the peculiar condition of the country, be referred to a Special Committee of One from each State." The resolution was adopted; and, two days after, the Committee was appointed. Mr. Boteler having expressed a desire to be omitted from the Committee – of which he would, by courtesy, have been chairman – his request was granted, and Mr. Corwin, of Ohio, appointed to that place. The Committee being filled and named, the member appointed for Florida (Mr. Hawkins) asked to be excused from serving, saying he "believed the time for compromise had passed forever."

On the question of excusing Mr. Hawkins, an animated discussion arose, in which Mr. Vallandigham participated. His remarks on this question, made on the 10th of December, contain the following incidental but important defense of the rights and interests of the West. He said:

> But, I repeat, sir, there is not, upon your Committee, one solitary Representative east of the Rocky Mountains, of that mighty host, numbering one million six hundred thousand men, which, for so many years, has stood as a vast breakwater against the winds and waves of sectionalism; and upon whose constituent elements, at least, this country must still so much depend in the great events which are thronging thick upon us, for all hope of preservation now or of restoration hereafter. Sir, is any man here insane enough to imagine, for a moment, that this great Northern and Western Democracy – constituting an essential part, and by far the most numerous part, of that great Democratic party which, for half a century, molded the policy and con-

trolled the destinies of this Republic; that party which gave to the country some of the brightest jewels of which she boasts; that party which placed upon your statute-books every important measure of enduring legislation from the beginning of the Government to this day – that such a section of such a party is to be thus utterly ignored, insulted, and thrust aside as of no value? I tell you, you mistake the character of the men you have to deal with. We are in a minority, indeed, to-day at the ballot-box, and we bow quietly, now, to the popular will thus expressed. We are defeated, but not conquered; and he is a fool in the wisdom of this world, who thinks that in the midst of the stirring and revolutionary times which are upon us, these sixteen hundred thousand men, born free and now the equals of their brethren – men whose every pulse throbs with the spirit of liberty – will tamely submit to be degraded to inferiority and reduced to political servitude. Never – never – while there is but one man left to strike a blow at the oppressor.

Sir, we love this Union; and more than that, we obey the Constitution. We are, here, a gallant little band of less than thirty men, but representing more than a million and a half of freemen. We are here to maintain the Constitution, which makes the Union, and to exact and yield that equality of rights which makes the Constitution worth maintaining. We are ready to do all and to suffer all in the cause of our – thank God! – yet common country; and by no vote or speech or act of ours, here or elsewhere, shall anything be done to defile or impair or to overthrow this the grandest temple of human liberty ever erected in any age. But we demand to worship at the very foot of the altar; and not, as servants and inferiors, in the outer courts of the edifice.

Sir, we of the North-west have a deeper interest in the preservation of this Government in its present form than any other section of the Union. Hemmed in, isolated, cut off from the sea-board, upon every side; a thousand miles and more from the mouth of the Mississippi, the free navigation of which, under the law of nations, we demand, and will have at every cost; with nothing else but our great inland seas, the lakes – and their outlet, too, through a foreign country – what is to be our destiny? Sir, we have fifteen hundred miles of Southern frontier, and but a little strip of eighty miles or less, from Virginia to Lake Erie, bounding us upon the east. Ohio is the isthmus that connects the South with the British Possessions, and the East with the West. The Rocky Mountains separate us from the Pacific. Where is to be our outlet? What are we to do when you shall have broken up and destroyed this Government? We are seven States now, with fourteen Senators and fifty-one Representatives, and a population of nine millions. We have an empire equal in area to the third of all Europe, and we do not mean to be a dependency or province either of the East or of the South; nor yet an inferior or second-rate power upon this continent; and if we cannot secure a maritime boundary upon other terms, we will cleave our way to the sea-coast with the sword. A nation of warriors we may be; a tribe of shepherds never.

No. XIV. Votes Upon the Various Compromise Measures. – On the 27th of February, 1861, the House proceeded to vote on the various Compromise Propositions before it.

Mr. Kellogg, of Illinois, had submitted a proposition similar to the Missouri Compromise of 1820, but to be embodied in the Constitution. It was rejected – yeas 33, nays 158. All the yeas were Democrats and Constitutional-Union men, except Mr. Kellogg himself. Mr. Vallandigham voted for the Proposition. – *Congressional Globe*, p. 1260.

The question then recurred on the "Crittenden Propositions," offered in the House by Mr. Clement, of Virginia, in the form of a motion to submit them to the people of the United States. It was these propositions which Mr. Davis and Mr. Toombs both declared would be satisfactory to the South and avert secession – (*Douglas' speech,* January 13, 1861. *Appendix to Congressional Globe*, p. 41.) And, as in the Senate, so also in the House, they were rejected, and by a vote of yeas 80, nays 113, every Democrat and Southern man, except Hindman, of Arkansas, voting for them, and every Republican, without one single exception, voting against them. Mr. Vallandigham voted aye. The following is a list of the yeas and nays:

> Yeas – Messrs. Adrain, William C. Anderson, Avery, Barr, Barrett, Bocock, Bolder, Bouligny, Brabson, Branch, Briggs, Bristow, Brown, Buroh, Burnett, Horace F. Clark, John B. Clark, John Cochrane, Cox, James Craig, Burton Craige, John G. Davis, De Jarnette, Dimmick, Edmundson, English, Florence, Fouko, Garnett, Gilmer, Hamilton, J. Morrison Harris, John T. Harris, Hatton, Holman, William Howard, Hughes, Jenkins, Kunkle, Larabee, James M. Leach, Leake, Logan, Maclay, Mallory, Charles D. Martin, Elbert S. Martin, Maynard, McClernand, McKenty, Millson, Montgomery, Laban T. Moore, Isaac N. Morris, Nelson, Niblack, Noell, Peyton, Phelps, Pryor, Quarles, Riggs, James C. Robinson, Rust, Sickles, Simms, William Smith, William N. H. Smith, Stevenson, James A. Stewart, Stokes, Stout, Thomas, *Vallandigham,* Vance, Webster, Whitely, Winslow, Woodson, and Wright. – 80.
>
> Nays – Messrs. Charles F. Adams, Aldrich, Alley, Ashley, Babbitt, Beale, Bingham, Blair, Blake, Brayton, Buffinton, Burlingame, Burham, Butterfield, Campbell, Carey, Carter, Case, Coburn, Clark B. Cochrane, Colfax, Conkling, Conway, Corwin, Covode, H. Winter Davis, Dawes, Delano, Duell, Dunn, Edgerton, Edwards, Elliot, Ely, Etheridge, Farnsworth,

Fenton, Ferry, Foster, Frank, French, Gooch, Graham, Grow, Hale, Hall, Helmick, Hickman, Hindman, Hoard, William A Howard, Humphrey, Hutchins, Irvine, Junkin, Francis W. Kellogg, William Kellogg, Kenyon, Kilgore, Killinger, DeWitt C. Leach, Lee, Longnecker, Loomis, Lovejoy, Marston, McKean, McKnight, McPherson, Moorhead, Morrill, Morse, Nixon, Olin, Palmer, Perry, Pettit, Porter, Potter, Pottle, Edwin R. Reynolds, Rice, Christopher Robinson, Royce, Scranton, Sedgwick, Sherman, Somes, Spaulding, Spinner, Stanton, Stevens, William Stewart, Stratton, Tappan, Thayer, Theaker, Tomkins, Train, Trimble, Vandever, Van Wyck, Verree, Wade, Waldron, Walton, Cadwalader C. Washburne, Elihu B. Washburne, Wells, Wilson, Windom, Wood and Woodruff. – 113. – *Congressional Globe*, p. 1261.

Of the eighty who voted *for* compromise, nineteen are in either the Federal or Confederate army, while of the one hundred and thirteen who voted *against* compromise, only six; one of them being Hindman, now a Confederate general. The other five are in the Federal army.

No. XV. The Affair at Camp Upton. – A story to the effect that Mr. Vallandigham, when visiting a camp of Ohio soldiers, near Washington, was indignantly repelled, and driven from their lines, has been widely circulated. The telegraphic dispatch, from the agent of the Associated Press, relating to that disturbance, was substantially correct, except that the "disposition" referred to, was limited to a single company from Cleveland. But the dispatch appeared only in the papers of Washington, Baltimore and Philadelphia. It was suppressed beyond, eastward and westward. Many papers, unfriendly to Mr. Vallandigham, supplied the omission, not by copying the dispatch from newspapers that received it, but by giving their own version for popular use. Hence the perverted and exaggerated form the story assumed. The dispatch was as follows:

> Alexandria, July 7, 1861. Mr. Vallandigham, member of Congress from Ohio, visited the Ohio regiments to-day. While in the camp of the first regiment, a disposition was shown by many to oust him, and, notwithstanding the nerve and courage shown by Mr. Vallandigham, it is probable they would have succeeded, but for the protection afforded him by the Dayton companies, and a pass from General Scott. He finally retired to the camp of the second regiment, after declaring himself as good a Union man as any of them, and expressing his scorn for the mob spirit shown by his fellow-citizens.

No. XVI. Peace for the Sake of the Union. – On the 20th of August, 1861, in reply to the charge that he had said that "he was for peace before the Union," Mr. Vallandigham published a card denying it, in which the following statements occur:

> I never, either in my place in the House of Representatives, or anywhere else, said anything of the kind.
> It is a part of that mass of falsehood created and set afloat so persistently for the last few years, in regard to all that concerns me; and is of the same coinage as that other falsehood, that I once said that "Federal troops must pass over my dead body on their way South" – a speech of intense stupidity, which I never, at any time, in any place, in any shape or form, uttered in my life.
> But now, allow me, also, to say that I am for peace – speedy and honorable peace – because I am for the Union, and know, or think I know, that every hour of warfare by so much diminishes the hopes and chances of its restoration. I repeat with Douglas: "War is disunion. War is final, eternal separation;" and with Chatham: "My Lords, you cannot conquer America."

No. XVII. Slavery in the District of Columbia. – On the 11th of April, 1862, Mr. Vallandigham spoke and voted against the bill to abolish slavery in the District of Columbia. The following is an extract from his remarks:

> Had I no other reason, I am opposed to it, because I regard all this class of legislation as tending to prevent a restoration of the Union of these States as it was, and that is the grand object to which I look. I know well, that in a very little while the question will be between the old Union of these States – the Union as our fathers made it – or some new one, or some new unity of government, or eternal separation – disunion. To both these latter I am unalterably and unconditionally opposed. It is to the restoration of the Union as it was, in 1789, and continued for over seventy years, that I am bound to the last hour of my political and personal existence, if it be within the limits of possibility, to restore and maintain that Union.

No. XVIII. Peace Resolutions. – On the 16th of December, 1862, Mr. Vallandigham introduced the following resolutions into the House of Representatives; they were postponed for debate:

Resolved, 1. That the Union as it was must be restored and maintained forever, under the Constitution as it is – the fifth article, providing for amendments, included.

2. That no final treaty of peace, ending the present civil war, can be permitted to be made by the Executive, or any other person in the civil or military service of the United States, on any other basis than the integrity and entirety of the Federal Union, and of the States composing the same as at the beginning of hostilities, and upon that basis peace ought immediately to be made.

3. That the Government can never permit armed or hostile intervention by any foreign power, in regard to the present civil war.

4. That the unhappy civil war in which we are engaged was waged, in the beginning, professedly, "not in any spirit of oppression, or for any purpose of conquest or subjugation, or purpose of overthrowing or interfering with the rights or established institutions of the States, but to defend and maintain the supremacy of the Constitution, and to preserve the Union, with all the dignity, equality, and rights of the several States unimpaired," and was so understood and accepted by the people, and especially by the army and navy of the United States; and that, therefore, whoever shall pervert, or attempt to pervert, the same to a war of conquest and subjugation, or for the overthrowing or interfering with the rights or established institutions of any of the States, and to abolish slavery therein, or for the purpose of destroying or impairing the dignity, equality, or rights of any of the States, will be guilty of a flagrant breach of public faith, and of a high crime against the Constitution and the Union.

5. That whoever shall propose, by Federal authority, to extinguish any of the States of the Union, or to declare any of them extinguished, and to establish territorial governments, or permanent military governments within the same, will be deserving of the censure of this House and of the country.

6. That whoever shall attempt to establish a dictatorship in the United States, thereby superseding or suspending the constitutional authorities of the Union, or to clothe the President, or any other officer, civil or military, with dictatorial or arbitrary power, will be guilty of a high crime against the Constitution and the Union, and public liberty.

On the 22d of the same month, Mr, Vallandigham offered the following, which, also, went over for debate:

Resolved, That this House earnestly desire that the most speedy and effectual measures be taken for restoring peace in America, and that no time may be lost in proposing an immediate cessation of hostilities, in order to the speedy settlement of the unhappy controversies which brought about this unnecessary and injurious civil war, by just and adequate security against the return of like calamities in time to come; and this House desire to offer the most earnest assurances to the country, that they will in due time cheerfully co-operate with the Executive and the States for the restoration of the Union, by such explicit and most solemn amendments and provisions of the Constitution as may be found necessary for securing the rights of the several States and sections within the Union, under the Constitution.

On the next day, Mr. V. briefly referred to the foregoing resolution, as follows:

The resolution which I offered yesterday, and which lies over for debate, was originally part of the series submitted by me some time since, and which, as afterward modified, were postponed till the 6th of January. I did not offer it at the same time with the others, because I desired a separate vote upon them; and, through the kindness of the member from Illinois (Mr. Lovejoy) and his friends upon the other side of the House, my desire was promptly gratified, just as I anticipated. The resolutions were laid upon the table by a strict party vote, and thus the record for that great hereafter made up, and I am content.

And now let me add that the resolution of yesterday is but an almost exact transcript of an amendment to the address in answer to the King's speech, proposed in the House of Commons, on the 18th of November, 1777, by the Marquis of Granby, and supported by Lord John Cavendish, Mr. Burke, and the other British patriots of that day. Had I pressed it to a vote, its fate would, I doubt not, have been just the same as that of the amendment itself, which was rejected by the followers of Lord North, by a vote of 243 to 86, in the third year of the American war. That war, sir, as we all know, went on for four years longer, and ended at last in the eternal separation of the Thirteen Colonies from the British Crown. So far as I am concerned, no similar result shall be the issue of our present unhappy war.

But by speedy, honorable peace, conciliation, and adjustment alone, in my deliberate and most solemn judgment, now, as from the very first, can that calamity be averted.

No. XIX. The "Dead-Body" Falsehood. – An apology would be needed for alluding to so contemptible a matter as "the dead-body lie," were it not for its late revival in Congress.

Mr. Vallandigham is charged with having said at an Ohio caucus, in Washington, December, 1860, that "before Federal troops should be permitted to pass through the Miami Valley, they must march over his dead body." Soon after the charge was first made, he denied it, saying in a published card, "It is a speech of intense stupidity, which I never, at any time, in any place, in any shape or form, uttered in my life." An attempt has since been made to prove the charge by the certificates of Abolition members of Congress, who were at the caucus. On the other hand, Mr. Pendleton and Mr. Cox declared in the House, on the 28th of February, 1863, that they heard Mr. Vallandigham's remarks, on the occasion referred to, and that he used no such language. Mr. V. himself explained, in the same debate, that similar language was used about the same time in the Senate, by a Senator, whose remarks and his own were some months afterward confounded. – See *Congressional Globe*, 1860-61, p. 144.

We now add conclusive proof of the falsity of the charge from Abolition authority. The Washington correspondent of the Cincinnati *Commercial*, W. D. Bickham, on the 18th of December, the day after the caucus, telegraphed the following to that paper. Mr. B., it should be observed, was not at the caucus; he received his information only from those who have since certified to the lie. The heading is:

> Vallandigham re-defines and modifies his position. He is anxious that the Miami Valley shall not be the battle-ground between the North and the South.

The correspondent says:

> Vallandigham said, if South Carolina assailed the Government forts and killed troops, he would treat her as he would treat any other foreign nation under similar circumstances. But if war was waged on her merely to keep her in the Union, Republicans might fight the battle, *but should not make the Miami Valley the battle-grounds.*

The next day, the same correspondent wrote a report of the caucus debate, which appeared in the *Commercial*, of December 22, 1860. He says, his information was "carefully collated from both sides;" and it is substantially correct, except that Mr. Vallandigham declined to discuss the abstract right of secession. He says:

> Our friend Gurley took occasion to run a tilt in warlike vein, and our frank friend Vallandigham, who detests anything like an unfair advantage in politics, went to work with the sword, with which the North-west proposes "to cleave her way to the sea-shore" – under certain important conditions. "Vall" took his peculiar views of the case, and, according to his colleagues,

on the Democratic side of the House, *quite dispassionately* reviewed the premises, and concluded that a State has a right to secede, and what is commonly called "coercing a State" is not exactly the thing. If South Carolina murdered our troops at Fort Moultrie, he would treat her as a foreign enemy, but unless she committed some "overt act," he would not countenance war upon her [nobody proposed to do so]; and he gave notice that if there was war upon such conditions, the Republicans might fight the battle. *They might have transit through the Miami Valley, provided they would not disturb any body;* but they should not make the Miami Valley their battle-ground."

And yet, Edgerton, Gurley, Blake, Theaker, Ashley, Hutchins, and Bingham, two years afterward, have assumed to "certify" to the falsehood. They forgot the old saying, that a certain class of men ought to have good memories.

No. XX. Reception at Home. – On the 13th of March, 1863, Mr. Vallandigham returned to his home in Dayton, Ohio. An immense crowd met and welcomed him at the depot. It seemed as if every man, woman and child in the district had come out to do honor to this champion advocate of Constitutional rights. A reception speech was made by Hon. David A. Houk, in which, addressing Mr. Vallandigham, he said:

> You, sir, have been a faithful sentinel upon the watch-tower of public liberty, and in the darkest hour of the night, and when the storms of popular fury raged most fiercely, have kept the light of hope burning, and have promptly, fearlessly, and resolutely, sounded the alarm upon every approach to danger.
>
> An ancient Jewish King, upon a memorable occasion, called all the Princes of Israel, the captains, the stewards of all the substance of his household, and of his children, and all the valiant men unto Jerusalem.
>
> And when he had assembled them about him, he stood up and said: "Hear me, my brethren and my people; as for me, I had it in my heart to build a house of rest, for the ark of the covenant of the Lord, and for the footstool of our God, and had made ready for the building – but God said unto me, 'Thou shalt not build a house for my name, because thou hast been a man of war, and hast shed blood.'"
>
> *When the shattered temple of Constitutional liberty shall be reconstructed in this country, it will not be done by the men of blood.*
>
> You, sir, have not been unmindful of those divine admonitions, and of the promises of the gospel of peace, as uttered by Him who said: "Blessed are the peace-makers, for they shall be called the children of God."

After a handsome acknowledgment of this flattering welcome, Mr. V. said:

It is the determination of the Democratic party to maintain free speech, a free press, and a free ballot, at all hazards. I am for obedience to all laws, and for requiring the men in power to obey them. I would try all questions of Constitution and law before the Courts, and then enforce the decrees of the Courts. I am for trying all political questions by the ballot. I would resist no law by force, but would endure almost every other wrong as long as free discussion, free assemblages of the people, and a free ballot remain; but the moment they are attacked, I would resist. We have a right to change Administrations, policies, and parties, not by forcible revolution, but by the ballot-box; and this right must be maintained at all hazards.

Referring to the Conscription Bill, he said:

The three-hundred-dollar provision is a most unjust discrimination against the poor. I propose that the City Council of Dayton appropriate money enough, and vote a tax for it, to release the city from the draft, and thus spare the lives and limbs of those citizens who are too poor to pay. I would recommend the same measure to Cincinnati, Chicago, and other cities of the North. The tax will equalize the burden, and make the rich pay some part of that "last dollar." Three hundred dollars, too, is just the price fixed, by an Abolition Congress, for the emancipated negroes of the District of Columbia. *It is now the price of blood. The Administration says to every man between twenty and forty-five, three hundred dollars or your life.* A tax by every city, township and county is just the way to meet and equalize the demand.

No. XXI. Eight to Keep and Bear Arms. – On the 21st of March, 1863, a very large Democratic meeting was held at Hamilton, Ohio. Mr. Vallandigham was one of the speakers, and in the course of his remarks, commented, in the following terms, upon a military order recently issued at Indianapolis. He said:

I will not speak disrespectfully of Colonel Carrington. He and I served pleasantly together in the militia of Ohio, on the peace establishment (laughter), and I found him always gentlemanly in his deportment. I am glad to learn that he is still so regarded at Indianapolis. How could he have issued such an order? I know he is "great" on general orders; but such a one passes my comprehension. I am sure he cannot want to do wrong, for he must know that two years hence, under the legislation of the late Congress, a Democratic

President or Secretary of War – and who knows but I may be Secretary myself? (laughter and cheers) – can strike his name from the roll without even a why or wherefore. It should be well for all ambitious military gentlemen just now to recollect this small fact, and confine themselves strictly to their legal and Constitutional military duties, and to allow others to enjoy their opinions and civil rights unmolested. But to the order. Here it is:

"Headquarters United States Forces, Indianapolis, Ind., March 17, 1863. *General Order No.* 15. I. The habit of carrying arms upon the person has greatly increased" – Well, so it has, and in times of threats and danger like these, it ought to, and in spite of all "orders," it will increase – "And is prejudicial to peace and good order" – Sir, restore to us peace and good order, and we will lay aside all arms, and be glad of the chance. (Great applause.) "As well as a violation of civil law" – I deny it; but, if so, who gave authority to this gentleman to lecture on civil law in a military order?

"Especially at this time, it is unnecessary, impolitic, and dangerous." Was ever the like heard or read of before? "At this time" – at a time when Democrats are threatened with violence everywhere; when mobs are happening every day, and Democratic presses destroyed; when secret societies are being formed all over the country to stimulate to violence; when, at hotels and in depots, and in railroad cars and on the street corners, Democrats are scowled at and menaced, a military order coolly announces that it is unnecessary, impolitic, and dangerous to carry arms! And who signs this order? "Henry B. Carrington, Colonel 18th U. S. Infantry, *Commanding*" – Commanding what? The 18th U. S. *Infantry,* or at most the United States *forces* of Indiana – but not the people, the free white American citizens of American descent, not in the military service. That is the extent of his authority, and no more.

And now, sir, I hold in my hand a general order also – an order binding on all military men and all civilians alike – on colonels and generals and commanders-in-chief – State and Federal. (Applause.) Hear it: "*'The right of the people to keep and bear arms shall not be infringed.'* By order of the States and people of the United States. George Washington, commanding." (Great cheering.) That, sir, is General Order No. 1 – the Constitution of the United States. (Loud cheers.) Who now is to be obeyed – Carrington or Washington?

But I have another "order" yet. "The people have a right to *bear arms* for their *defense and security,* and the military shall be in strict subordination to the civil power." (Renewed cheering.) That, sir, is General Order No. 2 – the Constitution of Ohio, by order of the people of Ohio. Here, sir, are our warrants for keeping and bearing arms, and by the blessing of God, we mean to do it; and if the men in power undertake in an evil hour to demand them of us, we will return the Spartan answer, "Come and take them."

But Colonel Carrington's order proceeds: "The Major-General commanding the Department of the Ohio." Commanding whom, again I ask? Only the military forces of the Department of Ohio, but not a single citizen in it – "Having ordered that all sales of arms, powder, lead and percussion caps be prohibited until further orders." Where, sir, is the law for all that? Are we a conquered province governed by a military proconsul? And so then it has come to this, that the Constitution is now suspended by a military General Order, No. 15! Sir, the Constitutional right to keep and bear arms carries with it the right to buy and sell arms; and fire-arms are useless without powder, lead and percussion caps. It is our right to have them, and we mean to obey General Orders Nos. 1 and 2, instead of No. 15. (Loud applause.)

But I read further – "and that any violation of said order will be followed by the *confiscation* of the goods sold, and the seizure of the stock of the vender." Is the man deranged? *Confiscation,* indeed! Why, sir, the men who are clothed now with a little brief authority seem to think of nothing except taxation, emancipation, confiscation, conscription, and every other word ending in t-i-o-n. (Laughter.) But General Order No. 1 says, "No man shall be deprived of property without due process of law!" and General Order No. 1 says, "Private property shall ever be held inviolate, and every person, for an injury done him in his land, goods, person, or reputation, shall have remedy by due course of law." And though the writ of *habeas corpus* may be suspended, the writs of replevin and injunction cannot be. (Cries of "Good, good.")

But Order No. 15 proceeds: "And said order having been extended, by the Major-General, to cover the entire department, is hereby promulged." Yes, promulged – "for immediate observance throughout the State. Can military insolence go further? Is this the way the military is to be in strict subordination to the civil power? And does the colonel commanding the 18th U. S. Infantry thus undertake to "promulge" a general order suspending or abrogating the Constitution of the United States and of Indiana? Are we living in America or Austria?

And now the fitting commentary on all this attempt to disarm the white man, while public arms are being put into the hands of the negro, is in the second section of this General Order No. 15, alluding to the recent destruction of a Democratic printing press, by what the colonel commanding the 18th U.S. Infantry, drawing it mild after the fashion of Sarey Gamp, calls a "popular demonstration;" and yet not one of the perpetrators of this outrage, although soldiers, and under military law, have been punished, nor ever will be. Yet at just such a time of lawless violence, it is proposed that the people shall be disarmed. Never. (Loud cheers.)

Sir, I repeat now what I believe to be the true programme for these times: Try every question of law in your Courts, and every question of politics before the people, and through the ballot-box; maintain your Constitutional civil rights, at all hazards, against military usurpation. Let there be no resistance to law, but meet and repel all mobs and mob violence by force and arms on the spot. (Great and continued cheering.)

www.ingramcontent.com/pod-product-compliance
Lightning Source LLC
Chambersburg PA
CBHW080918170426
43201CB00016B/2181